Black Revolutionaries

SINCE 1970
Histories of Contemporary America

SERIES EDITORS

Lynn Itagaki, *University of Missouri*

Daniel Rivers, *Ohio State University*

FOUNDING EDITORS

Claire Potter, *The New School*

Renee Romano, *Oberlin College*

ADVISORY BOARD

Mary Dudziak, *University of Southern California*

Devin Fergus, *University of Missouri*

David Greenberg, *Rutgers University*

Shane Hamilton, *University of Georgia*

Jennifer Mittelstadt, *Rutgers University*

Stephen Pitti, *Yale University*

Robert Self, *Brown University*

Siva Vaidhyanathan, *University of Virginia*

Susan Ware, *General Editor, American National Biography*

Judy Wu, *Ohio State University*

Black Revolutionaries

A HISTORY OF THE
BLACK PANTHER PARTY

Joe Street

The University of Georgia Press
ATHENS

© 2024 by the University of Georgia Press
Athens, Georgia 30602
www.ugapress.org
All rights reserved
Set in 10/13 Kepler Std Regular by Kaelin Chappell Broaddus

Most University of Georgia Press titles are
available from popular e-book vendors.

Printed digitally

Library of Congress Cataloging-in-Publication Data

Names: Street, Joe, author.
Title: Black revolutionaries : a history of the Black Panther Party/
   Joe Street.
Other titles: History of the Black Panther Party
Description: Athens : The University of Georgia Press, [2024] |
   Series: Since 1970: histories of contemporary america series |
   Includes bibliographical references and index.
Identifiers: LCCN 2024000344 (print) | LCCN 2024000345 (ebook) |
   ISBN 9780820366944 (hardback) | ISBN 9780820366951 (paperback) |
   ISBN 9780820366968 (epub) | ISBN 9780820366975 (pdf)
Subjects: LCSH: Black Panther Party—History. | African Americans—
   Politics and government—20th century. | African Americans—
   Civil rights—History—20th century. | Civil rights movements—
   United States—History—20th century. | United States—
   Race relations—History—20th century.
Classification: LCC E185.615 .S7247 2024 (print) | LCC E185.615 (ebook) | DDC
   322.4/20973—dc23/eng/20240229
LC record available at https://lccn.loc.gov/2024000344
LC ebook record available at https://lccn.loc.gov/2024000345

This book is for Barbara: socialist, feminist,
political activist, inspirational Nanny,
and the best Mum I could ever have wished for.

CONTENTS

ACKNOWLEDGMENTS ix
PROLOGUE xi

INTRODUCTION 1

Part I. Intellectual History

CHAPTER ONE The BPP's Intellectual Territory 19
CHAPTER TWO The Gendered World of the BPP 36
CHAPTER THREE Black Panther Political Philosophy 55

Part II. Community Activism

CHAPTER FOUR The BPP in the Street 73
CHAPTER FIVE The BPP's Social Programs and Local Chapters 87
CHAPTER SIX The Cal-Pac Boycott 101
CHAPTER SEVEN Bobby Seale for Mayor! 112

Part III. State Repression

CHAPTER EIGHT The Trial of Huey P. Newton 131
CHAPTER NINE The FBI and the BPP 151
CHAPTER TEN The Prison and the (Un)making of the BPP 167
EPILOGUE Remembering the BPP 185

NOTES 195
BIBLIOGRAPHY 237
INDEX 251

ACKNOWLEDGMENTS

I grew up in a household stuffed with radical literature, and the BPP has been in my thoughts for longer than I can remember. It has taught me more than I could have ever hoped to learn in terms of solidarity, fighting oppression, and working toward a better world. I cannot escape the facts of my own life, though. As a middle-class, white, heterosexual, cisgender British man I possess an immense amount of privilege. This doubtless influences my own position with respect to the BPP in particular and African American history in a wider sense. I try within the pages of this book to be as fair to the historical actors involved as I can, and especially to those without the privileges from which I benefit. Where I am critical of members of the BPP, I hope that my criticism is reasonable but more importantly that it not be seen as a personal attack from on high. My criticism reflects my belief that historical writing is at its best when it does not shy from posing awkward questions and that if it is to have meaning it must not wish away problematic events, documents, or other traces of the past. I remain in awe of all those who joined, supported, or aligned themselves with the BPP, and I wrote this book to attempt a critical analysis of their organization within a generally positive framework. In this, I hope that I have respected both the BPP itself and its members, most notably its insistence that struggle against oppression in all its forms should be front and center in all our lives.

I wish to thank many people who helped place this book in your hands. Sadly, as ever, none of the mistakes contained within it can be attributed to them. First and foremost, Lynn Itagaki and Devin Fergus have been immense sources of support. Their friendship has been fundamental as well. Both went so far beyond the call of duty that I cannot thank them enough: they are true friends. Alongside Lynn, Daniel Rivers proved another true friend, soothing my furrowed brow at key moments and helping ensure that I forged ahead even when I could not see the path that I was on, let alone its destination. I could not have asked for better series editors. The same goes for Mick Gusinde-Duffy, who was a tower of strength and central to ensuring that I finished this book, and Lori Rider, whose copyediting was quite simply brilliant. Thank you, all of you!

The anonymous readers of the book offered hugely detailed and constructive critiques that helped improve it beyond measure. They helped me see the manuscript through new eyes and I hope that they can see their influence throughout the pages that follow. I thank them from the bottom of my heart.

They were ably assisted by folks who generously read drafts of various chapters, commented on my ideas, or simply shared their time. The feedback and encouragement of Anne-Marie Angelo, Zoe Colley, Jim Hall, Simon Hall, Eamonn Kelly, George Lewis, Dan Matlin, Jo Metcalf, John Narayan, Christopher Phelps, and Zoe Trodd spurred me along and added extra dimensions to the book. Thank you. Elsewhere, the postgraduate work of Ellie White and Chris Jones helped immensely, and the good folk who attended my talks at various conferences and symposia helped me clarify my ideas. Veterans Bob Brown and Emory Douglas gave their time willingly; their encouragement was vital at two crucial points, now sadly some time ago! I hope that they and all the veterans who read this book feel that it does their immense contribution to history justice. While Professor Clayborne Carson will not remember our lunch together, it helped me find my voice as a historian. Laura Visser-Maessen and Jorrit van den Berk were hugely supportive in editing an article about the BPP in 1968 that helped me work through a knotty issue; similarly, the editors of the *Pacific Historical Review*, and especially Brenda Frink, offered great advice as I thought about Huey P. Newton for an article in their esteemed journal. Chapters 8 and 10 include revised material from these publications.

Thank you also to Robert Cook (who has the ill fortune to have been enduring my prose since the mid-1990s; incredibly, he still speaks to me), Sue Currell, Martin Halliwell, Ben Houston, Bill Issel, Peter Ling, Simon Topping, Stephen Tuck, and Clive Webb for their friendship and wise counsel. At Northumbria, the Americanists Brian Ward, Randall Stephens, Dave Gleeson, Henry Knight Lozano, and Paddy Andelic listened patiently and offered friendship, camaraderie, good advice, impeccable soundtrack choices, and Simpsons memes. As important, I don't know where I'd be without the comradeship of my UCU comrades, especially Adam Hansen.

As ever, the final thank you goes to my family. Of my vast array of nieces and nephews, Phoebe, Thomas, Elliot, and Mairead argued vehemently that I would be a terrible uncle if I did not mention them specifically, so enjoy reading your names, kids! As this book's dedication suggests, I wouldn't be here (quite literally) were it not for my Mum. Knowing that Dad and Anna are always there for me makes my heart burst with love too. My sisters, Jen and Tes, remain as fabulous as ever. Above all, Ruth and Carys fill my life with warmth, joy, and love; I love them both completely.

PROLOGUE

> The BPP to me was an organization that said we mean something to the world. The BPP taught the people that our ancestors made contribution to the world, we are valued, and we are somebody. And that was too powerful for the establishment to accept. That was too much power to give to Blacks.
> —Unidentified BPP veteran, 2013

The Black Panther Party is uniquely significant.[1] So effective was it at outlining its critique of American racism and capitalism that the FBI at one point considered it the (white) American public's most dangerous enemy, and worried that the fabric of society would be torn apart by this group of militarized African American revolutionaries. On the other hand, many American leftists held the BPP in awe and hoped to emulate the audacity with which its members challenged the status quo. As the white radical Cathy Wilkerson recalled, "I think in our hearts what all of us wanted to be was a Black Panther."[2]

While Wilkerson's comment hints at the white Left's romantic and occasionally patronizing relationship with Blackness—after all, being a Black Panther placed one in a uniquely vulnerable position—it also points to the hold that the BPP has over the popular imagination. Frankly, any assessment of the most eulogized and demonized decade in the twentieth century must reckon with the BPP's history. This history is also firmly enmeshed in our popular culture. Rappers from Public Enemy's Chuck D and Tupac Shakur (the son of a Panther family) to Kendrick Lamar cite the BPP as an influence, sometimes explicitly, sometimes implicitly. Documentary films, most notably Stanley Nelson's 2015 *The Black Panthers: Vanguard of the Revolution*, enable popular audiences to engage with the BPP's knotty history. Fictional films also treat the BPP's history with sensitivity, from Mario Van Peebles's *Panther* (1995) to Tanya Hamilton's *Night Catches Us* (2010), with the latter detailing the long-term impact of the BPP on its former members. A sequence of feature films such as Ryan Coogler's *Fruitvale Station* (2013) explore contemporary African American life in the BPP's birthplace in Oakland, California, obliquely and sometimes directly referencing the BPP's legacy.

Two blockbuster events confirm the position that the BPP occupies in the African American imagination. Beyoncé Knowles's 2016 Super Bowl halftime show presented the singer and her female dance troupe in leather jackets, berets perched on natural hairstyles. Referencing a famous photograph of BPP founders Bobby Seale and Huey P. Newton, Beyoncé sported two bandoliers crossing her chest as she sang "Formation." Few commentators missed the key signifiers, especially when the troupe very briefly formed a (Malcolm) "X" figure on the field.[3]

While based on the Marvel Comics character who had no relation to the BPP, Oakland native Ryan Coogler's *Black Panther* (2018) could not help but cite the BPP's history. The movie relocated the birthplace and hometown of Eric "Killmonger" Stevens, the titular character's cousin and main antagonist, to the BPP's home. Significantly, a copy of the famous poster of BPP founder Huey P. Newton sitting in a wicker chair hangs on a wall of Killmonger's family home. Radicalized by his upbringing, Killmonger follows in his father's footsteps in calling for revolution. He plans to use the superior weapons technology of *Black Panther*'s hidden state, Wakanda, to help oppressed people around the world overthrow their oppressors, stating that his observation of white colonial power enabled him to develop the strategy for victory: another subtle hint at the BPP's importance to the film. Michael B. Jordan—whose portrayal of Oscar Grant, the Oaklander murdered by police, in *Fruitvale Station* attracted widespread acclaim—took inspiration from Newton and Malcolm X for his portrayal of Killmonger.[4] He receives his comeuppance at the end of the film, when Wakanda's hero T'Challa/Black Panther defeats him in combat. Thus, the nearest the film comes to an authentic Black Panther learns of the futility of a revolutionary response to white supremacy. T'Challa takes the mortally wounded Killmonger to watch the sun set over Wakanda before musing that the Wakandans possess the means to heal him. Killmonger refuses. He offers one last defiant gesture: "just bury me in the ocean, with my ancestors who jumped from the ships. 'Cause they knew death was better than bondage."[5] His decision to accept death as a consequence of his actions references Newton's concept of revolutionary suicide, but more significantly, his internationalism—a central theme of his critique of Wakanda's refusal to engage with the outside world—transforms T'Challa's previous isolationism, initiating a new era of Wakandan foreign policy.

Even though these events stand apart from the BPP, their explicit references, and the debates that followed, prompt further consideration of the meaning of the BPP in the twenty-first century. More importantly, coupled with the BPP's echoes elsewhere in scholarly and popular culture, they confirm that the BPP is an essential part of world history.

Black Revolutionaries

INTRODUCTION

A feverish crowd gathered in Oakland on a sunny Wednesday afternoon in August 1970 to welcome their hero. Traffic outside the Alameda County Courthouse stalled as the throng surged toward the courthouse doors. As lawyers and the district attorney haggled over the bail fee, the crowd chanted and sang while some individuals heartily debated police officers. At 2:05 the focus of their gathering entered the blazing sunshine. Imprisoned since 1967 for the voluntary manslaughter of a police officer, he was perhaps the most recognizable African American radical of the times, almost ironically so given his separation from the organization he cofounded less than four years earlier. Buffeted by the clamoring crowds, he was forced to clamber on top of a nearby car to address them.[1]

Previously trapped by the state, Huey P. Newton was now a prisoner of his fame. The *New York Times* reported his people "swarm[ing] around him. They trampled one another in their frenzied attempts to touch him. They screamed and they shouted. And some of them cried. . . . Their admiration border[ed] on worship."[2] Visibly moved by the gathering and bothered by the heat, he removed his shirt to reveal his muscular physique, honed during his incarceration, and suggest that he was now more physically powerful than ever. Only smatterings of his short speech, punctuated by responses of "Right on!" could be heard amid the tumult. Newton insisted that "I am weak but together we are strong. . . . The power is with the people!" before urging everybody to disperse, suggesting that he understood that the people's power was not as strong as the Oakland police's.[3]

The Black Panther Party peaked at this moment. Less than three years before, Newton faced the gas chamber, with the organization little more than a name. It had achieved instant fame and notoriety in May 1967 for a spectacular "invasion" of the California State Capitol in Sacramento to protest a bill that would end its members' right to bear arms in public. But it soon withered to little more than a handful of loyalists. Newton's arrest for murder—publicized with photographs of him shackled to a hospital gurney, while a nurse and a police officer ignored his gunshot wounds—reinvigorated it. A campaign to free him brought thousands of new members, and many more declared their support through monetary donations, sympathy demonstrations, or merely by raising a fist in the air and shouting "Free Huey." The return of its founder and leading light suggested that the BPP would now cement itself as the most significant radical organization in the world. Yet this promise went unfulfilled. Four years later, Newton fled the country under suspicion of murder with the BPP reduced once again to a small cadre that only grew smaller after Newton's return to the United States in 1977. Within a few years the BPP was dead and Newton under investigation for fraudulent use of federal funds.

The BPP formed in the wake of the 1965 Voting Rights Act, commonly hailed as the crowning glory of the African American civil rights movement, and the Watts Rebellion, often understood as the moment when the urban centers of the North fully articulated their resentment at the failure of 1960s liberalism to alleviate poverty and social exclusion. It received acres of press coverage before fading, apparently leaving little behind of the revolution that it promised, leading one commentator to dismiss the organization as a media-generated phenomenon.[4] Yet the history of the BPP was far more complicated, significant, and troubling than this short precis suggests. In truth, the BPP reveals much about American politics, history, and culture in the middle of the twentieth century. It exemplified the revolutionary fervor of the late 1960s. Where the civil rights movement focused on social justice and racial integration, the BPP immersed itself in Marxist, Black nationalist, anticolonial, and internationalist traditions. As important, it saw through the hypocrisy that drove American law and policing. The crime reporter Jill Leovy argues that one of the major legacies of the urban rebellions of the 1960s was "a deep skepticism toward bureaucratic justice that echoes to the present day."[5] The BPP articulated this skepticism better than any other organization, before or since. As the American government effectively abandoned the inner cities in the decades that followed, many residents reacted by attempting to police the cities themselves.[6] Again, the BPP exemplified this response, and its public protests against police brutality are vital for an understanding of public space and public protest in the 1960s. Such activities rendered the BPP an international sensation, bringing African American radicalism to a global audience while symbolically uniting its members and supporters with the worldwide anticolonial struggle. The BPP was also the most heavily targeted radical group by the FBI's counterintelligence program and endured extensive disruption activities by police forces across the nation. The attempt to destroy the BPP reveals how law enforcement agencies clamped down on radical political groups, and particularly on African American communities throughout the nation, and indicates the centrality of law-and-order conservatism and repression to American politics. The response of its members to this repression reminds us that state repression impacted at an organizational and psychological level, and that it reverberated long afterward.

While the BPP did not recapture the zeitgeist after Newton's release, its experience of the 1970s reflected numerous transformations in African American politics and uniquely illuminates the wider political culture of the nation as the 1960s faded into history. Retreating from open advocacy of revolution, the BPP engaged wholeheartedly with community organizing, a leading paradigm of leftist political activism in the 1970s. In running candidates for political office and helping pave the way for a generation of African American mayors, the BPP placed itself at the forefront of a major progression in African American politics. Yet the BPP's shift into mainstream electioneering and community activism reveals how the parameters for radical political action contracted in the 1970s. As a case study, the BPP also causes us to question the role and impact of charismatic leaders on "their" organizations. Following Newton's arrest, the BPP's major aim became winning his freedom; once he returned, it looked to him for leadership. Beset by FBI surveillance and suffering from the aftereffects of months of solitary confinement, Newton could not live up to these expectations. Even though the BPP's grassroots activism flourished between 1969 and 1973, the organization entered a terminal decline in the mid-1970s, particularly once its activists exhausted themselves attempting to elect Newton's cofounder, Bobby Seale, to high office in Oakland.

As this suggests, the BPP's history is essential for an understanding of African American grassroots politics and protest, racial injustice, and police brutality in the post-1965 era. This importance and influence extends far beyond the BPP's organizational lifespan. The deaths of Eric Garner, Freddie Gray, Breonna Taylor, and many, many others as a consequence of police brutality are proof enough that Black people continue to suffer disproportionately at the hands of those whose duty is to protect and serve. Protesters involved with #BlackLivesMatter explicitly referenced the BPP when confronting police officers. By recording the police on cellphones, they created a twenty-first-century echo of the BPP's celebrated police patrols. They explicitly informed the police of their monitoring technique, and like the BPP, they transformed scenes of arrest or police-citizen confrontation into public spectacles involving an unspoken but profound negotiation over the nature of public power and control of the streets. Some activists also revived the BPP's analysis of the violence inherent in American racism. Bree Newsome, for example, argued that African Americans lived with violence every day of their lives: "our kids being shuffled from schools into prison is violence. Kids being hungry is violence," she stated.[7] As troublingly, the Trump presidency legitimized white nationalism. Trump's uniquely dystopian inaugural address talked of inner cities riddled with poverty, crime, and drugs. While designed to recall the failures of

Black Panther Party locations

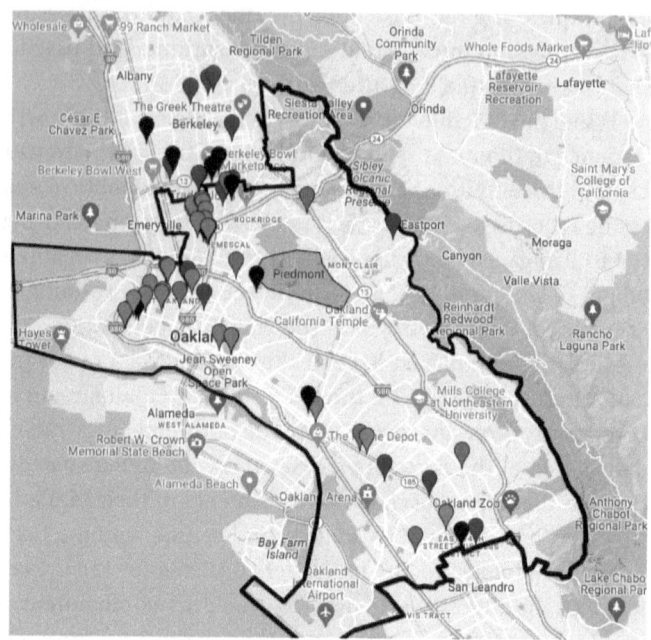

Redlining California

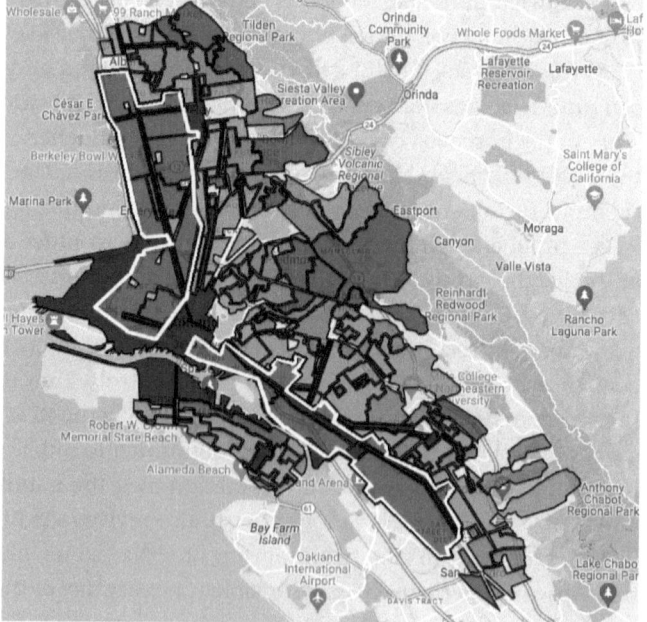

previous administrations, such comments reveal a larger failure of the American political system, one that the BPP itself highlighted half a century before.

Two maps starkly illustrate the world of the BPP. The first identifies major areas of BPP activity. The black line represents the boundary of the city of Oakland; the flags denote major BPP sites of interest such as BPP offices, including temporary offices established for the 1973 election campaign, houses, and locations of BPP protests and events.

The second denotes the areas graded by the Federal Housing Authority in 1934.[8] The key areas are ringed with white lines: the FHA considered these areas to house an "undesirable population," often without regular incomes, in poor quality housing, and with poor amenities and transportation.[9] The FHA's opinion gave mortgage lenders an easy guide to consult, enabling them to restrict loans to poor and Black customers and focus their lending on affluent areas. As pernicious, it ensured that white homebuyers were guided toward certain areas; Black homebuyers, meanwhile, were restricted to others and found mortgages more difficult to obtain, dooming them to a life of renting or seeking out loans from disreputable or usurious lenders.[10] Even a cursory glance at the maps reveals that the BPP was operating almost exclusively in the "redlined" areas characterized by much higher poverty levels and poor municipal services and housing, leading to a series of social and economic problems such as higher crime and lower life expectancy, educational achievement, and employment levels. Of particular note are the areas to Oakland's west side, which was designated a slum in 1937, and the corridor of BPP activity toward the city's northern border, designated by the FHA as an area with a high "infiltration of undesirables" and "colored" residents. The sections on either side of the thoroughfare were essentially written off as potential areas for investment.[11]

The Oakland BPP's location was not unique. Chapters across the nation established their headquarters in similar areas. In New York, the Harlem chapter was headquartered on Seventh Avenue, at the core of an area designated red by the FHA.[12] Brooklyn's headquarters similarly lay in the middle of a redlined area on Sutter Avenue; likewise, the BPP's newspaper distribution office on the East Coast and the Jamaica branch office sat within a redlined area. In Chicago, a huge redlined area surrounded the BPP headquarters on West Madison Street. The BPP's Los Angeles headquarters, meanwhile, sat in a narrow strip of redlined areas running north to south through Watts, surrounded by low-quality housing occupied by working-class people.[13] Similar congruencies lie in the BPP's offices in other cities such as Philadelphia and New Orleans (Seattle's lay in a relatively well-to-do area, only five blocks from a redlined district).[14] A high African American population and a declining or absent white population characterized all of these areas. It is therefore no stretch to argue that the BPP was primarily an inner-city phenomenon.

The BPP's embeddedness in such locations profoundly influenced its members' understanding of the Black community. Thus, when they spoke of "our Black community," they spoke of an inner-city, working-class, economically marginalized community trapped in poorly maintained, often rented housing, ill served by local amenities, and facing limited employment opportunities after being failed by the local educational facilities. Such residents found themselves excluded from mainstream political discourse even as the civil rights movement brought legal rights and a sense of self to huge numbers of African American citizens. Crucially, these communities faced police brutality and racism on a regular, if not daily, basis.[15] As Ronald Freeman recalled, he joined the BPP because "we were being shot down in the streets.... We had to develop self-defense groups to defend our communities."[16] Similarly, the BPP's famed survival programs were established to provide for these same communities. Consequently, when the BPP—and hence this book—referred to the Black community, it spoke not only of an imagined community defined by race but one that sat at the intersections of class, wealth, location, and an experience of vicious white oppression.

A Brief History of the BPP

Incorporated in 1852, Oakland grew to a city of nearly 300,000 residents by the New Deal, less than 3 percent of whom were Black. Federally supported industry flourished as the country headed into World War II, rendering Oakland a major destination for economic migrants and swelling the population by roughly 100,000, with its African American population increasing by over 400 percent.[17] Despite its vibrant, if schismatic, trade union movement, Oakland suffered in the postwar years as deindustrialization took hold and whites lit out for the suburbs, resulting in the city becoming nearly one-quarter Black by the 1960s, with many Oakland Blacks hemmed in by de facto residential segregation.[18] Notably, a number of families of future Panthers migrated to the Bay Area in the decades before the 1960s.[19] Thanks to this migration, their children already had experience making huge changes to their lives. Migration thus helped create the psychological, social, economic, and cultural circumstances in which the idea of a BPP could percolate. As they grew to adulthood, these children of migrants possessed the sense that, like their parents, they could change the circumstances around them; they chose political transformation rather than geographical relocation.

By the mid-1960s, racial tension and economic instability divided Oakland between wealthier and whiter residents in the hills to the city's east and a poorer, more racially diverse population who lived in the flatlands and complained bitterly about maltreatment from the Oakland Police Department. Rich whites meanwhile resented "their" tax dollars being spent on the poor.

The journalist Sol Stern concluded soon before the BPP's foundation that the city was on the verge of a Watts-style uprising. He also noted a large number of youthful African American political organizers actively agitating for change in a city failed by 1960s liberalism.[20] Merritt College, in the heart of Oakland's Black community, was one of the major hubs for this activist generation. While not an official campus organization, the Afro-American Association was central to Merritt's life. It evolved from a Black student union formed by Howard University graduate Khalid Monsour (formerly Donald Warden) at the University of California Berkeley campus in 1961. Initially a reading group, it soon broadened its horizons, introducing its members—which numbered over two hundred—to the thought of Robert F. Williams, Malcolm X, and other political radicals. AAA members helped found one of the first Black revolutionary journals of the period, *Soulbook*, which published poetry, articles on Frantz Fanon and Malcolm X, and broadsides promising revolution.[21] AAA member Huey P. Newton and his friend Bobby Seale studied at Merritt. Both were active with various campus groups, including the Revolutionary Action Movement and the Soul Students Advisory Council. Frustrated by the tendency of these groups to shy away from public action, they split and formed the BPP. They soon began recruiting among Oakland's African American population and started patrolling the police after collecting a small number of guns. By January 1967 the BPP possessed an office on Grove Street, the major thoroughfare near Merritt. After offering protection to Malcolm X's widow, Betty Shabazz, during a visit to San Francisco in February, the BPP began attracting serious attention from local press, the police, and Eldridge Cleaver, an ex-con writer for the New Left magazine *Ramparts*, who joined the organization soon afterward.

The death of a teenager named Denzil Dowell at the hands of police in nearby Richmond prompted the BPP to sponsor a series of protest rallies and publish a newsletter.[22] On May 2, 1967, it conducted one of the most sensational events of the 1960s, entering the California State Capitol to protest a gun control law that responded to its members' early forays into the community. Despite this, the BPP withered until October when Newton was arrested and charged with the murder of an Oakland police officer, precipitating an international campaign that rendered him a 1960s icon. Supporters set up BPP chapters across the country as the BPP's newsletter morphed into a weekly newspaper that became essential reading for American radicals. By the end of 1968, BPP chapters were operational in over twenty American cities, and the party was represented in many more—enough that the BPP itself could not put an exact figure on the number of local groups it had spawned.[23] The rapid expansion of the party afforded these chapters considerable autonomy over their activities, enabling individual Panthers to make their own assessment of and develop responses to the particular circumstances facing their local communities. Meanwhile, in Oakland, Cleaver helped broker an alliance with the Peace and Freedom Party, a group of anti-Vietnam War activists and white radicals, and pushed for the BPP to adopt a more paramilitary pose. An alliance with the Student Nonviolent Coordinating Committee, one of the decade's emblematic civil rights–Black Power organizations, was announced in February 1968, although it foundered following various disagreements. In April, two days after Dr. Martin Luther King Jr. was assassinated, Cleaver led a botched attack on the Oakland police that resulted in his capture and the death of the BPP's first recruit, Bobby Hutton.

By 1969, with Cleaver exiled in Cuba and Newton in prison, the BPP's activities shifted toward a broader campaign for African American self-sufficiency. Spearheaded by the free breakfast for children program, which offered thousands of cooked breakfasts, its social programs provided a focus for new recruits and the potential for the BPP to remodel itself as a community institution, and proved one of its most treasured legacies. It also attracted the attention of the FBI, which engaged in a major counterintelligence operation. Police targeted individual Panthers for harassment, with frequent arrests depriving the BPP of core activists and bail fees consuming the BPP's finances to the detriment of its social programs, which J. Edgar Hoover highlighted as the most subversive of its activities. Estimates suggest that law enforcement agents killed more than twenty BPP members. The whirlwind of violence peaked in 1969, with the deaths of Los Angeles BPP organizers Alprentice "Bunchy" Carter and John Huggins following a period of FBI-abetted tension, and the police assassination of Chicago BPP activists Mark Clark and Fred Hampton. Even so, thousands were flocking to the BPP, prompting an internal purge of members it suspected of foul play, a tactic that was influenced by FBI infiltration but did little to alleviate a sense of paranoia that increasingly affected the organization.[24]

Following the quashing of his conviction in August 1970, Newton was retried twice but never convicted. Promising to reinvigorate the BPP, he soon discovered that the organization he returned to was unrecognizable, filled with thousands of strangers who appeared to either venerate or distrust him. Soon after his release, Jonathan Jackson, brother of BPP prison activist George Jackson, was killed during an attempt to foment revolution in Marin County, California. In February 1971, tensions between Newton and Cleaver boiled over. Cleaver—now living in Algeria—was expelled, alongside his closest supporters. Prompted by the practical success of the social programs and Newton's new focus on "intercommunalism" as the BPP's driving theoretical force, the early 1970s saw the BPP immersing itself in Oakland's social, religious, and political life. It built bridges with local churches and began relocating its nationwide members to Oakland. BPP candidates were elected to various local offices, and in 1973 Bobby Seale ran for mayor and Elaine Brown for city council. The unsuccessful campaigns consumed the BPP, reducing its activist base after exhausted members resigned from the organization. Newton departed for Cuba the following year under suspicion of the murder of an Oakland woman, shortly after expelling Seale. Brown took charge, promoting numerous female Panthers while attempting to render the BPP a key player in Bay Area politics, working to aid Jerry Brown's election as governor of California and Lionel Wilson's as mayor of Oakland.[25] Newton's return prompted Brown's departure in 1977 and initiated the BPP's final phase. Increasingly reliant on government funds won by its community school—run by Ericka Huggins, one of the BPP's most gifted and long-standing activists—the BPP dwindled to the extent that by the end of the decade it was little more than a name. By 1980, even that name was defunct. In 1982 the last BPP community program, its community school, closed following revelations of embezzlement and fraud involving Newton, who was by now flailing amid a debilitating drug addiction.

Analyzing the BPP

Organizational histories tend to focus on the first five years of the BPP's history, following a chronology that emphasizes a rise-and-fall narrative, in which the BPP grows to international prominence before unraveling after Newton's release from prison.[26] A sequence of interpretative studies add nuance to particular aspects of BPP history, while broadening the chronology to include a more detailed analysis of the BPP in the 1970s.[27] Meanwhile, a plethora of shorter studies trace the activities of BPP chapters outside Oakland while emphasizing individual chapters' social activism beyond the 1960s.[28] Biographical studies are dominated by Judson Jeffries's intellectual biography of Newton, while Justin Gifford's detailed study of Eldridge Cleaver's life supplants Kathleen Rout's literary biography.[29] Panther memoirs, meanwhile, combine to create a tapestry of BPP grassroots activism.[30]

Building on this, *Black Revolutionaries* is not a traditional narrative history. Instead, it analyzes certain events in depth while deliberately overlooking others. Like the historian Ward Churchill, it insists that any analysis of the BPP must "excavate the understandings" of the party's work, "no matter how abbreviated" the successes of this work were.[31] It also takes influence from Agnès Varda's approach in her 1968 documentary, *Black Panthers*.[32] Varda's presentation of a BPP meeting as an open forum where BPP members debated BPP policy while a phalanx of Panthers paraded in formation and various leaders took the microphone to outline BPP policy demonstrates the many facets of the BPP. As the vibrancy of the meeting suggests, at numerous points in its history, the BPP offered the possibility of creating a new world. We must not be blind to the possibilities inherent to this vision. Yet this vision—and the BPP's successes—must be subject to rigorous analysis if we are fully to understand its meaning. As important, we must consider the BPP's program in as variegated a manner as possible. For example, some critical studies erroneously suggest that the BPP engaged with criminality for criminality's sake and that such activities were evidence of its members' almost sociopathic tendencies. The BPP's relationship with underground activity is better approached as an assertion of the BPP's deep distrust of American law enforcement, a critique of the civil rights movement's faith in the American legal and political system to bring about meaningful change, and an attempt to redraw the parameters of Black protest, one that drew influence from anticolonial philosophers such as Frantz Fanon.

Similarly, a chronological narrative of BPP history offers fine insights into the BPP's development but provides fewer opportunities to isolate and analyze the individual influences, events, or ideologies at play in the BPP's history. For example, a focused assessment of the prison experiences of key BPP members across the nation and at different points in BPP history enables a greater understanding of the role prison played in shaping the BPP. On a different level, evaluating the BPP's intellectual history enables us to reconsider the shifts in BPP ideology. Running separately, a consideration of BPP activism demonstrates how individual chapters and members responded to, reacted against, or even ignored this ideological steer as they developed their own activist programs. As important, a sustained examination of the disruption campaign led by police departments in cahoots with the FBI precisely demonstrates the extent to which the BPP's fate lay outside its own control. As this suggests, when one approaches the BPP's history within different frameworks, a more complex, multifaceted, and perhaps even more challenging and disruptive history emerges.

The book is driven by the BPP's archival record, combining both friendly and antagonistic sources from official and unofficial bodies, including published and unpublished oral histories with BPP veterans and observers, and the FBI's extensive surveillance files on the BPP and its leadership. All sources come with caveats concerning their reliability, and none more so than the FBI's, due to its organizational culture, ideological assumptions, and operational methodology. FBI agents made extensive use of material supplied by informants. Many of these informants were recruited because they had criminal charges over their heads. The promise of money coupled with the threat of jail compelled such people to work on the FBI's behalf but also encouraged embellishment and a tendency to tell their handlers what they thought their handlers wanted to hear. In turn, these handlers enthusiastically received such "evidence" because it would enable them to win more support and funds for operations against their targets; after all, the successful prosecution of a raid could lead to career advancement, and the more resources they had at their disposal, the greater the chances of success. Confirmation bias thus haunts FBI sources, allied to agents' willingness to embellish, misrepresent, and lie to advance their own agendas.

While oral history sources have fewer problematic layers attached to them, they also require cautious treatment. For the BPP, they are invaluable in bringing to light undocumented events, not least because until the early 1970s the BPP lacked a consistent approach to recordkeeping. They enable historians to shift focus from leadership to a grassroots approach that properly acknowledges the contribution of ordinary members to the BPP's successes. Perhaps most important, they reveal the emotional world inhabited by BPP activists that paper records rarely document. Leading from this, oral histories enable historians to evaluate how transformative membership was for BPP members, which demolishes the simplistic notion that the BPP was a failure because it did not achieve all the aims set out in its Ten-Point Platform and Program. Yet they retain their limitations, as the following passage suggests:

> [Harold Taylor (interviewee)]: Somebody bombed the Us Organization's office and another house was shot up really bad.
> [Curtis Austin (interviewer)]: Somebody bombed it?
> H. T.: Yeah, somebody bombed it.
> C. A.: Was it a member of the Black Panther Party?
> H. T.: I couldn't say.
> C. A.: Okay.[33]

Taylor's understandable reticence most obviously relates to the potential identification of unprosecuted parties. Alongside this, though, it points to the psychological trauma experienced by BPP members during times of high stress, indicating that such events might be too upsetting to recall, even decades later. As BPP veteran Claudia Chesson-Williams observes, "Talking about these things is bringing up all of these feelings, things that I haven't thought about or touched on for a long time"; this process could be discombobulating and even traumatic in itself.[34] As Austin's acceptance of Taylor's desire for silence demonstrates, some topics remain off limits and impossible to access even to the most skilled, sympathetic, and trustworthy interviewers.

More problematic, as any competent oral historian will report, human memory is not as reliable as we like to think. Each telling of a story is slightly different from the other. As individuals age, their memories morph, sometimes to take account of present circumstances, sometimes in response to external stimuli (such as an interviewer or from reading about the topic under discussion), and sometimes because of the brain's aging or later reevaluations of their own life. Similarly, the frequency with which many BPP veterans are interviewed has the potential to allow certain memories and mis-memories to calcify. Bobby Seale's recollections of the early days of the BPP in a 1988 interview and for the preparation of a 2016 book contain numerous similarities but also crucial differences, such as the extra detail Seale adds in the later interview for particular episodes, which might suggest him benefiting from the many publications that appeared in the intervening decades. Both obviously augment the account generated by Seale in conversation with Art Goldberg and others that formed the basis of his first memoir, *Seize the Time*.[35] Similarly, like countless other historical actors, Seale and his comrades are very aware of their own historical legacy. Oral histories are thus a process of assertion as well as remembrance, where individuals remind their interlocutors of their role as historical actors. As this suggests, the oral history subject changes through their life, and their recollections do not remain static.

Historians must weigh the impressionistic value of oral histories against their limitations. Astute readers will note the shortage of original oral histories in this book when compared with many recent BPP histories. This is not to deny the importance of the rank-and-file veterans; indeed, the book argues that they are central to the BPP's greatest successes. Instead, it constitutes acknowledgment of the vast array of oral histories on record and their immense contribution to BPP history. In using over fifty oral histories culled from various published, online, and archival sources alongside the publications of historians such as (but by no means exclusively) Curtis Austin, Joshua Bloom and Waldo E. Martin, Judson Jeffries, Donna Murch, and Robyn Spencer, who gathered hundreds of oral testimonies in their research, the book attests to the importance of BPP oral histories. It also appears at a liminal moment for students of the BPP. With most veterans entering old age or having already passed away, the BPP's story is turning definitively from memory to history. Soon there will be no eyewitnesses to the BPP alive, and future historians will be reliant on the extant record to aid their analysis. This book therefore has one foot in the BPP's memory and one in its future history: it both casts its eye over the plethora of oral histories and anticipates a new phase in BPP studies.

Three themes provide the book's core structure: intellectual history, community activism, and state repression. Each exists in a dialectical relationship with the others, in which the apparent tensions between their approaches (and the conclusions that might emerge from such approaches) resolve themselves to offer a more complex understanding of the BPP's history. So, while it is essential to understand the political-philosophical influences that acted on the BPP and its leaders' own ideas about the struggle, this knowledge must be placed within the context of the members' interaction with these ideas and the BPP's wider praxis, for, as the book's second part suggests, members and branches developed their own critical approaches to the BPP's intellectual and political worlds. Similarly, an understanding of the repression that the BPP endured heightens our awareness of the relationship between the BPP's profound intellectual and activist challenges to American racialized capitalism and the sustained and disproportionate attack its members suffered from the forces of reaction. As such, this section reinforces the book's central claim surrounding the heroism of BPP members in fighting so hard and so long for a better world.

The book's first part locates the organization beyond the intellectual confines of the African American struggle for civil rights. From the moment they joined, members were instructed to engage with key texts that influenced the party's founders and that would help inform its development. One of the earliest recruits, David Hilliard, remembers Newton encouraging him to read Fanon to help him understand the BPP's political philosophy.[36] Yet political education did not merely involve Panthers absorbing books; classes were also important forums for discussion and interaction, where members analyzed, debated, and thought about their and the BPP's place in the international struggle. Most important, they were vital spaces where members developed a critique of their immediate surroundings and developed their own solutions to the problems faced by the people in their communities.[37]

As chapter 1 outlines, BPP members engaged wholeheartedly with a broad collection of leftist and anticolonial texts, all of which related more closely to the worldwide human rights struggle than domestic civil rights activism. The thought of Malcolm X and Robert F. Williams united with the BPP's reading of Marxist revolutionaries like Ernesto "Che" Guevara, Frantz Fanon, and Mao Zedong to position the BPP within a rich intellectual world. This world was informed by elements of revolutionary theory, Marxist praxis, Black nationalist activism, and anticolonialism, while also reflecting the ideas of numerous female intellectuals from Ida B. Wells to Claudia Jones.

Yet the BPP's world was not simply dominated by the books its members read: BPP members also created this world. Part 2 explicitly examines the sociopolitical world created by BPP activism, whereas the two remaining chapters in part 1 concentrate on the thought of BPP members. Chapter 2 demonstrates that the membership and the leadership often had wildly diverging responses to key philosophical issues facing the BPP. It focuses on the BPP's gender politics, pitting Eldridge Cleaver's macho conception of the BPP's role in the radical community against female BPP activists, who developed a very different conception of the roles of men and women in the party. BPP women created an independent space for African American women members to assert themselves and consider their intersectional status in the party and the wider society, while also being subjected to the macho posturing and attendant antediluvian attitudes of some of their male comrades. So, while the masculinist stance advocated by Cleaver and some of his peers animated certain aspects of the BPP's political and social activism, others were defined by a far less macho gender politics. These tensions informed BPP activism throughout its history.

Huey P. Newton, meanwhile, styled himself as the BPP's chief theoretician. His work exerted considerable influence over the BPP's direction, from his early diktats to later, more obtuse theoretical considerations of capitalism, including an attempt to redefine Marxist internationalism as revolutionary intercommunalism. Chapter 3 highlights both Newton's important insights and the major shortcomings in his thought (including his rhetorical weaknesses) alongside the intellectual history of a wider group of Panthers including Kathleen Cleaver and Fred Hampton, to demonstrate that Newton was by no means alone in attempting to think through the BPP's ideology and praxis.

The book's second theme amplifies the underlying suggestions of part 1: that BPP chapters worked with considerable autonomy, and that their own analysis of local circumstances was as important to their activism as the macro-analysis of the BPP's leadership cadre. This section argues that, from its first police patrols to its last major attempt at political activism in the 1973 mayoral election, the BPP occupied the city's streets with a unique chutzpah. The BPP's retreat from its early belligerence to a more benign focus on serving the people defines the ebbing of the radical tide in the United States that crested with the BPP's most celebrated interventions into American politics. Reacting to various stimuli, including the response of state and federal authorities to the BPP's early activism, the party eventually conceded that the revolution it advocated could only be achieved if it first accepted the reality of electoral democracy. As such, this section reveals how the BPP's collective view of the imminence of the revolution developed into a more patient understanding that the revolution would take years to arrive.

The BPP's early police patrols possessed a profound symbolic meaning and destabilizing impact, one that observers often overlook. The power of these events—explored in chapter 4—explains why the BPP provoked such an intense backlash. This deepens our understanding of the development of African American protest in the 1960s and reveals the extent to which police officers not only feared Black violence but also suspected that African American people possessed a death wish, a racist misconception of human psychology that the BPP deliberately exploited. As the BPP endured a belligerent response from local police forces and the FBI, such actions ceded to a patient and careful attempt to reform American welfare through parallel structures such as health clinics, breakfast clubs, and food giveaways. These activities, informed by local activists' analysis of community needs, drove many BPP chapters outside Oakland even in the face of stiff repression from the police and FBI, a history that drives chapter 5's analysis.

In 1971, following the refusal of the president of California State Package Store and Tavern Owners Association (Cal-Pac) to make regular donations to the BPP, Newton announced a retaliatory boycott. Designed to create a new income stream for the BPP, the Cal-Pac boycott proved singularly controversial and threatened to alienate the BPP from the very community that it sought to mobilize. It proved a problematic test case for Newton's reanalysis of Black capitalism that was published weeks before the boycott began. The problems experienced by the BPP during the Cal-Pac boycott underscore the importance of the dialogic relationship between the BPP's leaders and rank-and-file, most notably demonstrating the importance for the BPP of winning a stronger base within the Black community. Chapter 6 presents the Cal-Pac boycott as a major turning point for the BPP, positioning it amid similar economic initiatives in Black America such as Operation Breadbasket, while revealing the narrowing gap between the BPP's practices and mainstream African American politics. The last major action of the BPP before its spiral into political obscurity reinforced this shift. The 1973 mayoral election saw Bobby Seale take the incumbent, John Reading, to a runoff. The subject of chapter 7, this election developed the electoral base from which Lionel Wilson became the first African American mayor in Oakland's history. More important, it demonstrated the vitality of the BPP's grassroots activism. Yet even as it promised a brighter future for Black Oakland, it exhausted the BPP, prompting the departure of enough burned-out activists to reduce the party to a shadow of its former self.

The book's third theme explains why the BPP failed to foment a revolution. The disruption of the BPP is essential to an understanding of the BPP's history: it ranged from a series of incarcerations beginning in 1967 designed to decapitate the organization, through innumerable FBI counterintelligence operations targeted at members across the nation, and includes Newton's trial for the murder of Oakland police officer John Frey, the central event in BPP history. As chapter 8 reveals, the trial highlights the extent of the California legal system's institutional racism and the BPP's vital role in revealing and challenging it. The defense strategy of Newton's attorney, Charles Garry, became a template for other defenses of Black radicals in the 1970s, while a vast "Free Huey" campaign brought the BPP to international attention and elevated Newton to the status of a divine martyr. Unfortunately, this proved a double-edged sword, as demonstrated by the FBI's concerted effort to destroy both Newton and the BPP.

A full evaluation of the FBI's campaign is impossible because of the sheer breadth of its activities and the destruction of many FBI records in the wake of COINTELPRO's 1971 suspension. Chapter 9 therefore focuses on select case studies to reveal the depth and impact of the FBI's actions. In Los Angeles, "Bunchy" Carter and John Huggins were murdered in broad daylight. In Chicago, Mark Clark and Fred Hampton were murdered by police in a nighttime raid. In New Haven, the torture and murder of BPP member Alex Rackley after he was falsely accused of being an FBI informant led to an attempt to frame BPP leaders Bobby Seale and Ericka Huggins, even though Rackley's accuser was himself linked to the FBI.

Infiltration and counterintelligence were not the only method used to disrupt the BPP's activities. The party saw scores of members incarcerated, and some remained imprisoned for decades after the BPP disbanded. The archival record here again privileges the experience of prominent Panthers, and Cleaver and Newton especially. The chapter uses these case studies not to reinforce such a focus but as exemplars of the kind of experiences endured by dozens, even hundreds of Panthers across the decades. This stretched from those who were only briefly imprisoned to those such as Mumia Abu-Jamal or the Angola Three who suffered decades of imprisonment, often in solitary confinement, because of their BPP affiliation. Importantly, however, the chapter argues that the timing of these particular imprisonments exerted a defining influence on the BPP's development during crucial moments in its history. In this, it suggests that prison helped shape the BPP in numerous ways. Eldridge Cleaver's experience of the California prison system's rehabilitative project prior to 1966, for example, had two major impacts: the first in shaping his own political, cultural, and perhaps even psychological outlook, and the second in making him a 1960s icon. Cleaver's notoriety led to the end of attempts in California to reform and rehabilitate Black convicts. Seale's imprisonments deprived the BPP of its most skilled organizer at certain critical moments. Newton's experience of prison was even harsher and more tragic. He endured years of solitary confinement that deprived the BPP of its founder and irrevocably reshaped his psychology. Finally, prison radicalized George Jackson, convinced him to join the BPP, and eventually killed him. The BPP's eulogies to Jackson and his brother Jonathan offer further confirmation of the importance of the prison to the party's development.

The eulogizing of the Jackson brothers begs consideration of the way in which veterans, historians, and the public remember the BPP, the topic of the book's epilogue. As the BPP receded into history, veterans engaged in a major memory-creation project involving conferences and memorials, the publication of memoirs, and other activities. This reified a commemorative interpretation of the BPP focused on social activism and personal sacrifice that valorizes BPP activists but also subtly undercuts the transformative potential that the BPP represented at its peak: a reading that reflects the hegemonic power of neoliberalism in the twenty-first century. As this suggests, key aspects of BPP memory ironically echo the triumphal narrative of racial progress that the BPP itself questioned. Yet even amid this, one simple fact remains: the memory and history of the BPP are fundamental to an understanding of recent American history.

PART I

Intellectual History

CHAPTER ONE

The BPP's Intellectual Territory

In September 1891, the *Free Speech* of Memphis, Tennessee, printed an uncompromising editorial highlighting the "true spark of manhood" evinced by the Black residents of Georgetown, Kentucky. In response to the lynching of a Black man, they set fire to the town. "Not until the Negro rises in his might and takes a hand in resenting such cold-blooded murders, if he has to burn down whole towns, will a halt be called in wholesale lynching."[1] These words were likely written by the newspaper's indefatigable editor, Ida B. Wells. Her warning to white Americans was clear; to Black Americans she promised that "sit[ting] tamely by" would simply lead to them forever being known as "a race of cowards."[2] Aware, however, that merely standing up and fighting would not be enough, she hinted that only armed self-defense would level the playing field between the outnumbered Black population and their white oppressors.[3] Wells was not the first to call for armed self-defense, nor would she be the last, but her insistence that only the threat of violence would prevent violence would reverberate throughout the twentieth century and become a constituent part of the intellectual world of the Black Panther Party.

This intellectual world most explicitly included Marxists such as Mao, Fanon, and Guevara, alongside Black nationalist icons such as Malcolm X and Robert F. Williams. Bobby Seale stated clearly: "I'd read *Wretched of the Earth* six times. I knew [Frantz] Fanon was right."[4] Huey P. Newton identified Fanon, Chairman Mao, and Ernesto "Che" Guevara as "kinsmen" who "saw clearly" that oppression was a violent phenomenon.[5] As this suggests, the Black Panther Party was steeped in revolutionary theory, albeit of a highly masculine kind: the BPP's first book list, published in September 1968, lacked even one book written by a woman. This list was headed by *The Autobiography of Malcolm X* and Fanon's *The Wretched of the Earth*; it included works by and on Marcus Garvey; studies of Black America by various historians; William Patterson's excoriating *We Charge Genocide*; and numerous leftist and Marxist texts including Herbert Aptheker's and C. L. R. James's studies of slave revolts,

19

and W. E. B. Du Bois's *Black Reconstruction*.[6] While the list offers an indispensable guide to the intellectual world of the BPP, Newton and Seale's elevation of Fanon, Guevara, Mao, Malcolm X, and Williams positions them as most important for in-depth evaluation, particularly so because of the defining influence they had on the BPP as it took shape.

As the historian Nikhil Pal Singh indicates, the BPP's immersion in this literature enabled it to position itself outside the paradigm established by the mainstream civil rights movement that pressed for change within the American system, and toward an internationalist anticolonial and radical intellectual tradition.[7] Yet, while generally acknowledging their impact, BPP scholars tend to avoid extensive evaluation of these influences.[8] Like many late 1960s radicals, the BPP developed a critique of American hegemonic capitalism, took a skeptical view of American democracy, and took inspiration from various revolutionary struggles across the globe. That these struggles were central concerns of anticolonial thinkers offered the BPP a gateway into alternative accounts of white supremacy, one that was bolstered by Malcolm X's critique of the civil rights movement and his increasing interest in the anticolonial struggle in 1964 and 1965. This forged an intellectual gap between the BPP and the civil rights mainstream, while simultaneously positioning it within the global, anticolonial New Left.

From the two great icons of 1960s African American radicalism, Malcolm X and Williams—both of whom acknowledged the significance of anticolonialism to the African American struggle—the BPP learned the importance of armed self-defense in the United States. Fanon's account of the Algerian Revolution expanded this to the world beyond North America, and Chairman Mao confirmed the centrality of the gun to liberation struggles and the immediacy of aphoristic sloganeering. Guevara, meanwhile, offered a potent example of the value of vanguardism and of the romantic element of revolutionary activism. Where Malcolm X and Williams highlighted the value of racial unity in a country riddled with white racists and hypocritical liberals, Guevara and Fanon's Marxism reminded the BPP not to dismiss interracial alliances. As important, perhaps, and reflecting the times, the overwhelmingly masculine aura of all the works other than Mao's emphasized adult male agency within the revolution.

The BPP's Intellectual Roots

As Seale and Newton suggest, it begins with Fanon. Born in Martinique in 1925, Fanon became influenced by a schoolteacher, Aimé Césaire, whose pioneering work on negritude became a lifelong inspiration. After joining the French army, he traveled to Algeria, learning there of colonialism's iniquities. At the University of Lyon, he studied dentistry and immersed himself in philosophy and psychoanalysis. His *Black Skin, White Masks* (1952) quickly became a classic anticolonial text. The following year he qualified as a psychiatrist and set out to practice in Algeria. He quickly realized that colonialism had even infected the hospitals, where staff simply assumed that Algerians suffering from mental problems were savage rather than unwell. Fanon instead linked his patients' afflictions to the impact of colonialism and racism, and he concluded that the Algerians' lived experience triggered their mental disturbances. Around the same time, he became involved in the Algerian war for independence. After the French expelled him, he effectively became a roving ambassador for the Front de Libération Nationale. He continued to work even after being diagnosed with leukemia and died shortly after his next book was published. So explosive was it that in December 1961 Paris police, considering it a threat to national security, seized the entire stock held by Fanon's publisher. Nevertheless, *The Wretched of the Earth* soon joined *Black Skin, White Masks* as a classic.[9]

A classic it might be, but *The Wretched of the Earth* is also misunderstood. Fanon's biographer David Macey argues that very soon after his death in 1961 Fanon became known as an "apostle of violence."[10] Yet this was certainly not the entirety of *The Wretched of the Earth*, a close reading of which is vital for an understanding of the BPP's ideology. The BPP's understanding of the text ran deep, as suggested by the fact that Newton kept a copy of the book on hand when he was awaiting trial in 1968 and by David Hilliard's determination to develop a deep understanding of its contents, which led him to conclude that Fanon "provided us with our most important theoretical model."[11] Its first chapter reveals Fanon's notion that armed struggle and disorder are central to the process of decolonization, and his gendered view that decolonization creates "new men."[12] Colonialism separates any locality into two distinct and mutually exclusive sectors: one for the colonized and one for the colonizers. The colonizers maintain control by herding the colonized into poor-quality, high-occupancy housing, much like America's inner cities were segregated by redlining practices. The threat of violence cements this division, which is policed by humans and a built environment designed to facilitate oppression, embodied in the panoptic barracks from which the oppressors observed the locals' everyday business. The colonized people thus see a world in which violence represents both coercion and control. Consequently, for Fanon, violence is central to the overthrow of the colonizers: a people who are oppressed through violence will logically be forced to choose violence to fight for their liberty. And this violence will symbolically cleanse them of colonialism.[13]

Aware of the potential of the indigenous people to revolt, the colonizers attempt to win over the minds of the native intelligentsia. This process has its successes, according to Fanon, who acidly comments that the many locals who envy the settlers' lives demonstrate merely how colonialism has corrupted their minds. Similarly, he presents nonviolence as a bourgeois plot to divert the struggle, an analysis that chimed with many BPP members' skepticism of the African American civil rights movement. Fanon argues that nationalist leaders emerge during this stage, when the initial outbreaks of violence create new power relations. The urgency of the message these people convey and their links to the people temporarily enable them to strike blows for the independence movement, which, he asserts, endures even if such leaders find themselves imprisoned.[14] Ultimately, the locals are drawn toward such rebels and the groups they represent because of the hopelessness of native life under colonial rule. "You could be sure of a new recruit," Fanon states, "when these individuals could not return to the colonial system." These people, he declares, find their freedom "in and through violence," and this violence is crucial in keeping morale high.[15]

So powerful is this chapter that generations of readers take it as the essence and totality of Fanon's thought, abetted by Jean-Paul Sartre's introduction to the original English translation that presented the book as a howl of pain and a battle cry, thus encouraging a simplistic reading of the text.[16] Sartre overlooked Fanon's insistence that violence, itself a response to the violence of the oppressors, only becomes viable as a last resort.[17] As important, he ignored Fanon's argument that violence is not only a consequence of colonialism but part of a revolutionary process that takes place on numerous fronts. More subtle readers, such as the BPP's members, understood the relationship between the explosive first chapter and the later chapters that, building on the work of generations of Marxists who debated the value of isolated, individual acts of violence, argued for a disciplined program of armed anticolonial struggle.

Chapter 2 focuses on class relations. Fanon notes that the working classes form the principal backbone of independence movements. The middle class and the peasantry are either too close to the oppressor or too reactionary to become revolutionary cadres. As the struggle begins, however, nationalist movements overcome the divide-and-rule strategy of the colonizers.[18] At this point Fanon reveals the importance of the lumpenproletariat to the struggle, an observation that became a major influence on the BPP's recruitment strategy. Marx defined lumpen proles as a "disintegrated mass" of the undesirable, the unemployed, and the unlawful who aided the Bonapartist counterrevolution.[19] For Fanon, however, these "classless idlers will by militant and decisive action discover the path that leads to nationhood."[20] Their exclusion from capitalism's bounties exceeds even that of the working class, thus increasing their revolutionary potential, provided that their rage at their exclusion could be channeled into revolutionary fervor. This adaptation of Marxian class analysis to colonial Africa resonated in Oakland, where Seale and Newton saw large numbers of almost permanently unemployed African American men forced to operate in both lawful and unlawful spheres. Yet it also subtly references a fellow internationalist Marxist in highlighting the revolutionary potential of society's most excluded. The Trinidadian activist-intellectual Claudia Jones concluded in 1949 that Black female domestic workers suffered from "super-exploitation," thus occupying a highly precarious position but one that could also be radicalizing.[21] The exploitation they faced, Jones suggests, ensured that they had less to lose when it came to protesting their situation, suggesting that these domestic workers could become the vanguard of the struggle.[22]

Jones is, of course, but one figure in a much longer and richer intellectual tradition of national and international Black women thinkers and organizers overlooked by the BPP's founders but whose thought would become part of the BPP's intellectual hinterland. Anna Julia Cooper, for example, considered the Black body—with all its intersectional identities—the crucial location in which emancipatory discourse and activism could take place.[23] Anticipating critiques of the Second Wave of American Feminism made by members of the BPP in the late 1960s and early 1970s, Cooper upbraided white feminists for failing to challenge racial as well as gender prejudice.[24] Similarly, as the historian Brittney Cooper argues, the National Association of Colored Women "laid the foundation for debates ... about what it means to properly perform and inhabit the categories of Black manhood and Black womanhood."[25] Amy Jacques-Garvey united nationalism with feminism to produce "community feminism," predicated on "assisting both the men and women in their lives." She insisted vehemently that women be accepted as intellectual as well as activist leaders in the Pan-African struggle.[26] As the Cold War became chillier, meanwhile, the members of the Sojourners for Truth and Justice developed transnational links with other groups fighting against colonialism and racism.[27] That the BPP founders marginalized the rich intellectual history of Black women—of which this is merely a thumbnail sketch—brings into sharp relief their highly masculine view of the world around them.

To return to Fanon, *Wretched*'s discussion then identifies the emergence of a new phase of the struggle, underpinned by national unity as the people discover that their common experience of oppression is more important than their internecine disputes. Fanon here suggests that colonialism breeds nationalism. Once this nationalism becomes apparent to the colonial forces, they turn their violence onto the indigenous people, which initiates the guerrilla warfare phase of the struggle. Here, a war of position emerges. Aware of the dangers that lumpen activists could lead the uprising down the wrong path as per Marx's interpretation, Fanon points out that education is vital to the struggle and states that a leadership cadre must ensure that the lumpen's energy is channeled in the right direction—advice that influenced the creation of the BPP's political education program. The chapter's final pages note the problematic nature of a racially defined struggle and argue that the nationalist leaders must become organic intellectuals by immersing themselves in the lives of the people.[28] Again, the BPP applied this to the Black American struggle, calling on African American politicians to reimmerse themselves in their communities and denouncing liberal African American leaders for their obeisance to the white power structure.[29] The contrast with organic leaders such as Seale and Newton was almost too obvious to point out.

Fanon's third chapter opens by stating that the nationalism that emerges in the colonial situation is a "crude and fragile travesty"—"the nation is passed over for the race, and the tribe is preferred to the state." This is a consequence of both the legacy of colonialism and the intellectual laziness of the indigenous middle class. Fanon's class analysis directs his awareness of the "pitfalls of national consciousness."[30] During this phase, the native middle class becomes an intermediary between the colonizers and the colonized. Driven by economic imperative, it tries to retain its elevated position in colonial society by integrating itself into the colonial-capitalist system.[31] This attempt to "replace the foreigner" exchanges colonial tension for national rivalries, a position that is easily exploited by nationalists who foment divides between whiter and blacker Africans and who treat the African working class with much the same disdain as the colonials. In Fanon's book, the nationalists' failure to reject capitalism also leads to their attempting to attract foreign capital to aid their economies, which itself exacerbates class tensions, not least because foreign capital would conform to its own class interests. The national period is thus merely a stage in a longer revolutionary process—national consciousness a step toward political and social consciousness. Ultimately, nationalism is an idea without substance, its historical role complete once nationhood has been achieved. For the revolution to develop, the national party needs to become the "direct expression of the masses."[32] The masses will not respond to the leadership simply dictating to them. Instead, they must develop the awareness that they are the crucial forces in the revolution. Each and every individual must become involved in the struggle: "every onlooker is either a coward or a traitor," concludes Fanon.[33]

Wretched's fourth chapter focuses on culture. Fanon reminds his readers that culture might not put food on the table, but it remains central to the revolutionary struggle. He objects to the regressive tendencies of many cultural movements, many of which took refuge in an idealized vision of Africa as the mother of human culture. Alluring as this vision is, for Fanon it merely diverts energies from the revolution, a quality that renders this culture similar to Marx's vision of religion as a "sigh of the oppressed creature" that does little to alleviate the material basis of oppression.[34] A "fighting" culture is consequently necessary, not least because stories about the past are useless to the individual when "the knife is at his throat." This is a culture that directly affects the revolution, created by revolutionaries who have devoted their lives to the struggle.[35]

In the last substantial chapter of *Wretched*, Fanon discusses the relationship between colonialism and mental disorders in a collection of case notes from the mid-1950s, accompanied by an essay on what he termed the "North-African syndrome."[36] Here he concludes that the large numbers of mental disorders treated by psychologists and psychiatrists in the colonies is clear evidence of the impact of colonialism on the human psyche. It is almost as if the unreality of the political-social situation causes mental breakdowns, helped by the methods through which colonists declare, reinforce, and control the feeling of inferiority among the indigenous people.[37] Furiously, heartbreakingly, Fanon details the human cost of colonialism's brutality. His brief conclusion, with its echoes of *The Communist Manifesto*, reasserts the need for a complete overthrow of the colonial world. Fanon's final call is for Africans to "turn over a new leaf... work out new concepts, and try to set afoot a new man," thus creating a new world.[38]

The Wretched of the Earth's English translation first appeared in the United States in 1965 and immediately received national attention.[39] By 1967, San Francisco's Success Book Store, a haven for African American bibliophiles, reported the book on its best-selling list. Within a year, over 185,000 copies of *Wretched* were circulating nationally.[40] Seale and Newton repeatedly read one of those copies. They saw many parallels between Fanon's colonial world and the East Bay. They understood that, much like colonial Algiers, the East Bay had been separated into "white" and "black" zones, with whites enjoying the high life in suburban enclaves while Blacks overpopulated the inner cities of Oakland and Richmond. They witnessed and experienced the dehumanization of African Americans by the police and the overt and covert methods by which the police and other oppressors made local residents feel second class. They also knew that the Oakland Police Department, which maintained the so-called peace, was largely staffed by white men who lived far from the areas they policed. These men were often brutal and frequently used dehumanizing, racist language—in Fanon's words, "the language of pure force"—when dealing with the local citizenry.[41] Meanwhile, working-class African Americans were treated as raw material for a system that produced goods they could not afford to buy. So where Fanon suggests that colonialism built and sustained European capitalism, it was no stretch to suggest that slavery and Black exploitation built and sustained American capitalism. No wonder that Oakland's Black population was wont to lash out.

According to Seale, *The Wretched of the Earth* immediately resonated because of its insistence that the lumpenproletariat become the shock troops of the revolution.[42] Both he and Newton were already influenced by the ex-convict Malcolm X, had been on the wrong side of the law, and understood what life was like for lumpen African American men. The BPP saw lumpen activity not as an end in itself but as a means through which American capitalism could be undermined and the revolution actuated; such actions "light the way," as Fanon argued, for others to follow.[43] Fanon thus elevated Newton and Seale to the level of active agents in a revolutionary process. As important, Fanon confirmed to them that words were meaningless without action, helping propel them from their study groups to street activity. Newton later wrote of his admiration for Fanon's notion of the "Year of the Boomerang," the third phase of violence, when it is turned on the oppressor.[44] Fanon's theory of armed struggle exerted great influence as the idea for the BPP percolated in their minds, but Newton and Seale both understood that Fanon's violence was far from nihilistic. "We used to underline," said Seale, "everything that Fanon said about violence . . . how spontaneous violence educates those who are in a position with skills to lead the people to what needs to be done."[45] Here Seale demonstrated the BPP's understanding of violence as process, that random acts of violence would lead to a more disciplined, focused attack on the state. Both he and Newton followed Fanon's gendered understanding of the anticolonial struggle, centering men and masculine action in the liberation struggle. Moreover, *Wretched*'s anger reflected Seale's and Newton's anger at the forces that oppressed them. It was consequently logical for them to consider Fanon's description of the colonial world as an analogy that could be applied to urban Black America, itself a reminder that *Wretched* is only nominally about Algeria; instead, it should be approached as a book about the worldwide struggle against colonialism and foreign exploitation. In the revolutionary imaginary, Algeria and California were far closer than mere geography suggested.

As if to compress the distance between Algiers and Oakland even further, Gillo Pontecorvo's incendiary *The Battle of Algiers* (1965) provided further evidence of the validity of armed resistance to colonialism. One of the most celebrated films of the decade, it depicted in quasi-documentary fashion the guerrilla war in the Algerian Revolution.[46] Don Cox testified that he watched the film numerous times before departing for exile in Algiers. Emory Douglas, the BPP's minister for culture, called it the single most influential film of his life, while Regina Jennings highlights its centrality to the BPP's induction program for new members.[47] The film played at festivals in New York City and in Los Angeles, where it attracted the attention of the local BPP chapter. It also played in San Francisco to BPP sympathizers from the local Black Student Union. In May 1968 it began a fourteen-week run in Chicago. Local activists Bobby Rush, Bob Brown, and Tommy Carter took many lessons from the film. The Detroit chapter put on their own screenings for the community. New York Panthers watched the film, as did some of their police surveillers.[48]

Its appeal to the BPP was clear. Not only did it depict an Algiers separated into European and native sections, it portrayed the transformation of the colonial apparatus from civil police to military paratroopers, and their attempt to create a panoptic surveillance structure to monitor locals. Like Fanon, the film condemned the colonial French at a systematic level, presenting their violence as another product of colonialism. As important, it revealed the vast superiority the French enjoyed in terms of resources, an advantage that did not prevent the Algerians from taking up arms, instead influencing them to adopt guerrilla techniques. Despite the apparent defeat of the Algerians in the titular battle, the film suggests that their immersion in their local surroundings was fundamental to their eventual success. The BPP recruits' knowledge of the inner cities could prove similarly decisive, as they knew how to exploit the built environment of the inner cities to prevent capture, patrol the police, and if necessary conduct guerrilla operations. Significantly, the film ends by observing the pyrrhic nature of the French victory in Algiers—a lesson that could prove instructive when BPP members experienced their own setbacks.

The Algerian Revolution, however, was far from the sole influence on the BPP. Seale and Newton took Robert F. Williams's *Negroes with Guns* very seriously. Indeed, in many senses it too presented a practical demonstration of some of Fanon's theories about armed struggle. The title itself offered an inspiring vision of African American self-determination and strength. The contents were equally explosive, detailing Williams's experience of leading an NAACP chapter in Monroe, North Carolina, before being forced into exile after being accused of kidnapping a white couple during a night in which he feared Monroe was on the verge of a racial pogrom.[49] Williams's response to white terror was revolutionary, he suggested, since it forced "the enemy, who is a moral weakling and coward ... [to] work for a respectable compromise."[50] He finished his book asserting that self-defense was "an American tradition," not far from the infamous claim by Jamil Abdullah al Amin (formerly H. Rap Brown) that violence was as American as cherry pie.[51]

Building on Ida B. Wells's understanding of the power inherent in the mere threat of retaliatory violence, Williams's treatise reveals the physical and subversive power that gun-wielding African Americans held. Williams and his comrades were picketing a segregated swimming pool when a white mob threatened them. Rather than taking solace in nonviolence or promising to overcome through song, the protesters aimed guns at their attackers. The atmosphere changed as the mob and local police immediately retreated. Williams's promise to meet violence with violence ironically averted violence and caused a significant shift in the psychology of Monroe's Black and white communities. Williams concluded that he and his comrades gained the respect of their white neighbors as a result of their willingness to stand tall. The threat of violence similarly kept the police honest; only the threat of mutually assured destruction kept the peace.[52]

Yet *Negroes with Guns* was more than simply a declaration of the right to self-defense. Williams presents nonviolence as a perfectly appropriate protest method but asserts that when the rule of law breaks down, an individual retains the right to self-protection, a message that echoed Fanon. For Williams, any system of racism was based on violence, and so it was appropriate to use the threat of fighting back to tackle it. Raising the threat of retaliation, Williams argued, revealed the enemy's cowardice, since only now would he be willing to make concessions.[53] For him, the rapid decline in Monroe Ku Klux Klan activity following his intervention was clear evidence of the value of the self-defense strategy. By contrast, the lack of concerted action from established civil rights groups such as the NAACP enmeshed them in the problem, which the NAACP in particular deepened through its failure to attract working-class people in the South. This was compounded by the naivete of the nonviolent protesters who descended on Monroe in August 1961. Their arrival, in Williams's account, merely emboldened the white racists. Coupled with Dr. Martin Luther King's heavily publicized denunciation of Williams, this revealed that the bourgeois civil rights leadership and their organizations could not contend with the increasingly brutal defense of segregation exercised by white supremacists.[54] Williams's call, then, was to abandon a civil rights struggle and fight for a human rights struggle, thus positioning Black Americans in the global movement against white supremacy. That Williams recruited heavily among local veterans—some of whom had fought abroad—and those who loitered in local pool halls, who frequented local beauty parlors, who labored for whites, or who were unemployed offered both a contrast to the NAACP's disinterest in the masses and a practical example of Fanonist organizing. His battle with the aging, middle-class NAACP hierarchy reminded him and his readers that Black elites blunted the revolutionary edge of the freedom struggle while playing into the hypocritical hands of white liberals. This also informed Williams's argument that economic disadvantage lay at the core of the problems facing the African American community, reinforcing Fanon's suggestion that class interests were crucial in defining the revolutionary struggle.[55]

Williams's influence over the BPP extended further. His involvement in the notorious "Kissing Case" demonstrated that supposedly minor local events could, in the right circumstances and with the right publicity, become major international sensations. "Rebellion," he resolved, "ferments in modern youth," offering a distant echo of the African American intellectual and formerly enslaved Anna Julia Cooper's insistence that youthful vigor was essential in driving Black Americans toward a better future.[56] This understanding surely gave Newton and Seale further confidence in their decision to recruit young men and women to the BPP. As important, once Williams's struggle reached the national press and came to the attention of the NAACP's national office, he grasped the importance of taking control of the narrative. His regular newsletter, *The Crusader*, countered the propaganda of the NAACP and the mainstream press. An avowed internationalist and keen student of history, he peppered *The Crusader* with articles about the Cuban Revolution long before he fled there, and he eulogized the militant abolitionist John Brown as the only white person he truly admired—an admiration that he shared with Malcolm X.[57] Not coincidentally, the BPP realized that its confrontational tactics needed a publicity outlet that countered the mainstream press.

While *Negroes with Guns* established Williams as both an activist and an intellectual force, his actions in the street suggested that he might be a "crazy Negro," unbound by the customs and conventions of society, prepared to take whatever action he felt necessary to uphold his own honor and protect himself. Backed into the corner by Monroe's racists, Williams's willingness to wield the gun suggested to his white antagonists that he was prepared to die fighting, and this apparent recklessness caused them to question their own attachment to life. With nothing to lose, he might lash out with disastrous consequences for them should they escalate the confrontation. To readers like Seale and Newton, Williams's ability to wrestle control of situations from white racists provided an object lesson in how to behave when faced by white supremacists.

Negroes with Guns was also a heavily masculine text. Although Williams was keen to involve local women in the struggle, the regular citation of traditionally masculine notions of strength, protection, and power suggests that his was a gendered struggle, one that chimed with Newton and Seale's gendered world. Its first page opens with Williams arguing that his primary objective in taking up arms was to protect the community's wives, children, and homes, thus presenting self-defense as a masculine action to protect the family unit. By contrast, the Klan forcing a Black woman to "dance at pistol point" clearly demonstrated its members' cowardice and depravity.[58] Importantly, however, without a (Black) man to protect her, she was at their mercy. Similarly, Williams illustrates his rejection of legal strategies to punish racists with two accounts of physical and sexual assaults on Black women. His conclusion was to "meet violence with violence" to "defend our women and children" when it became apparent that legal appeals would fail.[59] This retrograde focus on men as the protectors of the family (and by extension the Black community) offered extra purpose for men who felt emasculated by white social, political, and economic dominance, enabling them to express their masculinity while fighting white oppression. Yet it also reduced women's agency. Williams's conception of "strong people" was thus far less capacious than, for example, his peer Ella Baker, whose oft-cited adage "strong people don't need strong leaders" encapsulated her insistence that democratic movements needed to empower their members and work with them rather than on their behalf, not to mention her adamant opposition to patriarchal assumptions about masculinity and femininity.[60]

Like Williams, Guevara was fully prepared to take up arms to fight for his beliefs. In many ways, he was the new man that Fanon longed for. For him, guerrilla movements (or *focos*) should only be promoted where the ruling power has no constitutional legality. Provided this criterion is met, then insurrectionary forces can create the conditions for a revolutionary struggle. Such forces could be composed of as few as thirty men and work most effectively when they were in tune with the masses.[61] Guevara believed that these men were best placed if they lived in the sierras, or the rural mountains. Importantly, however, he insisted that focos operated best with a collection of male representatives of the local population, another suggestion that influenced Newton and Seale's recruitment strategy. Their low numbers meant that focos could move easily, outwitting larger but slower-moving forces. Again, this would be facilitated by local people, who would be drawn into the struggle when they assisted the rebels or misdirected their enemies. Guevara's foco theory thus aligned with Fanon's assertion of the centrality of the lumpenproletariat to the revolution, offering further confirmation that the BPP was in the vanguard of a worldwide revolutionary movement. Perhaps as important, Guevara's demise and apotheosis in 1967, not long after Newton's arrest following John Frey's death, was proof of the doomed romanticism of Guevara's revolutionary ambitions and of the power of the revolutionary icon in New Left hearts and minds. Within a few years, Newton himself was advocating the notion of revolutionary suicide, a welcoming of death that he presented as the hallmark of the true revolutionary. Guevara's influence over this concept cannot be discounted, and the example of his demise offers a crucial rejoinder to Fanon's lament that a "death reflex" led some colonial subjects toward a sense of fatality and suicidal behavior, which simply confirmed to the colonists that these people were less than human.[62]

Like any self-respecting African American radicals, Newton and Seale venerated another martyred radical. The contours of Malcolm X's life are familiar: the petty criminal who joined the Nation of Islam and became its most famed and controversial speaker before being assassinated not long after he departed the group. This obviously oversimplifies the many complexities of his life and ignores his vital contribution to Black history. His fierce denunciations of white hypocrisy, Black nonviolence, and American party politics brought him opprobrium from the mainstream media but proved inspirational to countless people across the globe. Many subsequent activists turned to his work for political insight and inspiration, ensuring that his legacy continued to inform African American politics long after his death.

His primary goal, he said, was to bring about the "complete independence of people of African descent here in the Western Hemisphere, and first here in the United States . . . by any means necessary."[63] Like Fanon, Malcolm X saw revolution brewing and understood the revolutionary capabilities of the lumpenproletariat.[64] Like Williams, he was an internationalist. His overseas visits convinced him both of the "wisdom and strength" of Africans through history and eventually of the myopia of racial separatism. He was particularly taken with the attempt by the 1955 Bandung Conference participants to sweep away that which divided nonwhite peoples, and he later welcomed Fidel Castro to Harlem.[65] The effect of the foreign travels on Malcolm X—and particularly his first trip of 1964 to Africa—was profound. He returned home believing that Black Americans had a strong relationship with the other nonwhite peoples of the world, and certain that he could charge the United States with violating the UN's Charter on Human Rights. This plan was received warmly in Africa, confirming to him the inseparability of the African American and worldwide struggles.[66] It also positioned Malcolm X within an informal network of American activists who wielded the Cold War and decolonization as weapons within the African American struggle. This network included the Sojourners for Truth and Justice and the Universal Association of Ethiopian Women (UAEW). Led by Queen Mother Audley Moore and Dara Abubakari, the UAEW issued a formal claim to the United Nations for reparations for slavery in 1959. Like Fanon, Moore and Abubakari concluded that Black Americans were a colonized people and saw the decolonization process as about not only politics, money, and land but also freeing themselves from psychological oppression.[67] The links between the UAEW and the BPP ran deeper, though: Moore mentored Malcolm X, helping him understand the importance of looking to Africa; she supported Robert F. Williams; and she was a leading light in the Revolutionary Action Movement (RAM), the organization that helped nurture Bobby Seale among other future BPP members, albeit in Philadelphia rather than the Bay Area.[68]

Soon after his return from Africa in 1964, Malcolm X established the Organization of Afro-American Unity to help promote his broadening internationalist vision. The Socialist Workers Party through the Militant Labor Forum sponsored a series of talks in New York City, bringing him to a white leftist audience that welcomed his occasional denunciations of Western capitalism and racism.[69] Whites were excluded from OAAU meetings because Malcolm X felt that their presence would inhibit the Black members' "discovery of what *they* need to do, and particularly of what *they can* do—for themselves, working by themselves, among their own kind, in their own communities."[70] Not coincidentally, the BPP accepted white support but not white members. Here, the BPP also echoed Robert F. Williams's skepticism toward integration both in its blunting of the radical edge of the racial struggle and its own implicit suggestion that Black Americans needed to assimilate into white America. Once again, though, this reflects a deeper tradition in Black thought going back centuries and moving far beyond the national boundaries of the United States.[71]

The implication of such a position was clear: such advocates sought not to integrate into an unjust society but instead play a key role in transforming that society by taking control of their own institutions. In asserting that whites were not the standard to which they ought to aspire, they posed pointed questions about white society that white integrationists often preferred not to ask. Malcolm X's understanding of Black nationalism shaped the BPP's call for the Black community to retain control of its own institutions. To him, Black nationalism was a form of interest-group politics that would enable Black Americans to take control of their destiny.[72] It incorporated a simple political philosophy: "the black man should control the politics and the politicians in his community."[73] A Black voting bloc to support candidates independent of the Republicans and the Democrats would give the community a political voice. Financially, the Black community should control its own economy, from its grocery stores to its banks, and should spend its money in this community rather than allowing the African American dollar to flow out. Socially, Black nationalism worked toward eradicating the ills that debased the Black community.[74] The OAAU program encompassed a wider educational, cultural, political, social, and economic plan to uplift the community. Community control of local schools was deemed essential for its children to develop self-respect and protect their identity as Black Americans. This was part of a campaign to launch a "cultural revolution to unbrainwash an entire people," unite the African American community, and inculcate closer identification with the diaspora.[75] Finally, so important was the right to self-defense that it was the sole statement on OAAU membership cards.[76]

The Early BPP's Intellectual Development

The Black Panther Party Ten-Point Platform and Program quickly became a classic radical text. According to Seale, Newton articulated every word, apparently spontaneously in October 1966, before Newton's brother Melvin smoothed out some of the language.[77] The printed version of the Platform and Program appeared in 1967 and was amended in May 1968 and summer 1969. Its list of demands echoed a similar platform drawn up by Malcolm X for the Nation of Islam in 1963, focusing on demands for freedom for all Black people including those in prison, an end to police brutality, a call for equal justice and employment opportunities, and proper educational opportunities for Black children.[78] The Platform and Program also demanded an end to white robbery of the Black community (amended to capitalist robbery in 1969); decent housing for all; exemption from military service for Black men; and a final call for "land, bread, housing, education, clothing, justice, and peace." A second section fleshed out these demands, arguing that only the ability to determine their destiny constituted freedom; that the federal government was responsible for full employment and that it had stolen so much from the Black community that reparations were essential. It also asserted that Black renters retained the right to expropriate substandard housing from their landlords; that knowledge of the self was vital to personhood; and that a racist government had no right to expect Black men to kill other nonwhite peoples. Citing the Second Amendment, the document declared the right to bear arms and form self-defense groups to prevent police oppression before touching on constitutional themes by declaring that no Black convict had received a fair trial by jury of their peers. Its final section quoted the Declaration of Independence as final proof that the BPP drew on a long tradition of humanist and American patriotic protest.[79] In 1968, the two sections were combined to link the demands and beliefs more explicitly, and a demand for a United Nations–sponsored plebiscite for African Americans to determine their national destiny was appended to the final point. This was first to give Black Americans the opportunity to put their feelings about sovereignty on record, and second to bring UN observers into the United States to provide a further bulwark against white-on-Black violence.[80] Once again, this positioned the BPP within a larger, internationalist, Cold War tradition.

The original draft of the Platform and Program might appear to elevate race over class and thus suggest that Malcolm X's analysis exerted the greatest influence on the nascent BPP. Yet elements of other influences poke through. The BPP's assertion of self-defense rights also draws from Williams, while the insistence that Black convicts be released reflects a subtle Fanonism and also suggests the BPP's awareness of the potential of the lumpenproletariat for the struggle. As this suggests, the Platform and Program serves as a succinct primer to BPP thought and was a crucial document for educating new Panthers. Importantly, however, its minor revisions did not quite match the transformations in BPP praxis, nor could it encompass the full complexity of BPP thought.[81]

Not long after forming the BPP, Newton and Seale came across *Quotations from Chairman Mao Tse-Tung*, the famous "Little Red Book." The collection of aphorisms and short extracts from Mao's lengthy publication list offered further confirmation of much of the theory that the founders had already absorbed, particularly in terms of the value of discipline in a revolutionary struggle and Mao's much-cited axiom that power flows from a gun. Prior to forming the BPP, Bobby Seale was briefly active in RAM, an organization that was well versed in Maoist theory, so it is possible that Seale encountered Mao's work through RAM and its Oakland front organization, the Soul Students Advisory Council. He claims that he quickly grew frustrated at RAM's rigid and hypocritical class politics, so any assessment of the organization's influence on his intellectual history must be accompanied by caveats.[82] Yet they share common interests. At a national level RAM outlined a program that advocated the creation of freedom schools, cooperative economics, rifle clubs, and a guerrilla army. All were to become central features of BPP praxis. While the BPP rejected its racial essentialism, RAM's internationalism, coupled with its insistence that African Americans understand themselves as victims of a colonial oppressor, also became important to the BPP.

Perhaps as important as the ideological and political influence the BPP drew from the Little Red Book was its form. Separated into thirty-three relatively self-contained chapters, the book includes over four hundred short quotations. It touches on many aspects of Marxist-Leninist theory, from the role of the party to discipline, imperialism, internationalism, solidarity, education, criticism, culture, and the necessity of intellectual study. For Mao, war was the "highest form of struggle" and inevitable in the revolutionary struggle.[83] Its practitioners should be spirited, courageous, fearless, and determined; diligent, frugal, and self-reliant; modest, self-abnegating, and disciplined. Such dictums lent themselves well to political slogans. His pithiness stood in sharp contrast to the density of Fanon's prose and Malcolm X's speeches, and BPP rhetoric came replete with similarly epigrammatic slogans such as "Power to the People" that echoed Mao's ability to reduce complex political theory to a memorable phrase.

Mao highlights the importance of educating the peasantry to win them over to the revolution, illustrating to the BPP that Marxist thought could be flexible on the topic of the revolution's vanguard. Indeed, education is a key element for Mao in ensuring discipline, ideological unity, and success. Self-criticism and the dialectical method were crucial to ensuring the longevity of the revolution. Mao insisted that a revolutionary culture was essential, asserted that women should be equal, and positioned young people in the revolution's vanguard.[84] Significantly, however, Seale prefers to talk of Mao's initial influence in somewhat more capitalist terms:

> we found a way to make money by selling *The Little Red Book* . . . for three or four weeks before we even opened it. . . . We'd buy it for 20 cents and sell it for a buck . . . because we needed funds, financial support. And one day after all of this selling of this book, we sit down and start reading this book and at one point in there it says, "Do not steal, not even a needle in a piece of thread from the people." We thought that was great.[85]

Seale also suggests that Cleaver—who was quite possibly the most Maoist of the BPP hierarchy—had to be educated in Maoism when he dismissed the idea of a free breakfast program as "sissy." "Always serve the people," retorted Seale, perhaps in more literal fashion than Mao intended.[86] After selling the Red Books, Seale reports that "Huey had us practicing the principles. And we used Fanon and Malcolm X. . . . Huey integrated all these principles of the other revolutionaries. We taught from all these materials, and from Che Guevara too."[87]

Combined, these influences created the intellectual world that forged the BPP. Their common insistence that revolutionary deeds were necessary for liberation—assertions that might be traced back to Marx's own axiom stating that "philosophers have only interpreted the world, in various ways; the point is to change it"—profoundly influenced Newton and Seale in particular: both men regularly lambasted supposed comrades who preferred thought or argument over action.[88] Despite Mao's insistence that women were equal in the struggle, this action would be led by men, whom the BPP considered were best placed to pick up the gun, and supposedly least likely to falter when violence erupted. The very physicality of the police in Oakland constituted a stark reminder that only the strongest and fittest would be able to overpower the occupying force. Seale and Newton were also profoundly influenced by the élan with which Marxist revolutionaries expressed themselves, whether it be in literary terms or in their physical being. Ultimately, BPP thought was best expressed through practice, and is exemplified by Newton's behavior in public. Echoes of Williams's very public display of Black Power can be distinguished in Newton's chutzpah when faced with a crowd of belligerent observers and local police, as demonstrated in numerous events around the Bay Area.[89] Like Guevara, the BPP's members adopted a uniform that was at once functional and romantic, while dedicating their lives to the struggle. Like Malcolm X and Fanon, they immersed themselves in the lives of, and spoke directly to, ordinary African American people, and like Mao they were convinced that political power could flow from the gun. Yet where Malcolm X and Williams suggested that Black unity was central, the BPP blended revolutionary Black nationalism with class analysis. As this suggests, Newton and Seale flexibly applied these theorists to the Oakland of the late 1960s. Similarly, their observation of the development of thinkers like Malcolm X informed their conviction that their revolution would always be developing in response to the changing situations in which the BPP found itself. Their ideas would follow suit.

CHAPTER TWO

The Gendered World of the BPP

A 1968 meeting among Detroit's chapter descended into outrage when one male insisted that a female comrade be silent while he spoke, to demonstrate the respect he was due as a man. According to an eyewitness, the woman jumped onto the table at which he sat. Drawing on her BPP training, she drew a pistol and aimed it directly at him. Informing the doubtless startled sexist that nobody would be silencing her, she won a swift apology.[1] This brief episode exemplifies many of the tensions between male chauvinism and female empowerment within the BPP, and confirms that debates over the politics of gender were present throughout party ranks. The female Panther's willingness to frighten her supposed comrade into submission and pointed refusal to concern herself with hurting his feelings (and potentially even his body) reflects how deeply members embraced the BPP's ideas about assertiveness, pride, and equality. As important, her preparedness to put her body on the line demonstrates quite literally how BPP women enacted the BPP's positioning of the human body at the vanguard of the challenge to racism at the same time as they challenged internal assumptions about male dominance and female submissiveness. Her insistence on seizing and exercising her right to speak rendered her and her female comrades more visible and powerful than her sexist adversary could ever have countenanced, reinforcing the sense that female members challenged many assumptions about their second-class status, not least those surrounding their supposed corporeal vulnerability. In positioning her body above his and wielding the gun as such, she—like many female BPP members—upended her male comrades' assumption that he was the more powerful in the male-female relationship.

As the episode also suggests, female members were often subject to sexist assumptions and demands; they challenged and overcame these barriers through many different means, including using the party's own ideas, to fight sexism from within. These sexist assumptions impacted almost all aspects of the BPP's praxis from the exclusion of women in the BPP's 1968 list of essential texts onward.[2] Indeed, early editions of *The Black Panther* suggest that sexism was never far from—and often on—the surface in the BPP.[3] The early emphasis on armed patrols was bolstered by the BPP's Williams-esque call for more recruits: "BLACK MEN!!! It is your duty to your women and children, to your mothers and sisters, to investigate the program of the PARTY."[4] Soon after the party's protest at the state capitol, Newton argued that Black men had been taught to consider themselves inferior. Battered by a combination of economic oppression, social exclusion, and unrealistic expectations, Black men did not receive the respect necessary for them to become fully fledged men. Their sense of self was further eroded by the breadwinning status of their wives, their physical inability to protect home and family, and their dependence on the white man for food, employment, education, and leadership. This, Newton suggested, rendered Black men little more than slaves.[5] The unexpressed resolution to this identity crisis was, of course, to join the BPP and take up the gun.

Even though many female Panthers entered a highly masculine environment, they carved out intellectual, activist, organizational, social, and political spaces that were essential to the party's development. This became increasingly important as state repression resulted in a relative decline in male membership in the BPP while women rose to fill important positions throughout the party. According to a number of male Panthers, rank-and-file women in the party held a surer grasp of politics and history than their male counterparts and possessed better organizational skills.[6] Tarika Lewis, the first female recruit, maintains that she performed exactly the same function as her male counterparts, even as the BPP attempted to recruit only women who could type, presumably to offer secretarial support. She played a central role in producing the early issues of *The Black Panther* and was soon joined by Kathleen Cleaver, who made many essential contributions to the BPP's house publication. Women thus embodied a dialectic, facing down men's expectations to produce a new synthesis in the form of a Black female revolutionary. Barbara Easley Cox's experience underscores this dialectical tension. She was ordered to relocate to Philadelphia before her husband ordered her back to San Francisco. Such disruption is suggestive of male Panthers' attempts to dominate the lives of their female comrades and partners. She also participated in security operations when she was heavily pregnant. In combining the role of expectant mother and revolutionary activist, Easley Cox demonstrates the vital importance of rank-and-file women to the BPP's daily activities, not to mention the immense burdens placed on individual members in the midst of a concerted campaign of state repression, even as these members contended with huge personal battles.[7]

As these examples suggest, women in the BPP faced numerous masculinist expectations and prejudices, positioning their struggles at the intersection of the campaigns against racial, class, sex, and gender oppression. Their response broadened the BPP's revolutionary ideology considerably, demonstrating the centrality of challenge and criticism within the party and illustrating the transformative impact of the BPP for its members. Yet the gender ideology of the BPP as constructed by its men, and particularly from men in leadership positions who wielded considerable influence at key points in the BPP's history, remains worthy of consideration. This both outlines the internal forces that impacted women's activities and underlines the importance of their demolition of these very forces.

Eldridge Cleaver took an almost macho attitude toward the revolutionary struggle and the role of men and women in overthrowing capitalism. With Huey P. Newton in jail, as minister for information he assumed de facto leadership of the party in late 1967. The BPP's structure hindered rank-and-file attempts to challenge or question him, and as the most visible and one of the most articulate Panthers, the media naturally gravitated toward him. His influence helps explain why, notwithstanding Emory Douglas's and Tarika Lewis's progressive depiction of women in the artwork that adorned the BPP's newspaper, women's roles in the revolution received less attention than they deserved in the paper until his departure for Cuba in November 1968.[8] His 1967 critique of female beauty contests aptly demonstrates his chauvinism. In denouncing them as a "sick thing" and a "racist ritual" he observed that competitions such as Miss America "brainwashed" people and acted as an insult to the "women of the Third World" who were ritually excluded from such competitions. Yet his solution was not so much to attack the objectification of women but to establish a rival Miss Third World Contest.[9] Obviously, this suggestion was infused with the BPP's "Black Is Beautiful" slogan, but its failure to appreciate the iniquity of the objectification of women illustrates Cleaver's failure to comprehend gender discrimination. He, however, was not alone in reflecting the male chauvinism of the 1960s; many male Panthers followed suit. Newton's own "Fear and Doubt," written in mid-1967, perfectly demonstrates the early BPP's gendered world. It opens on a highly gendered note: "The lower socio-economic Black male is a man of confusion."[10] Newton here only mentions women as childbearers or maids, their fates determined by biology and socioeconomic status. Newton's determinism even results in his arguing that any wife whose husband was not able to be the main breadwinner would view him as "quite worthless," presumably because of her resentment at having to leave the domestic sphere.[11] Such attitudes ensured that female Panthers contended with a gender ideology that they sought to overthrow.

BPP Feminism

It almost goes without saying that women became essential to the BPP's operation. For example, alongside a number of other early female recruits, Kathleen Cleaver became one of the early BPP's most important organizers. One of the few Panthers who previously worked for the Student Nonviolent Coordinating Committee (SNCC), she drew influence from uncompromising civil rights activists such as Gloria Richardson and Diane Nash rather than the male leftists lauded by her male comrades.[12] While Cleaver never met SNCC's guiding inspiration, Ella Baker, she cannot have avoided Baker's influence, especially her keen understanding of the relationship between racial oppression and economic inequality and her identification with poor and working-class people at the expense of her own class status.[13] As this suggests, Baker was keenly aware of the role capitalism played in creating and maintaining an unequal society, and of the failures of African American organizations that leaned into rather than resisted class stratification in Black America.[14] As her biographer Barbara Ransby observes, her inculcation of a questioning attitude toward society's structures led many SNCC activists to begin questioning gendered norms and assumptions, particularly over men's and women's roles in the movement.[15] Deep within her life, moreover, lay a foreshadowing of one of the BPP's most important recruitment methods. When working in Shreveport, Louisiana, she spent considerable time with a man known as "Papa Tight," renowned for his almost permanent presence at a local barbecue joint. Aware that his status as a local raconteur afforded him great insight into the local community's ideas, Baker listened carefully to him, in stark contrast to her former colleagues in the NAACP. Indeed, some twenty years previously, she had attempted to move the NAACP toward activism in the pool halls and bars, arguing that it needed to rid itself of its condescending attitude toward working-class people and puts its name "on the lips of all the people."[16]

Baker's life's work thus offers another thread linking the BPP to broader and deeper intellectual and activist traditions. Through their public activism, they positioned themselves at the vanguard of the campaign for change. They embodied Anna Julia Cooper's insistence that white feminism utterly failed Black women and her arguments that to judge Black progress exclusively on men's experiences was lamentably myopic.[17] Of course, Cooper did not transcend class prejudice in her focus on racial uplift, but her understanding of the Black movement's exclusion of women and the feminist movement's exclusion of Black women prefigured analyses made by 1960s radicals. Queen Mother Moore, for example, considered second-wave American feminists hopelessly white and middle-class.[18] Kay Lindsey, writing in Toni Cade Bambara's *The Black Woman* anthology, insisted that Black women were systematically excluded from the highly masculine Black movement and the lily-white feminist movement. For her, the revolution needed to destroy not only racial oppression but also the family—a link to the communal living among BPP members.[19] Bambara herself noted that women were often constrained by men's insistence that a tough woman was "a rough mamma, a strident bitch, a ballbreaker, a castrator"— derogatory terms that denigrated women and discouraged them from taking action.[20]

Cleaver brought her experience to bear on the BPP almost immediately on her November 1967 arrival. While playing a central role in the development of the BPP newspaper, she became the first woman on the Central Committee and was one of the Free Huey campaign's most familiar faces. In the face of her husband's dismissive attitude, she conceived the BPP march on the Alameda County Courthouse on the first day of Newton's murder trial, a key staging post on the BPP's rise to international prominence. Aware of the fundamental value of communication to an activist group, she became a key BPP publicist, while the media gravitated toward her as an articulate and authoritative voice.[21] It is no stretch to argue that Kathleen Cleaver was fundamental to the BPP's stabilization and growth at a critical moment in its history. And yet, like many other revolutionary women, she faced a barrage of gendered expectations, as Agnès Varda's 1968 BPP documentary confirms. It introduces Cleaver primarily as a wife rather than an activist in her own right. The interview proceeds with Cleaver outlining her views of Black beauty and women's roles in the party, the latter a question that perplexed her, for similar inquiries were never made of male comrades.[22] Consequently, Varda's deliberate emphasizing of women's contribution to the party combines with a depiction of the normative assumptions about political revolutions supposedly being men's business. While such approaches reflected contemporary gendered assumptions in eliciting discussion of beauty issues only among its women interviewees, like Cleaver these women's responses demonstrate how BPP women wrapped all aspects of their lives in their political outlook. Cleaver patiently outlined how she and other Panther women were engaged in a process of reclaiming African American beauty amid the considerable pressures faced by women from a beauty-industrial complex that privileged white while denigrating Black beauty. For her and her comrades, natural hairstyles signified their political beliefs; one unnamed Panther observed that her involvement with the BPP prompted her to change her hairstyle to better reflect her political development. As this suggests, they held a subtle and deeply complex understanding of the relationship between cultural expressions and political beliefs.

The documentary thus presents the framing of female Panthers and their response to such framing in a dialectical fashion. Indeed, the extent to which the documentary subtly challenges normative assumptions about the BPP's masculine, military bearing remains remarkable. While the expected Panther drills and discussions of guns are present, they follow an impressionistic opening to the documentary that emphasizes the joy amid a community gathering that features live music and animated conversation among the set-piece speeches, where children dance alongside teenagers and adults, and where women feature prominently, leading some singing and watching over the gathering. It takes nearly two minutes for a voice-over to inform viewers that this is not a picnic but a political gathering. The BPP thus appears much more egalitarian, the women possessing much more agency, than most viewers would expect, a message reinforced by Huey P. Newton's insistence in a prison interview that "the role of the black woman in the Black Panther Party is exactly the same as the man: that we make no distinction whatsoever. Women hold ranking positions in the Party, they are all instructed in our military training, they are expected to perform duties—not on a sex level—but just as a Party member and a revolutionary."[23] Such comments demonstrate that female Panthers provided a profound challenge to Newton's masculinist ideas as articulated in "Fear and Doubt," and that he responded positively.

Even so, readers of early articles in *The Black Panther* might be lulled into thinking that BPP women accepted certain patriarchal assumptions. Judy Hart, for example, entreated Black women to provide their men with "a base, an anchor, a refuge, a shelter, a haven, a place of peace, a home and institution of strength," sentiments that were echoed by Linda Greene just over a year later. Revolutionary women, Greene argued, had to be their man's "everything ... a worker ... a mother ... a companion, intellectual, spiritual, mental, and physical.... She is the strength of the struggle ... [who] does not distract the men with whom she works." And when her "Black man" makes his needs known to her, "she will and does seek them out." Gloria Bartholomew similarly urged her sisters to "stand behind" their men, so as to hold them up should they fall.[24] Such comments underscore BPP women's intellectual flexibility and strategic willingness to defer certain struggles in favor of others, and perhaps even their understanding of the fragility of the male ego in their tacit recognition of certain patriarchal traits. They demonstrate that BPP women were at pains not to present themselves as threats to their male counterparts. As important, they confirm the extra burdens assumed by Panther women, who played central roles in both revolutionary activity and the family or domestic unit. Building on this, as the historian Ashley Farmer observes, they engaged themselves in a process of redefining African American womanhood, with Greene in particular arguing that revolutionary women transcended the male-female binary to create a new archetype of the revolutionary, embodying both traditionally masculine qualities such as militancy alongside traditionally feminine qualities such as empathy.[25]

In 1971 Elaine Brown insisted that "as women, we suffer under pressure of our class, the pressure of our race, and as women. We have three levels of oppression."[26] Here, Brown reveals the centrality to her life of the intersections between her identities as a woman, an African American woman, a revolutionary from a working-class background who attended private schools, and a former student activist, not to mention a respected BPP member. Like her, Panther women contended with multiple forms of oppression. As Brown suggests, they used differential consciousness to navigate their way through party life, revealing how their intersecting identities enabled them to (in the words of the feminist scholar Chela Sandoval) "read the current situation of power and of self-consciously choosing and adopting the ideological form best suited to push against its configurations."[27] In this, BPP women adapted themselves to conform to certain expectations so they might carve out important spaces for themselves and to broaden the BPP's ideological framework. They thus chose which oppression to fight at particular moments and which to subordinate temporarily to achieve a tactical victory amid a broader strategic goal, and drew on particular facets of their identities at particular times to win each.

Recent reappraisals of African American female voices have convincingly demonstrated the deep roots of the intersectional approach to understanding the many social and political factors that combined to form the oppression faced by working-class, Black, left-wing activist women. Amy Jacques-Garvey, for example, considered her role as Marcus Garvey's wife—in which she occupied a traditionally female, domestic role—to complement her public role as a prominent woman and her insistence that all Black women be empowered to involve themselves in political activities. As the historian Ula Taylor argues, Jacques-Garvey worked to unify Garveyite nationalism with feminism.[28] Before her, Mary Church Terrell insisted that African American women's advancement was unsurpassed by any other people, on account of the combined weight of racial and gender oppression that they faced.[29] Like them, the Sojourners for Truth and Justice developed an intersectional approach to racial and gender oppression.[30] Similarly, Claudia Jones understood that Black working-class women experienced the sharpest point of white supremacy and thus were ideally positioned to lead the fight against it.[31]

Understanding both the importance of an intersectional analysis and BPP women's differential consciousness adds crucial nuance to the infamous opening lines of Brown's autobiography: "I have all the guns and all the money. I can withstand challenge from without and from within." Brown was about to give a speech to the massed ranks of party members who were, she states, "at my command." Her declaration of "supreme power," she wrote, "felt natural."[32] Irrespective of whether Brown spoke these precise words—and given the necessary caveats about autobiographical accounts, we cannot be certain she did—their position in her autobiography reveals their importance to the image Brown wished to project. They might at first suggest that Brown had absorbed an obsession with power and strength. Yet this was also an expression of resilience in the face of male hostility and resentment at her elevation, and an articulation of her awareness that she needed to demonstrate strength and power to win over skeptical (male) Panthers. It suggests that female Panthers like Brown transcended the limitations placed on them by men's willingness to wield epithets like "strident" to denounce, isolate, and undermine activist women.

By 1969, and reflecting the growing female Panther contingent, discussion of gender in the BPP's newspaper shifted considerably, becoming even more prominent following Elaine Brown's appointment to the editor's chair in 1970. In May, Southern California BPP activist June Culberson called on the party's men to let go of their emotional hang-ups about female equality. A first step toward this goal was to end the use of the term "Pantherette," a patronizing diminutive that suggested a two-tier membership of real (male) Panthers and subordinate (female) Pantherettes.[33] Jackie Harper from New York City later insisted that female Panthers be accepted as revolutionaries, suggesting that, in her branch, Culberson's article fell on deaf ears.[34] Elsewhere in New York City, Afeni Shakur, foreshadowing her son Tupac's career, contributed a poem that demonstrated the conflicting demands facing female revolutionaries:

> One of these days when I've got more time
> I'm gonna pick up a gun and shoot me some swine
> I can't do right now cause I got three kids
> And an evil husband who won't let me get involved.[35]

Shakur witnessed the struggles of revolutionary women to be taken seriously. The experience of BPP membership led her and Joan Bird to question patriarchal assumptions about women's roles and consider their own failure to challenge these assumptions from the start of their involvement in the struggle, demonstrating the extent to which the BPP's revolution enabled women to reconsider and transform their own internalized attitudes alongside their position in the wider society, indicating further that the BPP incubated a sense of the importance of intersectionality to its female members.[36]

Ida Walston, meanwhile, argued that the BPP enabled women like her not to "stand with my brothers ... [but to] truly be [their] comrade."[37] Like Walston, women writers in *The Black Panther* insisted on gender equality and were at pains to assert the importance of the female role in the struggle. Aware that they were writing for an audience of women and men, the writers worded their statements carefully. Their assertions of female strength were calibrated in such a way as not to threaten male BPP comrades but instead assure them that BPP women saw female revolutionary strength in harmony with that of men. As Hart suggested, the revolution would convince wavering women to abandon bourgeois trappings and enter into a new life: "His total commitment to his life is an invitation to the black woman to join with him in the pursuit of a life together."[38] Here, Hart offers echoes of Amy Jacques-Garvey's "community feminism" that saw essentially no conflict between domestic life and political activity.[39] Her final clause is essential: the "life together" is one based on the ideals of the revolution, which included a commitment to erasing inequalities and to valorizing the quality of interpersonal relations for the party's members. Such awareness doubtless informed Connie Felder's decision to run the South Baltimore office soon after the extradition of the chapter's defense captain, John Clark. Even though Clark respected her qualities enough to insist that she succeed him, a rival male Panther insisted that a man take on Clark's role. Rather than threaten the internal harmony in the chapter, Felder chose to step into the organizational role, allowing her male comrade—with whom she had previously clashed—to live out his masculinist fantasies while she performed an equally important role.[40]

Two articles that appeared in *The Black Panther* in mid-1969 illustrate the complexities of both the struggle faced by BPP women and their responses. The first reprinted an interview with a collective of "Panther Sisters" in the radical Bay Area publication *The Movement*. That they attempted to speak as a largely anonymous collective illustrates both the assumption that women were second-class Panthers and the problems that BPP women confronted when attempting to articulate themselves. Yet more important, it anticipates the collectivity that defined African American feminist groups such as the Combahee River Collective and reflects the development of the BPP's broader intellectual climate alongside the collective living that helped incubate members' political sensibilities. This latter point cannot be understated: as the scholar Patricia Hill Collins suggests, the base of Black feminists' societal and political structure lies in the quality of interpersonal relations they develop through their activism.[41] The need for low-cost housing and office space resulted in the BPP blurring the distinction between home and work, family and friends. BPP members of both genders shared these spaces, and while tensions existed over the usual domestic arrangements, roles, and responsibilities, as the "Panther Sisters" reveal, they also facilitated many Panther women's political development through the simple fact of living alongside each other and wrought a true community where a more private method of habitation might have isolated the women. The domestic arrangements in Los Angeles, for example, spurred Ericka Huggins to develop group discussions on sexism in the party.[42] Elsewhere, physical proximity facilitated ongoing political discussions between Panthers throughout their involvement in the party. As such, Panther women might not have been seeking to destroy the family unit, as per Kay Lindsey's incendiary polemic in Toni Cade's *The Black Woman* anthology, but in living communal lives as Panthers they most certainly offered an alternative vision of community life.[43]

While the Sisters agreed that gender relations in the BPP were improving, they acknowledged that the BPP could do more. By definition, the BPP's revolution required female liberation, they argued, yet they remained adamant that the BPP's internal hierarchical structure should be respected even as the organization needed to deconstruct male chauvinism.[44] In overlooking the close relationship between rigid hierarchies and masculine dominance, and suggesting that the BPP need not immediately enact the revolution that it hoped to spread to the world, the women thus announced their acceptance of the BPP's foco theory while also suggesting that, by elevating women into positions within this hierarchy, the BPP could strike a blow against male oppression. Yet in predicting that the struggle against male chauvinism would take decades, the women tacitly acknowledged their preparedness to elevate the BPP's struggle against racial oppression over a campaign for gender equality.

Despite their collective pseudonym, the "Sisters" were not homogenous. They debated the notion that women and men were mutually compatible, some arguing that women were men's "other half" with others noting that men and women could not "operate as two halves." "Our men have been sort of castrated, you know," one argued, reflecting contemporary debates over the generations-long impact of slavery and racism on Black American men, while suggesting that sex ought not define an individual's role in the revolution. Indeed, assertive action by women was, according to one sister, fundamental: only by refusing menial or submissive roles could women begin the revolution. African American women's unpaid and unnoticed labor was thus incorporated into the revolution, and their refusal to take on such work redefined as a general strike, rendering women's emancipation integral to the broader socialist revolution. The women pointed to Ericka Huggins as a key inspiration. She, they argued, helped raise the political consciousness of party members through all her activities, which itself raised awareness of the centrality of male chauvinism to American capitalism and the need to overthrow both if the revolution is to be complete. Broadening their horizons, they concluded that "the success of the revolution depends upon the women." As this indicates, through their activities and their discursive strategies, not to mention their negotiation of personal relationships, BPP women strategically but subtly and gradually won over their male comrades through demonstrations of their physical, philosophical, and ideological commitment to the struggle.

This careful negotiation between asserting the revolutionary capabilities of women and assuaging male comrades also characterized Candi Robinson's views, as expressed in the other major article from 1969. Of Panther women she said, "We too are strong. We too are a threat to the oppressive enemy." The intriguing inclusion of "too" in these sentences initially hints that Robinson thought women stood primarily but subordinately in comparison to men. Yet approaching it through the prism of interpersonal relationships suggests that Robinson's article instead is more a reminder that women should be considered equal and that the revolution was one that fought for gender equality.

The "too," significantly, operates not to alienate men but to remind them that her article is a call to revolutionaries of both sexes. A woman's role involved educating her male comrades to expand the revolution through their example and through their relationships with these men. Nevertheless, biological determinism remained an important touchstone, for Robinson also argued, "Our men need, want and will love the beautiful children that come from our fruitful wombs."[45]

Meanwhile, BPP member DC argued that monogamous relationships provided the most appropriate family unit for Panther babies, with Panther women being expected to be responsible for the children who were conceived in Panther unions.[46] Given BPP women's general assertions of gender equality alongside DC's acknowledgment, one would expect the BPP to back a woman's right to contraception. Again, however, diversity of opinion remained, as Judi Douglas revealed in 1970. Rather than offering women control over their biology, as per most feminist interpretations, Douglas wielded a somewhat nationalist argument that the pill was "the weapon of the pigs who have tried through the means of 'birth control' to stifle" the Black population.[47] She considered it an "underhanded form of genocide" that constituted a danger to the health of women who took it, deemphasizing the feminist argument in favor of a critique of the American state's use of contraception as a racialized weapon, one that obliquely referenced the forced sterilization of Black women across the South in the preceding decades.[48] Only in 1972 did the BPP engage in open debate over the issue of birth control and the impact of pregnancy and motherhood on female Panthers' ability to perform parental *and* BPP duties. Alongside this observation, Audrea Jones noted the depressing tendency of male Panthers to assume that the responsibility for birth control lay only with women. By 1974, Newton was insisting that all Panthers practice birth control, perhaps to prevent the BPP from losing members to maternity and paternity duties.[49]

Illustrating how BPP membership prompted women to question vast swathes of their own experiences and lives, Stephania Tyson reconsidered her entire life after being chastised for wearing a wig, which some Panthers considered a bourgeois affectation.[50] For her it was a temporary solution, but it prompted her to reassess the "knots on the head" her parents gave her, which led to the operation on her brain that necessitated her head being shaved. This led to further thoughts about her incremental absorption of BPP ideology through political education classes. Tyson's experience indicates how deeply involvement with the BPP affected many women. That Tyson felt compelled to discuss such tremendously personal issues in the pages of *The Black Panther* is highly significant, revealing that Tyson felt bonded enough to the group to share such an experience, doubly so given that not long before, the publication included a piece that claimed that African American women were "selfish and subjective." This article's anonymous author blamed women's attitudes for relationship problems experienced by party members and claimed that women emasculated men by failing to appreciate male struggles in white America: "When the Black man starts to talk about getting some guns and offing some white pig... his woman starts to fall apart.... To a great extent, her attitude explains the high rate of divorce among Panthers."[51] The public airing of such prehistoric attitudes renders it unsurprising that women spoke out relatively rarely, thus elevating the importance of Tyson's contribution.

These conflicting opinions reflect the struggles women experienced in the BPP, particularly in their negotiation between traditional and revolutionary roles. The common thread running through their accounts is the centrality of personal experience. Very few Panther women adopted a depersonalized approach in their BPP writing. In this, they asserted that the personal was the political. As important, in their centering of individual experience as the wellspring of political awakening and in their insistence that personal feelings and emotions were central features of political activity, they reflected core features of second-wave feminism even if they rejected the implicit (and sometimes explicit) race and class assumptions of that second wave.

BPP Masculinism

By 1970, Kathleen Cleaver's husband, Eldridge, was living in Algeria and becoming an ever more distant influence on the party. Yet his gender politics loom large over the BPP's history. His presence helps illustrate why it was so important for female members to articulate themselves. In 1969, Kathleen Cleaver wrote in the radical journal *Ramparts* of her first meeting with her future husband, at which he "exuded strength, power, force in his very physical being" as he "walked the earth like a king."[52] An initial reading might suggest that Cleaver internalized gendered understandings of masculinity. Yet the article was part of *Ramparts*'s crusade to highlight the injustice of the California authorities' treatment of Eldridge Cleaver. Its gendered language was a rhetorical ploy that demonstrated to readers that prison would diminish him while reinforcing his mythical qualities. The primary focus, after all, was to win his freedom rather than deconstruct his toxic masculinity.

Eldridge Cleaver joined the BPP in February 1967 when it was still only a minor group. Already on the *Ramparts* staff, he helped establish the BPP as one of the most visible protest groups of the time. His genius was to subordinate the BPP's organization to the Free Huey campaign, elevating the BPP founder to the status of a living god while forging links with radical groups across the globe. Manhood was his lifelong obsession, and he often expressed his gender views in sexualized terms. Of one of his schoolteachers he wrote: "We wanted to fuck her, to suck her tits." After she racially abused him for verbally abusing a white schoolgirl, "my feeling for her was no longer the warm desire of the lover. What I felt for her was the lust/hatred of the rapist."[53] Even disregarding Cleaver's aim to shock and the speed with which he turned to thoughts of sexual violence, his notion that a lover would simply want to "fuck" and "suck" a woman suggests a narrow view of consensual sexual relationships. *Soul on Ice*, his 1968 collection of prison letters and essays, was only the most well-known of his attempts to define a politics of masculinity. His often-quoted aphorism "We shall have our manhood . . . or the earth will be leveled by our attempts to gain it" was among the least controversial statements in the book, which also included a foul homophobic assault on James Baldwin.[54] Even worse, Cleaver's discussion of insurrectionary rape demonstrated his belief that male heterosexuality, power, and dominance were firmly entwined. His realization of the horrific implications of this attitude so deconstructed his self-image that he turned to writing to save himself. Such self-flagellation purged Cleaver of many—but not all—of these destructive attitudes.[55] Heterosexual masculinity, reinforced by male physical dominance, lay at the core of his vision, and his faith in physical dominance undergirded his understanding of male power. During his first long prison stint in the 1950s, he concluded that his Christian upbringing transformed him "into a softy. . . . I wanted to become tougher" while insisting that his position as the dominant partner in his homosexual experiences enabled him to "remain a man"—the unwritten implication being that subordinate partners lost any claims to manhood.[56] Prison rendered him an archetypal individualist lumpen prole. Yet by his December 1966 release, he was channeling his energies toward broader aims: "I knew perfectly well that I was going to war."[57]

Cleaver was a driving force behind the February 1967 Bay Area memorial to Malcolm X, at which he told an audience of several hundred, "If Malcolm X can die, we can die. We are proud to be black and we don't hide behind our women."[58] Cleaver's use of the possessive offers another indication of his view of male-female relations. This masculinist approach to the Black struggle is discernible in his first recollections of Newton. Cleaver had his back to the door from which a fully armed Newton entered at their first encounter. Cleaver's eyes were drawn elsewhere: "There was a deep female gleam leaping out of one of the women's eyes. . . . I had never seen it before in my life: the total admiration of a black woman for a black man."[59] Cleaver's recollection juxtaposed Newton's aggression with the woman's passivity, suggesting that her almost sexual response contrasted starkly with the awkwardness of Cleaver's fellow men. Their discomfort at the woman's awed response to a "real" man appears as further proof of the BPP's virility, the ideal Black woman's submissiveness, and the impotence of nonviolent men, appealing to Cleaver's belief that Black men should seize their manhood through displays of power and cunning.

The event that precipitated Cleaver's departure from the United States perhaps encapsulates his macho approach to the revolution and offers important insights into his gendered view of the BPP and revolutionary activity. On April 6, 1968, in response to the assassination of Dr. Martin Luther King Jr., Cleaver wrote his "Requiem for Nonviolence." "Now," he concluded, "there is [only] the gun and the bomb, dynamite and the knife."[60] Later that evening, he claimed, he planned to collect a rifle and kill the first Oakland police officer he encountered. An alternative account has Cleaver attempting to relocate some of the BPP's weapons cache before a police raid, while the FBI claimed he told his comrades that the BPP would strike at the police first. Caught short on this trip, Cleaver was apprehended while urinating, whereupon a shoot-out began.[61] Cleaver later recalled agreeing that armed insurrection was "irrational"; he and a small group of Panthers instead committed to a small ambush. At approximately 9:00 p.m., Cleaver and BPP treasurer Bobby Hutton were sitting in a car on Twenty-Eighth Street and Union. A patrol car approached and before its occupants could act, Cleaver and Hutton "got out and just started shooting."[62]

Cleaver's masculinism shines through his recollections of what followed. He described his comrades "stand[ing] up as black men inside of Babylon" and giving the police "a taste of their own medicine."[63] BPP member Warren Wells and Officer Richard Jensen were wounded before the police besieged Cleaver and Hutton in a nearby basement. Cleaver stripped naked after being hit in the chest by a tear gas canister and recalled feeling "an *impotent* rage" before announcing their surrender.[64] After they exited, police officers shot Hutton through his lower back. While he was in a kneeling position, they shot him twice in the legs and once in the head, killing him instantly. According to observers, Hutton did not remove his clothes; the police used this as a pretext to shoot and kill, arguing that he was not merely concealing his modesty.[65] His wish to preserve his decency might be juxtaposed with Cleaver's willingness to show his manhood, literally and figuratively. Soon after, *The Black Panther* printed photographs of the shoot-out's aftermath, including the near destruction of the house in which Hutton spent his final moments.[66] Newton lionized Hutton for his "infinite love for his people," while a BPP leaflet placed him alongside Malcolm X and Dr. King in the African American pantheon. Cleaver was arrested and beaten, his bail set at $50,000. To complete the outrage, a grand jury exonerated Hutton's killers.[67]

Cleaver presented physical strength as the key determinant of power during his 1968 campaign for president. His stump speeches regularly featured a crowd-pleasing challenge to Governor Reagan. Rejecting the obvious ploy of challenging Reagan to a debate, the Arkansan turned to the traditional southern method of resolving disputes of honor: a duel. Cleaver was so certain that he could beat the Republican that he was quite prepared to abandon using pistols for a more intimate method of combat, promising to beat Reagan to death with a marshmallow if need be. He rhetorically wielded the candy to add levity and absurdity to his threat, but underneath this lay his certainly that physical strength rather than intellectual prowess would enable him to subdue a man nearly twenty-five years his senior. Such rhetoric delighted and appalled crowds, something the FBI attempted to use to its advantage by sending transcripts to those who otherwise might be tempted to book Cleaver for a speaking appearance.[68] It is, of course, impossible to prove whether this tactic succeeded, but the mere fact of the FBI's intention indicates the extent to which the BPP could not control the dissemination of its message.

Cleaver's gendered view of political struggle crystallized in October 1968, in a speech mere weeks after the New York Radical Women invaded the Miss America pageant to dramatize the objectification of women in American culture. Toward the end, he remarked, "I have one more thing to say and it's not to all you ugly men in the audience."[69] Notwithstanding his somewhat judgmental claims about his male listeners' aesthetic qualities, such a statement suggested that the previous portion of the speech—which engaged with explicitly political themes—was not designed for women's ears, maybe even that they lacked the intellectual capacity to comprehend it. The following section was "for the ladies," he said, before condescending to them that what he was about to say was very serious. "You have the power to bring a squeaking halt to a lot of things. . . . We say that political power, revolutionary power grows out of the lips of a pussy." This comment must have provoked uproar because Cleaver was moved to plead with his audience to "cool it." Sex, he said, could be reactionary or conservative. But if it was done with a real revolutionary, then it was itself revolutionary. "You can put them under more pressure than I can," he told the women. "You can cut off their sugar." And, if these men still did not "act right," then there would be queues of revolutionary men ready to "come to your aid in your hour of need."

While Cleaver was wont to use ribaldry and outrage as fuel for his speeches, "pussy power" went far further. He sought to shock audiences into recalibrating their attitude toward free love but in doing so revealed a deeper, more troubling attitude. While he had quelled his fantasies of sexual assault, he remained wedded to the notion that women should be sexually and personally submissive and express their sexuality only with men. Cleaver offered no consideration that any woman might prefer to share her time or sex life with other women, not to mention the fact that some revolutionary men might have preferred to sleep with men. There was no room here for revolutionary political, social, intellectual, cultural, or economic action on the part of women; instead, they remained men's playthings: a patriarchal and heteronormative understanding of sexuality, and one that aids an understanding of why BPP women used subtle means to fight their corner rather than wage all-out war on Panther patriarchy.

When Cleaver learned of his comrade Ericka Huggins's dreadful experience in prison, he indirectly repudiated "pussy power" in arguing that her resistance to the physical and psychic onslaught of prison constituted a "stinging rebuke" to male chauvinism.[70] Yet even this deeper understanding of female revolutionary capacity remained wedded to his belief that physical and mental might defined the revolutionary. He omitted mention of even more significant examples of Huggins's revolutionary qualities such as her courageous response to her husband's assassination, her attempt to build a BPP chapter in Connecticut, and her organizing inside prison walls. Cleaver thus suggested that the revolution would be enacted through acts of individual will rather than through coordinated, transformational action; prison, he thought, cut Huggins into a diamond-hard revolutionary, a process far removed from that which created the new men and women envisaged by Guevara, revolutionaries who, like Huggins, possessed a "large dose of humanity."[71] It suggests that Cleaver had not moved far from his attachment to Sergey Nechayev's *Catechism of the Revolutionist*, which emphasized a single-minded, individualist, almost ascetic devotion to the revolution.[72] It also contrasts starkly with Huggins's recollections. Prison enabled her to rediscover her sense of self, file down the "edges in [her] heart," and recommence organizing. As part of the prison-based Sister Love Collective, she used hairdressing as a means of facilitating communication, to enable prisoners to "feel whole and complete and beautiful again."[73] This power of organizing and the revolutionary's love for her people proved the source of her fortitude.

Cleaver's reductive conception of female agency was shared by other male Panthers. Bobby Seale devoted a section of *Seize the Time* to women's roles, outlining the party's commitment to gender equality. Sadly, he could not transcend heteronormative approaches to sexuality, arguing that the BPP sought "to build a society where someday a man and a woman can relate to each other totally on the basis of natural attraction."[74] A series of parables outlined Seale's uncritical attitude toward male sexuality. In the first, a small group of Panther women reject the advances of some men, saying, "The only way you can get close to me is to get hip to some of the real ideology of the Black Panther Party." Seale comments that only this action motivated the men to join.[75] However well intentioned, this episode suggests that the women's allure was the chief weapon in their recruitment strategy. Disregarding Seale's suggestion that men operate according to the whims of their libido, it says little about the women's political activism.

A second incident is even more curious. One night Seale was awakened by a female comrade who presented him with a moral quandary. She wanted to sleep with a comrade but was concerned that he could not recite the Ten-Point Platform and Program. Seale reassured her that a verbatim account was not as important as being able to articulate its meaning. Duly reassured, the

Panther retreated to her bedroom, only to discover that her paramour had redirected his attention to a more compliant comrade. Notably, Seale did not criticize the male Panther.

If this was not evidence enough, his final anecdote confirmed his complacency concerning male sexual predators. A female Panther made a complaint about an attempted rape by a fellow Panther. On investigating, Seale discovered that the woman had invited the man to sleep alongside her, fully clothed. Seale concluded that, because the woman was able to resist his advances, the man was merely trying "to get a little *too* close," rather than attempting sexual assault. Seale suggested that, in the future, "the brother must learn that he has no right to use any kind of force on that sister, and she must watch herself for her own attitude, and not see everything he's doing as force."[76] The problem, therefore, equally lay with the victims as with the aggressors. So while Seale insisted that Panthers who attempted to call women counterrevolutionary for not sleeping with them were themselves the counterrevolutionaries, he was unable to commit fully to a feminist defense of women's rights and remained wedded to the notions that women were predominantly sexual beings and that there was no room for homosexual activity in the revolution.

Seale's complacency disguises somewhat the toxicity faced by Panther women. Regina Jennings, for example, was subjected to a prolonged campaign of harassment by her captain, who refused to accept that she might not desire his sexual advances. The BPP's Central Committee lambasted her for bourgeois attitudes before her captain had her transferred to national headquarters, where Jennings suffered yet more sexism and harassment.[77] Jennings's experience highlights the power imbalances that lay at the BPP's core and the unwillingness of the Central Committee to challenge dangerous assumptions of some members. The legitimizing of Jennings's captain's behavior suggests that the BPP had much to learn when it came to sexual and gender inequality.

Gender and Sexuality in the Post-1970 Party

Thankfully, BPP masculinism was far from hegemonic. Johnny Spain considered *Soul on Ice* "disgusting," for example.[78] In August 1970 Huey P. Newton admitted that the BPP's system of revolutionary values needed expansion, so he called for working coalitions with women's and gay liberation groups. This rendered the BPP the first major African American organization to declare common cause with gay rights.[79] Newton identified fear and insecurity as the root causes of reactionary sentiments among Panther men.[80] Their attempts to silence gay and female voices isolated the BPP from natural allies. In this way his statement repudiated Cleaver's gender ideology. Of course, that Newton had to issue such a statement indicates that the BPP had not been proactive enough in both forging alliances and correcting its internal contradictions. After all, the previous year saw Landon Williams positioning homosexuality and prostitution alongside organized crime as "filthy contamination[s]" wrought by capitalism.[81]

Elaine Brown's recollections of this period confirm that a gulf occasionally existed between the BPP's ideals and the reality its members experienced and detail the extraordinary lengths some party women went to assert themselves. Soon after her return from a visit to China in September 1971, a Los Angeles Panther subjected her to a grotesque nightlong beating for allegedly sleeping with another Panther. The episode prompted Brown to wonder why she relied so much on "the power of men" and remained in an organization that was so dominated by men and guns.[82] The BPP did not punish her attacker. Newton even dismissed Brown's beating as "not really party business" before chastising her for getting into a vulnerable position in the first place, reinforcing the sense that sexual assaults were the fault of victims rather than aggressors. When Brown succeeded Newton, however, she took the opportunity for revenge and had her assailant beaten to a pulp.[83]

Brown's fortitude doubtless helped her rise in the organization. Not long after falling in love with Newton, she realized that he seemed "the other part of my soul. Connected to him," she recalled, "I was a new force."[84] She remained dedicated to Newton for seven years, even though he compelled her to act against her better instincts, placed her in dangerous situations, and failed to commit to her. Yet in winning Newton's trust, she became a respected BPP leader and used her position to promote female comrades: it is no coincidence, for example, that Ericka Huggins succeeded her as editor of *The Black Panther*.[85] As this suggests, both in becoming the BPP's leader and elevating women to its Central Committee, Brown carved out important spaces for BPP women. At the start of the 1970s, she was insistent that she was no feminist, on the grounds that sexism was far less urgent a problem than capitalism and racism. As the decade wore on, however, she grew to appreciate the importance of feminism to Black women's struggles. Sadly, it seems that she was only partially successful in fighting BPP sexism: not long before leaving, she claims to have noticed that the party was riven along gender lines.[86] It is also highly significant that her departure from the BPP enabled her to reconnect with her daughter and finally assume her role as a mother, illustrating the all-encompassing demands of life in the party.

Brown was not alone in her uncertainty about the applicability of mainstream feminist thought to the BPP's world. Even in retrospect some Panther women could not agree on their identities as feminists. Huggins found it inconceivable that a woman in the BPP could not be a feminist, whereas Safiya Bukhari felt that being a revolutionary involved going far beyond mere feminism.[87] Assata Shakur noted, "A lot of us adopted that kind of macho type style in order to survive," adding another layer of meaning to the gun-toting female

Detroit Panther.[88] This reflected the fact that chauvinism was never far from the BPP's surface. As Bukhari observed, while the BPP had a regulatory system that theoretically prevented men from using gender to oppress women, it often failed in practice.[89] And yet, in sharing their personal experiences and acknowledging the intersectional nature of the oppression they faced and their response to it, BPP women articulated a distinct BPP feminist approach. Furthermore, as the BPP's ideology developed, shifting from nationalism, through anticolonial socialism, into intercommunalism, they outlined an increasingly complex definition of BPP revolutionary womanhood, one that encompassed warriors, mothers, artists, editors, and all points in between, often within one female body.

Ultimately, gender and sex were key battlegrounds both within the BPP and in its struggle with American society, underscoring the necessity for Newton to order that the BPP make clear its support for women's liberation and gay liberation. In particular, Eldridge Cleaver's hostility toward both groups necessitated rebuttal if the BPP was to remain at the vanguard of a New Left that was beginning to grapple with these very issues, since his stance severely undercut the BPP's claims to advocacy of "all power to all people." Female Panthers were at the forefront of this rebuttal, asserting their rights to play a central role in the revolution. Within this lay a more personal struggle, for within the BPP, women were forced to battle not only with the class and racial struggle engaged *by* the party but also with the struggle *within* the party. They thus had to transform not only the external world but the internal worlds of the BPP and its individual members themselves. They might have joined hoping to change the world around them but ended up also changing the world within. Ericka Huggins forcefully argued that "women ran the party, [while] men thought they did," an observation that strikes to the core of many male delusions of grandeur and positions the BPP alongside numerous radical groups whose males did not fully comprehend the importance of their female comrades.[90] Malika Adams later argued that BPP women's "consciousness about ourselves as women was very underdeveloped for the most part.... We didn't see ourselves as separate from the brothers.... I don't know that we really saw ourselves as women.... I think we saw ourselves in the eyes of men. The men defined pretty much what we were."[91] The evidence suggests, however, that as Safiya Bukhari reflected, the BPP might not have "completed the task of eradicating sexist attitudes within the Party and in the community. But we did bring the problem out in the open and put the question on the floor."[92] Its gendered world proved much more complex than men considered it to be and demonstrates how women expanded the struggle into realms that many of their male comrades could not comprehend.

CHAPTER THREE

BPP Political Philosophy

Eldridge Cleaver said that he fell in love with the BPP at first sight, at a meeting between various Bay Area African American groups at a time when he hoped to reinvigorate Malcolm X's Organization of Afro American Unity. He doubted his comrades' ability to organize a suitable commemoration of Malcolm X's death and preparedness to offer protection for their honored guest, Sister Betty Shabazz. As the meeting droned on Cleaver moved from despair to anger. Then the front door opened: "I . . . saw the most beautiful sight I had ever seen: four black men wearing black berets, powder blue shirts, black leather jackets, black trousers, shiny black shoes—and each with a gun!" When asked how these interlopers intended to contribute to the memorial, their leader said, "It doesn't matter. . . . Our message is one and the same. . . . We're going to talk about political power growing out of the barrel of a gun."[1] These men of action stood in sharp contrast to the idlers alongside Cleaver. In promising to protect Shabazz, they symbolically became Malcolm X's successors. As important, they reminded Cleaver of the phallocentric power of the gun and the centrality of masculine strength to the Black struggle. The BPP had arrived.

By the time of Shabazz's arrival, Cleaver considered the BPP friends. When Newton faced down the police outside the *Ramparts* office while she and he met inside, Cleaver inwardly testified to Newton's masculine prowess: "You're the baddest motherfucker I've ever seen!"[2] From then on, Cleaver was a Black Panther, as suggested by his comments to a television reporter: when asked about the BPP, he used the first-person plural throughout.[3] As this suggests, that the BPP was made up of armed and potent men was hugely appealing to him. He soon became editor of the BPP's newspaper, using it to elevate Newton to legendary proportions while transforming the newspaper into a seminal journal of the radical underground and becoming the party's chief spokesman.[4] Newton's arrest provided the moment for Cleaver to allow his rage to bubble to the surface. "Huey sent our spirits soaring when he laid Officer John

55

Frey out," he wrote. "He took [our] dreams . . . and shaped them into bullets." From the moment that Frey's death became public knowledge, Newton became a legend, a symbol, "containing the potential of epic proportions that would lead us in war."[5] To him, the new members who flocked to the organization were preparing for this war, and they would be abetted by thousands of whites.[6] In the interregnum between Newton's arrest and arraignment, the BPP's newspaper returned from a four-month hiatus with a front-page editorial, "Huey Must Be Set Free!" which had all the hallmarks of Cleaver's pen: "Huey Newton is a child of Malcolm X" who willingly "laid his life on the line so that 20,000,000 black people can find out just where they are at."[7] From this point, he was referred to as "Huey," the familiar used to demonstrate both his affinity with the people and their identification with him. Thus began Newton's deification.

In 1970, Cleaver insisted that Newton alone gave the BPP "a firm ideological foundation."[8] On one level, Cleaver was right, in that the BPP designated Newton its chief theoretician. Yet it overlooks the intellectual leadership offered by other Panthers and the extent to which Newton's ideological guidance was subject to challenge. Cleaver himself was one such individual, but as important, rank-and-file members also took the opportunity to develop and articulate their own ideas about the BPP's direction. This became particularly important during Newton's incarceration as the party experienced a near exponential membership rise. Their contributions to the BPP's intellectual world illustrate the extent to which members helped refine BPP political theory as the organization grew. The debates they engaged in illuminate the extent to which members grappled with the ideas they encountered in the BPP's reading groups.

Newton's release initiated a period in BPP history where his influence began to dominate the party's overarching intellectual direction. As chapters 4 through 7 suggest, BPP activism did not exist merely in response to Newton's ideas; instead, it relied on activists' analysis of local circumstances and their ability to conduct the necessary work. Nevertheless, such responses sat within an overarching ideological framework informed by Newton's writings that themselves emerged from his isolation from the party and the communities in which it operated. While the BPP's debates during the 1960s focused on the party's immediate challenge to American capitalism, Newton's return prompted greater consideration of the party's long-term goals, not least through the organization's observation of the abatement of the revolutionary fervor of the late 1960s.

BPP Ideology in the 1960s

For Cleaver, Newton rendered BPP ideology the ultimate expression of the African American experience and carved a new intellectual space for Black America, specifically in guiding the BPP toward organizing the African American lumpenproletariat. In applying Fanon's ideas to the American situation, he positioned the BPP in the modern anticolonial struggle, liberating the African American struggle from racist European intellectual traditions.[9] Executive Mandate Number One, first issued at the BPP's Sacramento protest, was the first major demonstration of the BPP's rhetorical brilliance. Its historical sweep encompassed the African American experience of slavery, the violence that underpinned American segregation, the civil rights struggles of the 1960s, the genocide of the American Indians, internment of Japanese Americans in the 1940s, and even atomic diplomacy. These references combined to apocalyptic effect, warning that Black Americans were close to being railroaded toward their destruction. The mandate noted bitterly that, despite all the peaceful protesting, political lobbying, praying, and petitioning, the tyrannical grip of white America over Black showed no sign of loosening. After outlining this dystopia, it arrived at a stark conclusion. The people, it stated, "must draw the line": armed struggle was the only option.[10] The mandate here drew on Fanon's argument that violence is appropriate when other forms of protest fail. Like Robert F. Williams, it suggested that the rule of law had broken down, and the Mulford Bill was further evidence that the state intended to ensure that its police met minimal resistance as it extended its repression of Black people. The mandate thus positioned California at the forefront of the racial struggle and the BPP at the very heart of 1960s protest.

Cleaver himself, meanwhile, began to apply his vision for Black liberation to the BPP. The pages of *The Black Panther* overflowed with analyses of Black oppression and resistance. Its second edition included three articles from an anonymous Panther who was present at both Sacramento and the confrontation at the *Ramparts* office. They lambast the white media, denounce "perverted whites" for wishing to consort with African American prostitutes, and talk of creating a new Black man amid the "blind, worn out crippled whore" that is the United States. These latter angles reflect themes in *Soul on Ice*, rendering Cleaver a likely author.[11] This edition also published for the first time the iconic photograph of Newton in a wicker chair, brandishing a shotgun and a spear, with spent cartridges at his feet—another indication of Cleaver's growing influence on the party, for he did more than any other individual to construct this image.[12] By midsummer Cleaver's demands for "real black power" were incorporating the first references to the BPP's application of Fanon's analysis of settler colonialism.[13]

The pages of *The Black Panther* indicate that this was a transitional phase for the BPP. Earl Anthony, prior to his sideline as an FBI informant, offered a critique of suburbanization within a Fanonist framework. Drawing on the BPP's notion of community control, Anthony argued that white flight necessitated Black Americans wresting control of the inner cities from their former neighbors.[14] In similar fashion, Cleaver called on his comrades to "smash police terror and domestic colonialism" while denouncing the Socialist Workers Party's attempts to organize in the Black community.[15] The same issue saw the BPP's second "World of Black Folks" column include an item about Africa, for the first time positioning the anticolonial struggle amid reports of African American uprisings, anticipating the newspaper's regular page of global revolutionary news.[16] Nevertheless, other Panthers' analyses suggest that Black nationalism remained a core ideological approach; Carl Mack, for example, argued that "Black America is definitely a nation within a nation."[17]

Such comments gradually ceded ground as the BPP's Marxist analyses grew, which coincided with the BPP employing the white leftist attorney Charles Garry to lead Newton's defense. Some African American lawyers denounced the BPP for employing Garry purely on racial grounds; as Kathleen Cleaver and Bobby Seale acidly observed, these turncoats served their own class interests by failing to offer unqualified support to the liberation struggle. Seale reserved his greatest ire for John D. George, who not only criticized Garry's hiring but also came close to selling out Seale during Seale's February 1968 trial. "I do not believe," Seale concluded, "that one black lawyer in the area, with their comfortable middle-class positions, would have filed a federal suit against the City of Oakland," as Garry had.[18] Their ideological fidelity to American capitalism and desire for career advancement simply overwhelmed their commitment to the Black and working-class people they supposedly represented. That same year, George Murray demonstrated the deepening ideological approach of many rank-and-file Panthers. In May he asserted that nationalism was central to the BPP's mission, but by September he was incorporating "all people of color" into his vision.[19] Fanon's elevation was cemented soon afterward, when a contributor declared that Fanon's ideas helped the BPP comprehend the relationship between colonialism and the warped justice African Americans experienced in the American legal system. By now, *The Wretched of the Earth* was second only to Malcolm X's autobiography on the BPP's reading list.[20] Soon thereafter, Landon Williams examined eighteenth-century American colonialism: the parallels were clear.[21]

Separated from the quotidian activities of the party and severely restricted from human interaction, Newton spent his prison time reading and thinking. His prison writings include entreaties to the anti-Vietnam War movement, other African American radicals, and the burgeoning Panther ranks.[22] They were also central to the BPP's leftward drift. Building on the internationalism of Executive Mandate Number One and informed by numerous leftist icons, Newton's thought grew capacious. Using the Cuban Revolution as a model, "The Correct Handing of a Revolution" presents the vanguard party as the essential vehicle that would lead the people away from inchoate protest toward guerrilla warfare, a message he repeated in an interview with the radical publication *The Movement*. As important, Newton identified *The Wretched of the Earth* as the guide to the "correct approach," before telling the *San Francisco Examiner* that the BPP's goal was to gain "some control of the means of production"—a clear indication of his deepening interest in Marxism.[23] White capitalism, he argued, had failed. To achieve power, he concluded, Black Americans needed to take up arms or support armed groups.[24] He then expanded Fanon's internal colonialism analogy, arguing that the power structure, and specifically a small number of capitalist companies, exploited all Americans.[25]

Cleaver's analysis of Newton's arrest further demonstrated the broadening of the BPP's vision.[26] This was a watershed moment, he argued, after which the police would no longer be able to kill African American people with impunity.[27] Yet the consistent pressure from law authorities distanced Cleaver from the rank-and-file, culminating in his departure from the United States in November 1968. With Bobby Seale facing charges of conspiracy and riot stemming from the 1968 Democratic National Convention, coupled with the BPP's transformation into a nationwide organization, spaces opened for other BPP leaders to occupy. Those who wrote in the BPP's newspaper intensified the party's critique of the United States. During 1968, they usually identified racism and capitalism as the core evils, but some described American police forces using "gestapo" tactics and denounced San Francisco's Democratic mayor Joseph Alioto as a fascist.[28] This term became increasingly important to BPP rhetoric during 1968. Kathleen Cleaver, for example, argued that America's "right-wing fascist element" was engaged in a plot to destroy the BPP leadership.[29] She was the first to use "fascism" in a headline later that year, leading the BPP's minister for culture, Emory Douglas, to employ a swastika as a signifier in his artwork the following month.[30] In slight contrast, their fellow BPP leaders were wont to remain focused on colonial analyses and used the prism of racism to analyze American authoritarianism. Cleaver's husband, for example, expanded Fanon's understanding of spatial relations to the relationship between Black America's "urban dungeons" and the "imperialism of the white Suburbs."[31] As this suggests, these critiques operated within a wider definition of the United States as a racist society.

The BPP's plan for a national United Front against Fascism (UFAF) conference in Oakland confirmed the centrality of anti-fascist rhetoric to the BPP. In May 1969, *The Black Panther* splashed "Fascism in America" across its front page. Here the BPP defined fascism as "the power of finance capital itself," illustrating it with gun-toting American police.[32] An excerpt from Georgi Dimitroff's speech at the 1935 congress of the Communist International that outlined the necessity of a united front against fascism formed the issue's centerfold.[33] This use of "fascism" reflected similar usage by 1960s European radicals who largely employed it as a synonym for authoritarianism and occasionally imperialism; its rhetorical power rendered it an emotive and resonant slogan, posing the eternal question: which side are you on?[34] Notably, the BPP first used the word as a major headline in response to police violence against mostly white students rather than African American residents, three months after the *Berkeley Barb* first put it in a headline.[35] This suggests that the term made up part of an attempt to broaden the BPP's support among white Bay Area radicals. Its use peaked in July 1969 with the UFAF, which was designed to prompt debate over "a concrete program of cooperation" between American anti-fascists over freeing the country's political prisoners (including Newton), opposing demagogic "law-and-order" politicians, and fully implicating the American courts in the "fascistization" of the country.[36] As the BPP was gearing up for the conference, Seale—who specialized in broad analyses of the social situation while inclining toward peaceful solutions to American racism—coined the pithy slogan "Racism plus capitalism breeds fascism"—an echo of the BPP's broader use of the term as a synonym rather than as a systematic theoretical framework.[37]

By 1969, party ideology as expressed in the newspaper solidified. In case readers were not convinced by Sacramento's branch lauding Mao or a panegyric to guerrilla warriors in Algeria, Cuba, and China, David Hilliard told readers that the BPP were Marxists.[38] Elbert "Big Man" Howard extolled Maoism and Cleaver combined Fanonism with Malcolm X's ideas about community control, outlining "community imperialism" as a central feature of American domestic politics.[39] Echoing this synthesis, a special edition of *The Black Panther* reminded comrades of Malcolm X's importance to Black America while also celebrating Ho Chi Minh's birthday.[40] The Chicago branch admitted in May 1969 that it began with a racist approach to organizing but that careful study led it toward coalitions with white working-class groups—a consequence of Fanon, Mao, and Malcolm X's centrality to its political education classes.[41] Demonstrating the far-reaching impact of these classes, Ed Williams from Illinois wrote in the same issue of the ills of domestic imperialism, capitalism, and class exploitation, prominently citing Fanon as an influence.[42]

For Fred Hampton, however, theory was inextricable from praxis. As he pointed out, Newton did not become a major figure merely by talking about oppression. Similarly, the BPP's free breakfast program was important not because of its relationship with theory but because it provided food to whomever needed it. This, he said, was far more popular with the people in the communities whom Chicago's BPP served and offered a concrete foundation for the BPP's political education program. Hampton argued that the BPP's friends would not necessarily defend socialism or communism as abstractions but would the breakfast program because it was a practical realization of these concepts. In this, his approach reflected Landon Williams's observation that "we've been trained in this country so that whenever we see the word communist ... most black people will be startled but yet they see the word capitalism and it more or less doesn't phase them at all ... [because] it's just an everyday word."[43] Through education, organization, and action, the revolutionaries could, Hampton suggested, effect profound change, both in terms of normalizing the words "socialism" and "communism" and in applying them to the inner cities.

This ability to articulate the principles that informed BPP praxis in accessible terms helped render Hampton such a powerful figure. While his oratory reflected the influence of Leninist vanguardism, the Chicago branch's activities in organizing Chicago's young people—particularly with the NAACP—and insistence on developing a broad front for the revolution alongside a multiracial conglomeration of groups representing the disaffected, poor, excluded, and oppressed of Chicago, coupled with the presence of numerous women in significant leadership roles position it within broader organizing traditions. Chicago's BPP chapter pioneered alliance building across the radical spectrum, bringing white students and Appalachian migrants, Chicano/a activists, Puerto Ricans, and even some "greasers" into the BPP's orbit. Indeed, this approach to organizing helps illuminate the theoretical framework that underpinned Hampton's notorious statement concerning killing all police to achieve complete satisfaction.[44] The BPP, Hampton argued here, had not moved against the police because it was aware that it did not yet have the numbers to achieve a successful revolution. Only when the entire population was radicalized through education and organization could they challenge the police. Thus, while individual action might lead to some satisfaction, and group action a little more, only mass, organized action would lead to total satisfaction—an analysis that hints at the influence of Fanon's critique of spontaneous violence. Yet that this analysis was couched in terms of the satisfaction to be derived from killing police rendered it easy for the BPP's opponents to dismiss it as a call for insurrection. Thus, while Hampton might have been speaking metaphorically, listeners—and especially critics—could take his claim literally: an illustration of the dangers of loose rhetoric and the ease with which observers could wring their own meanings out of BPP activists' words.

By the end of 1969, with Cleaver and Hilliard reiterating the centrality of Marxism-Leninism to the BPP, the organization's ideological stance had solidified into a staunch opposition to domestic fascism and capitalism, a defense of internationalism, and promotion of domestic socialism, leavened with its enduring commitment to community control and self-defense.[45] Reflecting Hampton, Seale urged the creation of a rainbow coalition of forces to "smash [domestic] imperialism."[46] At this point, the growth of the party and the need to convey information between the chapters across the nation shifted the newspaper's focus slightly to reports from the branches. Thus the more theoretical discussions that characterized the period between 1967 and 1968 ceded to reportage—notably of the social programs—and entreaties from the rank-and-file to support imprisoned comrades. Crucially, however, international news remained a central feature, reminding readers of the BPP's relationship with global struggles against white, imperial, and colonial oppression.

Newton's Return

Newton's release from prison reinvigorated the BPP's ideological discussions. Remarkably, given the pressure on him, Newton constructed a large body of work in the subsequent years. Unfortunately, however, his intellectual ambitions increasingly overwhelmed his articulacy, in part because of his personal experiences and in part because he labored under an immense burden to be the great revolutionary leader and genius of the BPP.[47] This burden led Newton toward a tortuous rhetorical style that often obscured his message. At its best, Newton's thought offered intriguing new directions for the BPP; at its worst it merely constituted—in Newton's own words—"a conglomeration of gibberish."[48]

Almost immediately after returning to public life in 1970 he offered BPP manpower to aid the Vietnamese National Liberation Front. A month later, he offered the BPP's support to the Palestinian cause.[49] His August 1970 message to the women's liberation and gay liberation movements potentially placed the BPP at the vanguard of 1970s social protest while also distancing him from Cleaver's homophobia. Notably, Newton made clear parallels between gay people and the lumpenproletariat, arguing that as potentially the most oppressed group in society, they could also be its "most revolutionary." This was followed by a declaration of opposition to the repression of homosexual people submitted to the Revolutionary People's Constitutional Convention (RPCC).[50] Taken together, these statements indicate Newton's desire to broaden the BPP's campaign and his keenness to reconsider his ideas about nationhood, nationality, and solidarity. Yet the failure of the party to follow Newton's laudable words with demonstrable action is perhaps as revealing. If nothing else, Newton's message to the gay liberation movement alerted the FBI to another opportunity to exploit differences of opinion within the party: Newton's statement received no further discussion in *The Black Panther*. The immediate aftermath only saw Joan Bird and Afeni Shakur remind readers that male chauvinism was a relic of capitalism and that their experience of "socialistic living" revealed the combined importance of women's and Black liberation.[51] Beyond these comments, the newspaper continued to focus on Black liberation issues, suggesting that if there was a furor it remained private.

The radical lawyer and activist Mark Lane interviewed Newton at length soon after his release. Opening with Newton's insistence that the United States was now a supranational entity because of its domination of international capital(ism), the interview confirmed that Newton sought a transformation of world society. Drawing on Fanon and Marx, he critiqued the African liberation movement for failing to overthrow capitalism and denounced the Pan-African Congress as a bourgeois talking-shop.[52] Arguing that leadership-centered organizations generate dependence on a single individual, he embraced Lane's suggestion that his own death would not matter in the wider sense, foreshadowing his concept of revolutionary suicide.[53] He rejected the suggestion that the BPP's social programs were reformist rather than revolutionary, arguing that such parallel structures facilitated community control of institutions and complemented the BPP's quest to educate the masses about the necessity for revolutionary action. In the short term, he accepted, they alleviated the most acute symptoms of capitalism's extremes, but when reinforced by other elements of the BPP's praxis they pointed the way to the cure. He unapologetically accepted that the BPP would sometimes obtain food for its breakfast programs by any means necessary, justifying expropriation on the grounds that it served a transformative goal.[54] When told of allegations that the BPP would distract the authorities by organizing demonstrations to coincide with robberies, he stuck an intrigued tone: "I don't know anything about [that] . . . but it's an interesting idea."[55] While he rejected the notion that individual expropriation was justifiable, Newton argued that an individual expropriating "what is rightfully his" or killing a police officer was "a pure act" because of its political connotations.[56] This offers a fleeting glimpse of the intellectual confusion that increasingly affected him. Indeed, as the interview progressed he descended into digressions and abstraction.[57] This tendency to ramble often confused listeners, as his friend J. Herman Blake later highlighted: "During his discourse[s] . . . I knew where we started but had no idea where we were or how the explanation would end. . . . He would eventually get to his point. . . . I learned to be patient."[58]

Newton's abstruse tendencies became fully apparent in a sequence of speeches he gave after his release. In September he made his first major post-prison public appearance, at the RPCC in Philadelphia. Newton's speech was almost legendarily lackluster. "By the time he was done," writes George Katsiaficas, a sympathizer among the dwindling number who listened to the entire speech, "our disappointment in him was already palpable," which itself related to the contrast between Newton's abstract concerns and the stentorian tones of New York BPP activist Michael Tabor, who preceded him.[59]

In November Newton spoke before a Michigan crowd that included six FBI informants, two of whom commented that the speech was too long-winded to contemplate taking notes. Starting with a long evaluation of the "contradiction" between the BPP and the League of Revolutionary Workers, Newton discussed the transformation of matter, the nature of acculturation, Marxist dialectics, and the end of Russian feudalism before arriving at his new concept of intercommunalism.[60] Following a reprise at the University of Michigan the following day, the FBI reported a disappointed audience member grumbling, "You spent two hours talking about Lenin and Marx and everything that is in books and didn't inform these people about what's happening right here to blacks? . . . That's a real problem."[61] This was followed by a pair of speeches on the East Coast.[62] The first, at Boston College, was republished in *The Black Panther* and in Newton's *To Die for the People*, indicating that Newton considered it among his best speeches of this period. Its opening section included a florid discussion of the relationship between objectivity and subjectivity, which he claimed constituted the union of theory and practice that the BPP embodied.[63] Nations were now "communities of the world," he argued, and revolutionary intercommunalism would enable the seizure of the means of production before redistributing technology and wealth in an egalitarian fashion. Newton concluded by denouncing Black and white capitalism before predicting that revolutionary intercommunalism would create a value system that harmonized human relations.[64]

The following day saw Newton declaring amazement that some of his audience had walked out, before pondering whether the sun might not rise tomorrow because it was "not tied to the past."[65] Again he outlined revolutionary intercommunalism before launching into confused statements such as:

> To have a racist man you have to have a man with a purpose to better his physical conditions and therefore he will adapt spiritual justifications. Anything that is intangible is spiritual, all things that are solid and tangible are material. So therefore, I say the cause is greater than the effect, and if, in fact, the material situation causes racism which is a value and an attitude, that in order to rid the world of racism we must change the physical structure.[66]

Such "incoherent . . . rambling," according to the FBI's source, led roughly a quarter of the audience to decamp.[67]

Conceptually, little that Newton described was problematic. His insistence that the human world comprised a sequence of interrelated communities rested on core Marxist approaches in that it accepted that class and economics overrode nationality when applied to human behavior and that it responded to a global economy that was dominated by Western capitalism and American cultural imperialism to the extent that national boundaries were fading.[68] No other country could compete with U.S. technological or market power, and consequently no country could guarantee its own sovereignty amid the United States' ceaseless quest for market domination and the resultant flow of capital to American corporations. The people of the world, Newton asserted, were as vulnerable to U.S. domination, be it technological, military, or economic, as the Black American population. This common enemy therefore gave these communities a reason to unite through the common experience of their victimhood.[69] Subsequent developments confirm the validity of Newton's argument that supranational corporations undermined national sovereignty through complex financial structures. The neoliberal economic paradigm, coupled with the acceleration of automation and computerization, enabled such corporations to dispense with both large workforces and tax obligations, destabilizing the world economy and reducing millions of workers to precarity as they were forced to compete for work in a deregulated global market.[70] Yet Newton's understanding of the fate of the nation-state was too abstract to be embraced by 1970s audiences. In attempting to deconstruct this essential feature of their worldview, Newton was guilty of vaulting intellectual ambition, echoed in the failure of the BPP's Ideological Institute.[71] It seems as though Newton eventually accepted the problems in his description of intercommunalism. When pressed in July 1972 he admitted that it amounted to the following concept: "Really we're all just one community."[72] As later BPP activity suggests, the concept offered an overarching theory that informed BPP grassroots activity, even if its specifics remained somewhat abstruse.

The response to Newton's speeches did not deter Yale University sociologist Kai Erikson from inviting him to meet with his father, the esteemed psychologist and psychoanalyst Erik. The trial of Bobby Seale and Ericka Huggins for the murder of BPP activist Alex Rackley in New Haven provided an opportune moment to promote the BPP's philosophy. Newton spoke in the city before settling down with Erikson and a group of students who included at least one FBI informant, for two seminars that would be recorded and edited into a book, with a further Erikson-Newton meeting in Oakland adding extra perspective.[73] At the first, Newton outlined intercommunalism before describing the difference between idealists and materialists, and the nature of logic, reality, and biology. The published version stripped this hour-long opening statement to the core discussion of intercommunalism, which did little for the cogency of Newton's thought.[74] One student questioned whether the BPP should simplify its ideology to attract the masses, a suggestion that Newton appeared to welcome, commenting that he alone bore this burden (one that was shifted to the BPP in the book). A testy exchange followed in which Newton protested that he was from the ghetto himself. The student responded bluntly, "But you're intelligent," prompting an understandably outraged Newton to call for a recess.[75]

A further student comment encapsulated the problem facing Newton. They expressed disappointment that Newton had not been more confrontational, suggesting that Newton essentially recapitulated his Boston College speech.[76] Beneath this justified observation of the similarities between his Yale statements and the speech lies the suggestion that the student thought Newton could not think on his feet. Ultimately, it seems that Newton committed a cardinal sin for any university educator: he was boring. During a speech the following week Newton admitted as much, asking his audience to endure his "very boring speech" before a promised Q&A session began.[77]

Yet unpicking the students' comments reveals that Newton was not solely to blame. The bored student was surely not alone in expecting a particular "Huey P. Newton": perhaps the gun-toting, confrontational caricature of media mythology. It seems that the students were ignorant of the BPP's transformation since the heady days of 1968. Deeper still lies a more troubling issue. Located at the edge of one of New Haven's poorest and Blackest neighborhoods, Yale might have opened an Afro-American Studies department in 1968 but remained essentially an institution for wealthy whites.[78] The "but you're intelligent" student clearly held racist ideas about the intellectual acumen of Black Americans. It is not outside the realm of possibility that the students were expecting Newton to conform to their expectations of a lumpenproletarian African American man. In this sense, Newton was bound to fail unless he attempted a form of rabble-rousing that gelled with privileged whites' expectations of how Black men and radical activists should behave.

Eldridge Cleaver's expulsion less than three weeks later offered the party an opportunity. Having resolved the contradiction between Cleaver's view of the revolution and the party's activities, the BPP could, Newton wrote, return to its "original vision," one "structured by . . . the practical needs of the people."[79] Reminding his readers that he had no time for radicals who privileged theorizing over action, Newton argued that the BPP based its strategy on a "consistent ideology" through which it identified the best methods to begin the revolution. Newton concluded that Cleaver's attempt to develop alliances with white radicals was a dead end, for these radicals could not win enough whites to their cause; more problematic was Cleaver's adventurism. Similarly, Cleaver's profanity infected the party and further isolated it. Without Cleaver, the BPP was now able to "serve the people as advocates of their true interests."

Newton's discussion of Cleaver's defection prompted three imprisoned Panthers to debate the implications of Cleaver's expulsion.[80] Randy Williams accused Cleaver of trying to convert the BPP into a demagogic reactionary group, warning any remaining Cleaverites that "retribution is cold and final."[81] Earl Satcher argued that the BPP would benefit from a union of Newton's focus on survival programs alongside Cleaver's insistence on intensifying its guerrilla campaign.[82] The more skeptical Romaine Fitzgerald noted that guerrilla warfare could not overwhelm the military power of the United States.[83] As this discussion indicates, theoretical concerns continued to inform many Panthers' physical activities in the party.

Newton's claims of returning to the "original vision" of the party clash somewhat with his presentation of intercommunalism as a major innovation, signaling both a rejection of Cleaverism and a return to community-level organization. In this, he elided the disconnect between intercommunalism and the nationalist ideas that informed the 1966 BPP.[84] In rejecting the Panther whose thought was closest to white Marxists, Newton reconfigured the BPP's previous alliances with white radicals as a defection from the Black community. This pivot suggested that Newton sought to win over Black business owners, nonsocialists, and, importantly, churchgoers by elevating race over class. These new collaborations, he said, would enable the BPP "to squeeze as many contributions and compromises out of all the institutions as possible."[85]

Such comments became fully explicable in the wake of "Black Capitalism Re-Analyzed" and its realpolitik focus on the BPP's revenue streams. With donations from whites dwindling and the party's publishing arm reliant on a steady stream of publications for long-term success, the BPP needed to shift its fundraising to the Black community.[86] Given that businessmen were the most visible of the wealthier portions of that community, it made sense to align the BPP with their interests so that they might be encouraged to offer financial support.

Newton presented "Black Capitalism" as intrinsic to the BPP's "original vision."[87] The BPP's defection from the Black community was largely a consequence of its reliance on money from white philanthropists, many of whom inherited their wealth. This dependence on unearned profit, he argued, sat uneasily with the BPP's condemnation of Black capitalists, many of whom were small businessmen with precarious incomes. This led him to differentiate between white (corporate, wealthy) and Black (individual, unwealthy) capitalists. This enabled Newton to present Black capitalism as congruent with the BPP's early conception of community control. Newton argued that Black capitalists were akin to the national bourgeoisie in Fanon's interpretation of anticolonial struggle. Subverting Fanon's prediction that the bourgeoisie would supplant the colonialists, Newton argued that the community needed to support the Black capitalist, who ought to reciprocate by, for example, providing goods to the people through BPP survival programs. This process, Newton argued, would encourage the Black capitalist to negate capitalism's exploitative features and develop a mutually beneficial relationship with the community.

Consequently, while intercommunalism suggested that racial and class oppression was a function of modern capitalism, "Black Capitalism" suggested that a temporary affirmation of small-scale capitalism might not necessarily be as oppressive. Even so, a key question remained: how could Black capitalists be convinced to donate to a campaign that was ultimately designed to destroy their businesses? Newton addressed this later in 1972, arguing that Black Americans were no longer colonial subjects but an oppressed community. He concluded that George Padmore's suggestion that communism did not hold the solution to the problem of the color line led to a further dialectical proposition: that the antithesis of communism, capitalism, would therefore be good for Blacks. While he maintained that the revolution needed the "unity of all oppressed people," he was immediately concerned with uniting Black Americans.[88] The BPP's praxis thus encompassed a temporary accommodation with capitalism involving redistribution of its surpluses among the community, which would produce the dialectical tension that would undo capitalism in the longer term.

Newton's declining interest in class unity informed his long exegesis on Melvin Van Peebles's 1971 film *Sweet Sweetback's Baadassss Song*. A fable of self-discovery, revolution, and community, *Sweetback* was entrenched in urban California.[89] Its titular brother from the block, who was raised in a brothel, becomes a sex worker before maturing as a rebel after intervening to protect an African American revolutionary from being beaten by the police. Made by a solely African American film crew, *Sweetback* echoed Fanon's argument that the violence of the oppressor would rebound in the revolutionary struggle. More troublingly, Newton was also influenced by Francis Ford Coppola's *The Godfather* (1972), which, according to Panther activist Landon Williams, he repeatedly watched while high on cocaine. Newton's analysis relates to the development of a BPP underground wing that engaged in various illicit activities while its overground wing cultivated a more respectable image. As David Hilliard recounted, the BPP-owned nightclub cum restaurant, The Lamp Post, came to symbolize the new, Mafia-styled BPP: it was a legitimate "front" for various extralegal activities that took place behind its closed doors.[90]

Newton burnished his intellectual status with the publication of a collection of his writings, *To Die for the People*, in 1971. While it cemented Newton's identity as a 1960s icon, J. Herman Blake now argues that he ghostwrote "most" of its contents, commenting that "Huey had great ideas but he didn't articulate them well."[91] It would be apposite to suggest that Blake performed as amanuensis, helping present Newton's ideas more accessibly. Newton's 1973 autobiography, formally written with Blake's assistance, complemented Seale's *Seize the Time*, which cemented Newton's revolutionary credentials even as it coated his history with a thick layer of legend.[92] While *Revolutionary Suicide* did little to challenge Seale's impressionist account of the BPP's early years, it painted a more complex picture of Newton. Its harrowing description of Newton's experience in prison begged comparisons with *The Autobiography of Malcolm X* and indeed Malcolm X himself, particularly in its presentation of Newton's political awakening. Significantly, it presented Newton as a genuine intellectual, stressing his immersion in Plato, Fanon, Mao, and Guevara, his understanding of existentialism, psychology, and logical positivism, and his belief in Christianity's irrationality.[93]

Weeks prior to *Revolutionary Suicide*'s publication, Newton appeared on William F. Buckley's television discussion show *Firing Line*. After teasing Buckley with a question about whether the conservative would have supported the revolutionaries in the American war for independence, he outlined his conviction that "contradiction is the ruling principle of the universe," prompting Buckley to begin bickering with him.[94] Amid a rambling discussion of the Cuban Revolution, an irritated Buckley attempted to liven things up: "I don't know what you're talking about and I think you don't either."[95] Undeterred, Newton went on to discuss the nature of democracy, free speech, and the nature of power, prompting an outraged Buckley to claim that one of Newton's main problems was his "total incoherence," an accusation that amused Newton greatly.[96]

This proved Newton's last major public appearance as a high-profile political figure. The relevance of his work to the African American struggle waned as he became embroiled in legal cases and withdrew from political activism. Later intellectual works did not reach a wide audience during his lifetime.[97] Yet as he descended into cocaine addiction and various unsavory activities, nobody replaced him at the party's intellectual head. This reflected their inclinations as well as the roles they occupied and the duties they shared. Where Newton had ample time for reading and introspection, Panthers like Elaine Brown, Ericka Huggins, and others involved themselves in the quotidian necessities of party and community organization, while other party leaders drifted away, found themselves at the mercy of the American judicial system, or, like Fred Hampton, were killed. During Newton's 1967–70 absence, they helped internationalize the BPP's ideological stance while deepening the party's critique of American capitalism, all courtesy of their engagement with an array of leftist literature that helped theorize their lived experience. That they did this while also playing activist roles is testament to their devotion to the party's ideals.

Following his return to civilian life, Newton began to experience considerable mental distress because of his many months in solitary confinement. Taking refuge in his penthouse apartment, he grew alienated from the very people he was supposed to lead. His two major contributions to late Panther thought emerged from this psychological maelstrom. He presented intercommunalism as a major contribution to leftist thought. As he discovered, however, audiences could not relate to this highly abstract concept. While intercommunalism quietly declined in his thought, his feud with Eldridge Cleaver reached its climax. Ridding the BPP of one of its most influential and well-known figures represented both crisis and opportunity. While Cleaver's ability to attract press attention and white radical finance was essential to the

BPP's rise, his departure allowed the BPP to return to the Black community as a more socially aware and socially rooted group. Newton's reassessment of Black capitalism was part of this process, an attempt to reconcile the BPP with the Black community amid an admission that race needed to be elevated above class in the short to medium term. It also helped spur a period of BPP activism that briefly promised to position it as a key player in Oakland's politics. As such, BPP activism represents a tactical response positioned within a more ambitious strategic goal that remained critical of, even as it attempted to accommodate aspects of, American capitalism.

PART II

Community Activism

CHAPTER FOUR

The BPP in the Street

In 2016 Bobby Seale insisted that the BPP's early activities were attempts to "capture the imagination of the people."[1] Many such operations involved its small, overwhelmingly male membership occupying Oakland's streets and have become part of the BPP's mythology, often interpreted as a propaganda ploy and a way to attract attention to the organization's political platform.[2] They were, however, a far more complex attempt to transform power relations in Oakland and are best considered with reference to the relationship between space and power, and perhaps even as street theater. As important, they demonstrate the centrality of public actions to the modus operandi of the BPP.

According to Jean-Jacques Lebel, a Parisian *soixante-huitard*, the first stage of "*any* revolution is always theatrical"; while the BPP did not design its events as theater, they transformed the street into a stage.[3] Street theater is performed in the space the performers wish to transform, reacting to events that occur naturally or regularly, and like regular theater it removes its audience from the everyday, taking them to an alternative reality. For the theater scholar Jan Cohen-Cruz, street performance "creates visions of what society might be.... [It] invit[es] participation ... [and comprises] moments when a new consciousness is trying to come into being."[4] Street theater retains its power even when media coverage is absent. The Brazilian theater theorist Augusto Boal argued that this "invisible" theater profoundly impacts its witnesses, who talk about it, thus transforming it into legend.[5] A classic example occurred at the New York Stock Exchange in 1967. The Yippies tossed hundreds of dollar bills onto the trading floor, prompting the traders to scramble for the money. This response—which encapsulated their critique of capitalism and love of the absurd—delighted the Yippies, who used the lack of press coverage to shift the event into myth, allowing the public to develop their own fantasies of what occurred. As the Yippie Abbie Hoffman recalled, "The system cracked a little.... An image war had begun." Hoffman also noted that street theater "benefits from an edge of menace—a touch of potential violence," a perspective that helps an understanding of the BPP's street events.[6]

Little to no violence occurred during the BPP's early activities, but some observers interpreted the BPP's stance as a menace to social order. It began a war of position between the BPP and Oakland's police in the public arena of Oakland's streets.[7] As the philosopher Henri Lefebvre points out, space is "a means of control, and hence of domination, of power."[8] The control of space is highly contingent and based in part on physical relations between individuals or groups. It is the definitive place where power is exercised and challenged. Groups who lack access to the levers of power are often only able to claim their rightful place in society through public activities, an example being the mass marches of the African American civil rights movement. Fanon himself suggested that the lack of an effective political space for the natives helped propel them toward violence. In essence, their violence constitutes a desperate attempt to create this political space.[9]

In Oakland, public space was controlled by the city's police officers. The BPP set about uncovering the weakness that lay beneath local police officers' heavily armed exterior through a sequence of street activities intended to demonstrate that power actually lay with the people, anticipating similar assertions by the *soixante-huitards*.[10] These operations constituted a temporary occupation of public space that would anticipate a more permanent transformation and create a new public consciousness. As important, the visibility these events granted the BPP was crucial for its ambition to win the support of Oakland's residents. This helped fix the image of the BPP among the locals and wage an image war against Oakland's police state, although the ultimate effect was not quite what the BPP expected.

This image war began even before the party's formation. In March 1966 Bobby Seale was arrested for obstructing the sidewalk, an incident that cemented his and Newton's friendship and catalyzed their decision to form the BPP.[11] The two were walking down Telegraph Avenue, one of Berkeley's major thoroughfares, while Seale recited a poem, "Uncle Sammy Call Me Fulla Lucifer." Written by Ronald Stone, the poem appeared in *Soulbook*, the local periodical with deep links to the Revolutionary Action Movement.[12] Another friend encouraged Seale to stand on a chair to reprise it, and a crowd gathered to listen. Unfortunately, one of the observers was police officer Eugene Sabatini, who opposed this transformation of the "spatial economy" of Telegraph.[13] Since January the police department had been conducting frequent patrols of Telegraph in an effort to cleanse the area of its scruffier visitors in anticipation of an urban renewal project.[14] Positioning himself as the defender of Berkeley's moral values, Sabatini attempted to arrest Seale for "using loud and vulgar language in front of women and children."[15] Sabatini claims that Newton then hit him. An off-duty Oakland police officer who had been drinking alcohol nearby joined the fracas; meanwhile, it seems that Newton began tussling for Sabatini's gun.[16] The appearance of the police caused a fundamental shift in the atmosphere, teaching Newton and Seale a powerful lesson. The crowd became angry and started to intervene, some to subdue Newton, others to protect him and Seale. Both men were arrested. At the time they held leadership positions in the campus-based Soul Students Advisory Council. According to Seale, one of their comrades sequestered funds to bail them out and hire a lawyer. Accused of stealing the money, Newton and Seale concluded that the SSAC was little more than a talking shop, so they quit—a key moment in the BPP's prehistory.[17]

As important, the crowd's reaction suggested that defying the police could be a useful way to develop sympathy among local people. In this sense, the theatrical and symbolic value of the arrest far outweighed the monetary cost. Newton and Seale learned that they could open up cracks in the system: their resistance challenged the police's dominance and undercut the police's power to control the populace. By verbalizing their outrage so loudly, they claimed the public space of Telegraph Avenue for local residents, even if only briefly. Their witnesses doubtless talked about the incident, ensuring that it lingered in the memory as a demonstration of the people's power, one that was confirmed by its recounting in Seale's memoir.

A similar rebellious aura surrounded the BPP's early street activities. According to Seale, early in 1967 Newton and some comrades were traveling in a car, openly displaying rifles and shotguns. An Oakland police officer began tailing them, prompting the Panthers to discuss their tactics. Newton told them:

> The man is going to try to arrest you.... He's going to try to prove to all the people... around us here that we have no right with a gun. And he's going to arrest you on a traffic ticket and the people out in the community will think he arrested you because you've got the gun. We want to prove to the people that we've got a right to carry guns and they've got a right to arm themselves.[18]

Once both cars stopped, a heated debate ensued. By the time Newton exited the car and loaded his rifle, a crowd of onlookers had gathered. The police ordered them to disperse, provoking Newton to announce, "Don't go anywhere!... You have a right to observe an officer carrying out his duty.... As long as you stand a reasonable distance away, and you *are* a reasonable distance. *Don't go anywhere.*"[19] The police asked Newton what he intended to do with his weapon. Newton retorted, "What are you going to do with *your* gun? Because if you try to shoot at me, or if you try to take this gun, I'm going to shoot back at you, swine." "This blew the pigs' minds," remembered Seale.[20]

Newton proceeded to invite members of the crowd into the BPP's recently opened office to watch the scene through its picture window. As the crowd grew, Newton allowed more inside. "The brothers observing," Seale wrote,

> would see that those pigs were scared of that *big* gun.... Every time Huey would say, "If you shoot at me, swine, I'm shooting back," niggers would have to holler.... That would let Huey know that he was revolutionizing our culture.... And after *that*, we really began to patrol pigs then, because we got righteous recruits.[21]

Like the poetry incident, this episode destabilized the OPD's control of Oakland. Its success in demonstrating the limits of police power was crucial in emboldening the BPP and attracting the local community to its cause. As Tarika Lewis, one of the BPP's first recruits, recalls, the BPP were heroes: "Finally somebody had the courage to do something."[22] In this instance, the mere *threat* of violence raised the self-respect of the local community, emboldening them just as Fanon and Robert F. Williams had promised. It also demonstrated the power of words. Newton's autobiography mentions that his youthful belligerence developed in part because of his feebleness at "the dozens," a game of verbal dexterity in which two antagonists insult each other in the most disgusting and entertaining manner possible.[23] In trading slurs to dominate your opponent, the dozens were a way of performing power. Newton's verbal challenges to Bay Area police played a similar role by dehumanizing them as swine, a word that defined them as lower-status animals and associated them with porcine tendencies such as a disregard for human hygiene.

This event also begs consideration of the BPP's interpretation of the nature of power. Newton was surely aware that such actions only temporarily reconstructed power relationships, since the OPD would not want repeats of such insubordination. Yet the involvement of local people transformed individual performance into community protest. The street became both a performative space in which the BPP staged its vision of community power and an arena for the creation of a new form of community.[24] The BPP thus created a new public space in Oakland, free from police harassment. This redefinition of a public space previously considered to be the domain of the Oakland police was powerfully disruptive.

These actions soon spread. Newton's research into California law confirmed that state citizens could legally carry weapons openly and observe police carrying out their duties. Standing a safe distance from events, BPP members would watch arrests and loudly read out relevant sections from their California lawbooks (helpfully reprinted in the BPP's newspaper), ensuring that the arrested individuals knew of their right to silence and what information they were obliged or not obliged to give. They would ask the suspects directly whether they felt they were being harassed or abused.[25] Not long after the incident outside the BPP office, Newton, Seale, and Bobby Hutton were accosted by a police officer who proclaimed his disgust that they were holding firearms. Newton turned to the people and cited Fanon: "Come out, black people. Come on out and get to know about these racist dog swine who been controlling our community and occupying our community like a foreign troop."[26] Seale estimated that about seventy people gathered before more than a dozen police cruisers arrived, giving Newton a further opportunity to reeducate the community.[27] These observers theoretically ensured that the police conducted their duties professionally and legally. As important, they demonstrated the power wielded by civilians. Once the situation had resolved itself, BPP members distributed literature to those who remained, allowing them to spread the word about the BPP's successful insubordination.

While not openly defying the police, the BPP demonstrated that a higher power existed than the purely corporeal power of the police officer: after all, the police had to abide by the laws, and what better way to ensure this than by patrolling them? In doing so, the BPP members created unpredictable and participatory moments, transforming arrests into scenes of community confrontation, which is largely why the police found it so terrifying. The BPP thus created a new psychological space for residents and their occupying force: the police's power was now in question. As important, the public brandishing of firearms resulted in the BPP's members considering themselves equals, rather than subjects, of the police; their use of dehumanizing epithets reinforced this undermining process.[28] They also subtly satirized their own notion (borrowed from Mao) that power flowed out of the barrel of a gun, testing another Maoist axiom: "to get rid of the gun it is necessary to take up the gun."[29] Their stance rendered the armed police impotent in the face of the community's strength. "It was sometimes hilarious to see their reaction," Newton remembered. "They had always been cocky and sure of themselves as long as they had weapons to intimidate the unarmed community. When we equalized the situation, their real cowardice was exposed."[30] In demonstrating the fragility of the OPD's dominance, the BPP struck a major psychological blow against these paper tigers.

The BPP's actions transformed spectators into "spect-actors": observers who did not sit passively but became participants.[31] This challenged the ideology that ruled Oakland's streets where the community largely did what it was told by the OPD. Newton's actions brought the community into direct contact with the police at flashpoint moments. Knowing that the police did not possess the manpower to arrest everybody and that the mere presence of these individuals would cause the police to rethink their own actions, Newton dissolved the boundary between active agents and spectators. As Fanon argued, onlookers were either cowards or traitors; Newton was leading them toward the revolutionary struggle.[32] The transformation of a simple arrest procedure into a community event empowered residents, unifying them against their common oppressor and adding substance to the BPP's suggestion that any Black person could be a Black Panther.

Not all early BPP street activities were confrontational. During the BPP's earliest days Newton and Seale often worked at the North Oakland Poverty Center at 5550 Market Street, which gave them a good view of the intersection between one of Oakland's major arterial roads and Fifty-Fifth Street, which catered for Oakland's commuters and schoolchildren heading to and from Santa Fe Elementary School on Fifty-Fourth and Market. After learning that several children had been injured and one killed there, the BPP leaders resolved to act. The city council rebuffed the BPP's petition, so armed Panthers occupied the intersection and directed traffic to ensure pedestrian safety. Passing police officers soon relieved them, and within weeks, according to the BPP, traffic lights appeared, proving that occupying public space could force local government to act. As important, when replaced by the police, Newton and Seale used the opportunity to talk to observers about the BPP and the need for coordinated neighborhood action against white oppression.[33]

One of the BPP's most famous street actions occurred outside the *Ramparts* magazine office in February 1967. Newton and Seale heard that Betty Shabazz had been invited to San Francisco to attend a commemoration of her husband Malcolm X's life. Newton resolved to accompany Shabazz from San Francisco's airport to *Ramparts*'s Broadway office for a meeting with Eldridge Cleaver. The BPP's armed vanguard group made their presence felt by loudly asserting their constitutional right to bear arms in a public space.[34] Seale recalled seeing "people with their eyes all bugged out. 'What are these guys doing with these guns?'"[35] The airport's head of security attempted to remove them but, outwitted by their superior grasp of California law, backed down.[36]

Following the convoy's arrival at *Ramparts*, BPP comrades stood guard to prevent the police from entering the building. By the meeting's end the media had arrived. At Shabazz's request, Newton attempted to prevent cameras filming, which prompted the police to prepare for confrontation. According to Seale, Newton told the assembled Panthers to do the same. "And the next thing you know," Seale remembered, "we spread. I put my hand on my gun. The police says, 'Don't put your hand there.' I said, 'Don't you put your hand on your gun' . . . a real Mexican standoff."[37] Watching from a safe distance, Cleaver thought to himself, "Goddam, that nigger [Newton] is c-r-a-z-y," seconds before the police admitted defeat.[38] Here again, Newton reversed the power relationship that existed between police and residents. Normally, the police officer drew his gun and the resident backed down. Newton's reconstruction of this relationship threatened a wider pattern of rebellion in the Bay Area and constituted a huge symbolic victory.

In the aftermath, an agitated news reporter attempted to wrench an explanation from a departing Cleaver. Ever savvy, Cleaver told the reporter that Shabazz was no more in danger of assassination than any African American: "Many black people have been murdered outright here in America. And we see nothing happening to believe that this is going to stop."[39] The slightly rattled police spokesman, meanwhile, insisted that the SFPD was only present in an investigatory role. Subsequent news reports cemented the BPP's status, as did the inevitable *Ramparts* coverage, in which Sol Stern observed that the incident would have a major "political effect on the black community [because] of a few blacks openly carrying guns."[40] Stern correctly identified the deeper meaning of the gun as a tool for recruitment and radicalization, and as a performative symbol of political protest.

Two months later, the *San Francisco Examiner* ran a front-page story publicizing the BPP, the most prominent coverage the organization had yet received. As ever, the media's involvement proved double-edged. It obviously drew curious individuals closer to the party, which facilitated more police patrols. There were also, however, numerous problematic outcomes. First, as Seale pointed out, the article contained numerous misconceptions, including most dangerously that the BPP was antiwhite. It overwhelmingly presented the BPP as dangerous individuals who possessed—and were prepared to use—a large arsenal. Its attendant image soon became part of the BPP's iconography: Newton and Seale, clad in black berets and leather jackets, posing purposefully outside the BPP office. Newton toted a shotgun and wore a bandolier bristling with shells, reminiscent of the Zapatistas, while keen observers would have noted a pistol peeking out of Seale's jacket pocket and another gun slung over his shoulder.[41]

The gun constituted a major factor in the BPP's attraction to disaffected Oaklanders. As Sherwin Forte recalled, the presentation of a pistol at his second BPP meeting was a key moment in his life: "You pick it up and . . . you feel a little bit of power. You feel like you have some righteous equipment to begin to address these wrongs."[42] Indicating that the gun possessed an appeal that could transcend the BPP's gendered calls to action, Tarika Lewis asked two questions when she first encountered the party: can she join, and can she have a gun? This was not merely about the potential for violence that the gun represents; evidence now suggests that gun owners feel the very presence of a gun on their body offers a profound sense of security.[43] The members' feelings reflect their awareness of personal safety in an urban landscape dominated by police brutality alongside the psychological impact of its presence.

The gun was also central to the BPP's gesture of power, which is where Robert F. Williams's influence is most apparent. Williams's memoir details his use of the street as a stage for confrontation and the reversal of power relations in his town. The opening episode is perhaps the most astonishing. In June 1961, as picketing over access to the Monroe swimming pool escalated, Williams arrived at the scene carrying firearms in his car. He was immediately threatened by a baseball bat–wielding racist:

> I put an Army .45 up ... and pointed it right into his face and didn't say a word. He looked at the pistol and he didn't say anything. He started backing away from the car. Somebody in the crowd fired a pistol and the people again started to scream hysterically.... So I opened the door of the car and I put one foot on the ground and stood up in the door holding an Italian carbine.[44]

When a police officer challenged him, Williams "struck him in the face and knocked him back.... I told him we were not going to surrender to a mob." Another police officer tried to position himself to shoot Williams in the back but was deterred by one of Williams's comrades who "put a .45 in the policeman's face." Both police retreated. As significant, a local white supremacist was led away in tears, wailing pathetically that "the niggers have got guns, the niggers are armed and the police can't even arrest them!" Soon afterward, the chief of police allowed the protesters to depart without harm. This variation on mutually assured destruction ensured a tense truce in Monroe. Indeed, Williams maintained throughout his life that only the threat of violence prevented a pogrom. His reasoning was brutal: common law relied on a civilized society, and the white South was far from civilized. African Americans therefore needed to rely on the colorblind doctrine of "no duty to retreat," reclaiming the right to stand their ground when faced by a violent antagonist and, if necessary, kill to protect themselves.[45]

Negroes with Guns's representation of this episode is vital for an understanding of the BPP's attitude toward public protest. Newton's activities exhibit such similarities to Williams's that Williams must be acknowledged as a huge influence on not only the BPP's practical philosophy but also its performance of gun ownership and resistance. Moreover, the similarities in Seale's account of San Francisco's commuters expressing outrage and Williams's of the aged white supremacist suggest that the latter's account echoed in Seale's mind as he constructed his memoir.[46] The reaction of the stunned racist to Williams's display of weaponry surely influenced Newton and Seale's decision to make firearms visible tools in their public protests, enabling them to consider the impact of similar displays of weaponry on the OPD and specifically on its policing of Oakland's Black neighborhoods.

As important, the BPP's actions would galvanize the local community, emboldening people to assert control over their own public spaces, which itself should compel the OPD to protect and serve all of Oakland's citizens. Once the police confrontation became a public event, the BPP members—and Newton in particular—almost paradoxically found themselves more secure. The BPP's members would be protected from the police by the crowd, discombobulating the men who were used to deference and civility and causing them to question how they should quell this incipient revolution. Since Newton had not broken any laws, they could not lawfully arrest him. They could not abuse him because this would turn the crowd against them, again threatening their own safety. Even if they chose to detain him, there was no guarantee that they could remove him. They obviously could not shoot him because of the presence of witnesses and because of the threat to their own lives that Newton—in their parlance a "crazy" n-word—represented. In this, Newton anticipated a key aspect of Richard Nixon's Cold War geopolitical strategy. As Nixon told his chief of staff, "I call it the Madman Theory, Bob. I want the North Vietnamese to believe I've reached the point where I might do *anything* to stop the war. . . . We can't restrain him when he's angry—and he has his hand on the nuclear button."[47] Newton's potential reckless action could result in the police suffering injury or worse. He knew that, as a Black man, the police often considered him an irrational and irresponsible second-class citizen. The threat of mutually assured destruction that the gun represented made him feel more secure when dealing with the police. His actions presented a no-win situation for the oppressor. The dilemma he created for the police contained no plausible victory. The only option they had was to allow Newton to prevail, as any of the other options led to him winning, either through legal means, on the streets, or even in his martyrdom. Consequently, their only option was to accept the supremacy of the law of the streets and allow Newton to go about his business. Newton thus posed one of the most fundamental questions in any society: who holds power? His actions emboldened the community when they saw the embodiment of white power in their neighborhood being challenged. This symbolism—the image of power—was arguably more important for the BPP than any other outcome of their performance of the gun.

In April 1967 the BPP interrupted a meeting at the Richmond Office of Economic Opportunity. Contra Costa district attorney John Nejedly told the FBI of the decidedly intimidatory atmosphere that followed, which he correctly concluded was the BPP's aim.[48] This aura was doubtless reinforced by the group's uniforms. When on duty Panthers tended to adhere to the striking uniform adopted by Newton and Seale, paired with sunglasses if possible. Sunglasses were both utilitarian and theatrical, protecting the members' eyes while adding an impression of mystery and anonymity. The sight of a group of men wearing the same clothes, moreover, reinforced a sense of discipline and strength, competence and calmness, underlain with a sense of menace; their attention to sartorial detail was thus a metaphor for the seriousness with which they took their public duties, a hint at their strength, and an articulation of their masculinity. Yet the semiotics of the leather jacket run even deeper. It signified teenage rebellion, conjuring up images of Marlon Brando's antiauthoritarianism in *The Wild One* (1953) and James Dean's alienation in *Rebel without a Cause* (1955). This leather-jacketed group rejected traditional lines of deference, demonstrating its youthfulness, its danger, and the potential for menace. This sartorial choice also represented Walter Benjamin's "tiger's leap into the past": a metaphoric resurrection of the BPP's revolutionary ancestors, such as leather-clad Red Army units and Leon Trotsky's elite guard in the Russian Civil War.[49] Similarly, Seale remembers that he and Newton adopted the beret after watching a movie about French Resistance fighters in World War II who wore berets to signify their anti-fascist credentials.[50] Of course, the beret was also the chosen headgear of "Che" Guevara, popularized through Alberto Korda's legendary March 1960 photograph of the revolutionary at a Havana rally. Guevara adopted the beret early in the Cuban Revolution and wore it almost permanently thereafter.[51] While he did not become a major icon until his October 1967 assassination, anybody with an interest in the Cuban Revolution could interpret the hat as a signifier of the BPP's alignment with revolutionaries like him.

April's *Examiner* article centered the BPP in the Bay Area's popular consciousness. Within days, the obscure California assemblyman Donald Mulford, whose district included Berkeley and the wealthy section of Oakland, proposed a bill that would make it a misdemeanor to brandish a loaded weapon within city limits, thus criminalizing the BPP's open-carry police patrols.[52] The pinnacle of his political career, his bill eventually passed amid urban rebellions spreading across the nation following an uprising in Newark, New Jersey, with legislators expanding Mulford's bill to apply to any public place.[53]

The bill's announcement prompted Newton to propose that the BPP make a statement at the California state capitol. This would involve Panthers appearing at the capitol and Seale delivering Executive Mandate Number One, which he had written with Newton and Cleaver. Newton would not attend, as his parole terms prohibited involvement in such activities and BPP members worried that his temper might get the better of him, which could, in Sherwin Forte's words, lead to "bad things" happening.[54] Cleaver, then on parole, had *Ramparts* request that the Department of Corrections allow him to attend the legislature to report on the planned discussion of policing. As such, his presence directly related to his ongoing employment (itself necessary as an indication of his rehabilitation), but it also ensured continued media coverage for the BPP.[55] As this confirms, the protest was a meticulously planned operation.

On May 2, thirty armed Panthers piled out of their cars into the Sacramento sunshine. As they checked and loaded their weapons in accordance with California law, Governor Ronald Reagan met with some schoolchildren on the capitol lawn. Cameramen documenting Reagan's gathering noticed a potentially more telegenic story emerging as the BPP delegation approached the capitol building. Their decision to abandon the governor for this breaking news proved crucial to BPP history.[56] After brushing past an elderly sergeant-at-arms, Seale noticed that the white people in the building "moved and stepped aside, and I saw some with their mouths hanging open ... and they were saying with their eyes and their faces and expressions, 'Who in the hell are these niggers with these guns?'"[57]

Most of the Panthers had not visited Sacramento before, let alone the capitol. Unsurprisingly, they soon became hopelessly lost. After some confusion, they were guided toward the assembly floor. Seale was ushered in by a doorman who said, "Yes, sir, you *sure* can come in. Come right on in, sir! You have the *gun*!" "And he opened the door in a very humble manner," recalled Seale. "Like a servant. Like a vassal."[58] This civility and deference clearly indicated the power of the gun. The doorman metaphorically justified the BPP's strategy: the gun finally gave access to the American political process and enabled Seale and his comrades to bypass the many obstructions faced by African American protesters. It rendered the capitol, previously the defining site of power in the state, a space of political engagement and challenge.[59] The assemblymen were less obliging than their doormen, however, and amid uproar, the BPP delegates retired to an antechamber where Seale was filmed reading Executive Mandate Number One as a discomfited security guard resisted the urge to expel these upstarts.[60] Showing a keen eye for publicity, Seale reprised his oration on the steps of the capitol for the benefit of media representatives who remained outside.

This was a watershed moment. The BPP briefly wrestled access to the American system, at a speed that sharply contrasted with the years of rejection, filibustering, and violence that civil rights protesters endured. The moment of the delegation's entry onto the assembly floor rendered African Americans equal players in the American democratic experiment, offering evidence of the mandate's promise, even if only fleetingly. For participant Emory Douglas, the event provided a feeling of involvement in a national struggle that previously felt remote. BPP sympathizer Reginald Major went further: it was perhaps the most important protest ever witnessed in Sacramento, a moment that definitively exposed the gulf between Black and white America. The poet and playwright Amiri Baraka, then in residence at San Francisco State College, recalled that news of Sacramento caused Black students to "beam ... from one end of the campus to the other. . . . The real revolution is just around the corner, we felt."[61] As Newton ruefully noted, however, the firearms received more attention than the message that justified them.[62] A disgusted Reagan dismissed the activity as "ridiculous."[63] The BPP's protesters were arrested and six convicted of disrupting a legislative session, initiating a long period in which police sought to disarm BPP members at any opportunity. Seale was jailed for ninety days.[64] An outraged Mulford—who previously opposed similar gun control bills—declared that the bill would be toughened while pompously and mistakenly claiming that the invasion was a "direct attempt" at personal intimidation. Before signing it into law on July 28, lawmakers amended it to make possessing a loaded weapon in the state capitol a felony.⁶⁵

Luckily, Newton and his friend David Hilliard were not yet high on the OPD's priority list. To raise funds for their imprisoned comrades they bought a pound of marijuana to sell. A police car tailed them as they transported it. Hilliard recalls asking Newton how they should react if they were stopped. "We *shoot* them," replied Newton. "We don't give up our guns. We don't give up our dope."⁶⁶ Newton's confrontational pledge contrasts sharply with the denouement to the Sacramento protest, in which Seale ordered his comrades to accept rather than resist arrest. Of course, Newton was acting undercover and was observed by a single police officer; Seale and the Sacramento protesters were arrested in front of the media in the company of many police officers. In ensuring a peaceful end to the protest, Seale demonstrated the limits of the BPP's preparedness to undermine police authority. Yet the close relationship between these two events highlights the thin line that divided the BPP's forays into extralegal activity from their more lawful pursuits.

Soon after, Newton confirmed that the BPP's fears about his notoriety were not without foundation. In June he was arrested in Richmond for attempting to prevent a comrade being arrested.⁶⁷ A few weeks earlier, according to the OPD, some police officers were investigating reports that some North Oakland youths were toting a sawn-off shotgun. When the police arrived, the youths attempted to hide in a nearby house. Not much later Newton and another Panther arrived. Newton allegedly berated the police while holding a large dagger. He was arrested and charged with various offenses, and the knife was confiscated along with the gun carried by Newton's comrade.⁶⁸ Whether or not Newton threatened the police officers with a knife is debatable. No evidence other than their report remains. That he was not carrying a gun—which would have violated a parole order—proves that he was aware of his precarious legal position. And yet, if the police were correct, he gave them reason to charge him with wielding a deadly weapon. The alleged presence of the knife suggests that the OPD were prepared to apply the letter of the law to its fullest extent against the BPP, and if necessary to go beyond it.

Such episodes position Newton, and perhaps the BPP as a whole, as heirs to Staggerlee, the near mythical figure of African American folklore. As many versions of his tribute song attested, he was a bad man, feted for his preparedness to kill a man and accept the consequent punishment. Yet beneath the myth lies a keener parallel with the BPP. The evidence suggests that Stag killed Billy Lyons in an act of self-defense: we might approach it like the historian George Eberhart, as "a primeval cry in the wilderness by an emasculated class trapped in a dystopia orchestrated by whites."⁶⁹ Jail, to Staggerlee, was no different from the "free" world he inhabited as a Black man in a white society. So even this small assertion of power, however temporary it proved to be, might be considered a triumph.[70]

These assertions of power suggest that the BPP held a similar view of guns as the U.S. government had of nuclear weapons: they were primarily a deterrent rather than an active weapon. In 1967 Newton asserted that "ninety per cent of the reason we carried guns in the first place was educational."[71] He was also clear in his autobiography: "weapons were a recruiting device," and Sacramento was significant for drawing onlookers and the media to the BPP, enabling Seale to articulate the BPP's political message.[72] Notably, BPP leaders Newton, Seale, Hilliard, and Cleaver were involved in only two verifiable gun-related episodes during the 1960s: Newton was implicated in the death of OPD officer John Frey in 1967, and Cleaver participated in the shoot-out that resulted in Bobby Hutton's death. Significantly, only in the Hutton incident can the BPP be accused of instigating gun violence.

This reminds us that the BPP's street protests were both highly theatrical and performative, and authentic expressions of ideology and vision. Much like slaves who made symbolic protests by standing up to their masters in front of their fellow slaves, the BPP rendered the hidden transcript of police-public relations visible while galvanizing the community, disrupting the activities of the OPD and refashioning the concept of authority.[73] BPP activists thus revealed the limits of the OPD's local power. They also actuated another of Mao's axioms: "All reactionaries are paper tigers. In appearance, the reactionaries are terrifying, but in reality, they are not so powerful. . . . It is not the reactionaries but the people who are powerful."[74]

Street activities cemented the BPP in the East Bay Black community. In doing so, the BPP brought key elements of Fanonist theory into practice. By unifying and galvanizing the community, the BPP challenged the quasi-colonial domination of the inner city by the police, developed solidarity among the underclass, asserted their own right to their land, and opened a war of position between themselves and the occupying force, rendering the open spaces of Oakland's streets a prime location for cultural, political, and physical challenge.[75] In disrupting the normative police-media-civilian relationship, the BPP dislocated the process of arrest that had become almost ritualized in the Bay Area. Newton could rely on the police's fear that Oakland's African American residents were volatile and violent to his own advantage. As a "brother from the block" he had nothing to lose, so he could affect a stance that suggested to the police that, like Robert F. Williams, he was prepared for a shoot-out. This forced the police to reconsider their own vulnerability. Yet a second effect underlay this. The image war sensitized local police to their own fragile hegemony. In satirizing the OPD's shaky grasp of constitutional law and openly defying their authority, the BPP provoked the OPD to reassert itself by heightening surveillance and repression of the BPP, a development that hastened the BPP's decline.[76] The first impact came in the Mulford Act, which prompted the theoretical and practical development of the BPP. As the BPP pivoted from armed patrols, its arms—and its armed wing—went underground.[77] The symbolic politics of the street waned as the BPP drew influence from foco theory while expanding into other forms of community activism, broadening its war of position.

CHAPTER FIVE

Social Programs and Local Chapters

In March 1971 the FBI learned that Newton wanted the BPP's newspaper to stop referring to violence. Prior to this, the newspaper regularly offered readers guidance on responsible gun ownership, peaking with Cleaver loyalist Don Cox's multipart guide to establishing self-defense groups that included paeans to various weapons alongside admonishments to "attack them [pigs] at will." Such features suggested that weapons played a key role in BPP activities.[1] By 1971 Newton thought that the BPP's less confrontational direction needed more publicity. His decision related to his understanding that references to armed struggle drew attention away from other aspects of the BPP's activity, most notably its community activism.

The BPP's community programs had been growing for years. Free breakfasts started in Oakland in January 1969, with liberation schools following soon after. Named "survival programs" to highlight their ambition to sustain the community until the revolution was complete, they broadened the palette of the BPP's activities and educated the community about the BPP's wider goals while offering recruits a focus for their energies. They also attracted state repression.[2] Attempting to triangulate between critics of the BPP's revolutionary ambitions and radicals who believed that the shift to community activism constituted a retreat, *The Black Panther* insisted that the survival programs were neither revolutionary nor reformist. Such criticism even came from within: Bobby Seale claims that Eldridge Cleaver dismissed the free breakfasts in typical homophobic fashion as "sissy."[3] Their true character, the BPP insisted, would become clear with hindsight: "if they ... raise that united consciousness to struggle to the point of liberation, they will be revolutionary."[4]

As Panther Landon Williams argued, the survival programs represented a new front in the BPP's war against white supremacy. For Williams, they broke the vicious circle that bound African American people: "You're hungry because you're poor.... You're poor because you haven't got the best jobs.... You can't get the best jobs because you're uneducated, and you're uneducated be-

87

cause you didn't learn while you were in school ... [because] every time the teacher mentioned 5 apples or 6 bananas, your stomach growled."[5] The compound harms wrought by racism, poverty, underemployment, and hunger on people he served could not be alleviated by an education system predicated on the assumption that such problems did not exist. Breaking this cycle would fundamentally shift people's relationship with capitalism, liberating them from the profiteering that corrupted the provision of food and freeing them from one aspect of colonial domination. Providing free food was thus a revolutionary act, part of the process through which the BPP attempted to develop power and influence among the people it was organizing. By creating a parallel structure, the BPP created a new propaganda tool and highlighted that another, noncapitalist world was possible.

Relatedly, the debate concerning the revolutionary or reformist nature of these programs diverts us from appreciating their impact on members and their communities. The evidence suggests that the BPP's social programs had a transformative impact on many thousands of people. Panthers nationwide embodied Mao's dictum that revolutionaries should serve the people, providing a plethora of services to dozens of communities, with women playing central roles in both providing and coordinating such services.[6] Important in themselves, these programs were also a welcome distraction from the repression that BPP members faced. The Los Angeles chapter, for example, established a health care clinic soon after the murder of two leading members, named for one of their fallen: Alprentice "Bunchy" Carter. This was an apt initiative for channeling the comrades' grief into positive action toward the BPP's larger ambitions and to avoid a spiral of retaliatory violence.[7]

The sterling research of numerous historians into the BPP chapters outside Oakland offers an important counterpoint to the BPP's history in its hometown. Their analysis reveals the extent to which the BPP excited people across the United States and reminds us of the sacrifices members made as they attempted to fashion a new world. Yet the histories of these chapters also demonstrate the problems faced by the BPP as it developed. Kathleen Cleaver noted that, in the absence of a nationwide organizational structure, the party expanded chaotically in 1968. She suggests that, at a community level, the BPP represented what local organizers thought it represented rather than any grand vision from the Oakland headquarters. The brief history of an unapproved chapter in Cleveland, Ohio, stands as a reminder that, briefly, almost anybody could set themselves up as the local BPP. Marvin Wolf-Bey announced himself as Cleveland's BPP representative in September 1968. Lacking recognition from Oakland did not prevent him from attracting media attention until he was convicted of murder in July 1970. Meanwhile, another BPP group rose and fell in 1969 before a more sustainable organization developed.⁸ Elsewhere, Oakland normally withheld bestowing the name "Black Panther Party" on new chapters until they had proved their worth, typically through a level of activism that included selling the BPP's newspaper. Such management occasionally created tension: New York City's chapter chafed at Oakland's control of its fundraising and policy direction, with the fallout contributing to the departure of some members.⁹

A macro assessment of the activities of various BPP chapters demonstrates the lengths that Panthers took to serve the people and the widespread repression they faced. This constitutes an important counternarrative of the BPP that emphasizes individual party members' idealism and dedication, and the extent to which chapter autonomy created a grassroots BPP that existed in counterpoint to the party's media-driven popular image. This approach applies equally to Oakland's local activism as it does the other branches, emphasizing its grassroots activity and interaction with the local community.

Social Activism

A mere list of social programs indicates the breadth of the party's activities: food and clothing giveaways, busing programs for people to visit jailed relatives, children's liberation schools and adult political education programs, health care clinics, and even ambulance services. Some were short-lived, such as the social programs of the New Bedford, Massachusetts, BPP.¹⁰ Others lasted longer, thanks to the determination of individuals to resist both the repression they faced and the insistence of BPP headquarters in 1972 that members should relocate to Oakland.

The health care initiative was the BPP's most significant social program. Two of the BPP's key political influences—the trained physicians Fanon and Guevara—were keenly aware of the relationship between oppression and poor health care. By 1970 chapters were mandated to establish a medical clinic offering individual examinations and testing or inoculation for several diseases. Often reliant on donations of equipment and materials, they provided a startling range of services. In Milwaukee, for example, the BPP discovered that hospitals charged thirty-five dollars per blood bag; the chapter planned its own blood bank to undercut this extortion and challenge the commodification and marketization of human blood. Health clinics also became an important location for the transfer of knowledge and skills from experts to the community. This was fundamental to the BPP's ideas about community self-reliance and democratization. Finding that community members were frequently too preoccupied with work and family to prioritize their health, BPP clinics empowered them through services such as dietary advice, cervical smears, and sickle cell anemia testing. Such actions critiqued an economic system designed to extract as much labor from a human being as possible without caring for the impact this work had on their mind and body. More explicitly, it was informed by a very simple philosophy: that health care should be free for all.[11]

That the BPP increasingly sought government funding for some of its health care projects illustrates that the BPP's antigovernment stance reflected its antipathy to federal and state indifference to human health and well-being rather than a blanket condemnation of government. Yet beyond, the health clinics critiqued the American medical system, proving that low-cost health care was effective and popular. It showcased the economic and health benefits of preventive health care, proving that socialized medicine benefits society. If it did not quite constitute a revolutionary assault on capitalism, it demonstrated that the union of capitalism and medical care benefited capital much more than citizens. Put simply, as Los Angeles Panther Terry Kupers pointed out, the clinic enabled local people to receive the care not provided by professional services.[12]

BPP health activism demonstrates the party's genuine commitment to its community. In New York City BPP members went door to door offering health screenings, and a roving Free Health Center in Cleveland started in 1970.[13] In spite of regular police raids, Boston's clinic was only one of four that offered a comprehensive service to the city's African American residents.[14] Robert Heard won a $900,000 grant for a San Francisco drug education project, while Oakland BPP's Free Medical Research Health Clinic proposed a six-month drug education program where five counselors would teach the community about treatment services. By 1973 the BPP offered Oakland's children an extensive pediatric care program integrated with the local children's hospital.[15] At the 1972 Black Community Survival Conference, the BPP reported that it had tested nearly 3,700 Oaklanders for sickle cell anemia (and registered two thousand to vote) in its emblematic campaign against a disease that disproportionately affected individuals of African descent. The American health care system intensified the disease's impact: cost prevented people from getting tested and treated, resulting in the disease sitting at the intersection between genetics, class, and race. According to the BPP, over a hundred thousand people were tested nationwide in its project's first year.[16] That the Nixon administration passed the National Sickle Cell Anemia Control Act soon afterward confirmed the BPP's vanguard position even as it responded to the BPP's contention that white America's inattention to sickle cell anemia was tantamount to a biological war. Unfortunately, by 1974 numbers at the BPP's health clinics were dropping, partly because staff numbers were dwindling. Some volunteer doctors chafed at the rote learning in their political education classes, suggesting that the BPP geared political education to a specific constituency.[17]

The BPP's food and clothing initiatives were, if less transformative, equally emblematic of the party's desire to improve the material circumstances of

Black communities. Heavily publicized, clothing and food giveaways in locations across the nation boosted the BPP's community profile and enabled it to offer temporary relief while dramatizing the problems afflicting many communities, vividly contrasting the BPP's altruism with the avarice of businessmen.[18] Even the smallest chapters engaged: Indianapolis, despite having fewer than twenty active Panthers, gave away food and toys to children.[19] In using boycotts to facilitate free distribution of food and clothing alongside campaigning for social or economic concessions, the BPP subtly deepened Newton's reassessment of Black capitalism. By appropriating products from large businesses, the BPP exposed the surplus profits of capitalism. As per the health care campaign, this constituted a shift toward a dialectical stance, exposing capitalism's contradictions from within—in this case by revealing hunger and poverty amid abundance and prosperity. Exposing and remedying such contradictions lay behind the BPP's occasional use of primitive accumulation to supply food programs. In 1970 the expropriation of tons of frozen meat facilitated a massive food giveaway in Philadelphia.[20] Similarly, the Milwaukee Panthers were prepared to seize food from local businesses to supply the breakfast program. The BPP instinctively knew that alleviating the children's hunger was paramount. As Michael McGee recalled, "You didn't want to let them down."[21] In essence, such activities posed profound questions: which was the greater crime—stealing food or forcing children to go hungry—and how should a group that possessed little money fund this activity? Capitalism, after all, provides nothing for free.

Providing free breakfast for children became a regular activity in nearly forty locations. Also reliant on donations, breakfast programs were designed for children of low-income families and highlighted the politics of hunger more starkly than any other BPP activity. In Milwaukee the city was chastened enough to offer its own breakfast program in response; Portland's schoolchildren, meanwhile, rated the BPP's breakfasts superior to their schools' offerings.[22] Breakfasts were normally served from 7:00 a.m., ensuring that children received a nutritious, satiating start to the day that maximized their opportunities to engage with learning. BPP members observed the quiet time while the children ate before engaging them in activities such as singing (Panthers at one program retooled the "Na, na-na-na-na" refrain of Wilson Pickett's "Land of a Thousand Dances" as "Gun, pick up the gun, pick up the gun, and put the pigs on the run").[23] That the huge federal antipoverty initiatives of the time could not feed every child properly constituted a stunning indictment of American capitalism; that the BPP gathered enough spare food to do so further condemned a system that produced so much excess without the will to distribute it equitably.

The BPP deepened its educational activities through day care centers for small children and political education classes for members. The most notable of these initiatives were its liberation schools, with Oakland's being so successful that it even outlasted the BPP itself.[24] This school's roots lay in the decision of leading Panthers to remove their children from public schools over fears that they would face discrimination because of their parents' activities. By 1973 it was teaching upward of fifty students drawn from local communities. Independent of the BPP it developed a fine reputation for its holistic approach to children's education.[25] School staff were predominantly female, with its teaching staff drawn from volunteer teachers, students, and BPP members. Women in the school challenged gendered expectations that they were best suited to nurturing roles. As Ericka Huggins recalls, male school staff were as likely to perform these roles as their female counterparts, who were more likely to be making strategic decisions that dictated school policy.[26] The school thus constituted an important space for destabilizing gendered identities. It educated hundreds of students and engaged with thousands of Oakland residents through outreach activities. It attracted funds from philanthropic organizations and state and federal government and eventually offered a full curriculum without tuition fees, which extended even to tae kwon do. The school's ambition encompassed its students' educational achievement, socialization, and consciousness, aiming to inculcate pride in the communities that were often dismissed as crime-ridden and hopeless.[27] Its ethos centered on children's agency, building on the BPP's insistence that their pupils shared a sophisticated understanding of American capitalism. It also reflected the BPP's insistence that children possessed the means to become active agents in their own lives. Val Douglas, of the BPP's Vallejo school, stated, "We don't treat the children as little babies.... We relate to them as comrades."[28] Douglas's verb choice is crucial, revealing precisely how the BPP school engaged with children as political beings. As Douglas observed, children witnessed the impact of capitalism through their parents struggling to hold jobs and listening to them talking about their working lives. Her colleague, the pseudonymous "Mad," similarly lauded the children's political sensibilities, embodied in their instinctive support for working people and suspicion of the police. Field trips, during which children explored their localities, offered more opportunities to consider Black America's relationship with capitalism, also providing a practical expression of the school's motto: "The World is our Classroom."[29] As this suggests, applied learning lay at the curriculum's core. This included practicing writing skills through letters to jailed comrades; comprehension by reading the BPP newspaper; oratorical, money management, and persuasive skills in selling the newspaper; and numerous skills in producing their own newsletter. Through such activities, the BPP melded education with everyday life in American capitalism.[30] In encouraging collective mealtimes, group schoolwork, and a cohesive group identity, the school also subtly inducted young Panthers in the communal way of life pursued by many adult comrades. The children thus experienced BPP theory as realities and began to comprehend the ideological underpinnings of the world around them.

By the mid-1970s the Oakland school's curriculum shifted away from the BPP's political influence to a child-led, holistic approach, enabling them to study at their own pace in classroom groups organized by "level of instruction" rather than age. Demonstrating the school's independence and the BPP's decline, references to the organization in the teachers' handbooks dwindled to nothing by 1980. Yet continuities remained, such as the continued importance of field trips and the overarching ambition of presenting education as an emancipatory rather than inhibiting experience. As important, a decolonized curriculum ensured that students graduated with a deep knowledge of Black history. Indeed, they emerged from an institution staffed by powerful Black, male and female, role models.[31] *Jet* magazine's 1976 photo story about the Oakland school vividly depicted the children's joy at being educated by community members in topics to which they related. Significantly, former students attest to treasured lifelong memories, reinforcing the school's multigenerational impact on Oakland.[32]

On a less successful note, the BPP leased cable television channels in Oakland in 1972 while compelling the cable companies to employ more minority staff and offer scholarships to minority trainees. An Oakland "People's Book and Record Store" opened in 1973, although its financial success was questionable, as was the profitability of the BPP's Oakland restaurant, which lost the party over $20,000 in 1972.[33] Such struggles confirm the precarious economic situation facing small businesses in inner-city America. That the BPP was more successful at exposing the contradictions of capitalism through subversion than through establishing rival enterprises constitutes a salutary reminder of capitalism's brutal indifference.

The BPP's social programs illustrate the importance the BPP placed on highlighting the breadth and depth of, and the necessity for practical solutions to, the problems facing the urban poor. The Philadelphia chapter offered education classes, protested police brutality, ran a breakfast program and a lunch program, held food and clothing giveaways, ran a clinic, and worked with local gangs to reduce tension and violence in the community before shutting in 1973. BPP candidates also ran for city council in 1969.[34] In Winston-Salem the BPP ran a pest control program and provided an ambulance service alongside local churches, aware that transportation was frequently withheld from patients who could not prove they could afford the hospital's service. It also ran a breakfast program and loaned or donated money to the needy while uniting with locals to protest unfair evictions.[35] Numerous chapters instituted free busing programs to convey people to incarcerated relatives.[36] The cost of Milwaukee's illustrates how much money such programs needed. The chapter, which possessed a membership that fluctuated between ten and fifty, estimated that weekly visits cost over $600 per month and the breakfast program $300 per day. The chapter's clinic periodically closed due to lack of funds: its astronomic insurance bills constitute another critique of the American health care system. Panthers, meanwhile, resorted to begging to finance their programs and lived in communal spaces, sharing food to minimize costs, not least because they donated large portions of their income to party coffers—yet more evidence of the huge sacrifices they made.[37]

As this brief account indicates, while the BPP social programs' general orientation was centrally defined, individual chapters retained the power to dictate quotidian practice. Similarly, they demonstrate the extent to which BPP praxis challenged gendered norms, both within and without the party. Members based their work on their analysis of community needs and how best they could address these needs. In part, this developed through necessity because of their limited numbers, but members' willingness to challenge assumptions about what constituted "male" or "female" jobs offered a refreshing and important realization of their theoretical visions of a different world.

Local Chapter Life

Many Panthers donated more than time and money. Connie Felder's parents helped fill her new apartment with domestic items. She donated it all, alongside her car, to the Baltimore chapter—a simple demonstration of the immense dedication offered by BPP members.[38] Baltimore activist Steve McCutchen endured an emotional struggle between his old life and his new commitments. He was not alone in believing that "anyone who can't function full time is a community worker, not a Panther. Revolution is a full-time commitment."[39] This commitment often started before dawn, with breakfast programs needing staffing long before serving began; many members sold newspapers late into the evening. Wayne Pharr recalled a typical Los Angeles day: "Selling newspapers, attending political education classes, weapons training, and meeting and training . . . recruits[:] a twenty-four-hour, seven-day-a-week commitment."[40] Within days of joining the New York chapter, Jamal Joseph began reporting for training at 8:00 a.m. on Saturdays; within weeks, exhausting BPP work supplanted his regular activities. Later, he moved into a BPP house, working full time in addition to completing school, commitments that resulted in him developing stomach ulcers. Cheryl Foster's detailed notebook of her activities in Harlem offers further evidence of the time commitments members made to the BPP. Similarly, Mumia Abu-Jamal, who joined the Philadelphia chapter as a teenager, commented, "Party work was all that we did, all day, into the night."[41] The Philadelphia chapter was established without much encouragement from Oakland. Believing Oakland's indifference to be their first test, they threw themselves into multifarious activities before being granted official status in late 1968. As Abu-Jamal recalled, "It was a rare Panther who did one job. I wrote; I read; I edited; I shoveled sand for our sandbags; I sold papers; I worked security; I did all that I was ordered to do."[42] Women and men frequently shared the work burden throughout the party structure. Women leaders like Mary Rem in Des Moines, Audrea Jones in Boston, and Ericka Huggins in New Haven meanwhile demonstrate that men did not hold the monopoly as branch chiefs, with women similarly represented in key national positions, such as Joan Kelley, national coordinator of the free breakfast program.[43]

The members' intense commitment is aptly illustrated by Seattle's chapter, which formed in April 1968 and moved into its first headquarters "after a mysterious firebombing coaxed a reluctant landlord" to rent them a storefront. Initially, its activists concentrated on police brutality. Very quickly, however, their activities broadened to include a breakfast program, a liberation school, a busing to prison program, a health clinic, and a regular food giveaway.[44] Seattle Panthers also addressed various community problems while planning and executing more overtly revolutionary activities, including armed robbery, all achieved with a membership estimated at less than twenty.[45] Meanwhile, Detroit's thorough vetting process for new recruits limited the branch to fewer than fifty members. Alongside breakfast and busing programs, the chapter spent considerable effort ridding the community of drug dealers. It also combined with the short-lived Kansas City chapter—which itself ran a sequence of social programs—to provide health programs to local citizens.[46] Pressure emanated from Oakland for chapters not only to be active in the local community but also to channel funds to headquarters regularly. In 1973 headquarters instructed members to file for unemployment, use birth control, and donate ten dollars per week plus an additional ten dollars per month to party coffers.[47] Oakland organizers regretfully noted that their dedication to selling the newspaper resulted in workers devoting less time to campaigning and recruitment. Central to this problem was the mentality of many comrades. Morale, it seems, was in almost as bad a shape as the office's finances, with unpaid bills multiplying. Bill Jennings, meanwhile, would "straighten" things out with "some good old discipline" when his workers failed to meet expectations.[48]

Many chapters were reliant on a small core membership. Atlanta's chapter, for example, peaked at twenty-four core members in 1972. They instituted eight survival programs, including a school, day care, bussing, and medical care, amid regular police harassment. Unsurprisingly, overwork led some workers to develop stomach ulcers; elsewhere, members reported that their duties resulted in poor sleep and diet, anemia, and even pneumonia.[49] A series of memoranda from Oakland in 1972 illustrates the intense demands on members. Each week they studied for and participated in political education classes and assisted with voter registration when necessary. When appropriate, they wrote letters to incarcerated comrades, cleaned local streets, donated blood, shuttled children to and from the Child Development Center, and engaged in recreational activities with other Panthers. By 1974 members were expected to attend services at the BPP's Son of Man Temple and were even chastised for failing to sing and clap appropriately.[50]

BPP activism was not necessarily conducted without interference, a factor that surely influenced many members' lack of sleep and confirms that activism was firmly entwined with the repression that BPP members experienced. Police infiltrated the New Orleans chapter, expecting to uncover nefarious activities. Instead, the spies merely learned of the chapter's dedication to its social programs.[51] This activism obviously redirected BPP work from its early confrontational stance toward police. It enabled members to interact with local people, affording more opportunities to spread the BPP's message and influence while softening the gun-toting image so prevalent in the media. Yet once J. Edgar Hoover identified the breakfast program as the BPP's "best and most influential activity," the FBI inevitably targeted these programs.[52] Repression thus influenced the BPP's move toward social activism but also clamped down on this very activism.

The repression local chapters faced underscores the immense pressure faced by individual BPP organizers. As Harold Taylor observed, it was "completely nerve wracking" knowing that the police or the FBI lurked just out of sight, ready to pounce. "You question everything," living in a permanent state of exhausting vigilance, he said, "constantly covering your tracks" and ready to move house at a moment's notice.[53] Police and the FBI actions ranged from minor interruptions of BPP activities to major actions, including mass arrests and incarceration. In 1969 alone more than twenty raids on BPP offices occurred.[54] The stress and damage these events caused were compounded by the near constant awareness that a raid might occur and the inevitable fallout and painstaking rebuilding that followed. Among the most egregious of these actions was the arrest and charging of twenty-one New York City Panthers with conspiracy to bomb and assassinate police officers. New York's chapter had roughly five hundred members and ran highly effective social programs and an armed underground wing.[55] It was raided repeatedly on the pretext that it was engaged in terrorist activities, both before and after the arrest of the New York 21. Jamal Joseph, who was living with his grandmother, had his house raided by a SWAT team. He later learned that one of his mentors was an undercover agent. Police tortured Joan Bird for eighteen hours to elicit information. Even though only Kuwasi Balagoon was convicted of any crime, the operation thwarted the chapter's development. While in jail, Balagoon concluded that he ought to commit to guerrilla warfare; soon after, he immersed himself in the Black Liberation Army.[56]

The BLA emerged from the New York Panthers amid the intensification of the Cleaver-Newton feud. Many New York members adopted African names as an indication of their political and cultural sensibilities, a factor that widened the chapter's alienation from Oakland, which associated such renaming with cultural nationalist ostentation. Oakland's failure to offer the necessary support to the New York 21 caused further tension, exacerbated in February 1971 when Oakland parachuted in new leaders who rejected New York's Afrocentrism, with tragic outcomes. After Cleaver's expulsion, the BPP's Harlem and Bronx offices went into lockdown, fearing an attack from Newton's supporters. Soon afterward, Robert Webb, a relocated California Panther, was shot during an altercation with another Panther, prompting his new colleagues to allege that he was the victim of a Newton-ordered assassination. A number responded by heading underground, including Dhoruba Bin Wahad. Their first targets were local drug dealers followed by Sam Napier, who ran the BPP's newspaper distribution service, and who died in revenge for Webb's death. Two New York police officers followed on May 21. The New York underground's violent campaign peaked in 1973, when leading BLA figure Assata Shakur was captured and imprisoned after a shoot-out with police in New Jersey.[57] This history reveals that the capture of the New York 21 both stymied the development of BPP social activism and prompted some members to engage even more with underground activity, adding important context to any understanding of the relationship between the BPP and armed struggle.

The Los Angeles BPP chapter experienced a similar level of police interference, which thwarted the branch's social programs. Local activist Flores Forbes reports that in 1968 the infamously brutal Los Angeles police harassed him almost daily. The chapter itself was infiltrated from its inception: Earl Anthony was in the pay of the FBI when the chapter formed. Nevertheless, it managed to develop food and clothing giveaways, a health clinic, a busing program, a community center, and a breakfast program. Frank Diggs, one of the chapter's captains, was killed in mysterious circumstances, not long after expressing his concern that local police sought to divide him from his comrades. Informants also provided a floor plan of a Panther office that was raided in December 1969, an event that escalated into an hours-long gunfight mere days after a similar operation saw police execute Chicago Panthers Mark Clark and Fred Hampton. In the aftermath, Los Angeles police sadistically beat Panthers Wayne Pharr and Harold Taylor. The repression forced the Los Angeles Panthers into a defensive posture, leading one member, Walter Pope, to complain mid-1969 that the only response was to attack. Within weeks, he was dead.[58]

Similarly, local police targeted the Detroit chapter, infiltrating it soon after its inception. Police ransacked its headquarters after a police officer was killed, despite the BPP having no role in the event, and Panthers were regularly harassed, obstructing the chapter's fundraising attempts and ensnaring it in legal battles. Detroit police even attacked two Panthers and their mother outside their family home. The death of their defense captain, Michael Baynham, allegedly at the hands of either police or an infiltrator, led to the branch's mid-1969 collapse and subsequent reconfiguration as a more militarized group. Confrontations with the police peaked on October 24, 1970, when a BPP member killed a police officer amid a siege of the BPP's headquarters that resulted in the arrest of fifteen Panthers who were charged with conspiracy to murder. That none were convicted confirms the police as the guilty parties.[59] Again, this example suggests that armed activities did not simply emerge from BPP members' reading of Newton, Fanon, and Guevara but also in response to the very real threats to their lives from local police forces.

As this suggests, even the smallest chapters received a level of police harassment disproportionate to their supposed threat to law and order. A Milwaukee chapter leader was beaten by police for no reason one month after the chapter's formation; many other members were jailed on flimsy pretexts, peaking when three were jailed for twelve months in September 1969, leading to the chapter's collapse. When local activists revived the party in 1972, the FBI infiltrated it almost immediately.[60] Winston-Salem's chapter was also targeted by local police. The local community received letters smearing the BPP, the FBI attempted to sow dissent within the ranks, and the chapter argued that the FBI (unsuccessfully) tried to frame various Panthers for robbing a meat truck. The chapter headquarters burst into flames hours after branch members left for the RPCC—a quite stunning coincidence. The BPP accused the police of arson and using the fire as cover for confiscating party records. By mid-1971 almost constant interference resulted in chapter membership dwindling to below twenty. Perhaps worst is the fact that bail and legal fees diverted so much money from the BPP's community activity.[61] Baltimore BPP activists estimated that in 1970 the chapter spent over $350,000 on bail fees alone, money that might have funded its food and health care programs. Party ranks were infiltrated, its programs disrupted, and activists surveilled and harassed by police, who even attempted to frame seven local Panthers for murder.[62] Irrespective of the human cost of this intimidation, the astronomical financial costs—both for the police and the BPP—constitute a shocking indictment of federal and state repression of the BPP. Millions of dollars that might have been used to benefit disadvantaged Americans instead financed a repressive legal and policing system that ensured the continued oppression of these very people.

Police raids were frequent enough that many BPP members lived in a permanent state of vigilance. The Indianapolis office was invaded in December 1968 as part of a campaign of low-level police persecution and regular denunciations in the local press.[63] The Philadelphia chapter was first raided in summer 1969, firebombed in March 1970, and raided again in August, during which police destroyed its office, followed by raids on other BPP locations as the RPCC approached. A major municipal campaign against police brutality resulted, but the BPP chapter entered a terminal decline.[64] Des Moines members were accused of arson in October 1968. The case was dismissed, but BPP leaders suffered regular harassment afterward, severely constraining their activism. Their headquarters was bombed in April 1969, one week after police disrupted a rally to promote their breakfast program. Police were suspiciously close to the building immediately after the explosion. Seattle, meanwhile, endured frequent raids and police confrontations, reaching a nadir when police killed one comrade in October 1968 as he attempted to protect his mother.[65] A Cleveland confrontation in June 1970 presaged police illegally seizing office items. Local BPP activist Jimmy Slater believes that police infiltrated the branch and destroyed its health clinic, which led to the chapter's swift decline.[66] Similarly, three months after the Houston chapter's reformation, a police confrontation led to numerous arrests and the death of the chapter founder. This event dominated the second phase of the Houston BPP, as members and recruits rallied amid further police repression.[67] In September 1970 New Orleans Panthers discovered two police informants. Meanwhile, the police chief's hatred of their breakfast program precipitated a major shoot-out and two raids. Forty-five Panthers were imprisoned. A jury unanimously found them not guilty of all charges.[68]

That Panthers knew the police were wont to treat them as such yet remained dedicated to their work is testament to both the personal costs they suffered for their idealism and to their determination to put the BPP, and the African American population in a larger sense, before their own safety and security. It renders the social programs even more impressive. The establishment of such a wide range of beneficial programs across the nation would be cause for celebration among any activist organization; that the BPP successfully did so amid a prolonged, brutal, and destructive campaign to destroy it is uniquely impressive, awe-inspiring, even. This activism also informed the BPP's activities after it called its members to Oakland. As the organization shrank at a national level, remaining chapters benefited from the vast experience of members who had been battle-hardened, not only in resisting repression but also in operating many social projects.

At a theoretical level, the social programs highlight the trenchant critique of capitalism at the party's core, particularly the dialectics of BPP praxis. The survival programs suggest that chapters were operating intercommunally before Newton constructed the theory. Similarly, these programs offered a practical application of the BPP's position on capitalism long before the party hierarchy developed its theoretical conceptualization of the BPP's approach. As this itself suggests, then, BPP practice helped shape BPP theory as much as theory shaped practice.

Moving deeper, this begs reconsideration of the BPP's "survival pending revolution" definition of the programs, positioning the phrase more as a slogan than an accurate portrayal of the programs' praxis. The slogan underemphasizes the extent to which the programs critiqued capitalism and overlooks the fact that they operated anticapitalistically in redistributing the surpluses of capitalism (thus, as Fred Hampton suggested, enabling local communities to experience alternatives as well as capitalism's sharpest end). In this sense they reconceptualized the actions of the capitalist parasite: unlike what might be termed "traditional" parasitic actors (who suck profits out of the system for personal benefit), the BPP appropriated and redistributed surpluses to create situations that anticipated a postcapitalist America. Of course, the extent to which this could only operate under capitalism remains moot: the BPP merely highlighted dialectically how capitalism operated and how an alternative might function.

In practical terms, the educational program remains one of the party's most important legacies. It also offers an important prism through which to consider the BPP's relationship with ordinary people, and it reminds us of the shrinking of the BPP's geographical presence. With so few Panthers remaining after 1973, the school offered an opportunity to prolong the BPP's presence beyond the party's lifespan. While at first glance it might reflect the party's decline, it more importantly represents a testament to the BPP's ideals, and specifically through the alumni whose lives it indelibly marked. Using this prism vastly expands our understanding of the BPP's legacy, which becomes a model for using education as a tool for liberation as well as of political and social activism. The school's expansive, child-led curriculum is further evidence of the complexity of BPP ideology. At first glance the denuding of BPP ideology within this curriculum might indicate that the BPP's ideological stance did not gain traction among its pupils. Yet the school cannot be understood *without* the BPP. It was a shining example of the flexibility of the BPP's approach to liberation and the prime example of BPP members' awareness that the BPP needed a role in the community beyond its organizational life. Their reconsideration of the BPP's role—transforming it to an organization with a holistic vision of Black liberation—is perhaps the most profound example of the transformative experience of membership in and engagement with the BPP.

CHAPTER SIX

The Cal-Pac Boycott

Two events in the BPP's history bracketed Newton's most important theoretical work of the 1970s, "Black Capitalism Re-Analyzed." Soon after the BPP published Newton's essay, it made its first attempt to translate Newton's concept into action by boycotting the California State Package Store and Tavern Owners Association (Cal-Pac), a group of African American business owners. The Cal-Pac dispute suggests that Oakland's rank-and-file labored under a more top-down operational structure than most chapters, one that profoundly influenced the boycott.[1] As important, it was preceded by an equally significant event: Eldridge Cleaver's expulsion.

Following his 1968 departure from the United States, Cleaver traveled via Cuba to postindependence Algeria. Witnessing the impact of a Fanonist revolution, he became ever more committed to revolutionary adventurism. FBI wiretaps of telephone calls between Newton and Cleaver in late 1970 suggest that the tensions between the two were palpable but not insurmountable.[2] Newton was furious that three of the New York 21—Dhoruba Bin Wahad, Newton's former secretary Connie Matthews, and her husband Cetewayo Tabor—apparently absconded with money and a cache of BPP files that might have proved the BPP misused funds it received for the 21. They were formally expelled in February 1971 after they missed a court date, forfeiting $150,000 bail and prompting the judge to revoke bail for New York Panthers Joan Bird and the six months pregnant Afeni Shakur. As significant, the FBI drove a wedge between the New York Panthers and Oakland, alleging that Bin Wahad planned to assassinate Newton and that David Hilliard planned a similar operation against Bin Wahad, alongside a stream of disinformation letters to Newton, Cleaver, and others, designed to exacerbate tensions.[3]

Claiming to be aware of the brewing storm, Jim Dunbar invited Newton to appear on his *A.M. San Francisco* show on February 26, with Cleaver appearing via telephone. Clearly briefed on internal BPP matters, Dunbar prompted a heated discussion of the recent expulsions. The two resumed arguing in a private call afterward, in which Newton expelled Cleaver and raged over Cleaver's decision to flee the country while he "face[d] the gas [chamber]."[4] The FBI would have been pleased: Newton's line of attack directly reflected one of the schisms it hoped to exacerbate.[5] According to the FBI's wiretap, a telephone call a few days later merely enraged both parties: Newton accused Cleaver of cowardice in the Hutton shoot-out, Cleaver responded by criticizing Newton for shooting John Frey, then Newton accused Cleaver of killing BPP member Rahim (Clinton Smith).[6]

In print, Newton insisted that Cleaver led the BPP's alienation from the African American community, soon after an Emory Douglas caricature demolished Cleaver's reputation. The image, titled "April 6, 1968, 1218-28th St. Oakland, California" for the date and location of Hutton's death, presented Cleaver, arms raised in surrender, his body wizened and belly distended, naked save a pair of underpants languishing around his ankles, cowering behind Hutton fearlessly aiming a rifle at unseen assailants. A photograph of a baby adorns Hutton's cloak, reminding viewers that he was an innocent victim. Significantly, Cleaver was dismembered, articulating the BPP's belief that he was less of a man than his sixteen-year-old guardian. That Newton was concurrently attempting to drive the BPP away from Hutton's armed posture was less the point than Cleaver's spinelessness and cynical manipulation of his young companion and hence the BPP.[7] Feelings ran so deep that Newton planned a book-length indictment of his former comrade.[8] Their personal animus reflected and deepened the ideological gulf between Oakland and Cleaver's Algiers outpost, from which he insisted that insurrection remained a formidable weapon.[9]

The Cleaver-Newton split signified the BPP's departure from open advocacy of armed activity and, notwithstanding its long-term revolutionary agenda, a movement toward mainstream politics. In November 1971 *Ebony*'s editor, Lerone Bennett Jr., outlined his vision for the decade. Voicing themes outlined by the Atlanta think tank the Institute of the Black World, Bennett argued that the Black population needed employment, welfare, education, prison reform, and a health plan, facilitated by community control of its institutions and bolstered by a program to renew the community's "structures, energies, and values." Community mobilization would transform American political structures and "disengage" African American politics from "white people's arguments." The IBW had outlined a "Black Agenda Network" that advocated greater involvement in electoral politics to lay the foundations for a "permanent political movement" outside the Democratic and Republican Parties.[10] Reflecting the awareness that electoral success would not necessarily benefit the entire population, many 1970s African American nationalists thought control of Black community institutions would enable them to enter into political coalitions with other ethnic groups from a stronger position, while elected officials supported the real work of community control. This control, however, was based on the acceptance of capitalism. Local officials themselves were able to outflank such nationalist appeals by pointing to their electoral success: a reflection of the popular appeal of biracial, moderate politics.[11]

Soon after Bennett's speech, the *Washington Post* reported that the BPP had "put down its guns and is working within the system."[12] This came in the wake of the BPP's boycott of Cal-Pac, the most important practical demonstration of Newton's reanalysis of Black capitalism, one that precipitated the BPP's transformation from outsiders to participants in Oakland's daily political and economic life.[13] Beneath this, the boycott points to Newton's growing interest in Oakland's criminal underground and the BPP's struggle to redefine its understanding of capitalism while simultaneously upholding its fidelity to its own history and adopting practices that appear to align with a more reformist protest tradition. It demonstrates the BPP's awareness that a subtle but dialectical long-term, local campaign would highlight the contradictions inherent in capitalism and underpin a future revolution while also organizing the community.

As important, the boycott positioned the BPP alongside other post-1960s attempts to reinvigorate mass protest. Reflecting the gradual move of civil rights protest away from Dr. Martin Luther King's late 1960s economic critique and responding to Richard Nixon's promotion of affirmative action and Black capitalism, Jesse Jackson, for example, hoped to increase African American employment in large companies, encourage these companies to trade with African American businesses, and create franchises for African American businessmen. Like the BPP, Jackson was accused of extortion and racketeering, but he could point to massive increases in employment and investment as evidence of success.[14] Jackson's campaigns became a dominant feature of civil rights activism as the United States drifted rightward. Moving further forward, the director of a leading rights organization told a 1980s New York organizer: "The corporate experience. That's the real business of a civil rights organization these days.... We've got to forge links between business, government, and the inner city."[15] While the Cal-Pac boycott did not go as far in its acceptance of the "corporate experience," it signified an attempt to forge stronger bonds between African American businesses and the communities around them.

It also reflected the BPP's awareness of the ebbing of the radical tide. Affirmative action policies suggested that the federal government would tackle African American underemployment, African American candidates reaped the benefits of the 1965 Voting Rights Act, and the Democratic Party made bold steps to reform its internal structures, all of which gave a certain level of political power to Black America just as the moderate American Left marginalized its radical wing. This, allied to the expansion of higher education opportunities for African Americans, suggested that Black America's material circumstances could improve under capitalism. Meanwhile, "Vietnamization" drastically reduced American troop numbers and combat deaths in Vietnam, rendering the Vietnam War a less urgent concern. Such developments suggested that revolution was perhaps unnecessary.[16] A local campaign focused on the relationship between business and community could therefore demonstrate that, while its strategic vision remained, the BPP understood the need for small-scale, tactical campaigns—wars of position that would heighten the community's awareness of the contradictions inherent in capitalism.

Formed in 1960, Cal-Pac represented some of the state's African American nightclub, convenience store, and liquor store owners. The *Washington Post* suggested that the BPP boycott began after Cal-Pac's president, Bill Boyette, reneged on a deal struck with the BPP in his dispute with the supermarket chain Mayfair Markets. In this reading, Boyette enlisted the BPP to assist with a boycott because Mayfair refused to work with a delivery firm that employed Black deliverymen. Boyette agreed to make food donations, unaware that the BPP assumed this would be a regular arrangement. Cal-Pac denied that it requested the BPP's involvement, arguing that the BPP simply attached itself to the Mayfair boycott (although Boyette publicly thanked the BPP for its support).[17] Another interpretation places the boycott's roots in Newton's demand that Oakland Cal-Pac members make a weekly donation to the BPP. Boyette's refusal led the BPP to threaten to close down these businesses. To assuage the BPP, Boyette offered a large donation of food and milk. Newton insisted on regular cash donations and later ordered the BPP to start picketing Boyette's store on Grove Street, a few blocks south of the first BPP office.[18]

Such accounts overlook the boycott's relationship with "Black Capitalism Re-Analyzed." While the article did not mention the Mayfair dispute, it explicitly discussed the relationships between white and Black capitalism, and between capitalism and the Black community. If the BPP was to maintain its tradition of uniting words with action, it needed a practical demonstration of this theory. The success of Cal-Pac's Mayfair boycott, coupled with its calls for its suppliers to respond to the needs of the African American community, offered a perfect opportunity to piggyback on Boyette's success and highlight his contradictions, notably his failure to contribute financially to the community while presenting Cal-Pac as a concerned member of this community. The BPP thus aimed to present itself as Black Oakland's conscience and one of its most benevolent institutions, again reinforcing its insistence that capitalism could not liberate Black America.

Naturally, the FBI took a keen interest, believing that the BPP might be violating the anti-racketeering Hobbs Act. The issue revolved around whether Newton threatened Cal-Pac businesses with financial losses.[19] Its investigations uncovered recordings of meetings suggesting that Boyette's stubbornness was as much of a catalyst as Newton's belligerence. On July 22 Newton spoke about the survival programs before offering support for the Mayfair campaign. He invited the businessmen to make a regular donation to the BPP in return for advertisements in its newspaper. Knowing that any request for a specific amount of money might be considered extortion, he presented this arrangement as similar to Cal-Pac's with Mayfair. Following his departure, the businessmen expressed their concern that this constituted extortion, perhaps informed by Newton's accidental confession that the BPP needed financial support from African American businesses to survive, a consequence of its decision to refuse donations from white corporations and businesses. The businessmen concluded that Newton's request concealed the real purpose of the donations: to bankroll the BPP.[20]

Hostilities resumed on July 30, when Boyette formally offered a contribution of perishable foods that Newton rejected, claiming that the community's problems were far more entrenched, which was why the BPP demanded a regular contribution.[21] Cal-Pac's refusal to accede prompted Newton to walk out. Within twelve hours, BPP demonstrators appeared outside Cal-Pac stores while an outraged Bobby Seale denounced Boyette on television for failing to offer consistent support to the survival programs.[22] The generally sedate pickets took place almost every day until January 1972, featuring Panthers circling the sidewalk, some toting placards and copies of *The Black Panther*, others reading books or merely occupying the space.[23] According to Bobby Seale, the BPP provided wine to the alcoholics who frequented Boyette's stores, which temporarily halted the BPP's attempts to rid neighborhoods of alcoholism but prevented the drinkers from crossing picket lines, illustrating the difficulties the BPP had in treating all of the ills that beset Oakland's African American population. Crucially, the lack of violence and the picketers' decision not to prevent customers entering the stores ensured the lawfulness and geniality of these protests.[24]

The BPP's awareness of the power of the media remained acute, with television cameras capturing members giving away a truckload of food to people outside its main office and distributing shoes and food outside Boyette's store. *The Black Panther* alleged that Boyette raised prices on the days when welfare checks were distributed, suggesting that his price gouging was more exploitative of the community than he argued the BPP was of him.[25] Yet the protests' small scale suggests that Newton manufactured a crisis and wielded the BPP as a weapon to prove the relevance of "Black Capitalism Re-Analyzed" rather than enabling the rank-and-file to develop their own solutions.

In August Boyette charged Newton with extortion and took out a restraining order preventing picketers from harassing customers, complaining that some employees received threatening telephone calls, amid protests that lost him roughly $1,000 of trade each day.[26] Concurrently *The Black Panther* chastised Boyette for doing "what the big time white, racist capitalists do" in inviting the police to monitor the protesters, while pointedly advertising Calco

Building Material Supply, whose owner made regular contributions to survival programs.[27] The paper later observed that the "corporate capitalists" would not cover his losses when local people withheld their money. The boycott would remind him on what side his bread was buttered.[28] Newton, meanwhile, considered the praxis of "Black Capitalism Re-Analyzed." He presented the boycott within a wider strategy to unify the African American community's economic interests, before berating businessmen who refused to give financial support to the community as "profiteers."[29] Flyers distributed around Oakland reiterated the BPP's position, asserting that by donating to the survival programs, the capitalists would join "the vehicle we need to liberate our communities."[30]

On August 13 Newton appeared on Jim Dunbar's television show. He responded to Boyette—who spoke over the telephone—with a stream of interruptions, insisting that Black businessmen aid the community by making regular contributions to BPP programs. Seale also debated Boyette on the show, promising free advertising in *The Black Panther* to liquor stores who made regular contributions.[31] Boyette complained that he reserved the right to donate to whichever causes he chose, and that as a gainfully employed member of the community, he likely knew the community's needs better than Seale. His tone-deaf insinuation that the community only expressed its needs through consumerism and that a businessman was more attuned to the community than political activists did little to soften the BPP's stance, although Seale did lament that Cal-Pac too was a victim of white capitalism.[32] Seale also asserted that the BPP was merely spanking him as it would an errant child.[33] Such infantilizing did little to ease tensions, but the notion that Boyette was also a victim highlights the theoretical considerations underpinning the boycott. Beneath the personalization, Seale and Newton understood that monopoly capitalists who controlled his supply chain oppressed Boyette. Tactically, however, he offered a more tangible target than the abstract concept above him. Here the BPP demonstrated an acute awareness of the importance of bogeymen. It rendered Boyette an almost cartoonish villain, personifying the impersonal economic system that created the inequalities in American society, enabling the BPP to suggest that he related more to the capitalism than the Black in Black capitalism, even though this elided the thin profit margins of small businesses like his. Essentially, Boyette was an easy target around which the campaign could coalesce. His precarity made the boycott's goals achievable and thus illustrative of the BPP's understanding of the need for tactical victories to service a broader strategic campaign.

Local businesses, meanwhile, lined up behind Boyette. A conference designed to find common ground descended into acrimony when Newton threatened to impoverish Boyette. Boyette's supporters insisted that any donations to the BPP be fully accounted. The BPP, not famed for its bureaucratic diligence, refused.[34] By September, Cal-Pac formed an Ad Hoc Committee to Preserve Black Business that included representatives of the NAACP and the National Business League to support its claim that the BPP's demands were unfair. The committee called on businesses to show their support by patronizing Boyette's store while declaring support for some of the BPP's activities amid a more general complaint about Newton's behavior.[35] A relatively cordial September 10 meeting at the BPP's Lamp Post bar saw Newton claim that the BPP's strategy intended to "strengthen the business institution[s]" and offered BPP donations to struggling businesses in return for an endorsement. He presented this as the first salvo in a fight against larger, white businesses. It thus made sense to unite the victims before taking on the "real strongman." Local newspaper official Otho Green suggested that businesses that could not spare five dollars per week were unviable, while Newton promised that the BPP would help employees who were laid off because of the boycott.[36]

One FBI source claimed that Newton was prepared to end the boycott but an Ad Hoc Committee flyer so enraged him that he ordered picketing to resume.[37] Meanwhile, the FBI claimed that Newton admitted to Boyette that the boycott was a mistake but wanted "to save face" in threatening to widen the boycott.[38] Amid reports in the anti-BPP *Oakland Tribune* that the community was uniting against the BPP, Newton rejected Otho Green's proposed umbrella group for disbursing contributions. The *Tribune* also reminded readers of the disparity between Newton's opulent Lake Merritt residence and the impoverished areas surrounding Boyette's store. It even allowed Joseph Simmons of the Ad Hoc Committee to compare Newton to the deposed Cuban dictator Fulgencio Batista, a profoundly hurtful accusation given the BPP's admiration for the Cuban Revolution.[39]

In mid-October the BPP's minister for culture, Emory Douglas, applied his considerable talents to the boycott, depicting Boyette and *Oakland Tribune* owner William Knowland feeding on the blood of the Black community. Two weeks later, in a second piece, he represented Boyette and Knowland as Ku Klux Klan members engaged in a Halloween swindle. The "treat" they offered was a bottle of human blood.[40] Meanwhile, despite the attorney general concluding that the BPP had not violated the Hobbs Act, the NAACP's Roy Wilkins suggested in his nationally syndicated column that the BPP might have been acting illegally.[41] Wilkins remained connected to the Justice Department through his chairing of the inquiry into BPP organizer Fred Hampton's assassination, rendering this missive a public warning about the BPP's future conduct.[42] Eventually, the BPP's friend, Congressman Ron Dellums, forged a compromise in which a United Black Fund of the Bay Area would distribute funds from businesses to various local charitable causes including the BPP, while the BPP's friend Father Earl Neil would oversee the Ad Hoc Committee's donations to the BPP's survival programs. In return, the boycott would end.[43]

Dellums claimed that all parties were winners at the boycott's end, but Boyette looked and likely felt every inch the loser. He told KNBC News that the boycott reduced his income by 98 percent in the first month with takings eventually stabilizing at 30 percent of their usual level. His business friends, he said, saved his business. Happy at the resolution of another contradiction within the community, a relaxed Newton pledged to target white merchants next. Beneath his jubilation lay a more significant admission. He declared that the Black community needed to pull itself up "by our bootstraps"—tacit acceptance that his vision was now yoked to capitalism in the short to medium term.[44]

Newton presented the boycott's conclusion as the "first step [in] organizing a Black united community.... We will stop the rift between the so-called bourgeoisie and the so-called lower class blacks."[45] A letter told white businesses "operating in and draining" the Black community that they ought to "return at least a portion of our resources to us" in the form of regular tax-deductible donations.[46] Soon afterward, local white businessmen formed a New Oakland Committee, with a local judge, Lionel Wilson, leading its minority caucus.[47] The NOC's formation was prompted by a letter sent to white businesses around Oakland that requested "a regular, weekly donation of those resources which keep you 'successful' and keep us in poverty" to a newly created United Black Fund. This letter's references to a "long-standing contradiction" in the community, to "programs that will meet those real needs of our people"—both BPP rhetorical themes—and the suggestion that donors give money to specific BPP programs all point to its author's identity.[48]

The UBF made its first payment to the survival programs in February 1972; flyers soon appeared urging BPP supporters to shop at Boyette's store, a "business that support[s] our community."[49] Emory Douglas urged *The Black Panther*'s readers to support Boyette through a collage featuring a happy community member, carrying a paper bag full of free food adorned with a photograph of Boyette, no longer a bloodsucker but a bona fide businessman and contributor to the survival programs.[50] Meanwhile, the BPP turned its sights on white business, preparing for a confrontation with the NOC.[51] This initiative fittingly reveals the amount of change to which the business community could commit itself: the dialogue between Oakland's various interest groups it planned would take place only at an elite level.

The UBF's brief history offers a peculiar coda to the boycott. Within five months, it appears to have ceased operating.[52] Meanwhile, the BPP's ally Charles Garry incorporated the United Black Fund, Inc., presided over by Earl Neil, with Newton's brother Melvin its vice president and its secretary and treasurer Newton's secretary, Gwen Fountaine, working in an apartment that once housed Newton. Garry conducted its legal work, and every project it supported until October 1972 had been initiated by the BPP. Boyette's outraged friends concluded that the UBF was a BPP front, and aware that Seale planned to run for Oakland mayor, they plotted revenge.[53]

Meanwhile, Newton grew interested in reducing the BPP's tax burden.[54] He boasted that he paid no tax himself and of the tax-free status of the BPP's Stronghold corporation (despite documentary evidence to the contrary).[55] Evidence suggests that Stronghold was wholly legitimate, although hints remain that it shielded Newton from his tax obligations.[56] Nevertheless, BPP lawyer Martin Kenner expressed concern about the financial relationship between the two in mid-1972, including the use of Stronghold funds to pay BPP bills—a potential tax minefield, because the BPP was formally nonprofit and Stronghold a corporation. Worse, Stronghold needed approximately $9,000 per month merely to cover expenses, which included mortgages, leaseholds, or rent on over one dozen properties occupied by BPP members, leading Kenner to seek loans to ensure its continued operation. The BPP's only regular income comprised a trickle of book royalties—neither Newton's autobiography nor Seale's *Seize the Time* recouped their advances, for example—and advances on future publications.[57]

Meanwhile, the BPP hoped to revive the spirit of the Cal-Pac boycott by attempting to disrupt the filming of a movie set in Black Oakland. The FBI alleged that the BPP harried its producers for cash donations, demanded that they include party members in the cast, and asked for an oddly specific 37 percent of the film's profits. The BPP argued that, according to the tenets of Black capitalism, the film's producers ought to share the profits they reaped from the Black community.[58] Bobby Seale chastised them on television, while street protests provided a visual counterpoint. Newton, meanwhile, occasionally invited members of the cast and crew to his penthouse, where he would educate them about Black Power, leading to a donation of $5,000 to the BPP's survival programs.[59]

Such activities deepen our understanding of the BPP's relationship with American capitalism. Indeed, the Cal-Pac agreement contained striking similarities to Richard Nixon's Black capitalism in stressing the importance of small businesses. Its first clause highlighted the necessity of Black unity and the imperative to ensure the "economic health and well being of the black community," which it linked to the activities of community businesses. It then stated that "all blacks who earn profits from the black community" had an "emphatic social responsibility" to contribute to its "economic, social and survival programs."[60] This agreement implied a shift in the BPP's anticapitalist stance, one that reflected the praxis of its other social programs. The giveaways of essential items indicated that the BPP focused on critiquing the overproduction and unbalanced distribution inherent in capitalism. The Cal-Pac boycott operated on a similar theoretical basis, demonstrating that the BPP's praxis was becoming more flexible, certainly in the short term.

Thus, while at first glance Cal-Pac seems to anticipate *Ebony* journalist B. J. Mason's 1973 contention that the BPP was "shift[ing] to the middle," a deeper engagement with the dispute's theoretical underpinnings suggests that the BPP's horizons remained ambitious, if not as immediately apparent.[61] As Newton argued in dubbing the survival programs "survival pending revolution," the boycott ostensibly signaled the BPP's acceptance of the role of small capitalist enterprises. Yet beneath this, the boycott also hoped to elevate "consciousness and understanding," educating the community about capitalism's inequities and leading them on the path toward revolutionary activity—classical war of position aims.[62] It consequently positions the BPP to the left of many 1970s contemporaries who reconsidered their relationship with capitalism. While Jesse Jackson, for example, sought further integration within white capitalism, the BPP hoped to educate the Black capitalist about the precarity of their position in the wider capitalist tableau. They needed not only to serve their communities goods but also serve them more holistically. Black capitalists existed in a chain of reliance: above them the rapacious corporate capitalists who controlled the supply and cost of goods to the Black capitalist; below them the community that kept them in business. It therefore behooved them to limit their exploitation of the latter, since the former would not step in to save their businesses should demand slump. As such, the BPP did not anticipate Black entry into white corporate capitalism but instead sought to remind Black capitalists of the hierarchical and deeply racist nature of America's economic system.

Yet the boycott also hints at the binds that constricted the BPP. Newton insisted that the social programs needed regular donations. Single donations might be a useful public relations exercise for the donor but force the recipient to devote time to sourcing further donations—time that would be better spent on the social programs themselves. A single philanthropic gesture offers a moment for the businessman to demonstrate largess without challenging the structural inequities that their business contributes to and benefits from. Furthermore, once the BPP had collected single donations from all the small businesses in the locality, to whom would it turn? A subscription system, predicated on compulsion rather than voluntarism, was the only method of developing long-term sustainability for its social programs. In essence, the BPP called on Boyette to understand that he had a duty to the people who supported his business. Such tactics demanded a hiatus in the BPP's assault on capitalism, a temporary accommodation with a rapacious economic system that would enable the local community to survive as the BPP plotted longer-term strategic goals.

Of course, as Boyette suggested, regular financial donations are easier to mismanage than food. At a different level, however, the boycott indicates that the BPP, like many other African American activists who survived the 1960s, concluded that appeals to revolution would be less important in the 1970s than focusing on the food on the table. This adjustment derives from many roots, including Newton's attraction to the trappings of fame, his decision to abandon the gun, the growing death toll of Panthers, and the BPP's need to become a permanent institution sustained by multiple revenue streams emanating from the African American population. The BPP thus shifted its focus at a tactical level to immediate material circumstances, and away from open advocacy of revolt. Consequently, beneath the BPP's redeployment of its energies to focus on liberation in Oakland lay the understanding forged by the social programs, that American empire should first be tackled at the local level. So, while Newton's thought expanded to consider worldwide intercommunal wars of position, the BPP's praxis—informed by the membership's understanding of the importance of community-level action—narrowed to fight for the heart and soul of its hometown.

CHAPTER SEVEN

Bobby Seale for Mayor!

The first National Black Political Convention, held in Gary, Indiana, in March 1972, sought to forge a united front between various Black political groups and initiate a new era in African American electoral politics. The convention's location was symbolic: the first Black majority city in the Black Power era to elect a Black mayor. Richard Hatcher's success, based on his cross-class appeal to the Black electorate, provided the convention with a useful model for a new African American politics. Yet a painful reality lay beneath it: most cities did not have the African American population density to enable such success; instead, Black candidates in cities like Oakland remained reliant on cross-racial appeals.[1]

Despite its inevitable compromises, the BPP astutely offered relatively positive coverage, and an entire issue of *The Black Panther* for dissemination, of the National Black Political Agenda. Newton subsequently asked his congressman, Ron Dellums, to lobby for the BPP's inclusion in the convention's planned Black Assembly. Such positive actions conceal the BPP's minor role in the convention.[2] That the BPP accepted such a subordinate role might usefully be contrasted with its insistence on being at the very least the equal partner in its 1968 alliance with the Peace and Freedom Party.

Organizing the national African American vote faced a fundamental problem: voter activity. In the mid-1970s, approximately nine million African Americans were registered, but fewer than six million voted in the 1976 presidential election. This fed into the resurgence of coalition strategies, exemplified by Carl Stokes's success in Cleveland, Ohio.[3] In Los Angeles, Tom Bradley lost a 1969 runoff election thanks to his incumbent opponent Sam Yorty's shameless appeal to white racism, which informed his avoidance of racial politics in his successful 1973 campaign.[4] This included rejecting Bobby Seale's endorsement. Seale also sought municipal office that year. Described by the historian Robert Self as Oakland's "first truly grassroots municipal campaign" since the 1940s,

Seale's mayoral campaign was the BPP's last major contribution to American political history and reversed Newton's April 1971 promise that BPP candidates would "never run for political office."[5] As important, it represented a pioneering attempt to develop a class-based metropolitan Black Power.

The 1973 campaigns (Elaine Brown also ran for the city council) offered a major renewal opportunity for the BPP. Seale ran strongly enough to force the incumbent, John Reading, into a runoff. His ability to connect with a significant portion of Oakland's electorate revealed that the BPP could fashion a new image for itself and shrug off the influence of the increasingly erratic Newton. That the generally avuncular Republican, a seasoned campaigner who had won two previous elections, handsomely won the runoff was less the point than Seale's securing of a foundation for future electoral success. The BPP's campaigns were coupled with expanded social programs, such as free food packages for voters, confirming that the BPP had transcended its association with the gun. Furthermore, Lionel Wilson—who became Oakland's first African American mayor in 1977—undoubtedly benefited from the legacy of the BPP's voter registration drive: he won a similar number of votes to Seale.[6]

The decision to engage in electoral politics followed the BPP's quixotic nominations of Eldridge Cleaver for president and Newton for Congress in 1968. Somewhat unconvincingly, Cleaver argued that the candidacies "unit[ed] the revolutionary political arena with the conventional political arena, and thereby obliterat[ed] the distinction between the two."[7] By 1972 Elaine Brown concluded that Black Power had not challenged white hegemony; it was now time to seize power through the democratic process. With revolution seeming only a distant possibility, the BPP focused its energies on a winnable battle in Oakland. "Imagine us having the control of this city," Brown mused.[8] The front—and thus the revolution—would be broadened once a base of operations was secure.[9]

The BPP also learned important lessons in the 1972 presidential election. As was customary, California ballots included a raft of propositions. The BPP saw six as especially pertinent. Proposition 1 sought the issue and sale of $160 million in state bonds to fund public community colleges. Proposition 11 would amend the state constitution to include the right to privacy. Proposition 14 hoped to limit ad valorem property taxes and the use of property taxes to pay for welfare and education, cut state taxes on insurance companies and banks, and increase taxes on cigarettes and liquor. Proposition 17 hoped to reinstate the death penalty. Proposition 19 would remove state penalties for possessing marijuana for personal use. Finally, Proposition 22 threatened to outlaw strikes and boycotts organized by farmworkers.[10] The BPP declared "people's victor[ies]" in all but 17 and 19, concluding that the ballot box could reinforce community action against oppression.[11]

Ron Dellums's successful political career provided another model for building local influence. Elected to Berkeley's city council in 1967, Dellums quickly became an influential Bay Area figure. Like Newton, he was an Afro American Association veteran, well versed in Black nationalist ideology. Like Seale, he worked with underprivileged young people. Like many others, he spoke at Oakland's Free Huey rally in 1968. Yet he operated inside the Democratic political apparatus. In 1970 he ran in the Democratic primary for California's Seventh Congressional District, which encompassed most of Oakland and Berkeley. Assailing his opponent Jeffery Cohelan from the left, he denounced the Vietnam War, linking it to domestic poverty and racism, and supported a national health service, universal childcare, expanded federal job creation schemes, and an increase in social security. He also cleverly referenced the BPP's program, condemning American racism and regularly calling for greater community control of local police. Even almost unremittingly negative media coverage could not prevent his victory.[12]

Dellums's success—and the 1971 election as Berkeley's first African American mayor of his protégé, Warren Widener—confirmed that ambitious electoral campaigns could create coalitions of liberals and radicals, Blacks and whites, and that radicals like Dellums could flourish amid the hurly-burly of municipal politics, even in majority white districts. Moreover, ambitious Panthers would have noted that, once it became clear he was a winner, the Democratic hierarchy attached itself to Dellums. Meanwhile, many of his 1970 campaign workers turned to municipal politics, becoming a readymade network for future campaigners.[13]

Concluding that the city's Republican establishment rested on insecure foundations after noticing that George McGovern won more votes in Oakland than Richard Nixon in the presidential election, BPP comrade Art Goldberg recommended that the BPP follow Dellums's lead.[14] The BPP also benefited from the networks shaped by the survival programs and its newspaper's position as a community fixture. Yet not all the auguries were favorable. Some of Dellums's circle saw local businessman and broker of the BPP–Cal-Pac treaty, Otho Green, as their best hope for 1973.[15] Demographically, Oakland housed a wealthy, white, conservative "Bible Belt." "You have to be rich, white and Republican to win," lamented the chair of the Oakland Black Caucus.[16] As important, structural cronyism underpinned Republican political domination. No Democrat had been elected mayor since the first popular vote in 1953. The council tended to replace resigning members with kindred spirits ahead of the next election, giving them the manifold benefits of incumbency, including time to woo the conservative *Oakland Tribune*. Local business interests smoothed the path toward another term with generous funding. This was precisely the process by which Reading ascended to mayor. Initially a supporter of civil rights, he shifted rightward, becoming a law-and-order advocate and eventually criticizing Nixon for failing to curb federal spending on poverty programs. Desirous of running the city government like a business, he pushed a neoliberal pro-business agenda, not least because it benefited his own businesses.[17]

Oakland: A Base of Operation

The BPP insisted that, even though it was calling its active members to Oakland to concentrate action and resources at the community level, its long-term revolutionary vision remained. While the membership would shrink during this tactical retreat, a smaller and stronger BPP would emerge, one that benefited from the close interpersonal bonds that developed during its earliest days. This vanguard group, the BPP thought, would transform the local community.[18]

A series of articles in *The Black Panther* called "Oakland—A Base of Operation" outlined the theory behind the Seale-Brown campaigns. It presented Oakland's recent decline as a product of "deep structural contradictions within American urban capitalism and its color-class-caste system," indicting both 1960s liberalism and the American political economy in a wider sense as key failures.[19] In outlining this startling vision of Oakland's position in the American hegemon, "A Base of Operations" confirmed the BPP's continued immersion in leftist ideology, particularly its understanding of the colonial relationship between Black Oakland and white America:

> Oakland is . . . a center of operations for America's super-technological domination of the world. . . . Sitting on the northern coast of America's most militarized, industrialized, most technologically developed state, California, Oakland operates as a base for much of America's dirty work. . . . [A] close view of Oakland will reveal much about the decadence of America . . . and allow people to study closely the workings of the U.S. Empire with an eye toward its downfall and transformation.[20]

The series presented Black Oakland as a victim of systematic oppression, including a relocation plan for nine thousand residents to create a new housing project and post office building. Meanwhile the Bay Area Rapid Transit (BART) tracks weaved between Seventh and Fourth Streets before joining the Grove-Shafter Freeway, effectively bisecting Oakland roughly north-south from Fifty-First to Sixth Streets, forcing more poorer and Black residents to relocate.[21] For the BPP, BART was a "costly catastrophe," designed to benefit middle-class and corporate capitalists, funded by tax dollars that disproportionately came from lower-income earners and a $792 million bond issue, the interest from which lined the pockets of bankers. While BART trains visited affluent neighborhoods, the system failed to serve many others: West Oakland and San Francisco's traditionally African American Fillmore and Hunters Point areas housed only one stop. Worse, it failed to provide long-term jobs for low-income residents. Thus it simply reinforced Oakland's existing racial-caste system.[22]

The BPP's analysis revealed endemic unemployment, underemployment, and low pay, with 25 percent of Oakland's Black population reliant on welfare (compared to 8.4 percent of whites) and only government jobs preventing Black unemployment rising further.[23] Part 20 of the series denounced welfare as a vehicle for dehumanization. It presented plans to compel welfare recipients to accept menial jobs, often without pay, as a chilling dystopian vision of extractive capitalism.[24] The city's decision to build houses in the East Oakland Hills was likewise an expression of its willful inattention to the African American population and subservience to business, as demonstrated by its attempts to displace low-income residents of Oakland Housing Authority homes by elevating rents to attract middle-class replacements.[25] Similarly, the BPP lambasted Oakland's Mountain Village development, which was to incorporate 1,800 homes, a park, and a lake, noting that over 1,600 Oakland families were waiting for public housing, with thousands more seeking affordable private homes. None could afford to live in Mountain Village. Mayor Reading argued that more housing for richer Oaklanders would staunch the outflow of wealthy families, thus bolstering the tax base, yet the BPP charged that the project's cost would far exceed any projected tax revenues.[26]

The BPP concluded that Reading was in hock to big business, as demonstrated by the channeling of public money to developers like William Sparling who, *The Black Panther* alleged, did not "give a damn about" Oakland.[27] The lack of Black or female faces on the city council reinforced the sense that certain Oaklanders were taxed but not represented. Indeed, Reading's spending plans after a property tax rise revealed his priorities: boosting police and fire department pension funds, redeveloping the business district, and building car parks and a convention center. Meanwhile, schoolchildren sat in cramped, overcrowded classrooms while the Board of Education planned further cuts to teaching staff numbers.[28] In 1966 the BPP demanded an education that "exposes the true nature of this decadent American society ... that teaches us our true history and our role in the present-day society." The perilous state of public education in 1972 forced it to focus on the impact on educational achievement of outrages such as ballooning class sizes and administration costs.[29] All this suggested that Reading might exploit the federal government's revenue sharing plan, which promised federal funds to state governments, to benefit Oakland's wealthy whites. More ominously, the BPP feared that the federal government might impose conditions on how revenue sharing funds be spent—a damaging proposition for a Seale mayoralty.[30]

While Reading trumpeted Oakland's economic prosperity, the BPP revealed that flatlands residents remained as poor, oppressed, and exploited as ever.

On a wider scale, Oakland exported American military power while its power elite ignored its impoverished residents. As important, Reading's prosperity plan was predicated on the assumption that businesses and middle-income and wealthy residents would remain in Oakland provided that they were not unduly burdened by city taxes—in short, a neoliberal continuation of the colonial relationship between white America and Black Oakland.[31]

Aware of the symbiosis between mayoral leadership and grassroots support, the BPP adopted a hybrid top-down and bottom-up approach to municipal policymaking. In summer 1972 it ran candidates for the West Oakland Planning Committee, which coordinated Oakland's Model City antipoverty program, encouraging voter registration with food and clothing giveaways. Volunteers ferried voters to the polls, where sickle cell anemia testing was available. BPP campaigners distributed forty thousand leaflets while meet-and-greets and radio slots further disseminated their message, encapsulated in their "For righteous community control" slogan and a progressive gender mix. The voters rewarded the BPP with one-third of the committee's seats. The key theme of the flyers, however, presented the candidates as ordinary citizens whose BPP work expressed their concern for the community rather than an interest in revolution, reinforced by their sporting civilian clothing rather than typical BPP attire. This refashioning of their image was to prove hugely influential on the Seale campaign.[32]

By the end of 1972 the BPP held a majority on the Berkeley Community Development Council and was developing links with Women Organized for Political Action and the Black Students Alliance inside the Democratic Party, emphasizing how the BPP promoted an intersectional approach to overcoming the oppression faced by poor and minority groups.[33] The BPP also monitored the activities of the Berkeley Radicals umbrella group while running candidates for the United Bay Area Crusade Board, which provided funding for neighborhood services in Alameda County.[34] This mobilization was enough to compel Carl Olsen of Oakland's euphemistically titled Concerned Citizens Committee to call on Oakland's business community to support "local candidates blessed with at least some degree of responsibility, statesmanship and business experience."[35] Olsen's ostensibly race-blind platitudes gilded his call's racist undercurrents, echoing the dog-whistle politics of prominent conservatives. Foreshadowing the Reading campaign's undertones, he hinted that African American candidates were irresponsible, uncouth, financially illiterate interlopers, messages that Oakland's white voters decoded easily. Another "concerned citizen" informed Ron Dellums that Newton threatened a man who subsequently fled Oakland.[36] The BPP, in fact, deliberately removed Newton from the campaign. In April 1972, on the same day the BPP endorsed Shirley Chisholm's presidential campaign, he was arrested for beating a radio DJ.[37] Keeping him out of the limelight afterward proved one of the campaign's unheralded successes.

Running the Campaigns

While Seale's campaign received much of the attention, Brown's campaign in District 2—which, like Seale's, was spearheaded by two indefatigable female Panthers, Audrea Jones and Joan Kelley—was also significant, not least because it illustrates the many impediments BPP candidates faced. She ran against the first African American elected to public office in the city, the Republican Joshua Rose, who had been incumbent since completing Robert V. McKeen's term in 1964. His district lay east of downtown, incorporating parts of wealthier Oakland. In almost all respects, District 3, which included the BPP's heartlands in West Oakland and downtown, offered a greater chance of success, but its election was not due until 1975. Of the districts contested in 1973, District 4 included large sections of the hills, the wealthiest and whitest area in the city; Joseph Coto, whose campaign to become Oakland's first Mexican American councilman the BPP supported, ran in the heavily Chicano District 6. District 2 was therefore Brown's only realistic choice. She faced numerous hurdles, competing against a familiar figure with strong community roots courtesy of his links to the Oakland YMCA, and the *Tribune*'s endorsement presenting him as the establishment candidate.[38] She was attempting to gain access to a notoriously masculine world, fighting all the preconceptions that voters had about women operating in municipal politics. Finally, whatever name recognition she possessed was indelibly linked to the BPP, which had its own problems.

Oakland mayors were elected through an open, nonpartisan primary. If nobody won more than 50 percent of the vote, the two most popular contested a runoff. The gossip among Democratic elites in late 1972 suggested that Seale might split the Black vote, advantaging a moderate white Democrat. Meanwhile, Reading's incumbency, experience, and name recognition gave him significant advantages, although the Republican hierarchy was concerned should he not run because his favored son, Frank Ogawa, "just didn't measure up."[39] Reading boasted that Seale was no threat, predicting that the Panther would win no more than 20 percent of the vote, but he feared a runoff because of Oakland's large number of registered Democrats.[40]

The BPP set its campaign tone at its inaugural meeting at Saint Augustine's Episcopal Church: "Working together, we can make a change."[41] The campaign aimed to energize flatlands voters, with Seale promising "organization—not rhetoric."[42] Sited just north of the BPP's West Oakland heartland, the church represented a stable, supportive, multigenerational community, with impeccable liberal and antiracist credentials. It therefore signified an approach to coalition building rooted in Oakland's Black population. It relied on low-income donors for church funds, much like Seale's campaign: aside from large donations from the film producer Bert Schneider ($7,500) and Stronghold

($10,000), the BPP's 1973 campaigns received only $21,467.13 from donors who gave more than $500. This reinforced the BPP's independence from Oakland's political and business establishment but led to a shoestring budget that hindered the campaign.[43] As Election Day approached, complaints mounted from campaign workers who needed money, particularly for rent and telephone bills, illustrating the difficulties faced by grassroots election campaigns.[44]

In December the BPP offered its first major policy, Seniors for a Safe Environment (SAFE), a promise to escort seniors to and from banks when they received Social Security checks and were most vulnerable to personal theft. Charging the city with spending $55,000 on a helicopter that failed to protect senior citizens, the BPP proposed SAFE's future as a municipal round-the-clock service.[45] Drawing on the BPP's police patrols and social programs, monitoring the police and protecting the vulnerable while visibly positioning the BPP at the community's core, SAFE ran with some success. It represented a major attempt to soften the BPP's image while attacking the city's plan to grant panoptic authority to a pilot whose remit was likely to be racially coded in targeting Black crime rather than protecting Black people *from* crime. SAFE's grassroots approach contrasted sharply with this depersonalized service and demonstrated the party's awareness of the importance of the senior vote.

Broadening from SAFE, by February 1973 the BPP had a raft of policies. Demonstrating how social programs like the liberation schools and health care programs informed its analysis of American society, it hailed preventive medical care and opposed budget cuts for Oakland's schools. Meanwhile, the candidates advocated allocating federal revenue sharing funding to job training programs, revealing a debt to 1960s liberalism. Better job training, they said, led to higher income and employment levels, which boosted municipal tax revenues. Stressing that all Oaklanders, regardless of skills, had the right to a job, they also pushed for more minority employment in Oakland's port.[46]

Seale's initial campaign statement was typically bullish, opposing property tax increases; encouraging more teachers and assistants in schools; promising safety for seniors, better health care, housing, environmental control, and affirmative action on employment. Brown's was more emollient, focusing on her personal relationship with the issues Seale raised.[47] Seale emphasized his open government campaign, stressing his role in challenging the Oakland council's tradition of holding secret city council meetings—to which only the *Tribune* was invited—by opening them to the general press. Surprisingly, the *Tribune* endorsed the anti-secrecy campaign, which was voted into law soon afterward.[48] While the candidates were disappointed to discover that the council rejected Seale's enforcement measure to outlaw any decisions made in secret, the end of secret meetings was a major coup and evidence that Oakland's political system was gradually opening itself up to the popular insurgency.[49]

Reflecting the BPP's experience of previous elections, Seale and Brown tempered their popular image. Rarely seen not wearing a sharp suit, he attended church every Sunday and delighted in shooting the breeze with elderly worshippers. Campaign literature had Seale smiling, looking upward in hope, often surrounded by happy Oaklanders, in stark contrast to the stern, leather-jacketed Panther of legend. To underscore this image, Seale and Brown's literature urged voters to "elect two Democrats!"[50] Neither candidate's formal election statement mentioned the BPP, although Brown pointed to her three years editing a "major international newspaper" that clever readers would have identified as *The Black Panther*. Seale's campaign biography afforded the BPP only two sentences, focused on his friendship with Newton and their shared concern for Black America. By deemphasizing the candidates' BPP affiliations and disassociating them from Newton (the BPP cofounder did not even sign their nomination forms) the campaign presented Seale and Brown as professional community organizers, as their declared job titles suggested.[51] The BPP's campaign song, "This Little Light of Mine," further distanced the candidates from the BPP. Indelibly linked to the church and the nonviolent civil rights movement, the song offered an optimistic view of the individual's ability to make change, enveloped in a similarly positive view of human nature. It was accompanied by "Vote for Survival," a bespoke song that included the line "Vote for people's government that's righteous and fair."[52] Both were a far cry from the "Revolution has come, off the pig" refrain that echoed around the Free Huey demonstrations.

In March the BPP candidates unveiled a fourteen-point economic plan that fleshed out its ideas about revenue sharing. In 1972 Oakland received $4.5 million, a sum the candidates said was large enough to improve the city's housing stock and street lighting without affecting property taxes.[53] The Reading administration disagreed. Revenue sharing money was linked to population and tax revenues. With middle-class whites departing, Oakland stood to lose both. Tax rises, Reading's finance director concluded, were inevitable since the city needed more than $1.5 million per year to offset projected revenue sharing shortfalls.[54] To raise revenue, the Seale-Brown program proposed taxing private intangible stocks (effectively a wealth tax) at 1 percent; implementing a 5 to 10 percent capital gains tax on corporate property transfers, with small businesses and small homeowners exempt; transferring the city's cash deposits to higher-interest accounts; closing property tax loopholes exploited by so-called public utilities; increasing rent on the Oakland Coliseum; and doubling the city's transient occupancy tax on hotels and motels. This $20 million plan would fund SAFE, loans and grants to low-income families for housing, eight mobile health clinics, extra childcare places, improvements to street lighting in high-crime neighborhoods, and environmental and consumer protection projects.[55] This policy overwhelmingly taxed large businesses and the wealthy (a doubling of municipal golf course fees would fund recreational programs for residents who did not want to spoil a good walk), demonstrating the BPP's commitment to income and wealth redistribution.[56]

Echoing the BPP's 1966 Platform and Program call for community control of institutions, the candidates insisted that fire and police department employees reside in Oakland. This would challenge Black Oaklanders' suspicions that police entered Oakland only to dispense law and order. As important, it would boost tax revenues and improve reaction times when emergencies required the presence of off-duty staff.[57] Aware that Mexican Americans constituted Oakland's largest bilingual or non–English-speaking minority, Seale urged Reading to approve bilingual ballots, noting the *Castro v. State of California* Supreme Court decision that declared unconstitutional the requirement to speak English to vote. With many BPP activists working in the relevant areas of Oakland, this could attract thousands of voters, an ambition aided by a laudatory endorsement from Cesar Chavez and the United Farm Workers.[58]

Sadly, Seale did not win the endorsement of Oakland's Democrats or the *Oakland Tribune*.[59] That said, the newspaper eventually conceded that he was a "formidable figure" and begrudgingly concluded that his program was "imaginative," albeit on the same day that its editorial board unequivocally backed Reading.[60] Rival candidates enthusiastically reminded voters of the candidates' BPP affiliation while placing opposition to Seale at their core, effectively accepting his credibility and strength. John Sutter's flyers urged voters "Don't pick a Panther" before even mentioning Sutter's qualities.[61] Otho Green told voters that they could reelect Reading and receive four more years of indifference or "a Black Panther leader who has openly preached violence ... [and] *cannot possibly beat Mayor Reading*."[62] The only logical choice was to vote for the Democratic businessman, army veteran, and family man. The *Tribune* considered Green Reading's strongest challenger, believing that local Democratic power-brokers would line up behind his well-oiled machine. The *San Francisco Chronicle* acclaimed him as one of "a new breed of savvy black politicians," which suggested that he was moderate enough not to trouble the establishment.[63] Endorsed by various Democrats and union figures, Green promised to reduce crime, unemployment, and the cost of living while using his business skills to win a better revenue sharing settlement. Yet that his flyers denounced Seale and Reading before outlining any policies reveals his fundamentally defensive campaign. Similarly, his rejection of the Seale-Brown program merely reflected his opposition to raising business taxes, confirming him as a do-nothing corporate lackey.[64] Reading's literature, meanwhile, focused on his employment, economic, house-building, and crime-fighting record.[65] The BPP collected choice quotes from the incumbent, designed to highlight his sympathies. Two were damning: on Oakland's problems he shrugged, "All we can do is muddle through," whereas "business should be able to do what it wants to."[66]

Campaign Organization

With Oakland's population 49 percent white, 35 percent Black, and 16 percent "other," the BPP needed maximum African American voter registration.[67] It estimated that 25,000 unregistered voters lived in majority African American or Chicano areas—enough, it hoped, to create a victorious coalition. It sought to register 50,000 new voters by dividing up the city into sections and precincts, coupled with a citywide telephone hotline.[68] It split Oakland's flatlands into eight sections, each with a leader and six with a separate office, alongside campaign headquarters in South Oakland where local organizers coordinated activity.[69] Aware that winning the hills' wealthy white residents would be near impossible, it delegated a majority-white group of Berkeley students to canvas there.[70] The candidates endured a hectic schedule of meetings, debates, canvassing, food giveaways, and benefits. They regularly boarded municipal buses to distribute literature and preach to passengers.[71] Donations provided food or other necessities to people in areas where BPP support was weak, enabling recipients to see a different side of the BPP. Such a strategy would, the BPP hoped, counteract the political influence wielded by Oakland's affluent conservatives and enable the BPP to oppose plans for future municipal elections to be run on a district-by-district basis, as it feared the city's power structure would gerrymander the divisions to prevent any Black majority districts.[72]

The BPP worked hard to broaden its support among flatlands residents. Ericka Huggins forged links with groups such as Oakland's Tenants' Union and the Youth Citizenship Fund, with Elbert Howard reaching out to the Berkeley April Coalition. Their colleagues organized regular meetings with trade union representatives and church parishioners and leaders. Section 4 workers organized Oakland's large Chicano population on Joe Coto's behalf.[73] Translators and bilingual flyers highlighted Seale's support for bilingualism, his belief in uniting the city's "poor and oppressed communities," and Cesar Chavez's endorsement.[74] Other flyers proudly displayed the endorsement of the Alice B. Toklas Memorial Democratic Club, which defined itself as the Bay Area's only gay Democratic club. The BPP's platform on gay rights was straightforward: it would end job discrimination and police harassment, ensure equal housing rights, support a community center and clinic run by and for the gay community, and push for federal and state action against discrimination. "None of us are free," it stated in familiar terms, "until all of us are free."[75]

Illustrating the BPP's complex understanding of racial and class oppression in Oakland, it campaigned to strengthen California's "Pay While Voting" law, which had been so watered down that many employees did not exercise their polling-day rights because they had to petition their employer to receive time off. The BPP filed suit against ten companies, prompting them to display conspicuous notices outlining their employees' rights. In April Seale invited Reading to ensure that all Oakland's employed voters received two hours of paid leave on Election Day and instructed his lawyers to draft an ordinance.[76] That the BPP had already effectively won was less the point than the publicity that the campaign accrued from forcing Reading to comment. Seale's concern was a form of enlightened self-interest: municipal election participation historically fell below that in presidential elections, which was surely related to nonvoters' fears of a dispute with their employer over their rights. Further, by publicizing "Pay While Voting" rights, Seale hoped to boost the turnout of poorly paid voters, a constituency that was more likely to support him than Reading. It also offered extra publicity for the BPP campaign's central themes of open government, employment, and pay.[77]

The campaigns energized every layer of Oakland's BPP. Registrars flooded neighborhoods on certain days, heading to places of congregation such as supermarkets or laundromats to maximize registrants.[78] By January the party's "Innerparty Memorandums," which dictated the following week's priorities, elevated the election campaign above everything. Soon afterward, the BPP suspended its near permanent newspaper subscription drive and devoted its political education classes to voter registration techniques.[79] While this intensity was vital to the campaign, it took its toll. Even though he timetabled sleep between 12:00 p.m. and 8:00 a.m., Chuck McAllister regretfully noted that such a long rest was a rarity. He was not alone: many other volunteers struggled to juggle campaign commitments with family, jobs, or school.[80]

Given the BPP's history, the relative lack of police harassment is notable. One campaign worker was jailed in January 1973 and another arrested in April, while the BPP alleged that FBI agents harassed three campaigners.[81] Police accosted two Panthers for pasting posters on a condemned property. While they had the owner's verbal agreement, their failure to produce written proof resulted in them destroying the posters to avoid a misdemeanor charge. "Lesson learned," they concluded.[82] Seale claimed that an Otho Green supporter threatened to kill him unless he withdrew, a ploy that was so irrational that police or FBI involvement cannot be discounted. One bizarre incident suggested to Sherry Brown that provocateurs were active: she noticed a man berating some whites at a bus stop, ordering them to vote for Seale. She initially suspected that he was intoxicated but reflected that his behavior was not random enough for such an explanation. The most significant incident was a police raid of a campaign office on April 16. They confiscated some guns, marijuana, and lists of volunteers' names, and arrested fourteen sleeping people. Predictably, days later the charges of conspiracy and possession of illegal weapons and drugs were dropped.[83]

Police brutality earned Seale at least one vote, however. Bonnie Pickett reported fruitless conversations with one white male voter until one day when he announced that he had been arrested and beaten by police. In her words,

> Realizing the fact that even a misdemeanor conviction could cost him his job, his car, his house, and perhaps his wife; he had come to understand on a gut level what the Chairman and the BPP have been saying all along about police harassment and the prison system.... He was visibly moved as he concluded that... he was voting for Bobby.[84]

Unfortunately, his vote was not enough. Seale polled 21,329 votes, nearly four thousand more than Green but less than half of Reading's total, which was only 134 short of an absolute majority.[85] Brown lost in District 2, 34,866 votes to 55,811; Joe Coto won the District 6 runoff.[86]

Aftermath

After finishing fourth, John Sutter bitterly dismissed Seale as a "celebrity candidate." The failed candidate argued that this scared voters into voting tactically for Reading, prompted by a last-minute Reading mailshot that further emphasized the fear factor attached to a Seale mayoralty.[87] Sutter epitomizes the squeeze white Democrats faced in the Nixon era. Seale represented an increasingly assertive African American vote that many white voters considered a threat, particularly those who lived at the front lines of integration. Meanwhile radicals such as George McGovern's supporters were attempting to pull the Democrats leftward, alienating centrist voters. From this perspective, the fractures within Oakland's Democratic coalition worked to Reading's benefit.

The Black Panther concluded that approximately fifty thousand registered voters in Oakland's Black and Spanish-speaking neighborhoods did not vote. Reaching out to these disaffected, apathetic, or unresponsive voters would be crucial before the May 15 runoff. This was particularly apparent in Districts 4 and 6, where Seale ceded to Reading 28 percent to 41 percent and 12 percent to 61 percent, respectively, and in District 1, where only eighty of the four hundred registered people voted. Notably, Seale won only where Green ran well and performed poorest where Green was weak, suggesting that the candidates split the Democratic vote. More concerning, Reading polled over 29 percent of Oakland's African American vote, a staggering figure given Seale's campaign strategy. Four hundred precinct workers therefore conducted door-to-door canvassing, yet more evidence that grassroots action was at the campaign's core.[88]

Seale's campaign workers also needed to engage Green's and Sutter's middle-of-the-road supporters, who might have tired of Reading but resisted radical change. New flyers depicted Seale on picket lines alongside parents worried about daycare programs, supporting Oakland's social workers over forced work programs, backing BART workers in job discrimination claims, and backing workers' rights while explicitly linking Reading to the Nixon administration. In time for the runoff, Ron Dellums joined a list of prominent endorsers including Coretta Scott King and Jesse Jackson.[89] *The Black Panther* ran a "Base of Operations" special to remind readers of Reading's disregard for the Black community and unashamed courting of business. This it juxtaposed with photographs of a smiling Seale meeting and greeting the people.[90] The message was clear: Seale was independent of the federal government and big business; only he had the interests of Oakland's citizens rather than its corporate elites at heart.

In debate Reading reiterated his message of economic stability and downtown development while Seale focused on social investment, arguing that the people's needs trumped the interests of big business. Such tactics resulted in Reading warming to Seale as a candidate who refused to play the race card and instead fought on the issues.[91] Yet Reading's sentiments were not as ingenuous as this suggests. Reading knew that he could attract Oakland's more affluent Black population through his economic policies; this constituency might have been attracted to Seale in a race-first campaign. He could also rely on the loyalty of Oakland's older, affluent whites, a constituency that voted in far higher numbers than Seale's base. Such comments also offered a coded reminder to wavering whites of the possibility of an African American mayor. Consequently, Seale's willingness to fight an orthodox political campaign played into Reading's hands. Moreover, Reading's placatory words were a classic Republican ploy, elevating the candidate over the fray while his campaign literature fought dirtier. Essentially, this was another Republican campaign that presented the country in postracial terms while fighting to protect white supremacy.[92]

Even though Seale doubled his primary vote, Reading won a crushing victory: 77,476 to 43,719 on a turnout of 70 percent. In a city of 350,000 with 70 percent of its 175,000 registered voters Democrats, Seale was unable to prevent tens of thousands of regular Democrats abstaining or voting for a Republican. Turnout was highest in the Oakland Hills where Reading was strongest, revealing that white backlash was as important to the election as support for the BPP.[93] The BPP's figures indicated that while Seale carried four of the eight sections into which it had divided Oakland, the margins of victory did not offset heavy defeats elsewhere. In District 6, Seale polled under 25 percent, and in the heavily Spanish-speaking District 4, he scraped past Reading by under 150 votes.[94]

Seale's failure to carry moderate Democrats was a core reason for his defeat—in part because many voters considered the name "Black Panther Party" problematic—but campaign funding was more important: Reading outspent him two to one. No matter how well calibrated and how enthusiastically staffed, Seale's shoestring campaign simply could not compete.[95] Even in defeat, however, there was cause for celebration. The BPP had a further four years to convince flatlands residents that voting was worthwhile, and the campaign's networks and data could be used to increase BPP newspaper subscriptions.[96] Events across the Bay also offered hope. A middle-aged gay activist ran tenth in the election for San Francisco's Board of Supervisors. His response was simple: he cut his hair, stopped smoking marijuana, and gave up visiting bathhouses. Already thinking of his next campaign, Harvey Milk was ready to "play the game."[97] Set in this context, Seale winning more than forty thousand votes boded well. Sadly, however, the campaign's momentum dissipated. Volunteers dwindled and bills piled up as donations and newspaper sales fell.[98] Party meetings became focused on mundane issues such as business plans and newspaper distribution, further depressing interest. For Seale, the campaign was a logical culmination of his involvement with the party; to comrades he appeared lost afterward; to Newton, he became useless.[99]

In 1975 Elaine Brown ran unsuccessfully for city council before backing Lionel Wilson's 1977 run for mayor. His victory was accompanied by wins for progressives in city council and school board elections, including the city's first African American representative and first female auditor. Wilson was one of a swath of African American mayors who entered office in the mid-1970s. He was more moderate in office than the BPP hoped, a reflection of the support he attracted from white moderates and a consequence of 1978's notorious Proposition 13. These developments confirm the triumph of liberalism in the 1970s and suggest that the BPP's transformative vision remained a minority pursuit, even at the municipal level.[100]

By 1977 the BPP was in terminal decline. Wilson ordered an investigation of the BPP's Educational Opportunities Corp, which managed the BPP's school, uncovering problems with bookkeeping that threatened its ongoing receipt of government funds. It highlighted particular concerns about problems with the EOC's handling of cash and discrepancies between employee signatures on payroll checks and tax forms. In 1974 *Tribune* investigative reporters Pearl Stewart and Lance Williams uncovered evidence of fraud when the BPP secured bail for Newton and Robert Heard. By May 1978 the BPP faced IRS bills of over $250,000 for Stronghold's corporate taxes and more than $30,000 in property taxes.[101] Two months later a major investigative report appeared. Kate Coleman and Paul Avery's "The Party's Over" placed Newton at the core of a seedy BPP underbelly. Newton responded by threatening—but never actioning—a legal suit.[102]

The BPP was now reliant on street donations even to buy food for members. JoNina Abron's heartfelt 1980 letter to Newton revealed the extent to which it was exhausted. Many remaining members were heading into middle age and considering their post-BPP lives. The school, the only remaining community program, generated the BPP's only major source of finance, leading many members to take on part-time work. Lamenting that the BPP lacked a sense of purpose, Abron implored Newton to make a public statement about the party's direction.[103] None was forthcoming; indeed, Oakland's population was more likely to need protection from Newton. Embroiled in his second DUI case in six months, Newton had his own demons to confront.[104] Rudderless, the BPP limped into its twilight.

PART III

State Repression

CHAPTER EIGHT

The Trial of Huey P. Newton

John Frey had a distasteful reputation. Over six feet tall and 200 pounds, the imposing Oakland Police Department officer was renowned for a brutal attitude toward Black Oaklanders and a tendency to use racial epithets, despite only being in his post for roughly eighteen months. Many colleagues found him lacking the qualities they sought in a good cop. He was, however, reflective of the OPD's demography. Oakland's sworn police personnel in 1967 were 96 percent white, with many officers hailing from the southern states. These employees might have migrated north for employment reasons, but that these were overwhelmingly white men leaving the site of the civil rights revolution is surely significant.[1] As one local politician later said, the OPD was "no different from the most rabid, cracker police force in a small Mississippi town."[2] The BPP's description of the OPD as an occupying force, then, was no mere bluster.

Between 4:30 and 5:00 a.m. on October 28, 1967, Frey was patrolling the corner of Seventh and Willow Streets. This beat was unpopular with officers since it covered part of Oakland's red-light district and a few all-night venues, so Friday to Saturday patrols could expect some bother. Frey noticed a Volkswagen Beetle turn east onto Seventh. Upon radioing for backup, he learned that this was a BPP car. Newton and his friend Gene McKinney were in search of soul food. Newton stopped his car on the carriageway shoulder, near Campbell Street. Frey parked immediately behind. A second officer, Herbert Heanes, parked behind Frey's vehicle. At this point, the record becomes murky. On request, Newton apparently presented a registration document that revealed the car belonged to his girlfriend, LaVerne Williams. After a short conversation, Newton walked toward Frey's cruiser. He and Frey tussled by the driver's side of the police vehicle. Frey died of bullet wounds before medical help arrived. Heanes, who observed from the rear driver's side of his vehicle, was shot in his right arm, left chest, and left knee. Newton suffered a bullet wound to the abdomen and departed on foot with McKinney. Police found his bloodied

California lawbook near Frey's body.[3] What began as a relatively routine stop would come to dominate the lives of both Newton and the BPP.

Newton reappeared outside Oakland's Kaiser Hospital just before 6:00 a.m. The attending nurse called the police before admitting him. Twenty-five minutes later, he was placed on a gurney, and soon after a posse of Oakland police burst in and stretched his wound by handcuffing his hands above his head. According to Newton, they also beat him. Soon afterward, he was charged with murder. A conviction could lead to the death penalty, and with the number of police killed feloniously in the line of duty reaching an unprecedented number in 1967, the state would offer a vigorous fight.[4]

Carlton Goodlet, the publisher of the Bay Area's African American newspaper, the *Sun Reporter*, encouraged the radical leftist lawyer Charles Garry to defend Newton. A tough defense lawyer, he firmly believed that the American legal system was designed to preserve the status quo at the expense of insurgent minorities, and he considered the court a battleground where radicals like him could fight this imbalance.[5] He later said that he would normally begin representing a client by researching the laws that pertained to the case. For Newton, it was different: "I had to find out... what made him *be* a Huey P. Newton." They did not even discuss the shooting before the trial; instead Newton started by advising Garry to read Malcolm X and Fanon. Thus armed, Garry concluded that the trial could reveal the depth of racism in white America.[6] Newton understood the necessity of this strategy. When a journalist asked whether he would "beat the rap," Newton replied that he was not guilty. After the journalist pointed out the difference between beating the rap and being innocent, Newton playfully replied, "Well, we are going to have to revolutionize the court structure in this country."[7]

Garry knew that the evidence was inadequate for conviction. This, however, did not blind him to the trial's social context, including Black Power, the BPP's public image, and the urban rebellions of the previous summer, factors that, he believed, rendered the atmosphere poisonous enough that a jury might convict Newton. His strategy was therefore twofold: first, he would use the evidence to demonstrate reasonable doubts about who killed Frey. Second, he would use the trial to indict the American judicial system, publicize the BPP's political program, and call into question a society that produced the BPP. In doing so, he set a template that animated trials of African American radicals like Angela Davis and Soledad Brother Ruchell Magee that lasted through the 1970s.[8] As important, by keeping Newton in the public eye, he helped nurture a campaign that transformed the BPP into an international phenomenon. It is no exaggeration to state that Garry, whose firm sacrificed considerable income in assigning him to Newton, was fundamental in elevating the trial to the central event in the BPP's history.[9]

Garry felt that holding the trial in Alameda County was best, since it was home to a large Black population who would likely understand the BPP. This offered important ballast for the claim that Newton deserved a trial by his peers. As significant, it enabled BPP supporters to attend the courtroom or protest outside, which could counterbalance negative mainstream media coverage. Garry then filed suit against Kaiser Hospital for negligence and maltreatment before investigating Newton's grand jury.[10] The California legal system used grand juries to investigate potential criminal conduct and decide whether to bring official charges, to prevent frivolous or malicious prosecutions. These rarely used juries could compel witnesses to give evidence and order the production of relevant documents. Garry objected on various grounds. First, the defense could not present its case and cross-examine witnesses. Garry alleged that prosecutors were able to present privileged information to which the defense council was not privy that would encourage an indictment. Further, the jury was composed solely of the Superior Court judges' "cronies": wealthy whites who received five dollars per day plus expenses, not people who were representative of inner-city Oakland or who comprehended—let alone lived in—Newton's world.[11] While Garry could not compel the judge to dismiss the indictment, in opening this argument he empowered himself to pursue a defense that focused on the relationship between the forces of authority in Oakland and the people that suffered beneath them.

A "Free Huey" campaign outside the courthouse reinforced Garry's courtroom strategy by presenting Newton as the personification of the BPP's critique of American capitalism, helping ensure that the trial received maximum media coverage. Members of the party and the community were always present in the court's public gallery. This conveyed a twofold message, reminding Newton and the court that the BPP was watching and giving the press another opportunity to publicize the party.[12] A public gallery full of Black faces supporting a Black man facing a white judge, white lawyers, and a majority-white jury offered a daily reminder of the trial's racial subtext. Outside, a sequence of rallies rendered the area around the Alameda County Courthouse a site of public protest and legal contest for activists, the police, and the media.

A further tactic involved building a support infrastructure by reaching out to other organizations, notably the Peace and Freedom Party (PFP) and the Student Nonviolent Coordinating Committee (SNCC). In December 1967 it announced an alliance with the PFP, whose links with the antiwar, civil rights, and campus movements suggested that it shared the BPP's worldview. The alliance promised to boost the PFP's faltering voter registration quest, particularly among the Bay Area's Black population, also signifying the BPP's understanding that it might disrupt the nation's two-party system en route to the revolution.[13] It certainly brought great publicity: in the wake of its announcement, even the *Oakland Tribune* published the BPP's Ten-Point Platform and Program. The PFP also liberally distributed literature publicizing why the two groups were reaching across the racial divide. Its rationale was compelling: like the Vietcong, the BPP was struggling for liberation; it was therefore logical and imperative for the PFP to support the latter given its support of the former. As important, it accompanied the BPP's increasing immersion in leftist literature and particularly Fanon, repositioning the BPP on the radical Left and enabling it to escape a bind that faced some Black nationalists: if their stated aim was to reject racism, why would they use race as an exclusionary force within their own movement?[14] Its final benefit was to offer legitimacy. When Newton was arrested, the BPP was on the verge of collapse.[15] By the Free Huey campaign's conclusion, it was an international sensation with tens of thousands of supporters and members. The alliance confirmed that a significant portion of the Bay Area Left wanted to work alongside the BPP. In addition, it centered Cleaver at the party's core. Overwhelmingly, however, it ensured the vigorous pursuit of the Free Huey campaign and elevated its slogan to a rallying cry of the era.[16]

Despite the PFP's significantly larger membership, the BPP presented the alliance as a partnership of equals and hoped to use the PFP to organize the white community on its behalf.[17] The alliance's first benefit brought a $3,000 PFP donation to Newton's defense fund. The second was an immediate boost to the BPP's Free Huey demonstrations. In November, sixty Panthers appeared at Newton's second court appearance. A late December hearing saw roughly four hundred demonstrators, followed by a successful "Honkies for Huey" meeting.[18] By January, Bobby Seale sat on the PFP steering committee in Alameda County. He and Bob Avakian, representing the PFP's white radical caucus, agreed that the alliance ought to prioritize winning Newton's freedom. This abandoned the Free Huey campaign's early focus on getting a fair trial, reflecting Fanonist thinking: as colonial subjects African Americans would never receive a fair trial.[19] The PFP's March convention hotly debated a proposal to advocate "Free[ing] Huey Newton by any means necessary." While it overwhelmingly voted to "Free Huey Newton Now," it narrowly rejected the second clause, leading to a further amendment that appended "which would further the black liberation movement."[20] As this suggests, the PFP were willing supporters but by no means BPP puppets.

The BPP's coalition with SNCC further cemented its position within the radical movement. Newton inducted one of SNCC's greatest organizers, Kwame Ture (Stokely Carmichael), into the BPP in June 1967, giving him control of the BPP's activities in the eastern states. That the BPP had no structure in this region was of little concern: Ture had built the original Black Panther Party, the Lowndes County Freedom Organization, from scratch and had the charisma, contacts, and skills to repeat this feat on a wider scale.[21] By late 1967 the two organizations were negotiating a formal bond.[22] The arguments would rumble through 1968 as SNCC withered and the BPP focused more intently on freeing Newton.

Stills from *Huey!* (1968), depicting the Free Huey rally in Oakland. Above, left to right: unknown male (likely Don Cox), Seale, Newton's chair, Ture (who donned his dashiki before giving his speech), al Amin. Below, Newton on the wicker chair. Directed by Sally Pugh, American Documentary Films, San Francisco Bay Area Television Archive (SFBATA), https://diva.sfsu.edu/collections/sfbatv/bundles/191359.

Early 1968 saw the first large Free Huey rallies: two celebrations of Newton's birthday, one in Oakland on February 17, and one in Los Angeles the following day. The first was a mixed success. The Oakland Civic Auditorium, almost within earshot of Newton's cell at the Alameda County Courthouse, filled with a mixture of Black, white, young, and old. Berkeley's KPFA radio station recorded the meeting, which included speeches from Bob Avakian; SNCC's Ture, James Forman, and Jamil Abdullah al Amin (H. Rap Brown); and Newton's mother, Charles Garry, and the recently elected Ron Dellums. Famed for its radical political stance, KPFA's presence confirmed that the BPP now sat at the core of the Bay Area radical movement. At center stage stood the empty wicker chair that Newton occupied for his famous photoshoot with spear and rifle—a simple and powerful visual ploy to remind the audience of Newton's absence.[23] The second took place at the Sports Arena in Los Angeles, with Maulana Karenga, a former Afro American Association colleague of Newton and founder of the Black nationalist US Organization, and local pastor Thomas Kilgore replacing Dellums. A three-thousand-strong crowd, including six FBI informants and one agent, observed matters.[24]

The Black Panther lauded the Oakland rally as the "first liberated rally ever held in Babylon," but the speeches suggested tensions between its speakers.[25] Bobby Seale reminded the audience of the BPP's history and Newton's centrality to the African American struggle.[26] Pandemonium followed al Amin's address, which included crowd-pleasing swipes at Thurgood Marshall, Lyndon Johnson, and George Wallace before musing on the potential of a Black-led rainbow alliance of the dispossessed.[27] Anointed prime minister of Afro-America, Ture approached the lectern resplendent in a dashiki. His sartorial choice to eschew the traditional BPP uniform for attire more associated with Pan-Africanism underscored his philosophical distance from his new comrades, reinforced by an apocalyptic speech that gave little indication of his sympathies for the BPP's program beyond his support for Newton's release. Ture stressed the value of Black nationalism, concluding to a standing ovation, "The major enemy is the honky and his institutions of racism."[28] Schooled in the fissiparous atmosphere of leftist and civil rights organizations, Ture was a wily political operator, which is perhaps why he insisted that the BPP's ideology was "up for grabs" in 1968.[29] This comment exemplifies the struggles the BPP faced in trying to engage with other radical political groups.[30]

The speeches in Los Angeles reinforced the sense that the BPP was enmeshed in a struggle for the future of Black radicalism in California. While praising Newton as a "symbolic figure," Karenga echoed Ture in asserting that only nationalism offered the Black population a legitimate political ideology, before declaring: "Let's talk about how to get white people fighting each other.... Let them shoot each other... and after... we will have a better world."[31] Jamil Abdullah al Amin raised laughter that was loud enough even for the FBI to notice when he pondered, "The only thing that Huey Newton is guilty of, perhaps, is that he didn't tell me he was going down on the honkies that day." After repeating some of the themes of his Oakland speech, he concluded nihilistically, "We say freedom or death. Fuck it. Black Power, brother."[32] According to the FBI, Ture's speech was similarly reiterative aside from a suggestion that his audience prepare themselves to kill police in retribution should Newton be executed.[33]

The birthday galas, then, reveal the inconsistency in the public messages associated with the BPP early in the Free Huey campaign. Unable to dictate the content of their speeches, it needed to accept Ture and Karenga on their own terms. Observers such as the FBI and the press who sought to emphasize internecine disputes thus gathered useful material. The rallies also intensified police repression. Within one week Bobby Seale was arrested and charged with conspiracy to commit murder, and numerous other activists were stopped and searched, prompting Newton to mandate that all BPP members "acquire the technical equipment to defend their homes and their dependents."[34] Meanwhile, Eldridge Cleaver's *Soul on Ice* became an instant sensation, selling hundreds of thousands of copies and confirming Cleaver and the BPP's status as international icons.[35]

In January Newton gave his last interview without Charles Garry ready to correct any missteps. This meant the interviews could take place in the courthouse's attorney-client room rather than in the dramatic yet insalubrious setting of Newton's cell. Presenting him in less suggestive surroundings reframed Newton not as a criminal but as a free man, reinforcing his claims to innocence. Illustrating the BPP's rise, Newton's interviewers in March included KPFA, his comrade Eldridge Cleaver, and Joan Didion, whose spare journalistic style was attracting major attention. Didion's piece appeared in the *Saturday Evening Post* on May 4, raising Newton to another level of celebrity while being perfectly calibrated to appeal to the *Post*'s genteel readership.[36] Didion lamented Newton's preference for political statements over personal confession. "Almost everything . . . had that same odd ring of being a 'quotation,' a 'pronouncement,'" she sniffed before suggesting that she considered Newton little more than an "educational fun-fair machine . . . where pressing a button elicits great thoughts on selected subjects."[37]

> I kept wishing that he would talk about himself, hoping to break through the wall of rhetoric, but he seemed to be one of those autodidacts for whom all things specific and personal present themselves as minefields to be avoided even at the cost of coherence, for whom safety lies in generalization.[38]

Her desire to engage Newton—a man she had not previously met—at a highly personal level merely reveals Didion's youthful sense of white privilege. Similarly, her reference to Newton's education and its impact on his articulacy presents the interview as an exercise in condescension. Rather than celebrating Newton's determination to overcome the failures of Oakland's school system, it instead reinforced her readers' prejudices even as it brought the world of the BPP further into the suburban homes of middle America.

By May 1968, such was the BPP's repute that *Ramparts* editor David Welsh proposed that the Newton trial would "rock this rotten system to its foundations."[39] The BPP's newspaper went further still, asserting that the trial "marks the end of history."[40] Even Eldridge Cleaver's arrest in April did not contain the campaign: Seale and Kathleen Cleaver replaced him as spokespersons, while information flowed from the BPP through press conferences, *The Black Panther*, and flyers plastered across the Bay Area. The BPP even developed a speaker's kit, offering bite-sized histories of the party and its jailed leaders, and information on the BPP's various legal cases and their significance. This was designed to ensure that each BPP speaker could detail not only the trial but also a plethora of cases, ranging from police brutality to low-level harassment, involving BPP members, thus reinforcing Newton's position as a symbol of a wider system of repression.[41] Soon afterward, Seale compared Newton to Jesus, insisting that Newton "laid his life on the line" for "twenty million black people."[42] He also slyly indicted the American government, suggesting that Newton's life, like Jesus's, hung on the whims of a capricious legal system. Here began Newton's mythologization.

On the trial's July 15 opening, the *San Francisco Chronicle* described an "awesome outburst" of popular sentiment and a police baton charge outside the Alameda County Courthouse.[43] Thousands of supporters alongside the press and the FBI watched hundreds of chanting and fist-raising Panthers taking drills, presenting the BPP as a highly organized and regimented unit while making the courthouse appear occupied by ordinary Oaklanders. The demonstration reached fever pitch when Bob Avakian scaled a flagpole and was arrested on his return to earth with Old Glory, while the crowd chanted "Burn it!" hoping to outrage watching patriots.[44]

Unfortunately, the BPP could not maintain the momentum. Numbers dwindled and the demonstrations ceased before the end of the month.[45] The recently bailed Cleaver, meanwhile, met with the Cuban and Tanzanian delegations at the United Nations and promised that he and other BPP members were prepared to die "before seeing Huey Newton sentenced to death."[46] Following the broadening of the BPP's vision in the wake of Bobby Seale's arrest, the BPP called for UN observers to be placed in all American cities that had Black ghettos. "This action is necessary," the BPP newspaper stated, "because the racist power structure of this imperialist country is preparing to unleash a war of genocide against her black colonial subjects." Citing Malcolm X, the BPP promised to resist "by any means necessary, including revolutionary armed struggle. The hour of showdown for racist-imperialist America has dawned. The case of Huey P. Newton will be the spark that will set this showdown in motion."[47] These warnings were echoed elsewhere. The *Washington Post* mused that the trial could create the first martyr of the American Left since Sacco and Vanzetti.[48] The *Berkeley Barb*, in full apocalyptic mode, presented the trial as a pivotal moment in history, representing "life or death for the United States."[49] Newton thus became the preeminent symbol of revolution as the country reeled from the assassinations of Dr. Martin Luther King and Robert F. Kennedy.

Such extravagant language had its roots in BPP rhetoric. In February SNCC's James Forman outlined a taxonomy of retaliation should any militant leaders be assassinated: for his own death, he considered a fair price to be the destruction of ten "war factories," fifteen police stations, thirty power plants, one southern governor, two mayors, and five hundred police. "And I tell you this," he promised, "the sky is the limit if you kill Huey Newton," a slogan he repeated at February's Oakland rally.[50] By April, placards wielded by Newton sympathizers across the Bay Area read: "Free Huey, or the Sky's the Limit," and as Newton's jury considered its verdict, *The Black Panther*'s cover headline read similarly.[51]

The slogan was deceptively complex. "Free Huey" immediately condemned the trial. For the BPP, a jury of Newton's peers—people of "similar economic, social, religious, geographical, environmental, historical and racial background[s]"—was impossible to compile.[52] Thus, a guilty verdict would merely reflect a racist, iniquitous legal system. Bobby Seale explained that any claim for a fair trial represented "old white liberal[ism]" and an "endors[ement of] continued racism," a subtle swipe at the faith of the mainstream civil rights movement in using the law to address Black inequality. Kathleen Cleaver was even blunter: "Asking whether a black man can get a fair trial in America is tantamount to asking if a Jew could get a fair trial in Nazi Germany."[53]

"The sky's the limit," meanwhile, suggested that the BPP was prepared to use any means necessary to obtain justice, referencing the BPP's willingness to present arms in public. When pressed, though, Panthers exploited the statement's ambiguity, stating that "the sky's the limit" referred to their willingness to go to the highest court in the land to ensure Newton's liberty.[54] This echoed Charles Garry's courtroom strategy, in which he called Dr. J. Herman Blake of University of California Santa Cruz to testify about the gulf between the literal and metaphorical meanings of BPP rhetoric. Blake outlined the linguistic concept of signifying, a strategy often used by Black Americans in which one talks about one idea while having a different idea in mind. Blake noted that a group of young men might talk of a "fine day" when an attractive woman passes, to signify appreciation of the woman's beauty.[55] Applied to "the sky's the limit," signifying suggests that the BPP might not have apocalypse in mind. This claim rests on shaky foundations, however. The BPP considered the California judicial system to be racist, unfair, and unrepresentative. Nothing suggests that Supreme Court justices were any less so. Meanwhile, elsewhere, Seale promised that, should Newton not be freed, then "the sky is the limit around the world," including locations outside the Supreme Court's jurisdiction. Similarly, Cleaver told the *New York Times* that the BPP would do "anything within our power" to keep Newton alive.[56]

As this suggests, the slogan existed to alarm observers and rally supporters amid the revolutionary atmosphere of the time. It tapped into observers' fears of Black Power and supporters' desire to act against oppression. Allied to the press coverage of the rallies and the trial, it suggested that the BPP was tremendously powerful and presented the Panther sympathizers inside the courtroom as the tip of a revolutionary iceberg. It simultaneously transformed Newton into a martyr-in-waiting. Finally, following the chaotic Democratic National Convention and the third phase of the Tet Offensive wreaking havoc in Vietnam, the BPP's statement both exploited and contributed to a tense national atmosphere.

In court, Newton faced three charges: murdering Frey, assaulting Heanes with a deadly weapon, and kidnapping Dell Ross, who claimed that two men commandeered his car after the shooting. Garry moved to relocate the trial to the Oakland Civic Auditorium to maximize viewing opportunities for the public, and then to quash Newton's 1964 conviction for assault with a deadly weapon on the grounds that Newton had not received proper legal representation. Garry was fearful of two repercussions from this conviction: that the felony would influence the jury's approach to Newton, and that the prosecution would argue that Newton was on parole on October 28. Both motions were denied.[57]

Garry's subsequent tactic followed immediately. In the voir dire process, attorneys ask potential jurors about their understanding of issues related to the case, to compile a balanced and hopefully neutral jury. In theory, this should exclude anybody who might have decided on the accused's guilt or had personal ties to involved parties. In actuality, defense and prosecution used it to build a jury that they hoped would be advantageous to them. Garry attacked the unrepresentativeness of the jury system, raising motions that challenged the lack of Black members of the jury panel and highlighted the iniquitous and insidious nature of American racism. Using the findings of his research team, led by his cocounsel Fay Stender, which concluded bluntly, "America remains a racist society," he revealed that Alameda County voter rolls did not represent the local population, which was a consequence of the low numbers of registered African American voters. Building on the BPP's denunciation of the jury process, he argued that Newton was "virtually a stranger" to jurors who simply could not understand the circumstances that shaped him.[58] Garry also pointed to the Kerner Commission, which stated that white racism was a central cause of recent urban unrest, and to the impact of continued police harassment of the BPP since Newton's arrest. He later noted bitterly that, of the hundreds of potential jurors, none had read the Kerner Report and only one had even read about it. In a further tactic, Garry argued that the voir dire process was problematic, because attorneys did not receive enough time to discover whether potential jurors harbored racial prejudice. All his motions were denied.[59] Expecting this outcome, Garry's team prepared 290 questions for the jurors, ranging from questions about the BPP and Black Power to fair housing and the John Birch Society. They hoped to compel the judge to dismiss overtly unfriendly jurors for bias, thus reserving their twenty peremptory challenges for subtler jurors. It had the corollary benefit of reminding everybody that American racism lay at the trial's core.[60]

As if to confirm Garry's contention, the prosecuting assistant district attorney, Lowell Jensen, raised peremptory challenges against many Black members of the pool. Garry responded by insisting that the court record each juror's race, not least because he knew that a recent case against five Black men was declared a mistrial after the prosecution attempted to prevent any Black jurors being selected. Jensen also challenged jurors who lived in Berkeley because of the city's reputation for radical politics, and any juror who had serious reservations about the death penalty.[61] The Jensen-Garry battle proved to be a case study of contrasting approaches to criminal trials. Colder and more methodical than the flamboyant Garry, Jensen rarely indulged in repartee.[62]

To reinforce his team's contention that a fair trial was impossible, Garry used all his peremptory challenges. Using less would have constituted tacit approval of the jury and thus of its fairness. In using them up, he bolstered the political angle of his defense, which might become important should he need to appeal a guilty verdict. That Jensen used only fifteen of his added weight to this argument. Garry excused for cause the one person who admitted to being racist, alongside anybody who objected to Black Power; Jensen meanwhile rejected those who approved of Black Power. Typically, however, potential jurors offered bland, indifferent, and often ignorant answers to questions about race. Garry rejected suggestions that this was because his questions were too blunt, arguing that he wanted to prompt listening potential jurors to engage with the broader issue of white racism—including their own—*before* they answered for themselves. The jury eventually included David Harper, a Black Bank of America employee, and eleven other jurors including one Japanese American man, two Latina women (of seven women on the jury), and one Cuban immigrant, all of whom gave noncommittal answers to Garry's questions. For the Berkeley sociologist Robert Blauner, this proved that it was "perfectly acceptable" for people with "total ignorance and indifference to racial matters ... to judge the case of a Black militant leader." Accordingly—and damningly—"the type of person that is held up as ideal for a democratic citizenry—the concerned, knowledgeable, and politically active citizen—had the worse chance of all to become a final juror."[63]

At the trial's opening, Judge Friedman weakened Newton's case by decreeing that Newton's 1964 conviction constituted a felony and could be referenced if Newton testified. Jensen opened by arguing that Newton knew that LaVerne Williams's car contained some marijuana. Since this was a parole violation, Newton had a motive to give a false identity and resist arrest. By contrast, during his two-hour opening statement, Garry outlined Newton's biography and the circumstances that produced the BPP. He sketched the BPP's philosophy, in particular its approach to armed self-defense, and read the Ten-Point Platform and Program, before contending that the OPD deliberately targeted Newton because of these beliefs. Frey, he argued, stopped Newton's car hoping to fabricate a confrontation. He did not discuss Newton's arrest.[64] This tactic had the desired impact on at least one observer. Gilbert Moore, covering the trial for *Life* magazine, remembered thinking: "I'll bet a million dollars you shot John Frey. . . . [But] I hope to God he did shoot him."[65]

In the witness box, Frey's autopsy surgeon confirmed that Frey died from a shot from the rear that passed through his right lung before exiting his upper chest. Heanes recalled Frey asking Newton to exit his car and claimed that Newton started shooting when he and Frey were toward the rear of Frey's vehicle. This contradicted his grand jury testimony, which stated that Newton attacked Frey on being asked to leave the car. Heanes said that he was shot before he noticed that Frey and Newton were wounded, that he shot at Newton with his left hand, and that he was then shot in the chest. To the grand jury, he reported that Newton shot Frey in the back as Frey was falling to the ground. In cross-examination, Garry simply asked Heanes whether he shot Frey. Heanes revealed that he did not remember firing his gun twice and that he concentrated more on Frey and Newton than he did McKinney.[66] The former fact suggested that the pain might have impaired Heanes's cognition; the latter implied that he was aware of Frey's recklessness and Newton's reputation, or else he would have followed procedure and concentrated on McKinney. Garry and Newton then acted out Heanes's impression of the tussle, to demonstrate that Heanes could have shot Frey, before Heanes reiterated that he did not remember seeing Newton holding a gun. To foment doubt in the jurors' minds about who was present, Garry suggested that an unknown short man fired a gun. Heanes did not recall seeing this man. Adding to the confusion, Heanes failed to identify the color of the coat that Newton was wearing and agreed that he could not be impartial. Garry then wondered why neither officer frisked or handcuffed Newton, despite knowing that he occasionally carried firearms, and probed Heanes on his failure to follow protocol. Heanes ultimately confirmed that Frey did not arrest Newton until he refused to comply with the order to exit his vehicle. At no point did they inform Newton of the reason for his arrest: a breach of his constitutional rights.[67]

The prosecution hid the potentially most damaging witness, the Black bus driver Henry Grier, until the trial's first day. He had already given police a sworn statement claiming that, after turning his bus around to begin his eastbound route along Seventh Street, he saw Newton reach into his jacket and shoot Frey twice.[68] Rather than pursuing the unlikely argument that Grier was a racist, Garry focused on detail in a three-hour cross-examination. It revealed major discrepancies between Grier's testimony and his statement, including his estimated distance from the incident, his descriptions of Newton, the way in which Newton retrieved his gun, the hand with which Heanes shot his gun, and how Frey fell to the floor. More suspiciously, his description of Newton's clothes shifted from a light jacket (which matched the description in the transcripts of police radio dispatches) to a dark jacket and a light shirt, which reflected the color of the clothing collected as evidence. He also stated that streetlights lit the scene. None were present in October. Garry provided evidence that Grier tended to run his buses ahead of schedule, suggesting that he passed the scene before Frey apprehended Newton, before concluding that the police induced Grier to change his testimony.[69] Although Garry had no concrete evidence, the mere suggestion of manipulation pointed to the shadows a racist police department cast over the case. One unasked question was as important: if Grier was so close to a violent incident, why did he endanger his passengers by slowing down?

After Grier, several police witnesses confirmed that Williams's car contained a miniscule amount of marijuana. Dell Ross, who testified to the grand jury as the sole witness to his alleged kidnapping, followed. He invoked the Fifth Amendment, confirming only that he lived in Oakland and owned a car. As Garry recalled, "pandemonium broke out." Ross's attorney, Douglas Hill—who worked with a friend of Fay Stender—argued that, were his client to testify, he would incriminate himself and thus be considered an accessory after the fact to Frey's murder.[70] After a day's recess, Judge Friedman granted Ross immunity, but Ross kept quiet until Jensen and Friedman pushed him to declare that he could not remember the events, a position that rendered him immune from contempt of court. Ostensibly to refresh his memory, and over Garry's strenuous objections, Jensen then read out Ross's testimony. This ensured the jury knew its contents, even though it would be struck from the official record. Here Ross testified that two men jumped into his car and told him to drive to Thirty-Second and Chestnut (although it appears that Ross dropped them at Twenty-Sixth and Adeline). During the drive, one apparently said, "You shot two dudes." Jensen glossed over the discrepancy between this and Ross's police statement, which stated that the other man admitted to the shooting. Garry responded in cross-examination by playing a recording of his own July 28 interview with Ross. Here, Ross told Garry that he went along with the prosecutor's suggestions at the grand jury hearing because he feared prosecution for some parking tickets. He said that he did not see a gun in Newton's hands and that Newton did not speak in the car. Newton was acquitted of kidnapping—Garry's first major victory.[71]

The director of Oakland Police's crime laboratory, John Davis, testified next. Prior to the trial, he confirmed to Garry's team that Frey was shot three times in the front with regular velocity bullets, and twice with special high-velocity bullets at short range from the back, one of which killed him. These were bullets that Frey habitually used and were in his gun belt. Since Heanes was never as close to Frey, logic suggests that Newton shot Frey in the back. Frey's other wounds came either from Heanes's gun or an automatic 9mm weapon that was not used by the police, and like Frey's was never recovered. Police at the scene found one 9mm bullet embedded in Williams's car, and two 9mm casings and a live 9mm round inside. Given that there were numerous twenty-four-hour bars and restaurants, brothels, and a pool hall nearby, this was enough for Garry's extra shooter theory, even though Ross told him that he saw a gun in McKinney's belt during his supposed kidnapping.[72]

Davis acknowledged that Frey's gun had shot the bullet that wounded Heanes in the knee and another that became lodged in Williams's car. He also accepted that Heanes most likely shot Newton in the stomach. He reasoned that, had Frey shot him, Newton could not have wrestled the gun away.[73] The lack of concrete testimony suggests multiple possibilities. The tussle might have prompted Heanes to shoot, wounding Frey and thus allowing Newton to seize the gun before using Frey as a shield. Equally, Newton might have taken the gun before Heanes shot him. That Heanes had been shot in the right arm suggests that he was either an exceptional gun handler with his weaker hand or he shot Newton before shooting Frey with his weaker hand. Adding to the uncertainty, Davis affirmed that no tests had been conducted to ascertain whether Newton had fired a gun and that Newton's lawbook was not analyzed for fingerprints. Garry here implied that the OPD deliberately overlooked the tests because they knew they would not obtain the desired outcome.[74]

Other prosecution witnesses stated that investigators found less than 0.1 grams of marijuana in Newton's pocket—an amount so small that he would not have been aware of its presence. Newton's probation officer testified that he might have given Newton the impression that his probation expired on October 27.[75] This apparently minor point was crucial. Jensen argued that Newton knew that carrying a weapon or drugs while on probation would result in immediate conviction. He therefore had a motive to resist arrest. Moreover, if he was a felon carrying a concealed weapon, he would automatically be convicted of second-degree murder. Thomas Finch of Kaiser Hospital confirmed that Newton remained handcuffed to the gurney with his hands above his head for five minutes after receiving a tranquilizer dose. A nurse told the BPP that this ran contrary to every piece of medical advice she knew, while Garry privately denounced Finch as a "shit-ass," one of his favorite epithets.[76]

Garry sought to open holes in the prosecution witnesses' accounts and raise questions concerning Frey's relationship with the people he patrolled. He brought to the stand numerous Black Oaklanders who witnessed or suffered Frey's racial abuse. His first eyewitness was a passenger in Grier's bus who testified that he saw a civilian pinned against one of the cars as if a police officer was frisking him and that he heard shots after the bus had passed. Garry asked Newton's passenger, Gene McKinney, whether he shot at Heanes. McKinney took the Fifth Amendment and was jailed for six weeks for contempt. McKinney's nonanswer was enough, Garry hoped, to raise further doubts about the killer's identity, echoing the confusion that surrounded Henry Grier's and Dell Ross's testimonies.[77]

Newton then took the stand. Garry felt that his sincerity and articulacy would endear him to the jury and outweigh Jensen's focus on his past behavior, written statements, and prior convictions. Newton testified that the incident was relatively straightforward until the point at which he was shot. He could make this claim, he said, because Oakland police had stopped him some fifty times since the BPP's formation. He stated that he was wearing a black jacket and white shirt—casting doubts over the accuracy of the police radio description of his clothes—and denied possessing marijuana. He recalled Frey ordering him out of the car, frisking him roughly, then walking him to the patrol car, whereupon Frey manhandled and racially abused him. He remembered being shot before passing out and awakening at Kaiser Hospital, where the police racially and physically abused him. Such a memory lapse is entirely consistent with a form of amnesia that often overcomes individuals during moments of severe trauma.[78]

Jensen's cross-examination brought up Newton's 1964 conviction for stabbing Odell Lee with a deadly weapon, which resulted in six months in prison and three years' probation. Newton confirmed that his parole officer said his parole would expire on October 27. Jensen also referenced the altercation with Eugene Sabatini and other run-ins with local police. Sabatini testified in 1966 that Newton attempted to wrestle his gun away; Jensen hoped that the jury would speculate that Newton attempted to repeat this tactic.[79] He followed this by analyzing Newton's writing, citing "The Correct Handling of a Revolution" and a Sol Stern article about the BPP to suggest that Newton advocated shooting police officers. Jensen then had Newton read his poem "Guns Baby Guns!" after which Newton lamented the poem's poor quality. During the redirect, Garry invited Newton to expand on the BPP's relationship with various Black historical figures before leading him through a short bibliography of the philosophy he had read—prompting a surprised Friedman to question Newton on William James—and talking through the key features of the BPP's California lawbook. He was delighted with Newton's calm performance. Outside the court, Kwame Ture denounced the trial as part of a concerted effort to decapitate a revolutionary movement, suggesting that Garry had successfully melded it with the wider political atmosphere.[80]

Following Jensen's rebuttal witnesses, Garry called J. Herman Blake to the stand. Blake argued that signifying was common in the African American community, enabling Garry to suggest that readers not take Newton's work literally. So "Guns Baby Guns!" did not indicate that a "P-38 will open prison gates."[81] This, Garry hoped, would soften the impact of Panther rhetoric and remind the jury that whites failed to appreciate the contours of Black life in Oakland. Jensen's use of Newton's poetry was therefore another example of the failure of the white power structure to understand the BPP. Garry's final witness was Bernard Diamond, an expert in the relationship between bullet wounds and the brain, who testified that one could easily lose consciousness from a bullet wound to the stomach.[82]

Summing up, Garry implored the jury to assess the evidence dispassionately and ignore Jensen's attempts at deception. He demonstrated that Newton could never have concealed the gun that shot Frey in his jacket pockets. He argued that the police were so desperate to convict that they were prepared to plant marijuana on Newton to create a motive for violently resisting arrest. He demolished Grier's testimony before denouncing Heanes's refusal to meet him prior to testifying as another shameful example of police malfeasance. Positioning Newton's lawbook at the case's core, he claimed that Newton could not have wielded both the book and a pistol in his right hand, as Heanes and Grier suggested. The lawbook challenged the logic of their claim that Newton whirled around and started shooting before he was shot. After all, if he were knowingly breaking the law by carrying a concealed weapon, why would he have carried a lawbook at all? Garry then questioned why Frey did not handcuff such a dangerous man. He denounced the prosecution's case as a "diabolical" attempt to railroad an innocent man whom he compared to Jesus Christ and concluded expansively: "White America, listen! The answer is not to put Huey Newton in the gas chamber. . . . The answer is to wipe out the ghetto, the conditions of the ghetto, so that black brothers and sisters can live with dignity."[83]

Contrastingly, Jensen saw little relevance in the lawbook, since it was entirely plausible that Newton dropped it before shooting Frey. He denied manipulating Grier and outlined the consistencies linking Grier's and Heanes's testimonies. Judge Friedman instructed the jury that they could convict Newton for first- or second-degree murder, or for voluntary manslaughter. They could also choose to acquit and were to consider whether Newton's 1964 conviction constituted a prior felony.[84] During their deliberations, they asked to see the transcript of Grier's police statement. Once a copy was matched with the recording, Garry's team noticed an odd alteration: "I didn't get a clear picture, clear view of his face," became "I did get a clear picture."[85] Syntactic infelicity notwithstanding, it changed little since Newton accepted that he was present. Yet it transformed the trial, confirming that the police had manipulated sworn statements. Garry's team played the recording for the media, prompting Friedman to order the transcript corrected.[86]

Despite such indications that an acquittal was possible, the jury returned a verdict of voluntary manslaughter. Garry denounced it as "chickenshit," stating that either Newton shot Frey and was therefore guilty, or he did not and therefore was not guilty. Even when his outrage subsided, Garry maintained that the decision was inconsistent. That the jury concluded there was insufficient evidence to convict Newton of wounding Heanes added to the confusion. Newton urged readers of *The Black Panther* to forgive the jury and called on the Black community to wage a political, judicial, and publicity war while refraining from violent retribution, implicitly rejecting the "sky's the limit" promise. Harper later admitted that the jury settled on a compromise to prevent a retrial. None were convinced that Newton was guilty of first-degree murder, but four felt that he was guilty of second-degree murder. Another four desired an acquittal and the final four remained undecided. Harper's efforts brought them all into the fold, ensuring that Newton would not face the death penalty but instead would be subject to California's indeterminate sentencing law.[87]

Amid the shock of the verdict the BPP resolved to continue the Free Huey campaign, spurred perhaps by the reaction of the OPD. Two days after the verdict, two officers offloaded a volley of bullets into the BPP's Grove Street headquarters. The special issue of *The Black Panther* on September 14 retorted that the BPP would free Newton, with a portrait of the BPP leader on the masthead hovering above the "sky's the limit" slogan, with a rifle pictured beneath.[88] The Free Huey campaign then downshifted. With Newton removed to the prison in Vacaville and then San Luis Obispo, Oakland-based demonstrations lacked a focal point. Consequently, the BPP shifted focus to Newton's absence, mythologizing his role in the party's creation.[89] The desired impact was manifold. It presented Newton as a martyr and ensured that he remained in the minds of members and supporters. His physical absence paradoxically became the basis for his omnipresence, not least because his image adorned *The Black Panther*'s masthead each week, his profile eerily echoing Alberto Korda's image of Che Guevara. Shot from below and lit from the left, both men look sternly outward, suggestively to the viewer's left, and both sport berets, Guevara's trademark headgear.

While the FBI tried to prevent the rise of a Black messiah, the BPP attempted to render Newton the BPP's driving intellectual force, issuing a number of his writings in various radical publications.[90] Newton's prison writings might therefore be compared to Dr. Martin Luther King's "Letter from Birmingham Jail," disseminated as a tool through which to undermine the prevailing justice system while ensuring that jail did not remove the writer from the struggle. They demonstrate that the system had not beaten him and that his incarceration was only a temporary hiatus. Supporters could draw sustenance from his continued determination to fight while Newton himself had something to focus on during the long hours of solitary confinement. As important, such work burnished his intellectual credentials. While feted in radical circles for his activism, Newton was not renowned as an intellectual. Missives such as "Executive Mandate Number One" and "The Correct Handling of a Revolution"—both written before his conviction—confirm this as an underestimation. The first remains the greatest demonstration of the BPP's rhetorical brilliance. It positioned the BPP within a centuries-long, worldwide struggle against white supremacy before noting bitterly the failure of nonviolent protest during the 1960s. After drawing this dystopian tableau, it offers a stark, Fanonist conclusion: armed resistance was the only remaining option. "The Correct Handling of a Revolution," meanwhile, focused on the importance of the vanguard party to the revolution and urged readers to heed Fanon's *The Wretched of the Earth*.[91] A further sequence of publications allowed Newton to develop a broader platform for the BPP and new directions for it to pursue. His writings thus helped ensure that he lived up to his billing as a central figure in the African American struggle.

In February 1969 Berkeley's community theater hosted a birthday rally for over two thousand supporters who heard a recorded message from Newton promising a new offensive that would bring about the revolution. The BPP's friend, the Reverend Earl Neil, opined that the empty wicker chair onstage symbolized not only Newton's absence but the absence of any meaning in society without Newton.[92] Neil's mythmaking helped deepen the BPP's attempt to render Newton a living martyr. Where the empty wicker chair at the 1968 galas was an ominous vision of what might occur should the campaign fail, in 1969 the chair represented both Newton's physical absence and his omniscient, almost transcendent presence. By 1969 his apotheosis continued to give the BPP purpose but also ironically detached him from his own humanity. He was no longer capable of error, doubt, or vacillation. Such panegyrics were not confined to the BPP. In April 1969 New Left activist Stew Albert wrote, "Huey's greatness can not [sic] be locked up.... He took the best thoughts of the greatest minds the century has known and summed it up in a law book, a shot gun and a ten-point program.... Huey is a generator, the purest light of freedom our generation has produced."[93] This lauding was to have a major impact on Newton's postprison life.

Meanwhile, Newton's appeal bore fruit thanks to three technicalities: (1)

Friedman had not instructed the jury that Grier's "didn't" testimony had been a correction; (2) Jensen should not have read Ross's grand jury testimony in court; (3) Friedman should have instructed the jury that it could consider the notion that Newton was functionally unconscious and thus unaware of his actions when he shot Frey, and not simply operating under diminished responsibility.[94] Newton therefore qualified for a retrial for manslaughter.

Newton's official response was telling. While expressing gratitude to his legal team, he announced that popular opinion, expressed largely through the BPP's public actions, compelled the court to reverse his conviction. As important, his release did not constitute freedom: "I'm being transferred for institutional convenience, as they say, from maximum security to minimum security."[95] Freedom, he suggested, could only begin with the release of all African American political prisoners; moreover, as Malcolm X argued, America was for its Black population the prison. Indeed, the *New York Times*'s Earl Caldwell noticed something that might have chilled the BPP: during the trial, hundreds of Panthers marched in the streets; by August 5, 1970, significant numbers were in prison or dead.[96]

Two retrials proved inconclusive, leading Jensen to drop the case. Newton was free to move on, but questions remain about Frey's death. Prior to the retrials, Ed Keating published his account of the trial. *Free Huey* concluded that somebody fired a third gun during the incident. The jury's theory about the order of events also contains two major problems. David Harper told Gilbert Moore that the jury thought Heanes fired the first shot, after Frey pushed Newton to the floor. Frey then shot at Heanes, thinking that he was another aggressor. Newton took advantage to wrestle Frey. Heanes shot again, with his left hand, hitting Frey and forcing him to cede his gun to Newton, who then shot him in the back.[97] While outwardly logical, this does not account for the trajectory of the bullet that wounded Newton, which suggests that he was not on the floor but either standing or possibly falling, and that a wounded Newton rose from a prone position to wrestle Frey. Adding to the mystery, twenty years later, David Hilliard revealed that Dell Ross dropped McKinney and Newton near his house. Inside, Hilliard stripped Newton of his shirt and jacket and deposited him at Kaiser Hospital. After conferring with Eldridge Cleaver, he burned the clothes. Hilliard's memory might be faulty here, since John Davis spotted bullet holes in the front and back of Newton's shirt. He also noted a hole in the front of Newton's jacket that corresponded to the hole in Newton's shirt but could not be certain that it was large enough for a .38 bullet. A button that fell off Newton's jacket at the scene was similar to those that remained in the jacket.[98]

Such tangled memory simply amplifies the reasonable doubts that swirl around John Frey's death. These doubts, coupled with the police's determination to execute Newton, led the OPD to overplay its hand. The evidence that remains is perhaps enough for a conviction of voluntary manslaughter (although Newton's consciousness of his actions remains moot). Jensen and the police, however, set about gathering enough circumstantial and potentially false testimony to push for murder. This campaign ultimately worked to Garry's advantage, allowing him to deconstruct the prosecution's case for premeditation while wrapping the trial within a wider conspiracy against the BPP. As this suggests, the attempt to railroad Newton was part of an OPD campaign to destroy the BPP, which began as soon as the BPP began patrolling the police. Garry's defense might not have convinced the jurors of Newton's innocence, but it placed Newton's trial firmly within the BPP's political crusade, just as the Free Huey campaign built the party to hitherto unimagined significance. Meanwhile, J. Edgar Hoover plotted the FBI's next move, telling his agents that Newton's release "offers excellent opportunity for effective counterintelligence."[99]

CHAPTER NINE

The FBI and the BPP

Any assessment of the FBI's relationship with the BPP must begin with J. Edgar Hoover's instruction to agents in September 1970: "[The] purpose of counterintelligence action is to disrupt the BPP *and it is immaterial whether facts exist to substantiate the charge.*"[1] Hoover's determination to destroy the BPP overrode any consideration for upholding the Constitution, protecting the American people, and indeed facts themselves. The BPP was the target of 233 out of a total 295 FBI COINTELPRO activities that were part of its campaign against "Black Extremists."[2] Hoover's missive came in the wake of Richard Nixon's secret attempt to broaden the FBI's ability to engage in counterintelligence. The so-called Huston Plan would legalize break-ins, wiretapping, mail interception, and widespread use of informants. Even though the plan was not approved, the FBI continued to engage in such tactics without official sanction, and the BPP was one of its major victims. While the extent of the FBI's monitoring of the party is a boon to generations of historians thanks to its voluminous bureaucratic record and the failure of many FBI officials to destroy their records as per Hoover's orders, its effect on the BPP and its members was unremittingly negative.[3]

The FBI added Newton to its Security Index in May 1967, and within a year the Internal Revenue Service was investigating him.[4] The FBI's interference in the BPP's activities only escalated from there. This operated at almost innumerable levels, from the very basic atmosphere of suspicion that it fomented to the crippling of chapters and loss of lives. The pressure of constant surveillance helped push the BPP toward an almost cultlike internal dynamic where individuals were constantly monitored, had their behavior questioned, and were punished arbitrarily. The FBI's disruption of the BPP contrasts sharply with its failure to infiltrate the Weathermen, a group of white and largely middle-class revolutionaries who were far more reckless and dangerous than the BPP.[5] Numerous factors influenced this, but ultimately, two overrode the others: BPP members offered a forthright critique of American capitalism, and most of all, they were Black.

The BPP suffered infiltration at almost every level. FBI monitoring, for example, revealed the extent of the film producer Bert Schneider's largess, which ran to many thousands of dollars.[6] The FBI obtained records from the BPP's central committee and numerous confidential, high-level meetings, as well as financial records. One example demonstrates the extent of the authorities' reach. In 1992 the presidential candidate Ross Perot claimed that the Vietnamese sent some Black Panthers to kill him in 1969. The head of Dallas police intelligence issued a revealing denial: "It did not happen.... There were only about eight people here that belonged to the Black Panther Party. Two of those people worked for us."[7] Notwithstanding the information they furnished, their mere presence would have influenced the chapter's activities. In San Francisco, meanwhile, a "Black Panther Squad" monitored the BPP's headquarters, recruited low-level informers, and set up a wiretap. Their attempts to interview Panthers rendered no useful information, which says little for their powers of persuasion and much about the loyalty of local BPP members. Illustrating the layers of misinformation that surround FBI sources, one squad member maintained that it was "beyond question" that the FBI's strong stance against the BPP ensured that the BPP never achieved the level of influence it craved. And despite his protestations to the contrary, his superiors in Washington, D.C., claimed an informer at the highest level of the BPP by January 1970.[8]

In the 1970s Charles Garry, Ed Epstein, and Donald Freed engaged in a short dispute over the number of BPP members killed by the police and the FBI, a debate that missed the key point: one was too many.[9] The FBI was implicated in the deaths of at least five key BPP members. While FBI agents might not have pulled the trigger, their fingerprints run throughout the cases surrounding the deaths of Los Angeles Panthers John Huggins and Alprentice "Bunchy" Carter, New Haven's Alex Rackley, and Chicago's Fred Hampton and Mark Clark, their actions running from generating an atmosphere in which suspicion ruled to active subterfuge and incitement. These emblematic events demonstrate how the FBI disrupted the BPP. They also highlight the consequent human costs, extending far into the future, such as the mental health of FBI infiltrator William O'Neal, the paranoia that almost overwhelmed the BPP at various points, the mistrust that corroded many personal relationships, and the ultimate decline of the party amid bitter recriminations.

Los Angeles

The Black Student Union meeting at the University of California Los Angeles campus on a sunny January 17, 1969, was typically raucous. Discussions over the presentation of a new Black studies curriculum had been ongoing for some time. Los Angeles BPP members quarreled with members of a rival organization, US, over the identity of the program's leader. Following the meeting's conclusion, Alprentice Carter, known as Bunchy, noticed an US member threatening a BPP comrade, Elaine Brown. Within seconds of Brown leaving, students scattered as a volley of bullets killed Carter. The short gunfight that followed saw Carter's friend John Huggins mortally wounded. US member Larry Stiner suffered an injury; both he and his brother George surrendered to the police and were later sentenced to second-degree murder and conspiracy, although the evidence upholding their conviction edges toward the circumstantial.[10] According to agent Wesley Swearingen, the FBI intended to stage a drug deal that would provoke the BPP members' deaths, but events on the UCLA campus overtook these plans. The FBI informant Darthard Perry claimed that the shooter, US member Claude Hubert (who disappeared soon afterward), was also an FBI informant. Additionally he claimed that he spotted the Stiners at the local FBI office.[11] FBI agents might not have pulled the trigger—and Perry's claims surrounding Hubert and the Stiners seem fanciful—but the FBI certainly toxified the atmosphere in which the men were killed and helped keep tensions high in the months afterward.

US formed in Los Angeles soon after the Watts Rebellion. Like the BPP, it had roots in the Afro-American Association: its founder, Maulana Ron Karenga, chaired its Los Angeles chapter. Frustrated at the AAA's tendency to talk and not act, like Newton and Seale, he formed his own group.[12] Like the BPP, US maintained a small Black-only membership, demanded community control and campaigned to end the Black community's exploitation by the white man. It forged links with Black student unions and ran political education classes, arguing that class politics merely disguised the real issue at the heart of world politics: racism.[13]

Like the BPP, US laid claim to Malcolm X's self-defense legacy, embodied in its paramilitary wing, the Simba Wachanga. Karenga's philosophy held many echoes of Malcolm X's call for cultural revolution. He emphasized Africa's symbolic meaning and the intellectual legacy it bequeathed, which he thought could unite and inspire Black America.[14] Consciously echoing Malcolm X, US promised that a political revolution would only occur after a revolution in the African American mind and prioritized organizing around African culture. Karenga designed the Nguzo Saba, the Seven Principles of Blackness, to create an alternative cultural milieu for African Americans that did not rely on the institutions and beliefs that undergirded white American life. This was a more overtly nationalist philosophy than anything in the BPP's praxis. It revolved around unity, self-determination, collective work and responsibility, cooperative economics, Black greatness, creativity, and faith in the struggle. For Karenga, cultural activities provided firm foundations for the coming Black American revolution.[15]

Initially, US's relations with the BPP were cordial. Newton appeared at US's first Uhuru Day celebration in August 1967, and the BPP used an Emory Douglas portrait of US supporter Amiri Baraka as a fundraising tool until late 1968 (Baraka's groundbreaking study of jazz music, *Blues People*, remained on BPP reading lists until a similar time). US sponsored and provided security at the BPP's Los Angeles Free Huey rally. Nearly three months later, members of both organizations discussed how to quell racial tension in Los Angeles in the wake of Dr. Martin Luther King's assassination.[16]

Yet relations deteriorated. Some of the causes were philosophical. Fanon wrote compellingly of the shortcomings of nationalist parties in the anticolonial struggle and was particularly critical of their indifference toward attempting to transform economic relations, not least because of their middle-class leanings, a position that profoundly influenced the BPP's critique of Karenga. Bunchy Carter also took inspiration from his former Soledad prison mate, Eldridge Cleaver, in applying Marxist-influenced ideas such as recruiting lumpen men through stressing the BPP's revolutionary credentials.[17] Conversely, Karenga derided the BPP's willingness to forge alliances with white radicals, which he considered a betrayal of the Black movement. He scoffed at the BPP free breakfast and clinic programs, suggesting that the BPP was wasting its resources in providing an alternative option to services provided by state welfare and Medicare. His paradoxical willingness to meet with white authorities such as the Los Angeles Human Relations Commission, meanwhile, created tension. The BPP acidly noted that Karenga considered himself an intellectual who benefited from UCLA's white power structure, and unlike most Panthers, he merely learned street tongue rather than lived a street life, suggesting that class tensions fed into the rivalry.[18] As important, the BPP echoed Fanon's critique of the inability of nationalist leaders to become organic intellectuals in denouncing US for its intellectualized approach. From this perspective, elevating a cultural revolution over a political revolution abstracted and distracted from the realities facing Black America.

Yet these were not the only factors. Both groups held offices in the same corridor in the UCLA campus. Due to his seniority in the local activist network and leadership of the Black Congress umbrella group, Karenga justifiably considered himself preeminent in Los Angeles. According to Elaine Brown, US perceived BPP organizing in Los Angeles as a threat. Adding to the tension, several Los Angeles BPP recruits, including Carter, emerged from a prominent local gang, the Slausons. US, meanwhile, incorporated former members of the rival Gladiators. As such, urban gang culture influenced the organizations' relationship. US naturally envied the BPP's ability to attract media attention, which inevitably influenced African American public opinion. The BPP was jealous of the influence that Karenga held in Black Los Angeles. Its local organizers knew that the party had to outwit Karenga if it was to become the city's dominant force. The BPP had already achieved notoriety for its uncompromising treatment of other local nationalist groups, using intimidation to force the Black Panther Party of Northern California to disband, for example, and BPP operatives similarly threatened a Black Panther Political Party based in Los Angeles. Yet US was quite prepared to stand its ground.[19]

Crucially, one of the BPP's Los Angeles organizers was the FBI informant Earl Anthony, who encouraged the branch to move against US.[20] Meanwhile, near constant distribution of counterintelligence material aggravated relations. In late September 1968 George C. Moore, head of the FBI's racial intelligence division, advised the FBI to accelerate its anti-BPP operations. This, he argued, should involve more investigations, recruitment of informants, and disruption of activities, to lure the BPP into violent actions that would lead to arrests and increase suspicion between BPP leaders at national and local levels. Days later, a memo to FBI agents across the nation ordered them to "submit concrete suggestions as to proposed counterintelligence activity."[21] Two weeks later, the Los Angeles field office reported that the BPP was "out to kill" Karenga following the conclusion of Newton's appeal against his conviction. The office suggested that the FBI write to the BPP indicating that US's youth wing was aware of the assassination plan and was preparing to ambush the BPP's LA leaders. It also hoped to misinform the BPP's Oakland headquarters that the Los Angeles leadership were embezzling BPP funds and had no interest in freeing Newton. Its final suggestions were to submit misinformation to the PFP and Eldridge Cleaver to widen the splits within the BPP and between it and a key ally.[22]

While Hoover worried that overuse of such letters might be counterproductive, he found the suggestion concerning US "appealing" enough to greenlight both it and the plan to create suspicion about the Los Angeles chapter's financial probity. He received the materials for final approval in December. Meanwhile, US infiltrators were expelled from a BPP rally on November 3. According to the FBI, this prompted the BPP to discuss eliminating US outright.[23] Three weeks later, Hoover cheerfully informed his agents that "the struggle ... is taking on the aura of gang warfare with attendant threats of murder and reprisals." He invited field offices across the nation to "submit imaginative and hard-hitting counterintelligence measures aimed at crippling the BPP."[24] According to Darthard Perry, these activities included planting illegal weapons and contraband in BPP offices and framing the BPP activist Elmer "Geronimo" Pratt for murder.[25]

The veracity of the FBI's information concerning an assassination plot will never be confirmed. Yet that is not the point. Hoover's request licensed agents to construct situations that the FBI could exploit. Local agents knew of Hoover's racism and belief that the BPP was little more than a criminal gang. Irrespective of proof, the news that the BPP planned to murder a rival would have delighted Hoover. Local agents would have been able to play on this confirmation bias to earn kudos for creating this situation and gather more resources for further activities. Given also that agents could earn promotions by exploiting such situations, and informers more money from reporting on them (and perhaps embellishing said reports), the organizational culture of the FBI helped create, intensify, and prolong the circumstances that undermined BPP activity in Los Angeles.

At the end of November 1968, using information likely provided by their informers Larry Powell and Darthard Perry, the local FBI office reported that suspicions within the Los Angeles BPP were so high that any new member was suspected of being an US plant. The FBI's San Diego agents, meanwhile, prepared fake letters designed to deepen the BPP-US rift.[26] By January, however, the Los Angeles office discovered that the BPP had retreated from its feuding, in part because it feared that, should it move against him, Karenga's popularity in the local area could rebound on the BPP. On the eve of Huggins's and Carter's deaths, the FBI's Los Angeles agents told Hoover that the only activities they were undertaking were a fake subscription to *The Black Panther*, designed to suggest that the LA chapter was siphoning off funds, and distributing an anonymous letter designed to increase tensions between the BPP and the PFP.[27] Whether these protestations of innocence can be believed is moot—the damage had been done.

The local special agent in charge was somewhat coy in the aftermath of the killings, commenting only that the BPP was now planning to conduct some revenge killings and declining to identify the deaths as "tangible results" of FBI activity.[28] The FBI shifted its attention to interviewing various BPP members, in the hope that this would both disrupt the party's activities and sow more seeds of doubt among the membership about their comrades' integrity, for what could be more suspicious in the wake of the assassinations than a BPP member being invited to talk by a friendly FBI agent?[29] As ever, it would be near impossible for the members concerned to prove that they were *not* conspiring with the FBI, as Alex Rackley later discovered in New Haven.

Aware that any reconciliation would be problematic, since it might enable the rivals to discover the activities of their common enemy, the FBI distributed various cartoons around Los Angeles designed to inflame tensions before whispering to US that the BPP had bombed their San Diego office. Such cartoons depicted US as a cobra looming over various BPP leaders depicted as chickens; another literally placed the BPP in the hands of the local police. This helped scupper BPP-US talks that took place in March, aided by a homophobic cartoon in *The Black Panther* that depicted an egg-shaped Karenga enjoying sex with a fellow US member.[30] San Diego's FBI office continued to exert pressure with anonymous telephone calls spreading misinformation that certain BPP members were FBI agents in disguise. Gleefully, it reported that the city's BPP chapter "was so completely disrupted and so much suspicion, fear, and distrust has been interjected ... that the members have taken to running surveillances on one another in an attempt to determine who the 'police agents' are." The entire membership of the chapter was either in jail or "neutralized."[31]

During January 1969 the FBI in San Diego discovered that a local BPP member was pregnant by a fellow Panther. They suggested to Hoover that the FBI notify her parents and charge the male with statutory rape. By the end of February, with the parents apprised of the situation through an anonymous call, the young mother-to-be was in jail herself, a location where, the FBI maliciously opined, she could receive the correct prenatal care. Within two weeks, the FBI had seized all of the paper records of the local BPP branch. On a more unspeakable level, FBI operative Julius Butler was ordered to attack US member James Doss, which provoked a response from John Stark, an FBI agent in US, to murder the Panther John Savage. Unsurprisingly, by the end of 1969, San Diego Panthers disbanded the chapter.[32]

Tension between the BPP and US peaked again in August 1969. Amid a succession of violent confrontations between the two groups, US members killed the BPP member Sylvester Bell, prompting *The Black Panther* to declare that this proved that US was nothing more than a "division of the fascist police establishment."[33] An Emory Douglas cartoon on the cover of the newspaper was even blunter: as a pig dangled a bone wrapped in dollar bills, a Sambo-fied Karenga, complete with drool and lolling tongue, jumped out of his boots in a vain attempt to grasp the morsels. The pig sneered at Karenga, "Kill Black Panthers. Kill black people"; Karenga responded, "I just want to be to be like you Boss like you." In case readers were unsure of the symbolism, Douglas surrounded the pig with words such as "avaricious businessman; demagogic politician; fascist; racist; slave master; capitalist; degenerate; rapist." Karenga's equivalents included "bootlicker; slave; thug; fascist; murderer; traitor; Uncle Tom; racist; black capitalist; gangster."[34] No rapprochement would be possible.

This did not stop the LAPD, however. Having forced the BPP chapter to divert its resources from social programs through a concerted terror campaign, it launched a major assault on the BPP's Los Angeles headquarters. Eighty LAPD men, half of whom were in the SWAT team, descended on a building that housed fewer than fifteen Panthers at 5:00 a.m. on December 8, initiating a siege that concluded only with the BPP's surrender after four hours of fighting, which included the building being dynamited, tear-gassed, and riddled with bullets. Like their Chicago counterparts who assassinated Mark Clark and Fred Hampton, the LAPD had a floor plan of the BPP's offices that helped them plan their offensive. Staunch defense and some luck saved the lives of numerous LA Panthers, but the outcome was clear: the LAPD would respond brutally to any attempt by the BPP to organize in Los Angeles. That all six of the female Panthers arrested in the wake of the siege were physically injured attests to the LAPD's equal-opportunity brutality.[35]

New Haven

The FBI's ability to manipulate events in Southern California demonstrates that provocateurs could operate with more than a modicum of success within the relatively porous membership of the BPP. Such infiltration helped conjure a climate of suspicion within the BPP that accelerated internal tensions and intensified the stress experienced by members.[36] The murder of BPP member Alex Rackley further illuminates the impact of FBI infiltration and surveillance. The nineteen-year-old was tortured for approximately three days in the BPP's New Haven office, located in local member Warren Kimbro's apartment. Following this ordeal, on May 20, 1969, he was taken to the banks of Connecticut's Coginchaug River. On George Sams's orders, Kimbro and another local BPP member, Lonnie McLucas, shot him and left him to die at the river's edge. Sams had accused Rackley, who joined the party less than a year earlier after relocating from Florida, of being an FBI agent. His crime was apparently his inability to read. Sams was renowned in New York BPP circles for his short temper, violent tendencies, and disregard for rules and regulations. His behavior was so bad that he was expelled and only reinstated following his friend Kwame Ture's intervention. In New Haven he insinuated that Rackley was lying about much more than his reading abilities. Amid the tense atmosphere in the New Haven BPP, liars simply had to be FBI agents.[37] According to Paul Bass and Douglas Rae, Sams "evoked the paranoia" that consumed the BPP. After Ture's intervention to prevent Sams's expulsion, for example, and potentially misled by FBI counterintelligence, Newton accused Ture of being a CIA agent.[38]

By mid-1969 the New Haven chapter was so obsessed with infiltration that attempts to weed out snitches all but paralyzed its activities. Kimbro knew that local police had wiretapped the chapter. He would pretend to wave courteously at the plainclothes officers who sat in a car opposite his house and frequently paused his own telephone calls to say, "Pigs, we know you're listening."[39] The arrival of tough Panthers like Sams and Landon Williams—parachuted in to improve discipline—did little to ease tensions in the chapter: nobody dared question them because they had the authority to expel anybody whom they suspected. Soon after their arrival, they informed Huggins that they thought Rackley was a spy (although it is possible that they confused him with Alex McKiever, a Cleaver associate in New York's chapter).[40]

The BPP made an audio recording of Sams and Ericka Huggins discussing Rackley's torture soon after it concluded. They said that they outlined their suspicions before Sams aggressively questioned the terrified youngster and started disciplining him. The exhausted Rackley's response to this beating was apparently too cowardly for a Panther. After he stumbled through the Ten-Point Platform and Program, Huggins said, "We began to ask questions with a little force and the answers came out after a few buckets of hot water."[41] This water was not merely hot. It severely scalded Rackley, prompting him to give the names of various infiltrators in the New York BPP. At no point did his interlocutors attempt to work through his evidence or promise to corroborate it. Instead, Sams and Huggins appeared relatively satisfied at learning that so many New York Panthers were informers, perhaps because this confirmed their preexisting suspicions.

Immediately on discovering that Rackley was a BPP member, the local police turned to their informers. Within two days they raided the BPP's office and arrested Kimbro. Raids were also conducted on numerous BPP chapters nationwide. Tipped off as to its location, the police confiscated the murder weapon before arresting Kimbro's wife and numerous other Panthers, but not Sams. After being apprehended, McLucas accused Kimbro of being the killer.[42] Even though the police possessed no evidence that explicitly linked him to Rackley's death, Bobby Seale was arrested. Seale apparently visited the chapter during Rackley's torture but did not definitely witness anything. En route to New Haven for trial, Seale shared a fifth of whisky with New Haven's head of police intelligence, who claimed to be impressed enough by Seale's bonhomie to declare the Panther's innocence. After arriving in Connecticut, Seale received letters from the FBI intimating that the BPP was about to abandon him now that Newton had returned to active duty. So desperate was the FBI to put him behind bars that they offered Kimbro a place in the witness protection program in return for testimony that would prove Seale's guilt. Luckily, Kimbro was more interested in truth telling.[43]

In court Sams continued his counterintelligence campaign, claiming to the jury—which surprisingly included five African Americans—that Seale ordered Rackley's death and told other Panthers that he would have killed the man had Kimbro not. This mendacious testimony fell apart under cross-examination. The jury took two hours to confirm Seale's innocence. Huggins's decision took a further five days, with her testimony turning on her admission that she felt unable to speak out because of the power of men in the BPP. Only two jurors considered her guilty, leading to the judge declaring a mistrial and commenting that it would now be virtually impossible to select an unbiased jury.[44] Huggins's lawyer commented that informers and FBI agents riddled the New Haven chapter, further suggesting that Huggins was a victim of a frame-up. Kimbro received a life sentence, reduced to four years in October 1971. Fellow Panthers Rory Hithe and Landon Williams received suspended sentences after pleading guilty to conspiracy. Lonnie McLucas received twelve to fifteen years for conspiracy, but his lawyer filed a writ of habeas corpus, revealing the illegality of a wiretap that produced key evidence. The state decided to free him rather than reveal the methods used to entrap the Panther.[45]

The failed attempt to frame Seale and Huggins was far from the only evidence of police malfeasance in New Haven. The BPP chapter was relocated from Bridgeport in January 1969; within weeks it was under FBI surveillance, and within four months it was on its last legs. Police activity extended from sharing misinformation with the local press and various activists to allowing an informant's car to transport Rackley to his death. The police remained a step ahead when the BPP attempted to resurrect the New Haven chapter after the trial, and they instantly began monitoring the new leader, Doug Miranda, even sending a welcome party to kick down his apartment's front door. This was despite the San Francisco FBI reporting that BPP operations in Connecticut would be solely educational and propagandist. Unsurprisingly, Miranda could not reinvigorate the chapter.[46]

Sams's ability to win a position of considerable power demonstrates the BPP's instability during its rapid expansion. By 1969, aware of constant FBI monitoring, the party kept telephone calls to a minimum.[47] Chapters consequently held significant autonomy and communicated relatively rarely. The absence of a robust vetting system for new members also enabled Sams to ascend to a leadership role. The New Haven branch's brief period of growth coincided with a purge of members across the country, when the chapter—and indeed the national organization—was riven with interpersonal suspicion and paranoia.[48] Sams's domination of New Haven confirms that fear permeated the party. Because Sams was stronger willed, more violent, and more vocal than Rackley, he could define the younger man's characterization to the extent that no other Panthers spoke up for him. It is worth remembering that Sams's violence was itself not unusual. Physical discipline was used in various chapters on a regular basis, from slaps right up to beatings.[49] Ericka Huggins was clearly not in a position to oppose Sams. The branch's macho atmosphere, fueled and exploited by Sams, similarly prevented her from challenging him and gave him more latitude to dominate Rackley's final days.

Bass and Rae argue that there was "one insidious, debilitating effect of efforts like COINTELPRO: widespread, irretrievable suspicion."[50] Kiilu Nyasha, who was briefly a New Haven chapter member, agreed: "You can't take Rackley's murder out of the context of the paranoia that prevailed then."[51] As many social psychologists and historians acknowledge, rumors take on particular currency at times of uncertainty and often offer tempting explanations both of the situation and how to resolve it, filling gaps left when reliable information is absent. They are particularly alluring to people who have little trust in official sources of information.[52] In New Haven the BPP comprised a tightly knit core of fewer than a dozen people, around whom casual members orbited. In a constant state of high alert about police surveillance amid a national obsession with informers and agents provocateurs, and fearful of being accused themselves, members would have been highly susceptible to rumors, especially when the source was such a forceful individual. The police might not have pulled the trigger, but they ensured that all the conditions were present for Sams—who later admitted that he knew Rackley was an innocent scapegoat—to take such reprehensible actions.[53]

Chicago

A February 1969 article in the BPP's newspaper also likely informed events in New Haven. It reported that a man named Derek Phemster tried to infiltrate the BPP's Illinois chapter, toting a letter purportedly from Seale and David Hilliard, and declared he would take the chapter underground. Calls revealed that BPP headquarters knew nothing of him. William O'Neal, Illinois's head of security, questioned him, using unnamed "methods which proved very effective" in forcing Phemster to admit he was an FBI stooge, hinting that torture was a viable tactic for exposing infiltrators.[54] Adding to the depressing nature of this case, O'Neal was himself an FBI agent.

O'Neal's tangential role in Rackley's death was overshadowed by his central role in the most notorious murders of any BPP members: the assassinations of Mark Clark and Fred Hampton. Killed in a police raid of the BPP's Chicago offices in the early hours of December 4, 1969, Clark and Hampton became the most powerful symbols of the baleful impact of the FBI's war on the BPP. Where George Sams's disruption illustrates the extent to which an individual could dominate small chapters, O'Neal's case demonstrates how infiltrators were able to influence even the largest (Illinois's membership numbered over three hundred).[55]

At Mayor Richard Daley's behest, the FBI worked closely with the city's police to hobble the Windy City Panthers. The two shared information weekly, while undercover police observed BPP operations and infiltrated meetings, leading to four raids on the BPP's office in 1969 alone, including an unsuccessful attempt to find Sams. Meanwhile, the FBI recruited local journalist Ronald Koziol to weave a suitable spin on BPP activities. Koziol's tales, more lurid fiction than journalism, included a denunciation of the free breakfast program, an accusation of financial impropriety, and an allegation that the Communist Party funded the BPP.[56]

The FBI recruited O'Neal in 1967 or 1968 after he was involved in a car accident while joyriding. FBI agent Roy Mitchell considered forgetting about the incident but wanted payback. The nineteen-year-old O'Neal, who grew up wanting to be a police officer, became one of the earliest members of the Illinois chapter and almost instantly became security captain despite having no awareness of the party, let alone experience of political organizing. That he rose so quickly reminds us of the BPP's fluidity and its inability to vet recruits amid its rapid expansion. O'Neal also became a bodyguard to Fred Hampton, although Bobby Rush argues that Hampton doubted O'Neal's commitment because he seemed to prefer criminal activity over social programs.[57] His voluminous reports to the FBI meanwhile gave an extensive and intimate view of BPP operations. Somewhat ironically, he was responsible not only for security but also for weeding out informers and provocateurs. To facilitate this work, he even constructed an electric chair for torturing problematic individuals. He also observed negotiations between the BPP and the Black P Stone Nation (then called the Blackstone Rangers), discovering that the latter were prepared to defend their turf with violence, a development that led to the BPP building its own arsenal.[58]

According to O'Neal, the Chicago police escalated its anti-BPP operations after two police officers were killed and eight wounded in a November 1969 gun battle. Although O'Neal insisted that the killer, Jake Winters (who died in the incident), was operating without the chapter's authority, that he was a Panther was enough for the local police to seek revenge.[59] "No Quarter for Wild Beasts," thundered the *Chicago Tribune* two days later. "These murderous fanatics," it opined, "have declared war on society. They therefore have forfeited the right to considerations ordinary violators of the law might claim."[60] Such sentiments echoed the FBI's, which O'Neal discovered when the FBI tasked him with adding as much detail as he could to the floor plans of BPP buildings that he had already provided, including the location of weapons caches and where individual members slept each night. The BPP's members knew by now of the extent of surveillance, noticing cars following them and hearing the telltale "click" of the wiretap every time they used the telephone.[61] Mitchell might not have detailed the plans to O'Neal, but he made clear that a raid was imminent. Fatefully, O'Neal reported that Hampton's abilities as an organizer and leader lay behind much of the strength of the local chapter, and he provided a detailed plan of Hampton's apartment, where the BPP held many of its meetings. After allegedly drugging Hampton to sleep, Chicago police raided the apartment, riddling it with bullets before executing Hampton at point-blank range. Clark was shot five times from a longer distance. Four other BPP members were wounded. The FBI gave O'Neal a bonus of $300 for the "tremendous value" of the information he furnished.[62]

One press photographer snapped smiling Chicago police officers removing Hampton's body on a gurney. Reports suggested that many of their colleagues shared their happiness.[63] Their satisfaction lapsed into complacency, however. They hubristically failed to secure Hampton's apartment for two weeks, enabling the BPP to examine the evidence and invite members of the public to survey the scene. Clearly believing that its authority, links with the press, and ability to dominate the narrative would prevail over the BPP's rival interpretation, it allowed the BPP to transform Hampton's death into a battle that proved ruinous to its reputation.[64] Yet the lapse also confirms the extent to which the police and the FBI could control the narrative of events surrounding the BPP, prompting further questions about police and FBI culpability in other BPP "shoot-outs." The tragedy of Clark and Hampton's deaths was not only their loss but also the confirmation that the BPP was fighting numerous wars on many fronts, often against a whole wing of the federal and state apparatus.

Huey P. Newton told the journalist Mark Lane in September 1970 that he considered Hampton's death an opportunity to rededicate the BPP to the community and to its wider goals. He immediately followed this with an illuminating declaration of intent: "We will not be put in a state of dismay by the loss of a battle or by the murder of a man; *it will only increase our vigilance*, it will only increase our revolutionary fervor and we will fight on until the doom of the oppressor and until the victory of the people."[65] The BPP's rededication to revolution thus also focused on rooting out infiltrators. Such doubling down heightened the tension within party ranks, increased the pressure members experienced, and frayed personal relations.

O'Neal's testimony suggests that the FBI and the Chicago police were unable to inflame tensions between the BPP and the Blackstone Rangers to the extent they did in Los Angeles, in part because of the contrast between two key individuals. "Bunchy" Carter was adept at recruiting brothers off the block because of his Slauson reputation. In Chicago the BPP's membership had roots in Chicago's West and South Sides, including former Vice Lords members, students, former SNCC activists, and others. Hampton was an NAACP veteran with a background in social organizing. He worked assiduously to prevent internecine warfare, even after a BPP member was killed in Rangers territory.[66] Such facts suggest that Chicago's relatively heterogeneous membership was able to overcome tensions that remained as a legacy of members' gang affiliations, and that Hampton's history enabled him to overcome such tensions more easily than Carter. Of course, such skills likely increased the chance that the police would seek to remove him, to increase the likelihood that internecine warfare could surface. Yet their lackadaisical inattention to the murder scene swayed public opinion toward the BPP, limiting the likelihood of such tensions emerging.

The Hampton affair's coda involved further tragedy. By 1990 O'Neal was living under an assumed name. In the early morning of January 15, he was sharing a drink with his uncle Ben Heard, who noticed him acting oddly. At one point, he darted out of the house. A car driver saw him jump onto the nearby Eisenhower Expressway but could not avoid impact. Heard reported that O'Neal was never keen to talk about his past but also that he did not appear suicidal. The Cook County medical examiner's office disagreed.[67] Former BPP member Bobby Rush met O'Neal's death with understandable candor. "I feel no remorse," he said. "He committed a dreadful act."[68]

O'Neal was not merely implicated in Clark and Hampton's deaths, however. He was present when former Chicago police sergeant Stanley Robinson abducted Jeff Beard and went on to murder him in 1972. After Robinson was convicted of violating Beard's civil rights, the family filed suit against O'Neal for failing to prevent Beard's death. Not long after the original legal case concluded, he went into the witness protection program.[69] The personal guilt and the weight of these deaths must have lingered. Yet somehow the staff on a documentary series about the African American freedom struggle managed to convince him to be interviewed about Hampton and Clark's murders. While he spoke of his past using his assumed name to the *Chicago Tribune* in 1984, *The Eyes on the Prize* was a very different consideration. Broadcast nationwide in early 1987, it received universal critical acclaim. Three years later, an eight-part sequel continued the story of African American protest through the 1980s. A laudatory *New York Times* review pointed to O'Neal's interview as a "journalistic coup."[70]

The sixth episode, which heavily featured O'Neal's testimony, was scheduled for broadcast on February 19, 1990.[71] O'Neal would appear on camera, the first time in decades that his face and birth name were matched. One of the staff who witnessed the interview commented that O'Neal showed remorse but considered himself on the side of the angels, which somewhat downplays its content.[72] When asked about remorse, he talked extensively about his anger at the police and his realization that, had he been present, he would likely have been killed as well. "I didn't walk in there with guns. I didn't shoot him," he protested. When asked to return to his feelings about the event, he stuttered, "I can't do it again, I, I just can't.... It just, it won't" before the recording was cut. After recomposing himself, he admitted: "I don't have anything bad to say about [Hampton].... I, I'm sorry that he died like he did. He was, in my opinion, he was murdered by the Chicago Police Department, and I feel bad about that." Recalling that the FBI never asked him to monitor the BPP's social programs, he argued that they were primarily interested in criminal or violent activities. "No," he said, he did not regret the personal costs. Even so, he acknowledged that Hampton's death was a loss, not least because, despite their best efforts, they could not dig up any dirt on him whatsoever.[73] The looming broadcast of this interview, with the publicity that would follow, must be acknowledged when considering O'Neal's state of mind in January 1990. His twenty years living under the weight of the deaths simply increases the evidence that the Chicago police and the FBI cared not a jot for the human costs of their campaign to destroy the BPP.

In 1976 the BPP launched a major legal action against the FBI, the Justice Department, the CIA, and the IRS for conspiracy.[74] Its depositions cited raids of BPP properties in Los Angeles, Chicago, New Orleans, and Kansas City, alongside countless other counterintelligence activities. In 1977 the Cleavers sued the estate of J. Edgar Hoover, several FBI employees, Attorneys General John Mitchell and Richard Kleindienst, and other individuals, alleging deprivation of their human rights. Believing that the COINTELPRO against the BPP was targeted at preventing either Cleaver from becoming a "popular Black leader," the Cleavers argued that counterintelligence material caused the split in the BPP and alleged that the FBI conspired with San Francisco police to attempt to murder Kathleen Cleaver in August 1972.[75] That same year, on hearing that Frank Johnson was to be appointed as the new director of the FBI, Newton requested that the famously liberal judge use his new powers to disclose all the evidence of the FBI's illegal actions against the BPP and make an offer of monetary compensation to the "wrongfully injured parties."[76] Ill health prevented him from taking up the post, and Newton did not receive a response from Johnson's replacement, William Webster.[77]

A further case that erupted in 2011 offers an intriguing postscript to the tale of the FBI's relationship with the BPP. The journalist Seth Rosenfeld uncovered information that suggested to him that an early BPP sympathizer, Richard Aoki, was an informant. Aoki played a vital role in the BPP's infancy: he supplied two weapons, instantly doubling its cache, before selling the group its first Magnum pistol. Throughout his life, radical activists lauded him for his principles, integrity, and loyalty.[78] Born in the Bay Area in 1938, Aoki was subjected to the U.S. government's internment of Japanese Americans during World War II before enlisting in the army in 1957. Rosenfeld believed that the FBI recruited him around this time. By 1966 he was studying at Berkeley; Seale and Newton learned of him because of his militancy and large collection of weapons. Aoki himself claimed that he played an active role in the BPP's early days, helping with early recruitment efforts and police patrols, and becoming a field marshal and the BPP's first minister of education.[79]

Fred Ho, a writer and activist who knew Aoki, called Rosenfeld's accusations "calumnious."[80] He pointed to Aoki's lifelong dedication to the struggle and his role in building a radical student movement in the East Bay, arguing that the information he might have supplied to the FBI paled in comparison to the positive impact his activities had on Bay Area radicals. The historian Scott Kurashige, who met Aoki toward the end of the activist's life, felt that the evidence for Aoki's FBI connection was strongest before 1965 but observed that the aged Aoki still supported the campaign for social justice. Diane Fujino, who did not mention any links between Aoki and the FBI in her biography of Aoki, questioned the veracity of the documents, noting that Rosenfeld relied solely on notoriously inaccurate FBI material (Aoki's name was misspelled, for example). Panther veteran Elbert Howard dismissed Rosenfeld's charges as "ridiculous."[81] None, however, acknowledged that the Center for Investigative Reporting supported Rosenfeld's work. Its previous engagement with the BPP was even more explosive: it funded much of the reporting that underpinned Kate Coleman's exposé of Newton's excesses in the 1970s. Significantly, even though Coleman was highly critical of the BPP, she refused to countenance using FBI sources, considering them untrustworthy.[82]

Rosenfeld responded with further information culled from Aoki's FBI file, which suggested that he had not provided any valuable information during the BPP's formative period. This led Fred Ho to conclude that there was not a "shred of credible evidence" to suggest that Aoki was a stooge. Instead, it was Aoki leading the FBI a merry dance.[83] Certainly, that the FBI accepted that Aoki provided no useful information suggests that he was gaming the FBI, providing them with enough information to keep himself on the payroll but not being open about his many activities. It also rebuts any suggestions that the FBI were complicit in the process by which the BPP took up the gun and began patrolling the police—events that were fully implicated in the police surveillance of the BPP from very early in its life. Yet Aoki's case also reveals that, from its inception, the BPP operated in a location populated by FBI and police informants, and that even decades afterward, the issue reverberates in many veterans' lives. Moreover, it confirms that the FBI closely monitored the BPP's rise, peak, and decline. It is no stretch of the imagination to state that the BPP's history, and particularly its decline, is firmly entwined with the FBI. Indeed, neither organization can be fully understood without reference to the other.

CHAPTER TEN

Prison and the (Un)making of the BPP

"That's what America means: prison," stated Malcolm X.[1] Newton later elaborated: "The prison is simply a more distinctive form of entrapment within the massive walls of exploitation which is our experience in the United States." Beyond its synecdochic qualities, Newton suggested that the physical space of American prisons would incubate a revolution that would sweep through the nation.[2] As this suggests, prison became central to the Black radical struggle of the late 1960s and early 1970s. It affected the BPP in three major ways. At an organizational level, it removed many activists from party work while draining the BPP's resources through bail, legal fees, and related campaigns. At a personal level, dozens upon dozens of Panthers found themselves incarcerated, before, during, and after their involvement with the BPP, sometimes in solitary confinement. It affected their mental health while also generating a revolutionary fervor among others. As this suggests, the final impact of prison on the BPP was to shape the conditions and culture in which the organization emerged, developed, and ultimately declined.

The experiences of its leadership quartet exemplify the role that prison played in shaping and destroying the BPP. Eleven years in prison rehabilitated and radicalized the young Eldridge Cleaver, giving him the time and intellectual space to devote himself to writing, a process that helped render him one of the most visible public intellectuals of the late 1960s and the BPP's own Vladimir Lenin: a ruthless, clear-sighted vanguardist. Prison also confirmed to him that the most committed revolutionaries were either in, or had experience of, jail. Since prisoners were, almost by definition, lumpenproletariat, they were outcasts, had no stake in society, and were acutely aware of the capricious, racist, nature of American law enforcement and penal systems. They were thus ripe for revolutionary education. Prison, meanwhile, arguably defined Huey P. Newton's life. His early experiences behind bars convinced him that he possessed an almost superhuman fortitude. This belief was sorely tested between 1967 and 1970, an experience that scarred him and the BPP for life. Prison also robbed the BPP of Bobby Seale's considerable organizational and activist skills at critical points in its development. In August 1969 the absence of other BPP leaders due to prison and exile thrust David Hilliard into a leadership role. At a San Francisco rally three months later, he rhetorically threatened to kill Richard Nixon, prompting his arrest. He spent six months in prison and was later convicted of assault and imprisoned for an indefinite term. By the time of his release, he had been expelled from the BPP.[3]

Like many 1960s radicals, the BPP considered prison a tool through which the power structure confined and repressed political radicals. It was America in microcosm: an institution designed to oppress people of color, the poor, and those who challenged the status quo, by physically, legally, and philosophically removing them from society. Like the Nation of Islam, the BPP saw the prison as fertile recruitment ground. Its prison recruits would have experienced the sharpest end of American racialized capitalism, and with the BPP's encouragement they could be molded into the revolution's vanguard. Having experienced prison themselves, key BPP members had instant credibility when attempting to organize among young men; this credibility was deepened courtesy of their ability to form persuasive arguments surrounding the relationship between the prison, America, and political struggle. Moreover, their own personal trajectories, with their profound echoes of Malcolm X's, offered powerful examples of the radicalizing potential of prison. While most prisoners were not incarcerated for their political beliefs, the febrile atmosphere of the times, coupled with the BPP Ten-Point Platform and Program's demand that African American prisoners be freed because they had not received a fair and impartial trial by a jury of their peers, enabled the BPP, like many Bay Area radicals of the time, to present prisoners as victims of a political system dedicated to wiping out a poor, Black underclass.[4]

In this, the BPP founders understood that people like themselves could never become genuinely proletarian. American capitalism systematically excluded them through an education system that failed them, thus enabling an employment system to reject them because of their lack of qualifications. Without qualifications or a job, they could not join a union and so were further excluded from proletarianization. Corralled into ghettoes, they and their fellow unemployed were then exposed to the merciless racism of inner-city police forces who would brutalize them on the flimsiest of pretexts, collapsing the boundaries between unemployment and the label of criminal. Prison thus became an imprimatur of lumpenness and influenced the gender politics of the BPP's leadership, not least thanks to the overtly masculine atmosphere of the prisons they experienced. Seale and Newton, informed by their own experiences and knowledge of Malcolm X's life, saw it as both a location for the ultimate repression—and potentially extermination—of the Black underclass and as a site for renewal, the breeding ground of true revolutionaries among society's most excluded. And primus inter pares of this group was a man who, more than any other prominent Panther, found his life shaped by the prison.

Papa Rage

Cleaver later argued that prison definitively pushed him toward rebellion. "That's when I really began to be filled with hatred," he said. "I think I became much more violent in prison. I believe that prisons, in that sense, are schools for crime."[5] Prison undoubtedly schooled him. First imprisoned at eighteen years old, prison offered him his first engagement with radical literature in the form of Marx and Engels's *Communist Manifesto*, which in turn led him to read Nechayev's *Catechism of the Revolutionist* and Lenin. This did not necessarily aid his rehabilitation, however. According to the police, Cleaver escalated his activities to attempted murder and rape, leading to his incarceration in March 1958 for an indeterminate term of six months to fourteen years, which he spent at Folsom, San Quentin, and Soledad prisons and the California Men's Colony at San Luis Obispo. Here he became the most prominent beneficiary of the California prison system's experiment with rehabilitation techniques that involved offering prisoners work programs, along with group and individual therapy, to prepare them for life outside the prison and render them active participants in the prison regime. Redefined as residents, inmates underwent a barrage of psychological tests to ascertain the nature of the problems that underpinned their criminality before being encouraged to embark on a journey of self-discovery and reformation. Such tests signaled the fashionable belief that mental dysfunction was the primary reason for criminal behavior and furnished distorted evidence to confirm this belief. The plan inadvertently helped produce a radical political movement of which Cleaver was the key figure. Almost paradoxically, in allowing him to read Marxist literature, it unwittingly produced a revolutionary.[6]

The rehabilitative experiment and its fallout had three major outcomes, all related to the experiment's underestimation of the intelligence of the prisoners, who managed to subvert the process for their own ends. Many applied the program's suggestion that they deserved rehabilitation to their immediate surroundings, pushing for increased rights within and without the prison. Some argued simply and powerfully that they did not need rehabilitation. Instead, they argued, white America was at fault, and rehab itself fronted a sinister plan to crush crime and the social chaos that were direct consequences of a corrupt and repressive regime that worked to impoverish Black America. In encouraging socialization, the experiment also bred group identity, assisting the emergence of the Nation of Islam among California's prison population. By the 1960s, Black Americans made up 30 percent of California's prison population. While the Nation's converts were never more than a small minority, their influence far exceeded their numbers, not least because they demonstrated the value of unity.[7] These influences coalesced in future BPP leader Cleaver.

Cleaver was described as cooperative and successful in his educational program. He received psychiatric input, including countless hours of individual therapy, an experience he later described as "harrowing" but one that enabled him to develop an understanding of himself that might otherwise have eluded him.[8] After a series of unsuccessful parole applications, he converted to the Nation of Islam and by 1963 was a Nation Minister. He added a political edge to the prison's educational program, suggesting that, like Malcolm X, he chafed at the Nation's formal rejection of political activism. In mid-1963 he was transferred to Folsom prison, where he continued his political education while spending up to seventeen hours each day in his cell. His brief 1965 stay at the California Men's Colony merely led him to experience the unremitting psychological pressure of constant CCTV surveillance before he found himself back at his June 1954 to December 1956 home, Soledad prison. To subvert the prison education system and encourage his comrades to develop a thorough critique of American capitalism as well as racism, he began tutoring fellow inmates in Marxism and Leninism, using literature smuggled to him by the Progressive Labor Party.[9] Soon after his 1966 release, he became one of the BPP's most valuable and media-friendly orators: a salutary lesson to California's prison authorities about the ability of politicized African American prisoners to aggravate broader tensions inside and outside prison.

From his early twenties until he was thirty-one, then, Cleaver spent considerable time in two of California's most brutal prisons. This undoubtedly shaped him as a man. The jazz saxophonist Art Pepper spent two stretches at San Quentin at a similar time. He argued that racial hatred consumed everyday life in the prison and regularly erupted into violence. Enforced celibacy led many inmates toward homosexuality, with the threat of rape almost ever present. The guards engaged in psychological warfare while each prisoner sought weaknesses in the others to exploit. Pepper concluded that he had to protect himself by acting like a maniac. "I would have to kill myself rather than go through that again," he concluded.[10] As Pepper suggests, inmates had to put on a mask to save face, increasing the psychological pressure they endured. This involved a retreat behind heavily masculine codes of strength and power. Years of observing and participating in these rituals would doubtless have affected Cleaver's psyche, let alone the mere fact of being imprisoned for such a long period of time. Similarly, the prisons' atmosphere would have done little to reform his attitude toward women. Pepper suggests that the testosterone-fueled atmosphere resulted in inmates objectifying women. At San Quentin Cleaver campaigned against conjugal visits, since they discriminated against single inmates, and advocated for paying women to "minister to the needs" of well-behaved prisoners, who deserved as much "action" as their married counterparts. Meanwhile, his epistolary relationship with the white lawyer Beverly Axelrod, coupled with his therapy, encouraged him to shift his views from objectifying women as targets for sexual violence to objectifying them as the queens of the Black race.[11] Pepper also observed the quasi-military organization of the Black inmates.[12] Cleaver's observation of this—not to mention his potential involvement—hints at why he found the military bearing of the BPP so attractive. His immersion in Marxism and Malcolm X pointed to the conclusion that the United States was a prison. And if the United States was the prison, then maybe the techniques adopted by San Quentin's inmates and echoed by the BPP were most appropriate for survival. The prison thus helped shape Cleaver as a revolutionary.

Prison also decisively affected Cleaver's life following his involvement in Bobby Hutton's death. He spent two months at Vacaville prison. Facing the revocation of his parole, he fled the country in November 1968, relocating first to Cuba and then Algeria. During his transport to Cuba he endured two weeks confined to a cell-like cabin. According to Kathleen Cleaver, he lived in a state of almost permanent agitation. "His past was prison; his future was prison," she observed, hinting that he would never truly be free.[13] Evidence suggests that he became violent and abusive toward his wife and the comrades who followed him into exile. His ideas grew more apocalyptic as exile increasingly resembled prison. While the Algerian government formally recognized his status in June 1970, his inability to speak French prevented normal social interaction. He rarely left his lodgings; meanwhile, the heavily pregnant Kathleen Cleaver found herself similarly confined. Their tiny social circle was dominated by slightly eccentric American expatriates and six fellow BPP exiles whom Cleaver became adept at alienating through his authoritarian, sexist behavior.[14] The impact of FBI counterintelligence letters denouncing his comrades in Oakland and highlighting his own precarity doubtless contributed to his sense of confinement.[15] A summer 1970 "grand tour" of North Korea, Vietnam, and China merely confirmed his descent into brutishness. Meanwhile he denounced David Hilliard and his family as "so punked-out and gun-shy, they're making the vanguard look like a reformist bitch."[16] The BPP's armed, adventurist wing was thus the male partner in the BPP, another example of Cleaver's equating violence and power with manhood and masculinity. The twin themes of prison and macho revolutionary adventurism combined to edge him out of the BPP, abetted by three East Coast Panthers, Dhoruba Bin Wahad, Connie Matthews, and her husband Cetawayo Tabor, absconding in February 1971.

Prison thus shaped Cleaver's life as a Black Panther. It established the psychological and political circumstances that drew him toward the BPP, abetted his rise to prominence through removing Newton from BPP activities and allowing him the room to dominate the organization. It also informed the rift.

Cleaver's isolation in Algiers—a direct consequence of his fear of returning to prison—combined with the issue of the forfeiture of bail fees and Newton's resentment at his own treatment in prison to prompt a catastrophic breakdown in relations between the two BPP leaders during their fateful telephone call on Jim Dunbar's television show. Prison thus contributed to his separation and ultimate divorce from the organization.

The Organizer

Bobby Seale spent some time in a military stockade while in the U.S. Air Force and experienced the occasional short prison stretch, but beyond that, his youth was relatively unmarked by incarceration. That changed soon after he formed the BPP. He was one of the nineteen arrested at Sacramento and spent six months in Santa Rita prison. He used the time to spread the word about the BPP among other prisoners, later reflecting that the absence of sexual activity was the worst part of the experience. Significantly, his imprisonment coincided with a fallow period in the BPP's development at a crucial moment in its history, which was so marked that the FBI thought the organization was moribund.[17] It took the Newton trial to resuscitate the party. As important, where Seale's organizational skills had been instrumental in embedding the BPP in the community, Cleaver was less interested in grassroots development and more with cementing the party's national status, factors that profoundly influenced the BPP's development.

Seale was briefly imprisoned in February 1968 for conspiracy, but his third imprisonment was more shocking. He was charged with conspiracy and incitement to riot for a speech in Chicago during the 1968 Democratic National Convention. Matters were complicated by a murder charge related to Alex Rackley's death. He spent time in solitary confinement in San Francisco jail, before being transferred to Chicago. Denied both a postponement of the trial so that Charles Garry could attend after recovering from surgery and the opportunity to defend himself in Garry's absence, he frequently protested vocally during the hearing; each time he was admonished by Judge Hoffman.[18] Seale's fellow defendants attempted to lighten matters by hosting a birthday party on October 22. Sadly, the authorities arrested their cake. "They've arrested a cake but they can't arrest a revolution!" hailed Seale triumphantly.[19]

On October 29 Hoffman ordered Seale bound and gagged. Forcibly removed from court, Seale returned manacled to a metal chair with a gag around his mouth. The following day saw Seale chained to a wooden chair with duct tape over his mouth. A third day of gagging saw him nearly choke.[20] After the gag was removed, Seale continued to protest, but he was charged with contempt of court and sentenced to sixteen consecutive terms of three months' imprisonment. Meanwhile, the New Haven case rumbled on. Seale was extradited to Connecticut in March 1970. The state wished to prosecute Seale, Ericka Huggins, and Lonnie McLucas for Rackley's death; meanwhile the FBI set about smearing Huggins's and McLucas's lawyers. Kept in isolation for twelve months during the preliminaries, Seale was eventually acquitted and released in May 1971. As David Hilliard recalled, Seale's absence and inability to mediate between other BPP leaders played no small role in the BPP's inability to build on the Free Huey campaign.[21]

Unfree Huey

Although Seale protested that he was unscarred by the experience of solitary confinement, this cruel and unusual punishment must have affected him. The catastrophic impact of it on his fellow BPP founder indicates as much. Found guilty of voluntary manslaughter in September 1968, Newton remained in prison until August 5, 1970, spending much of this time alone. He claimed to have previously spent more than five months in solitary following his 1964 conviction for assault with a deadly weapon, another eleven months prior to his 1968 conviction, plus the twenty-two months afterward.[22] Even if Newton exaggerated the length of some of these periods, he endured isolation for a considerable period. Moreover, all his interpersonal interactions during his 1967 to 1970 stretch took place within the physical and psychological context of prison oppression and tension.

Newton's prison experience is also illustrative of the end of, and fallout from, California's rehabilitative experiment. Prison authorities, doubtless influenced by his association with the BPP and Cleaver, prevented him from leading, joining, and even informing any political movement among his fellow prisoners. Prison wardens, believing he had killed a police offer, were keener than normal to punish rather than rehabilitate. While Newton protested that he prevailed over his captors, his post-release behavior exhibits many of the symptoms that indicate psychological damage, suggesting that his descent into crime and drug addiction was firmly enmeshed in his prison experience, revealing the effect of prison on the decapitation of an African American radical movement. It must be acknowledged as a defining period in his life and as a key moment in the transformation of California's prisons into locations for the punishment of prisoners, one that defined the lives of many of Newton's imprisoned comrades, including Assata Shakur, Geronimo Pratt, and Mumia Abu-Jamal.

On a very simple level, prison isolated Newton. His solid steel cell in Oakland's Alameda County Jail, where he remained for much of his murder trial, measured roughly four by six feet. He was permitted visits from his lawyer, conducted some media interviews, and was in the courtroom during the trial; otherwise, he was cell bound. Almost immediately after conviction, he was transferred to California State Prison at Vacaville, roughly fifty miles north of Oakland. Other than during library or exercise yard visits, he could communicate only through a hole drilled in the wall of his four-by-six-foot cell. On October 30 he was transferred over two hundred miles south of Oakland to San Luis Obispo, where conditions were similar and where he remained until August 1970.[23]

A prison correctional counselor assessed Newton and offered two important conclusions. First, he felt that Newton did not possess a criminal orientation but that he responded violently only when personally threatened. More intriguingly, he argued that the BPP's self-defense philosophy was "a projection of his personality."[24] This pathologizing of the BPP's political platform offers a suggestive insight into the prison's construction of both Newton and the BPP. Yet it also reveals Newton's suspicion of attempts at psychological analysis. He tended to consider conversations with antagonists as battles of wits that rendered attempts at analysis hugely challenging. That he had absorbed *The Wretched of the Earth* also informed his bearing. The book's fifth chapter focuses on psychiatric problems faced by those under colonialism, arguing convincingly that colonial oppression wielded psychoanalysis as a tool.[25]

Newton faced severe constraints on his freedom of thought, expression, and association in prison. This was no place for reform or rehabilitation. Given that he identified his occupation as "community organizer" to Vacaville's Reception Guidance Center, the authorities unsurprisingly isolated him, fearing his ability to politicize prisoners and foment disorder.[26] Newton further isolated himself at San Luis Obispo by refusing to work unless he was paid minimum wage. Consequently, warders barred him from the education program and placed him in solitary, restricting his social interaction to visits from family, his law team, and later J. Herman Blake, with whom he collaborated on his autobiography. Compounding his isolation, warders habitually intercepted his mail, ransacked his cell, and stole his possessions.[27] This was merely part of the psychological abuse he endured. At Kaiser Hospital his police guards openly talked of cutting his feeding tube and told him that the gas chamber awaited. At San Quentin guards chanted "Dead man" at him regularly. At San Luis Obispo guards spread rumors about his mental state and taunted and harassed him whenever they could.[28]

Like Eldridge Cleaver, Newton refined his political ideas through essays, letters, and polemics written in San Luis Obispo. Life-writing exercises provided an opportunity for reflection, itself an important process. A crucial difference between the two remains, however: Beverly Axelrod used Cleaver's writing to offer a route to freedom by smuggling them out and giving them to Ed Keating, who distributed them widely.[29] Axelrod and Keating's network promised future employment for Cleaver at *Ramparts*, itself a prerequisite for winning parole, which doubtless aided Cleaver's forbearance. Newton's writing possessed less potential. His autobiography would take far longer to write and edit than Cleaver's brief pieces. As important, prison authorities had no interest in rehabilitating him and so ignored his ongoing published work. Consequently, while this writing enabled him to focus his mind on issues beyond prison, it offered little to aid his battle for corporeal freedom.

Newton later insisted that he proved his indestructible spirit while in prison. He recalled other prisoners in solitary at the Alameda County Jail screaming for release from the so-called soul-breaker. He lasted fifteen days. His celebrated 1970 article "Prison, Where Is Thy Victory"—which in referencing Corinthians 15:55 ("O grave, where is thy victory?") compared prison to death—argued that prison could only hold his body and not his mind. His autobiography maintains this insistence on victory, arguing that amid the prison's nightmarish unreality, he perfected the control of his thoughts, reconfiguring punishment as liberation.[30] Later, when told that solitary confinement "shakes a lot of men very deeply," Newton protested, "Not me."[31] Unfortunately, only after Newton's release did the debilitating psychological impact of prison become widely accepted. Academic studies of solitary confinement now almost unequivocally state that even short periods of isolation affect prisoners in many ways, ranging from discombobulation to severe psychosis, and including perceptual distortions, panic attacks, hypersensitivity, hypervigilance, impulsivity, emotional breakdowns, suicidal thoughts, and paranoia, with many sufferers finding even ordinary stimuli debilitating. Such patterns significantly reduce the prisoner's ability to reintegrate into civilian society, thus increasing the probability of recidivism. Significantly, most inmates refuse to admit to any of these experiences, thus reinforcing their isolation. For those with preexisting problems, the prognosis is even grimmer.[32]

Newton described solitary as "living hell" and "terrifying," recollections that undercut his claims of victory.[33] His autobiography hints at the psychological devils catalyzed by solitary:

> If you are not disciplined, a strange thing happens. The pleasant thought comes, and then another and another, like quick cuts flashing vividly across a movie screen. At first they are organized. Then they start to pick up speed.... The pleasant thoughts are not so pleasant now; they are horrible and grotesque caricatures, whirling around in your head. Stop! I heard myself say, stop, stop, stop.[34]

It is possible that a degree of artistic license taints this account. Yet Newton describes in almost uncanny detail several medically recognized symptoms of mental distress that only later received widespread acknowledgment.[35]

In 1978 Newton wryly recalled that solitary taught him the "value of meditation." This, it seems, was not so much a choice as a necessity. As he pointed out, "I had to achieve some insight into myself or get crushed."[36] Such a response echoes Ericka Huggins's reaction to prison. Imprisoned for over two years and placed in solitary whenever she was caught fraternizing, Huggins forced herself to confront both her pain at losing her husband and the psychological assault of solitary by writing poetry, learning meditation, and attempting to improve the lives of fellow prisoners. The space that she carved for reflection is reminiscent of Guevara's insistence that the "true revolutionary is guided by strong feelings of love."[37] Where for Newton meditation seems to have been a "fight-or-flight" response, for Huggins it became a route toward inner peace and deeper interpersonal relations. As she later reflected, "I will never be free if I don't feel free here in prison"—a complex statement about the relationship between the individual and her psychological and physical surroundings.[38]

The acclamation that surrounded his release in August 1970 indicates that Newton was expected to resume his duties without delay. Yet the themes that emerge from his recollections suggest that, like Cleaver, he experienced severe dislocation.[39] His absence brought thousands of people into the BPP, rendering it a major radical organization and one that was fashioned in the image of an absent leader who happened to be experiencing severe trauma. As Newton allegedly said to Huggins, "I didn't know this thing would get this big. And now I'm responsible for hundreds of people's lives. . . . I don't know if I can continue to do it."[40] Like many recently released prisoners, he had become so institutionalized that he struggled to remember what he should eat and when he should retire to bed.[41] "Even the sight of ordinary activities, such as cars stopping for traffic lights, some going in one direction, some in another, people in the street, was too much," he recalled. "I had literally forgotten how to live outside. . . . Ordinary life seemed hectic and chaotic, and quite overwhelming."[42]

Newton's struggle was likely exacerbated by the lack of any rehabilitative program and the reaction of his comrades, abetted by the FBI and Oakland's police department.[43] According to BPP historian Reginald Major, Newton the man and myth were by this point "completely intertwined."[44] "Thousands were waiting for deliverance," recalled Elaine Brown. "He was David with a stone in hand. . . . He had become a kind of homegrown messiah."[45] More disturbingly, friends and lawyers advised him to avoid appearing at large gatherings without significant protection. Constant police surveillance led the BPP to initiate twenty-four-hour protection. Within days of his release, the FBI instigated a misinformation campaign designed to "demythicise [sic] Newton, to hold him up to ridicule and tarnish his image among BPP members . . . and insinuate that he has been cooperating with police to gain his release."[46] Countless forged memos and letters that declared widespread dissatisfaction with his leadership appeared in his mailbox over the following months. "It appears," claimed an FBI agent in early 1971, that "Newton may be on the brink of mental collapse. . . . We must intensify our counterintelligence."[47] Evidence suggests that the agent's delight was justified and, more ominously, that the FBI possessed a source very close to Newton himself.[48]

In October 1970 Newton moved to a two-bedroom penthouse suite on the banks of Lake Merritt. This new home was a gilded cage. A doorman warded off undesirables, helped by a video security system that allowed Newton to monitor the entrance. More curiously, the apartment overlooked the Alameda County Jail. When told of this, Newton whispered, "You mean I can see the Soul Breaker, where I nearly died."[49] Within days, Newton installed a telescope on the viewing balcony, perpetually focused on the jailhouse. He claimed to gaze through it daily. Meanwhile the FBI bugged the apartment. Adding to his problems, the *San Francisco Examiner* published his address on its front page, allegedly at the behest of the Oakland Police Department. Widespread outrage prompted the BPP to increase Newton's personal protection, leading journalist Walt Thompson to observe that it had been easier to meet Newton in prison. The occasional burglary ensured that he always felt hounded, a situation the FBI intensified through occupying the apartment next door.[50]

Former inmates of maximum-security prisons frequently find the adjustment to freedom so tough that they seek a return to prison. Curiously, Newton discussed spending a short vacation at a hotel roughly a half mile from San Luis Obispo prison; on a daily level, he retreated into his apartment, even complaining that it had become a prison itself.[51] *Rolling Stone*'s Tim Findley noted these parallels:

> Newton still serves a sentence, perhaps more solitary now than he was in the state's cubicle. The much talked-about penthouse apartment ... is like a two-bedroom, two-bath cage in which Newton paces almost constantly, seldom going out.... It is a characterless apartment, devoid of clear personality and almost sterile, not unlike an opulent prison cell.[52]

Just as prison warders were wont to suggest that other prisoners wished to assault him, BPP members regularly reminded him of threats to his safety, encouraging permanent vigilance and reinforcing his isolation. His seclusion hindered his ability to lead the BPP, and he became further isolated following the poor reception for his speeches on the East Coast in November 1970, compounded by his decision to remain aloof from the rank-and-file.[53]

This amplified a quite paradoxical veneration of Huey P. Newton. His honorific title "The Servant of the People" was designed to demonstrate humility, selflessness, and devotion but inadvertently had a distancing effect. Whereas previously he was known as Huey, he would now be "The Servant," a name that stripped him of his individuality, elevated him to the status of the definitive "servant," and rendered him more of a mythical than human being.[54] Commemorating his thirtieth birthday, *The Black Panther* insisted that Newton "brought together the struggle led by Martin Luther King and the too-soon silenced ideas of Malcolm X; the marches in the South and the violent rebellions in the North.... [He came] out of prison ready to continue, on the street, to do the hard, the tedious, concrete work required to bring about the total liberation of oppressed people."[55] Such a portrayal reinforced Newton's isolation by presenting him as the sole unifying force behind the entire African American freedom struggle. Such encomiums, reinforced by the innumerable posters of Newton on the walls of the BPP's headquarters, simply burnished his legend and further yoked the party to him.[56]

Meanwhile, Newton became increasingly paranoid, hypervigilant, and hypersensitive. Ericka Huggins recalls him resembling "a caged animal that didn't want out of the cage and didn't want anybody in the cage.... You could get knocked over or slapped, depending upon the mood he was in."[57] He became convinced that assassins were lurking around every corner. Between 1972 and 1974 Newton was involved in numerous violent episodes, including barroom brawls, a widely reported pistol-whipping of a tailor, and allegedly the murder of Kathleen Smith. Each event appears to have been catalyzed by innocuous comments that Newton considered insulting.[58]

Drugs compounded Newton's paranoia. According to Elaine Brown, constant surveillance prevented him from sleeping well, leading him to use Ritalin to ward off tiredness. David Hilliard added that Newton enjoyed the drug's euphoric high.[59] The pharmacologically similar cocaine, regularly offered to Newton in tribute by various visitors, soon superseded it. Initially it ameliorated his shyness, boosted his ego, energized his brain and body, and offered relief and refuge, enabling him to forget about his responsibilities and allow his mind to roam freely, without the fetters of his myth.[60] Once he became a regular user, though, he entered a self-destructive cycle of compulsion and negative behavior. Aside from its ability to induce euphoria and arousal, cocaine can induce the body's normal physiological response to external threats, heightening anxiety or paranoia. Long-term use leads to a decline in its positive effects coupled with an intensification of its negative impacts, which include irritability, volatility, and a propensity toward violence, leading to dysphoria and often depression, which themselves produce more craving for the drug.[61]

In 1974 Newton expelled all but one of the Hilliard family, believing them to be at the core of a planned coup. Bobby Seale mysteriously departed two weeks later. Soon afterward, Newton went into hiding, resurfacing in Cuba, where he remained until 1977.[62] He returned after the publication of the U.S. Senate's Church Committee report, which offered further proof of the state's complicity in the BPP's decline. Newton read the report among other FBI materials while researching his UC Santa Cruz PhD dissertation, which concluded that an extensive counterintelligence program hobbled the BPP. Consequently, even his academic studies confirmed the monitoring of almost his every move. His use of cocaine following his return served to deepen his paranoia, as did the July 1978 appearance of Kate Coleman and Paul Avery's investigative report into the BPP. Their conclusions were devastating: criminality was rife in the BPP and Newton was central to the organization's decline.[63] As this suggests, prison continued to cast a shadow over Newton's life even long after his release, helping neutralize the BPP and ultimately enmeshing him in events that were fundamental to the organization's destruction.

The Brothers Jackson

Perhaps the most shocking example of the interlacing of the BPP and the prison, however, is the story of George and Jonathan Jackson. This history also complicates our understanding of the Newton-Cleaver split, reinforcing the notion that prison politics are vital to an understanding of the BPP. Given that Newton opposed Cleaver's insistence on the fundamentality of revolutionary violence to the struggle, his support for both George and Jonathan, whose writings and actions were far closer to Cleaver's position, seems peculiar but is explicable when placed within the wider context of the power struggle between the two BPP figureheads. Beyond this, the posthumous beatification of the Jacksons reinvigorated the popular assumption that the BPP threatened to bring chaos to not only the Bay Area but the nation at large.

George Jackson was involved in minor extralegal activities from his teenage years, culminating in a role in a gas station robbery that earned him a disproportionate indeterminate sentence of one year to life. He spent much of the subsequent decade shuttling between Soledad Correctional Training Facility in California's Central Valley and San Quentin, spending more than two-thirds of this time in solitary confinement, and refusing to engage wholeheartedly with all the rehabilitation schemes offered him, with one crucial exception. At Soledad, fellow prisoner W. L. Nolen introduced him to Marxist literature. Duly energized, Jackson developed a worldview that echoed the BPP's, not least in considering the United States a colonial power. He was in San Quentin when twelve hundred prisoners went on strike, which prompted a spasm of violence that caused the deaths of two white inmates. The authorities identified him as a ringleader and recommended isolation before removing him to Soledad. By 1969 the BPP's comrade Fay Stender had taken his case. Within a year Newton appointed him a BPP field marshal, hoping that he would boost recruitment in California's prison system. He might not have played a substantial role in the BPP's quotidian activities, but his involvement symbolized the close relationship between the BPP and the prison system.[64]

The death of Nolen and two other prisoners at the hands of Soledad guards in January 1970 ushered in the final act of Jackson's life. He was charged with the murder of a prison guard—supposedly killed in retaliation for Nolen's death—and faced the death penalty. Taking influence from Charles Garry's defense of Newton, Stender campaigned for Jackson's freedom alongside his fellow defendants Fleeta Drumgo and John Clutchette while denouncing the entire prison system as inherently racist and brutalizing. Meanwhile Jackson's younger brother Jonathan developed his own plan. His infamous actions on August 7, 1970, led to four deaths, including his own. David Hilliard recalls Cleaver offering unequivocal support, arguing that it provided the model for future BPP activities. Newton, Hilliard argues, was more skeptical: reflecting a more orthodox Fanonist position, he considered spontaneous action that did not mobilize the community or build up the BPP to be of little utility. Following his brother's death, George Jackson grew ever more apocalyptic. He declared his loyalty to the BPP, and Newton specifically, in February 1971 and willed the proceeds of his book of letters, *Soledad Brother*, to the organization. Six months later, in highly suspicious circumstances, prison guards shot and killed him.[65]

Soledad Brother proved popular in the nation's burgeoning prison population, not least through its uncompromising critique of the institution and assertion that prisoners could become the revolution's vanguard. On a theoretical level, it revealed Jackson's immersion in revolutionary Marxism, melding Fanon's view of the lumpenproletariat with Leninist vanguardism and Guevara's foco theory, while offering further context for his brother's failed insurrection. In this *Soledad Brother* echoes *Soul on Ice*, demonstrating how prison shaped many Black Californian radicals. Amid his increasingly apocalyptic political analysis, Jackson committed his life to the revolution and his heart to Angela Davis, a facet of the book that elevated its emotional and political heft.[66] Not long after his death, Jackson's *Blood in My Eye* followed *Soledad Brother* into print. More overtly political, it lacked the personal dimension that made its predecessor so moving, although the inclusion of an edited transcript of Newton's speech at Jackson's memorial service made explicit his links to the BPP. That the book earned the BPP a six-figure advance ensured that Jackson's legacy did not remain solely on the page.[67]

The BPP almost immediately set about sanctifying Jackson. Its first statement after his death alluded to Newton's and Malcolm X's argument that America was the prison while declaring that Jackson "was a supreme servant of the people because he gave his life, all that any human being can give, in the struggle for all oppressed people."[68] In suggesting that Jackson's actions comprised a logical reaction to San Quentin's inhumane conditions, the BPP suggested that the failed prison revolt merely reflected the brutality at the heart of American society and that the prison cultivated the prisoners' violence. The allusion to Christ, and Newton's own beatification, became a theme of the BPP's memorialization of Jackson and his brother while also subtly reminding readers of Newton's centrality to the party.

The men's funerals cemented their envelopment by the BPP and reinforced the notion that they were innocents struck down by an uncaring, racist system. At Jonathan's funeral Father Earl Neil echoed George Jackson, calling him a "manchild" who "offered his life for our liberation." An audibly moved Newton lauded him as "the best that humanity has produced," a warrior who placed the revolution "on a higher level."[69] Calling on his comrades to follow Jackson's example, he argued that Jackson fought in a war waged against Black people. Prisoners were therefore at the vanguard of the revolution. Newton's ongoing struggle with Cleaver informed this formal adoption of Jonathan Jackson as a Black Panther. Released from prison only days before Jackson's death, Newton was skeptical of the value of such adventurism, but in embracing Jackson posthumously he laid claim to a martyr, even though he remained skeptical that Jackson's actions had sufficiently mobilized the community. He also reinvigorated the BPP's heritage as apostles of revolution while outflanking Cleaver, a message that was reinforced soon afterward when San Quentin's BPP branch denounced Cleaver as a counterrevolutionary.[70]

Following the theme of freedom and release, George Jackson's memorial service welcomed visitors with Nina Simone's "I Wish I Knew How It Would Feel to Be Free." Echoing his brother's eulogies, Neil, Seale, and Newton stressed that George Jackson found freedom in death, first by willingly sacrificing himself for the liberation of his people and only second by demonstrating how to conduct a revolution. For Newton, he rested alongside Nat Turner, Gabriel Prosser, and Denmark Vesey. Such eulogies echoed *Soledad Brother* in emphasizing his emotional intelligence and humanity. This was the Jackson eulogized by Bob Dylan in his tribute single featuring a gospel chorus pealing "Lord, Lord, they cut George Jackson down."[71] Newton added a chilling, if muddled, conclusion: "We will fight on. We will tear his legs off, we'll tear his head off, and we'll take the example from George Jackson. In the name of love and in the name of freedom, with love as our guide, we will slit every throat that threatens the people and our children. We'll do it in the name of peace."[72]

The Black Panther went further. Its memorial issue presented Jackson as a revolutionary intellectual, mixing some of his letters and position papers with a March 1971 interview and letter from a grief-stricken Angela Davis. The interview reminded readers that Jackson thought prisoners were the revolution's vanguard but also that he leaned toward Cleaverism: "Although . . . I've gained a clearer understanding of the tie-in between political and military activities, *I still see my function as military*."[73] The newspaper also offered extensive coverage of Jackson's comrades, the Soledad Brothers, outlining their defense strategy in some detail, much as it had Newton's, placing particular emphasis on both the intolerable conditions under which they lived and their campaign against prison corruption and racism.[74] This had a threefold purpose: it informed readers about the case and its relationship to the wider oppression faced by Black Americans; it reinforced the argument that the prison was a crucial arena for the BPP's struggle; finally, it elevated the Soledad Brothers to the pantheon of innocent victims of state oppression. In the week of Jackson's death, *The Black Panther* devoted its central spread to a study of the centrality of incarceration to American racial oppression, and prison to the enslavement of Black America.[75] Events following Jackson's death confirm the prison as a crucial battleground for the BPP in 1971. A major uprising at Attica prison prompted Newton to affirm that the brutal suppression of the Attica prisoners left "no alternative but violent, armed resistance."[76] *The Black Panther* stated that Attica was merely symptomatic of a systemic problem, reinforcing the BPP's notion that the prison was simply the country-prison's maximum-security wing.[77]

In 1971 Jackson was arguably as famous as Cleaver was in 1968. Moreover, the manner of his death and the confusion surrounding its circumstances suggested that the maelstrom of the 1960s had not yet abated. To some observers he appeared as another agent of chaos who threatened to destabilize California, occupying much the same psychological and media space as the BPP had in 1967. The BPP's acceptance of his praxis thus held the potential to return the party to its status as Hoover's greatest threat to the country's internal security. Such notoriety was of course problematic, but it had the advantage in 1971 of permitting Newton to demonstrate that he was far from the reformist coward of Cleaver's accusations. Moreover, as BPP supporter Martin Kenner pointed out, Jackson's death, the attendant publicity, and the publication of Jackson's letters provided a perfect opportunity for the BPP to reassert itself within the Left, for the BPP's focus on the Black community since Newton's release was perfectly logical, but it meant the white Left found itself without ideological leadership.[78]

Yet it also speaks to the BPP's understanding of the power of image and images. In death Jackson was a far more powerful symbol than he ever had been in life. He might have been notorious inside the California prison system, but he led under one hundred prisoners. As events demonstrated, he was no threat to anybody outside San Quentin's walls, but the violence that swirled around him was powerful enough to remind ordinary Californians of the urban crisis, of Reagan's and Nixon's tirades against crime in the streets, and of the BPP's earlier swagger. His March 1971 interview, now part of his official memory, might have praised the BPP's social programs, and he might have willed the proceeds of his final book to these programs, but the manner of his death spoke to something more dangerous, more mythic—and more marketable.[79]

The prison, then, emerges as another contested site for the BPP. It was a space used by the state to remind the party of its powerlessness and its fragility. By decapitating the party through imprisoning its leadership, not to mention hundreds of rank-and-file Panthers, the state presented the prison as a key site for the unmaking of the BPP. In isolating and dehumanizing its leaders, the prison could stymie the intellectual, political, and organizational development of the BPP, thus fulfilling Hoover's ambition to destroy it. By imposing burdensome bail charges, prison also operated as a financial brake on the BPP, depriving it of crucial funds that might otherwise have funded further organizing efforts.

In particular, prison played a fundamental role in making and destroying Huey P. Newton. His incarceration followed a period in which African American prisoners exploited and subverted an attempt to remold them into model citizens. Their success at using this rehabilitative scheme to educate themselves about the corrupt society around them, and specifically Eldridge Cleaver's politicization of the experiment, convinced prison authorities that future prisoners should not be given the same opportunities. Newton was California's first high-profile African American prisoner to experience the return to the "Big House" concept of incarceration, one that exerted a defining influence on his later life and helped prevent, in the words of the FBI, the "rise of a messiah" who might "unify and electrify" Black America.[80] His case demonstrates the authorities' acute awareness of the importance of prison in the development of African American radical political movements, and their attempts to stymie the catalyzing of a second generation of inmate activists. The effect of the prison in first isolating and then undermining him played a key role in the BPP's decline after his release.

As important, the prison was a key site for the making of the BPP. Newton's incarceration was the central event in the BPP's development, propelling it—thanks in no small part to the organizational and publicity work of Kathleen and Eldridge Cleaver—to the height of its membership, influence, and fame. Arguably as important, the prison helped define the ideas, character, and mystique of several key BPP individuals. Most obviously, prison helped create Eldridge Cleaver's hypermasculine image, posture, and personality. His outlaw persona doubtless attracted him to the BPP just as he was similarly attracted by Newton's antiauthoritarianism and willingness to push the laws of the land to their very edge.

Yet George Jackson offers an alternative approach to understanding the BPP's relationship with the prison. Like Cleaver, his experience of prison helped define his view of the world around him. He read deeply during his long periods of solitude, developing a thorough and uncompromising critique of the capitalist system and his own position within it. As his fame grew, he became ever more attractive to the party. With Newton out of prison and the BPP hoping to translate the fervor of the Free Huey campaign into something more sustained and sustaining, Jackson appeared the perfect symbolic successor to the imprisoned Newton. The circumstances surrounding his imprisonment were even more outrageous than Newton's. Similarly, he was implicated in events that led to the death of an authority figure. As important, both defendants could impose a political reading on their case: Newton that he was unfairly targeted for his political beliefs, Jackson that the prison system had unlawfully killed his comrade. Both certainly felt that the dehumanized automatons of the system could justifiably be killed in the act of war. Jackson's death also offered the BPP the opportunity to create a new martyr to succeed Newton; this was especially welcome given that Newton's personal shortcomings were becoming apparent to the BPP's inner circle. Just as Newton issued a stream of directives from prison while his absence fueled his myth, Jackson's letters demonstrated how humanity could respond to inhumane conditions.

Jackson noted the centrality of prison to the BPP's praxis in June 1971, observing that the BPP offered free busing for prison visits as a fundamental component of its survival programs. He argued that the prison movement, which fought for the "liberation of political prisoners and the convict class in general . . . was from the outset fashioned" by the BPP. To him, that the BPP donated the first $10,000 to the Soledad Brothers' legal defense fund was further proof that the BPP and the prison movement were entwined.[81] That it made a major contribution to the destruction of the BPP as an active force in national politics is undeniable. It arguably broke Newton and doubtless many other Panthers. It also created Eldridge Cleaver and George Jackson, while attracting many more members to the BPP. More than this, though, the prison was both firmly enmeshed in the activities of the BPP and a site where it could make and even potentially renew itself. As such, the prison must be understood as a defining influence on the BPP.

EPILOGUE

Remembering the BPP

On March 7, 2015, President Barack Obama stood on the Edmund Pettus Bridge in Selma, Alabama, to honor the Americans who crossed that bridge fifty years earlier in the face of a posse of armed police. His speech cast the civil rights campaign as a moment of transcendence before he and forty thousand Americans, including numerous veterans of the campaign, crossed the bridge.[1] Eighteen months later, BPP veterans gathered in Oakland to commemorate their organization's fiftieth anniversary. Events included a free concert; museum exhibits, including wallpaper art by Sadie Bernette made of paper copies of her BPP activist father's FBI file; a gala dinner; a three-day conference; and a ceremony to dedicate Bobby Hutton Grove in DeFremery Park.[2]

The gulf between the two events speaks to the elevation of the civil rights movement and the relegation of the BPP in popular narratives of American history. That so many joined Obama crossing the Edmund Pettus Bridge while so few commemorated the BPP starkly illustrates both the sidelining of the BPP and white America's refusal to acknowledge the party's trenchant critique of American capitalism. As Rene de Guzman, the curator of the Oakland museum exhibit, commented, "The prevailing perception [of the BPP] is militant at best, criminal at worst."[3] That the BPP had to make do with the dedication of a small grove of trees rather than the entire park is evidence enough of the willful rejection of the BPP's claim to a major stake in American memory and the city of Oakland's keenness to deemphasize the organization's centrality to local history. This "forgetting" reflects the general tenor of public memorialization, which emphasizes a celebratory commemoration of the past and strips popular memory of the radicalism that the BPP embodies.

That said, even the BPP's own memorialization activities struggle to escape a similar framing. Recent years have witnessed veterans engaging in a memory creation process that valorizes the BPP's social activism, in large part to rebut the assumptions highlighted by de Guzman. For example, when asked by the Oakland Museum of California about the BPP's legacy, Tarika Lewis and Billy X. Jennings turned to the BPP's community activism, whereas Asali (formerly M. Gayle Dickson) talked of the BPP "bringing us to a place of harmony and balance."[4] Similarly, Ericka Huggins remembered: "My heart opened to new ways of being.... [The BPP] changed my understanding of generosity and passion because we *gave* all of the time."[5] Bobby Seale went further, insisting in 2016 that he was no socialist and that the BPP was only ever about community control.[6] Such remembrance, while vitally important in demonstrating the personal impact of the BPP, deemphasizes the BPP's critique of American capitalism and its revolutionary ambitions, steeped as they were in anticolonial and Marxist ideas. Even so, such memorial activities are essential: in 2017 a right-wing campaign forced the National Parks Service to withdraw funding of nearly $100,000 for a project to document the BPP's legacy led by University of California professor Ula Taylor.[7] As this suggests, BPP veterans again stand against the American Right, who would prefer the BPP to be forgotten completely.

BPP memorialization began in earnest soon after Huey P. Newton died, just before he planned a garage sale of his personal memorabilia to alleviate his perilous financial state. Within hours, the site of his death became a memorial. Newton's widow Fredricka and David Hilliard urged community members to rededicate themselves to a crusade against the social problems that bedeviled Newton and inner-city Oakland. Eventually, shock and grief gave way to a nuanced appreciation of his life. Mary Kennedy attended a wake with fellow former comrades at which she argued that Newton inspired the sacrifices made by hundreds of Panthers who gave their livelihoods, savings, and sometimes their lives to the party.[8] Newton's funeral, held at Allen Temple Baptist Church in South Oakland, was generally celebratory. A sequence of preachers claimed Newton for their God and promised him eternal peace while Jamil Abdullah al Amin (formerly H. Rap Brown) claimed him for Islam. Earl Neil, the BPP's first Christian friend, compared Newton to Moses. Consciously echoing the words of Dr. Martin Luther King, Alfred Smith concluded that Newton was now free. JoNina Abron promised that Newton's spirit would live "as long as there are hungry people, as there are homeless people, as there are victims of racism, sexism and all the other isms that oppress us."[9] Emory Douglas echoed these sentiments, mordantly commenting that no thug—as some critics had labeled Newton—would take the time to learn and deconstruct dialectical materialism. Not long after, former Panthers began discussing an activist response. Some formed People's Organized Response. Others planned a memorial issue of the BPP's newspaper that would presage their own reassessment of the BPP's history.[10]

Newton's death also prompted a major historiographical response. On its 1994 publication, Hugh Pearson's *The Shadow of the Panther* immediately became the most controversial study of the BPP. Mainstream and right-wing commentators received it warmly in reviews that were implicitly and occasionally explicitly antagonistic toward the BPP. More important, the book catalyzed a generation of BPP scholars who, starting with Errol Henderson's vociferous critique of Pearson's failings, set about constructing a more complex history of the BPP. This new wave, following the template set by historians of the civil rights movement who sought to highlight local struggles rather than leadership figures, shifted attention from Newton's individual shortcomings to the rank-and-file's social activism.[11]

BPP veterans, meanwhile, set about their own rebuttals. Following the publication of his autobiography, David Hilliard established BPP legacy tours in 1997, hoping to reconnect young people with BPP history through educational tours that would reveal the importance of the party's social programs. Wishing to bring BPP history alive while encouraging tourists to become engaged citizens, Hilliard stressed the present-day relevance of the BPP's activities. He was particularly bitter that the city of Oakland made no attempt to erect historical markers to the BPP, commenting in 1999 that "we literally put Oakland on the map."[12] Oakland's poet laureate, Ishmael Reed, agreed, musing that an Oakland road and park were named after the white supremacist Joaquin Miller, numerous local institutions memorialized the thief and mugger Jack London, and a street was named for the genocidal president Andrew Jackson. Given this, he continued, surely the city should be prepared to commemorate the BPP.[13]

Hilliard's tours regularly started at DeFremery Park, a key location for the BPP where early rallies were held and which the BPP renamed Bobby Hutton Memorial Park in 1967. This renaming was a multilayered attempt at memorialization. On one level, it memorialized their comrade and ensured that party members would not forget his name. Yet it was also a means through which the BPP's members could externalize their grief and assert that Hutton's death was not meaningless. This latter assertion dovetailed with the BPP's attempt to claim part of the city for itself. Its rallies and public meetings often took place at DeFremery Park because of its proximity to the BPP's early offices and its status as a public space in the heart of Oakland's Black community. It thus made sense to claim DeFremery for the BPP; meanwhile, using the death of a comrade as the focus for this reclamation gave the assertion greater moral authority and emotional heft. That the city largely ignored this renaming confirmed the BPP's outsider credentials.

As important, when Hutton was formally recognized in 2016, the city limited the memorial to a grove of trees. Thus, in refusing to allow the BPP to dominate a key green space, the city revealed its own ambivalence. By retaining the park's name, the city sidestepped the inevitable controversies that BPP antagonists would have manufactured. That it took nearly fifty years for the city to come to this decision suggests that enough time passed for the city to forget some—but not all—of the troubling questions raised by the BPP and the circumstances of Hutton's death, including the fact that he died at the hands of Oakland police. Sites of memory are as much about power as remembering, and the limiting of Hutton's memorial to a grove indicates the sidelining of the BPP within Oakland's metropolitan history and subtly reinforces the suggestion that the BPP's time has come and gone.[14] Notably, Hutton's official memorial lies far away from the location of his death, indicating the city of Oakland's desire not to engage with the circumstances of this event, which includes police brutality, gunfights, and ultimately murder. The lack of an easily identifiable public memorial at the site of Hutton's death is another reminder of the relationship between memory and forgetting. The disconnection between the location of Hutton's death and his memorial reinforces the BPP's insistence that Hutton was an innocent victim and chimes with the veterans' insistence that their BPP experiences were a time of personal growth and harmony. After all, what is more peaceful in the middle of an urban area than a grove of trees? Yet gatherings at the grove indicate the gulf between the city's attempt to forget Hutton and BPP veterans' desire to remember him, reflect on their past, rededicate themselves to political agitation, and inspire new generations of activists, indicating the complexities of the memorializing process.[15]

Hilliard's tours also visited the location of the Anti-Poverty Center where Newton and Seale laid down the Ten-Point Platform and Program and the nearby intersection where the BPP's first protest took place. Hilliard took his tourists to various BPP offices and homes, enabling them to see how the BPP emerged from and worked within a relatively tightly knit community. Before concluding, the tours visited the locations of the deaths of Hutton and Newton. Hilliard maintained that his friend was among the most brilliant men he had ever encountered, a "saint" who was also a chronic drug user.[16] This narrative was informed by his overcoming his own drug addiction, and his narrow escape from the post-BPP life that caused his friend's downfall.[17] Hilliard's ambivalence also reflects many veterans' struggles to come to terms with Newton's and the BPP's impact on their lives, their desire to create a digestible narrative for later generations, and the multilayered history of the BPP itself.

The tours emphasized two facets of BPP history. The first was the BPP's peak in the late 1960s. They visited only three 1970s locations: the Peralta Street headquarters, which opened in fall 1969; Newton's penthouse apartment; and Bill's Liquor Stores, the focal point of the Cal-Pac dispute. As important, Hilliard's narrative focused on the BPP's social activism. About Cal-Pac, Hilliard stressed that Bill Boyette's refusal to make a regular donation to the BPP's breakfast program ignited the boycott. Elsewhere, he highlighted the centrality of the social programs to the BPP's daily activities, believing these to be the major blind spot in the popular understanding of the party. Proudly citing his role in establishing the breakfast and health care programs, Hilliard pointed to the thousands whom the BPP tested for sickle cell anemia, before lamenting the fact that little had changed in Black Oakland since the BPP disappeared, hinting that the BPP's impact was more evanescent than he would have liked to admit while offering a coded critique of America's failure to respond to the BPP's call.[18]

Meanwhile, Hilliard reinterpreted Bobby Hutton's death. His autobiography presented it as the outcome of Eldridge Cleaver's plan to avenge Dr. Martin Luther King's death by killing a police officer. He told a 2004 tour that the authorities conspired to provoke the shoot-out amid rumors that Seale, Cleaver, and he were to be assassinated. Stating that Hutton, Cleaver, and he were transporting some food to a park in advance of a BPP rally, Hilliard told his 1999 audience that they were carrying guns because they feared attack before challenging his audience to write their student papers on the social programs and "get away from all this craziness about the guns because it wasn't about that. The guns were never the whole point."[19] Hilliard is quite correct to indicate that the gun was not present for terrorist purposes, but his statement underplays the extent to which the gun made up a significant component of the BPP's image. His refashioning of Hutton's death also relates to a wider issue in BPP studies. As the historian Ahmed Rahman points out, the focus on benign activities is partly a consequence of BPP veterans themselves. Those veterans who are most willing to put their experiences on record are more likely to be the overground Panthers than those engaged in underground activities. Sometimes the silences in the accounts collected by historians point to this.[20] So while Hilliard correctly notes that guns were not the entirety of the BPP, his renunciation of the gun deemphasizes the complexities of the BPP's relationship with firearms, reflecting a desire to shy away from controversies in the BPP's history.

Perhaps a more detailed consideration would be too nuanced for the tourists and teenagers on the tours. Similarly, to focus on problematic aspects of the BPP's history might have limited their appeal. After all, Hilliard admitted that they offered an opportunity to earn some money, with tourists paying twenty or twenty-five dollars per tour: "Cultural tourism," he said, "is a multibillion-dollar industry across the country." The BPP "is our primary asset, our history. We have nothing else to market."[21] These comments point to the impact of the last forty years on many BPP veterans' understanding of the relationship between the BPP and the communities that surrounded it. Whereas the BPP proved a stern critic of American capitalism, by the 1990s veterans such as Hilliard found themselves struggling to contend with capitalism's dominance. Talking of the BPP's history as a community asset at once reflects the importance of the BPP to Black Oakland but also suggests that these assets possess primarily economic value, and hence that the BPP is now a commodity. This commodification necessitates the denuding of the BPP's radical ambitions to appeal to a broad audience. Thus, the neoliberal era in which Hilliard lives, not to mention the ideological construction that no alternative to neoliberalism exists, requires him to focus on individual commitment and selfless community activism. The memory of the BPP's revolutionary anticapitalism thus cedes to its members' attempts at reform of local institutions and activism that did not as explicitly confront the prevailing economic, social, and political system.

Such comments also speak to the long-term impact of BPP affiliation for members. Hilliard's heartbreaking insistence that "we have nothing else to market" indicates the stigma attached to BPP membership in an increasingly harsh employment atmosphere where job candidates without many formal qualifications, with criminal records, or with gaps in their job record struggle against less interesting but perhaps more marketable applicants, not least those with white skin. Forced by neoliberalism to "market" themselves as economic agents, cultural tourism is one of the few viable options available to veterans like Hilliard, and a way to supplement inadequate incomes—yet another baleful legacy of neoliberalism. Their prime commodity is their personal history, and neoliberalism dictates that they monetize it.

Such considerations must inform any assessment of Hilliard's relationship with the voluminous records of the BPP. The journalist Kate Coleman—who has sniped at the BPP since the late 1970s—accused Hilliard of using the BPP's documentary record for financial gain. She threw a similar accusation at the Dr. Huey P. Newton Foundation, a charitable organization dedicated to teaching the message of the BPP, headed by Hilliard and Fredricka Newton.[22] In 2004 it trademarked a "Burn Baby Burn" "revolutionary" hot sauce and the Black Panther Party name for branded clothing, before filing suit against an online gift shop that was selling BPP-branded products.[23] Coleman noted that most of the foundation's income in 1995 and 1996 was distributed to unnamed consultants, concluding that its primary activity was administrating commercial deals to minimize tax. These years saw the foundation manage the sale to Stanford University of the Huey P. Newton archive, which documented the BPP's history. Coleman claimed that the sale brought the foundation $500,000.[24]

The notion that BPP history was now a marketable commodity in a neoliberal economy perhaps informed the generation of a raft of BPP memoirs. More important, however, party memoirists engaged in an active process of collective remembering, one that was as much about the individual's identity as their past. Memoirs offer the perfect form through which to assert an individual perspective on historical events and are particularly useful for revealing an emotional world that is often absent from archival records. Yet they are not completely unproblematic.[25] The problems inherent in human memory, from the simple act of forgetting to more complex processes where recollections shift and morph as the individual grows older and the stories they tell change as new emphases or evidence is added and other elements fade, doubtless influence all memoirs.

Elaine Brown's autobiography is the most notable of the BPP memoirs to present a partial and occasionally distorted view of the past, so much so that Kathleen Cleaver dismissed it for a "reckless disregard for the truth."[26] Given that Brown's presentation of Cleaver was less than flattering, Cleaver might be forgiven for settling a score in her assessment. Whereas David Hilliard's memoir supplemented his memories with interviews of family, friends, and comrades, thus creating a more rounded portrait of the man at the book's core, Brown's autobiography was seemingly constructed alone, including uncannily detailed conversations from twenty or even thirty years in the past. While readers might be skeptical about Brown's powers of recall, it is also difficult to disentangle fact from memory. Since Brown was undeniably present at certain events she depicts, and most readers were not, who might dispute the facts as presented? How can people who were not present prove that she was engaged in a process of literary reimagining? Indeed, attempts to do so often merely reveal the complexities of BPP history. The historian Margo Perkins, for example, attempted to tackle Brown's silence on the events leading to Bobby Seale's expulsion from the BPP in 1974. Siding with Hugh Pearson's salacious account, Perkins believes that Brown omitted the most shocking aspect of the incident. Unfortunately, Pearson's account relies on sources who were not present themselves. Perkins's unfamiliarity with the manifold problems of Pearson's reliance on inveterate BPP critic David Horowitz led her to trust a known antagonist over those who were present, including Seale himself.[27]

More mysterious was Brown's depiction of the death of Betty Van Patter, who disappeared shortly after Brown rescinded her appointment as the BPP's bookkeeper. After firing her, Brown questioned Van Patter's probity, alleging that she had a criminal record and suggesting that she might have been an FBI plant—accusations that appeared in the 1992 edition of her autobiography but not in subsequent printings. Van Patter's crime, it seems, was to analyze rather than merely balance the BPP books. Soon afterward, her body was found in the San Francisco Bay. After talking to the police, Horowitz became convinced that Brown ordered her death. Riddled with guilt because he first suggested Van Patter to the BPP, he grew apart from the BPP and headed along a neoconservative trajectory that grew increasingly fervid as he aged.[28] Brown's account outraged him, further confirming her—and by extension the BPP's—mendacity, an outrage that was compounded by the refusal of many historians to discuss the same events. That the notable exceptions, Curtis Austin and Robyn Spencer, observe evenhandedly that Brown was not charged in relation to Van Patter's death presumably enraged Horowitz even further.[29]

On a broader level, autobiographical accounts place the writer at the core of events and play a key role in maintaining the community of former members. This dialogic quality operates on several levels, beginning with the preparation of books such as Hilliard's, which rests on a series of interviews he and his coauthor Lewis Cole conducted.[30] Each published book then metaphorically speaks to existing memoirs and informs those that have yet to be written. Hilliard's and Brown's autobiographical accounts of criminality, abuse, and their later struggles to reckon with their BPP past, for example, opened the door for later Panther memoirists to discuss openly their roles in BPP activities and detail the fallout they experienced once they left the party. Later memoirists stressed personal rehabilitation, a complex reckoning with the past that suggested that their life in the party gave them both the skills with which they could later flourish and a keen sense of the importance of fighting for social justice in their professional and personal lives. They express regret for lost comrades and sometimes for others who became embroiled in the BPP's world, but the overriding sentiments are, quite rightly, pride in their role in events of historical importance and insistence that they attempted to bend the moral arc of the universe toward justice.

Recent Panther life stories tend to share a similar structure. They recount the author's early life, discussing how their early experiences led them to join the BPP. They then trace their involvement in the BPP, in sections often written with the pace and verve of a thriller. Many feature the Panther leadership only briefly, reflecting the relative autonomy of individual chapters and redressing the imbalances in Oakland- or Newton-centric histories, and most place a heavy emphasis on the importance of social programs to BPP praxis. As important, the accounts trace the writer's post-Panther life, often in searingly honest terms. Following Hilliard's lead, they include details of criminal activity or personal failings such as addiction or a failure to build a family life, which imply that the writer's post-BPP life was defined by the fallout from the intensity of their BPP membership.[31] The authors' lack of rancor and determination to start afresh without rejecting their past is often startling to read. Flores Forbes, for example, spent three years as a fugitive, during which time his father died, before being jailed for ten years because of his involvement in the BPP. Prison enabled him to focus on education, which led him to begin a life as an urban professional. The final scene in his autobiography is highly symbolic. Interviewed for the position of project manager for a major Harlem planning project, he is ordered to submit to a background check. The Department of Investigation contacts him, having discovered his extensive felony and prison record. "Well, what were you doing to compile such a record?" asks the investigator. Knowing that this will likely destroy his chances of employment, Forbes fearfully replies that he was active in the BPP for ten years. "Oh! Okay," comes the cheerfully unflustered response. "That answers that. Now let's move on to your taxes."[32] No longer haunted by his BPP past, Forbes progresses to his new life. His frank admission acts as a symbolic reconciliation of his new and old lives. Having come to terms with his BPP involvement, he discovers that it was not the impediment to his future that he feared. This final moment of the book—literally one of closure—is in its own quiet way a triumphant validation that echoes the post-BPP life of many veterans who drew on their experiences to pursue other forms of social activism.[33]

This notion of reconciliation also informs the veterans' periodic memorial gatherings. These meetings cultivated a memorial community and grew as the members entered old age, a period in any individual's life that prompts reflection. Yet while many veterans extolled the benefits of reconnecting with their past and their comrades, compared them to family reunions, and used them as opportunities to engage with and motivate younger generations of activists, others hinted at more disconcerting emotions.[34] Forbes compared the thirty-fifth anniversary reunion to a gathering of army veterans:

> Many of us suffer from old combat wounds (I have one), and all have had some degree of post-traumatic stress syndrome.... The 200 or so Panther veterans who showed up came for as many reasons. Some came to maintain contact with people they hadn't seen for decades and to share pictures and news of their families. Some came to find the answers to questions that no one wanted to answer years ago. Others were investigating and seeking a type of therapeutic closure, one that would satisfy and soothe the mental anguish we all shared for dead comrades, people still missing, and for political prisoners incarcerated for much too long.[35]

Such comments illustrate the thorny, ambivalence-drenched, and occasionally desolate process of remembering past activism and the costs it entailed. This past can be murky and unknowable, frightening and overwhelming, but the remembrance process also combines celebration, reevaluation, and lamentation for a past that casts a shadow over the present.[36] Notably, the BPP thirty-fifth anniversary meeting hosted two healing workshops. One, led by Kathleen Cleaver, was exclusive to female Panthers. The other, facilitated by Father Earl Neil, invited members to discuss the psychological trauma they experienced both in the party and after they left.[37] While many delegates greeted old comrades as long-lost friends, Neil's healing workshop, an intense experience for its participants, demonstrated both that emotional repair was necessary for many BPP veterans and that perhaps only fellow comrades offered the understanding and the supportive space to enable this repair. Cleaver's, meanwhile, illustrates the extra burdens often undertaken by Panther women and perhaps even the long-term impact of male chauvinism within the BPP.

Forbes also lamented the passing of time in entropic terms: "No longer the lean fighting men and women ... they were rounder, and most were graying and some had no hair at all."[38] With aging, it seems, came a more benign view of the BPP's activism. As NPR noted in its discussion of the fortieth-anniversary gathering, pride in community activism was far more important to the former members than militancy or armed self-defense.[39] Former Panther James Mott went further, offering a comparison that might have surprised his comrades back in the day:

> One of the greatest stories ever told talked about a man who fed thousands; I remember us having breakfast programs that fed thousands. Talked about a man who healed the sick; we had health clinics that healed the sick.... I know that we were on the right path and I know that we still are on the right path.[40]

Yvonne King offered a simpler encomium: "It was the best five years of my life."[41] In this, the BPP's former members wrestle control of the memory of the BPP for themselves in the face of public indifference or even approbation.

In some respects this points to the opinion of Lothario Lotho, one of the Bay Area's musical icons and master of ceremonies of Berkeley's annual Juneteenth festival, who told Ishmael Reed that Oakland is a "Blues City," arguing that, like the blues, it contains no hope.[42] Reed, who was completing a psychogeography of his adopted hometown, demurred, arguing that his perambulations revealed "that a certain class and dignity—even majesty—emerges from Oakland's history." Yet perhaps both overlook nuances in the blues where glimmers of optimism, humor, and camaraderie, but more important, resistance, struggle, and solidarity illuminate the darkness. More than anything else in Oakland's history, the BPP represents one of these sparks, shining brightly before being snuffed out, but lingering in the memory as a symbol of hope for a different, better future. Equally important, the Black Panther Party is not merely memory but also, as Reed suggests, history. Its radical history must never be forgotten.

NOTES

Prologue

1. BPP veteran, quoted in Pope and Flanagan, "Revolution for Breakfast," 465.
2. Quoted in Burrough, *Days of Rage*, 68.
3. Jessica Elgot, "Beyoncé Unleashes Black Panthers Homage at Super Bowl 50," *Guardian*, February 8, 2016, https://www.theguardian.com/music/2016/feb/08/beyonce-black-panthers-homage-black-lives-matter-super-bowl-50; Tim Kenneally, "Beyoncé's Super Bowl Tribute to Black Panthers Sparks Controversy, Protest," The Wrap, February 10, 2016, https://www.thewrap.com/beyonces-super-bowl-tribute-to-black-panthers-sparks-controversy-protest/#:~:text=The%20organizers%2C%20who%20go%20unnamed,Panthers%20regalia%20from%20decades%20ago.
4. Josh Eels, "The 'Black Panther' Revolution," *Rolling Stone*, February 18, 2019, https://www.rollingstone.com/movies/movie-features/the-black-panther-revolution-199536/.
5. Coogler and Cole, *Black Panther* screenplay, 117.

Introduction

1. Earl Caldwell, "Newton Is Freed on $50,000 Bail," *NYT*, August 6, 1970, 24.
2. Earl Caldwell, "Young White Army Rallies to Newton," *NYT*, August 7, 1970, 14.
3. "Huey P. Newton's Release from Prison," KPIX Eyewitness News, August 5, 1970, https://diva.sfsu.edu/collections/sfbatv/bundles/208428; Newton with Blake, *Revolutionary Suicide*, 312–13.
4. Pearson, *Shadow of the Panther*, 347.
5. Leovy, *Ghettoside*, 157.
6. Leovy, 158.
7. Quoted in Malloy, *Out of Oakland*, 248.
8. "BPP Locations," created by the author, https://drive.google.com/open?id=1UJo-4zIZ.gu8hJyjSKe7mfez9K530&usp=sharing; Josh Begley, "Redlining California, 1936–1939," https://joshbegley.com/redlining/. See also Mapping Inequality, https://dsl.richmond.edu/panorama/redlining/#loc=12/37.8100/-122.2135&opacity=0.8&city=oakland-ca.
9. Madrigal, "Racist Housing Policy."
10. Madrigal; Ta-Nehisi Coates, "The Case for Reparations," *Atlantic*, June 2014.
11. "Area Description," Oakland C-9 and Oakland D-7, February 2, 1937, embedded in Oakland redlining map at Mapping Inequality.
12. Arianne Hermida, "Mapping the Black Panther Party in Key Cities," Mapping American Social Movements Project, https://depts.washington.edu/moves/BPP_map-cities.shtml; Home Owners' Loan Corporation residential security map, New York, 1938, https://www.moma.org/interactives/exhibitions/2015/onewayticket/panel/48/history/.
13. Hermida, "Mapping"; Home Owners' Loan Corporation residential security

maps, New York, 1938, and Chicago, 1940, https://dsl.richmond.edu/panorama/redlining/#loc=13/41.883/-87.695&maps=0&city=chicago-il&area=D33&adview=full; Los Angeles, 1939, https://dsl.richmond.edu/panorama/redlining/#loc=11/33.945/-118.35&maps=0&city=los-angeles-ca&area=C144&adview=full.

14. Hermida, "Mapping"; Arend, *Showdown in Desire*, 6; Home Owners' Loan Corporation residential security maps, Philadelphia, 1937, https://dsl.richmond.edu/panorama/redlining/#loc=11/39.985/-75.175&maps=0&city=philadelphia-pa&area=D15&adview=full; New Orleans, 1939, https://dsl.richmond.edu/panorama/redlining/#loc=13/29.985/-90.104&maps=0&city=new-orleans-la&area=D22&adview=full; Seattle (n.d.), https://dsl.richmond.edu/panorama/redlining/#loc=13/47.609/-122.308&maps=0&city=seattle-wa&area=D4&adview=full.

15. "Let Us Organize to Defend Ourselves," *TBP*, April 25, 1972, 2.

16. Freeman quoted in Shih and Williams, *Black Panthers*, 73.

17. Johnson, *Second Gold Rush*, 14, 35, 53.

18. Sol Stern, "Trouble in an 'All America City'," *NYT Magazine*, July 10, 1966, 22; Johnson, "War as Watershed," 317–320, 323–25.

19. Murch, *Living for the City*, 42–46.

20. Stern, "Trouble in an 'All America City.'"

21. Newton with Blake, *Revolutionary Suicide*, 63, 71; Donald Warden, interview with Robert Martin, July 25, 1969, 32, 34, 40, 42, 44; Welton Smith, interview with Malaika Lumumba, January 30, 1970, 3, 11; Fred Lewis, interview with Lumumba, January 20, 1970, 6–9, 11; Ernie Allen, interview with Robert Wright, November 15, 1968, 1, 5, 7, all RJBOHC.

22. Murch, *Living for the City*, 143–44.

23. Bloom and Martin, *Black against Empire*, 159, 436n78.

24. Murch, *Living for the City*, 162, 186.

25. Brown, *Taste of Power*, 360–63, 371–73, 418–24, 436; Self, *American Babylon*, 310–12.

26. For example, Bloom and Martin, in *Black against Empire*, devote less than twenty of 401 pages to the period after 1970, arguing that the BPP was "disintegrating" by early 1971, with sections on the period after 1972 titled "Retreat" and "Unraveling." See 372–89, quotations on 373, 379, 381. Austin, *Up Against the Wall*, devotes twelve pages to the same period (320–32).

27. For example, Rhodes, *Framing the Black Panthers*; Self, *American Babylon*; Nelson, *Body and Soul*.

28. Jones, *Black Panther Party*; Cleaver and Katsiaficas, *Liberation, Imagination, and the Black Panther Party*; Lazerow and Williams, *In Search of the Black Panther Party*; Williams and Lazerow, *Liberated Territory*; Jeffries, *Comrades*; Jeffries, *On the Ground*; Jeffries, *Black Panther Party in a City Near You*. See also Street, "Historiography of the Black Panther Party."

29. Pearson, *Shadow of the Panther*; Jeffries, *Huey P. Newton*; Hilliard et al., *Huey*; Rout, *Eldridge Cleaver*; Gifford, *Revolution or Death*.

30. Among the best are Seale, *Seize the Time*; Brown, *Taste of Power*; Hilliard and Cole, *This Side of Glory*; Forbes, *Will You Die with Me?*; Dixon, *My People Are Rising*.

31. Ward Churchill, "To Disrupt, Discredit, and Destroy," in Cleaver and Katsiaficas, *Liberation, Imagination, and the Black Panther Party*, 116.

32. Varda, *Black Panthers*.

33. Austin, "Interview with Harold Taylor," 161–62.

34. Chesson-Williams oral history in Shih and Williams, *Black Panthers*, 14.

35. Bobby Seale interview conducted by Blackside Inc.; Shames and Seale, *Power to the People*, 22–23, 25–26; Seale, *Seize the Time*, ix, 47–48, 50–52, 79–84, 94–96, 107–15.

36. Hilliard and Cole, *This Side of Glory*, 119–21.

37. Mumia Abu-Jamal, "A Life in the Party," in Cleaver and Katsiaficas, *Liberation, Imagination, and the Black Panther Party*, 47; Claudia Chesson-Williams, Patrice Sims, and Ajamu Strivers oral histories in Shih and Williams, *Black Panthers*, 12, 131, 195–96; Pharr, *Nine Lives of a Black Panther*, 123; Dixon, *My People Are Rising*, 82, 88–89, 107.

Chapter 1. The BPP's Intellectual Territory

1. Quoted in Giddings, *Ida*, 172.

2. Quoted in McMurry, *To Keep the Waters Troubled*, 123 (first quotation), 121 (second quotation, originally appeared in *New York Freeman*, July 9, 1887).

3. McMurry, 136.

4. Seale, *Seize the Time*, 41.

5. Newton with Blake, *Revolutionary Suicide*, 116. See also Joseph, *Panther Baby*, 46; Abu-Jamal, *We Want Freedom*, 108, 248; Forbes, *Will You Die with Me?*, 31–32, 75–76, 146; Hilliard and Cole, *This Side of Glory*, 119–21, 152.

6. "Black Panther Party Book List," *TBP*, September 14, 1968, 3.

7. Nikhil Pal Singh, "The Black Panthers and the 'Undeveloped Country' of the Left," in Jones, *Black Panther Party*, 69, 70–71, 74.

8. Austin, *Up Against the Wall*, 33, 90, 140–41; Alkebulan, *Survival Pending Revolution*, 13–14; Bloom and Martin, *Black against Empire*, 31, 32, 63, 66–67, 75, 321, 420n69; Ogbar, *Black Power*, 81, 84–86, 94–96, 98–99; Rhodes, *Framing the Black Panthers*, 93–94, 108; Spencer, *Revolution Has Come*, 27–31, 36, 50; Murch, *Living for the City*, 133–34; Jeffries, *Huey P. Newton*, 14–16, 56, 125; Michael L. Clemons and Charles E. Jones, "Global Solidarity," in Cleaver and Katsiaficas, *Liberation, Imagination, and the Black Panther Party*, 188–92; Kathleen Neal Cleaver, "Back to Africa," in Jones, *Black Panther Party*, 214–16; Joel Wilson, "Invisible Cages," in Lazerow and Williams, *In Search of the Black Panther Party*, 197; Robert O. Self, "The Black Panther Party and the Long Civil Rights Era," in Lazerow and Williams, *In Search of the Black Panther Party*, 40, 44–45; Ahmad A. Rahman, "Marching Blind," in Williams and Lazerow, *Liberated Territory*, 199–200. As the brief page numbers suggest, these tend to underplay Singh's important evaluation of Fanon's and Williams's influences on the BPP. See Singh, "Black Panthers and the 'Undeveloped Country,'" 67–79. Malloy, *Out of Oakland* (18–34) is the major exception, although Malloy does not quite make clear enough how the BPP drew on these influences.

9. Nayar, *Frantz Fanon*, 15–25.

10. Macey, *Frantz Fanon*, 2.

11. Pearlman, *Sky's the Limit*, 352; Hilliard and Cole, *This Side of Glory*, 119–21, 152, 180, 183, quotation on 247.

12. Fanon, *Wretched*, 27–28.

13. Fanon, 29–31.

14. Fanon, 36–38, 41, 48, 50, 56–57.

15. Fanon, 67 (first quotation), 68 (second quotation), 74.

16. Sartre, preface to Fanon, *Wretched*, 7–26; Macey, *Frantz Fanon*, 465.

17. Gayatri Chakravorty Spivak in *Concerning Violence* at c. 3:00; Fanon, *Wretched*, 34–53, 56–57.

18. Fanon, *Wretched*, 86–92, 99–101.

19. Marx, *Eighteenth Brumaire of Louis Bonaparte*, chap. 5.
20. Fanon, *Wretched*, 103.
21. Jones, *End to the Neglect*, 4.
22. Erik S. McDuffie, "'No Small Amount of Change Could Do': Esther Cooper Jackson and the Making of a Black Left Feminist," in Gore et al., *Want to Start a Revolution?*, 34.
23. Cooper, *Beyond Respectability*, 7–8, 43.
24. Gaines, *Uplifting the Race*, 134.
25. Cooper, *Beyond Respectability*, 23.
26. Cameron, "New Negro Renaissance," 112; Taylor, "Negro Women Are Great Thinkers," 105, 110.
27. Castledine, "In a Solid Bond of Unity," 57–81.
28. Fanon, *Wretched*, 106–17.
29. "Black Politicians, Come Home!" *TBP*, May 15, 1967, 8; Emory Douglas, "Bedfellows," *TBP*, July 20, 1967, 7; "Bootlickers Gallery," *TBP*, July 20, 1967, 19.
30. Fanon, *Wretched*, 119.
31. Fanon, 120–23.
32. Fanon, 127–38, quotation on 151.
33. Fanon, 156–61, quotation on 161.
34. Marx, *Contribution to the Critique of Hegel's Philosophy of Right*, Introduction.
35. Fanon, *Wretched*, 167–79, 187–88, quotations on 179, 45.
36. Macey, *Frantz Fanon*, 454.
37. Fanon, *Wretched*, 237, 240–44, 248.
38. Fanon, 255.
39. Zolberg and Zolberg, "Americanization of Frantz Fanon," 50; "Books—Authors," *NYT*, April 12, 1965, 32; Victor Navasky, "Notes on the Underground," *NYT*, June 5, 1966, 59.
40. Lewis Nichols, "In and Out of Books," *NYT*, April 16, 1967, BR5; "The People's Choice," *NYT*, February 16, 1969, BRA28; Mel Watkins, "Black Is Marketable," *NYT*, February 16, 1969, BRA30; Lionel Abel, "Seven Heroes of the New Left," *NYT*, May 5, 1968, SM30–31.
41. Fanon, *Wretched*, 29.
42. Seale, *Seize the Time*, 47.
43. Fanon, *Wretched*, 54.
44. Fanon, 42, 48, 51; Newton with Blake, *Revolutionary Suicide*, 117.
45. Seale, *Seize the Time*, 51.
46. Reid, "Re-Viewing *The Battle of Algiers* with Germaine Tillion," 98; Bignardi, "Making of *The Battle of Algiers*," 15, 16, 22.
47. Harrison, "Based on Actual Events," 338; Safiya Bukhari, "An Interview with Donald Cox, Former Field Marshall, Black Panther Party," March 31, 1992, http://www.itsabouttimebpp.com/DC/htm/In_Memory_Of_Exiled_Fallen_Black_Panther_Party_Field_Marshall_Donald_DC_Cox.htm; Spencer, "Engendering the Black Freedom Struggle," 99; Douglas cited in Sohail Daulatzai, "The 50th Anniversary of 'The Battle of Algiers' and the Film's Impact on the Black Radical Imagination," AlterNet, October 18, 2016, https://www.alternet.org/2016/10/50th-anniversary-battle-algiers-and-films-impact-black-radical-imagination; Regina Jennings, "Why I Joined the Party: An Africana Womanist Reflection," in Jones, *Black Panther Party*, 261.
48. English, *Savage City*, 224, 422n224; Edith Evans Asbury, "Algerian Film Called Panther Guide," *NYT*, November 10, 1970, 51; Daulatzai, "50th Anniversary of 'The Battle of Algiers'"; Sohail Daulatzai, "How *The Battle of Algiers* Influenced Rage Against the Machine and L.A.'s Chicano Artist Community," *LA Weekly*, October 7, 2016, https://

www.laweekly.com/how-the-battle-of-algiers-influenced-rage-against-the-machine-and-l-a-s-chicano-artist-community/; William Minter interview with Sylvia Hill, September 23, http://www.noeasyvictories.org/interviews/int16_hill.php; Bob Brown, email to author, April 4, 2017; Rhodes and Jeffries, "Motor City Panthers" in Jeffries, *On the Ground*, 141; Rooney, "*The Battle of Algiers* and Colonial Analogy."

49. Tyson, *Radio Free Dixie*, 48, 53, 62–64, 78, 80, 92–140, 283–86, 302; Singh, "Black Panthers and the 'Undeveloped Country,'" 72; Newton with Blake, *Revolutionary Suicide*, 117; Seale, *Seize the Time*, 143.

50. Williams, *Negroes with Guns*, 4.

51. Williams, 72; Carson, *In Struggle*, 259–60.

52. Williams, *Negroes with Guns*, 6–12; Newton with Blake, *Revolutionary Suicide*, 112; Seale in Hampton and Fayer, *Voices of Freedom*, 365–66.

53. Williams, *Negroes with Guns*, 4, 17, 19, 25–26, 76, 78.

54. Williams, 19, 38, 40–45; Tyson, *Radio Free Dixie*, 214–16.

55. Williams, *Negroes with Guns*, 13, 14, 40, 74–75, 76.

56. Cooper, *Voice from the South*, 144; Cooper, *Beyond Respectability*, 23; Williams, *Negroes with Guns*, 21–24, quotation on 77.

57. Williams, *Negroes with Guns*, 29–30, 32–33, 81–82, 84; *Crusader*, April 23, 1960, 2–3; *Crusader*, June 11, 1960, 1–2; Mae Mallory, "Fidel Castro in New York," *Crusader*, October 8, 1960, 5–6; a sequence of *Crusader* articles between February and March 1961; Malcolm X, "The Second Rally of the OAAU," July 5, 1964, in Malcolm X, *By Any Means Necessary*, 81–82.

58. Williams, *Negroes with Guns*, 3, 17.

59. Williams, 24–26, quotation on 26.

60. Ransby, *Ella Baker and the Black Freedom Movement*, 188, 211–13, 216–17, 296.

61. Childs, "Historical Critique of the Emergence," 595, 604–5; Guevara, *Guerrilla Warfare*, 45, 48, 80–81, 157–58. Seale, *Seize the Time* (105) recalls reading Guevara during the BPP's earliest days. Only *Guerrilla Warfare* was available in English at this time.

62. Fanon, *Wretched*, 42.

63. Malcolm X, "Founding Rally of the OAAU," June 28, 1964, in Malcolm X, *By Any Means Necessary*, 37.

64. Malcolm X with Haley, *Autobiography*, 380–81, 422, 484–85; Malcolm X, "After the Bombing," in Malcolm X, *Malcolm X Speaks*, 158–60, 174–75.

65. Malcolm X with Haley, *Autobiography*, 339, 348–49, 354, 378; Goldman, *Death and Life of Malcolm X*, 76–77, 156, 175; Malcolm X, "Message to the Grass Roots," in Malcolm X, *Malcolm X Speaks*, 4 (quotation), 5–6; Haley, "The *Playboy* Interview: Malcolm X Speaks with Alex Haley," in Gallen, *Malcolm X*, 109–30; "Minister Malcolm: A Conversation with Kenneth B. Clark," in Gallen, *Malcolm X*, 131–143; DeCaro, *On the Side of My People*, 138–46, 162–64.

66. Malcolm X with Haley, *Autobiography*, 435–56, 461–62, 469–70; Goldman, *Death and Life of Malcolm X*, 156–58, 180, 183–91, 240–41; DeCaro, *On the Side of My People*, 204–20; Malcolm X, "Black Revolution," April 8, 1964, in Breitman, *Malcolm X Speaks*, 53–54.

67. McDuffie, "I Wanted a Communist Philosophy," 185–87; Farmer, "Mothers of Pan-Africanism," 282; Farmer, *Remaking Black Power*, 23.

68. McDuffie, "I Wanted a Communist Philosophy," 186.

69. DeCaro, *On the Side of My People*, 240–42; Perry, *Malcolm*, 277–97; Goldman, *Death and Life of Malcolm X*, 161–62, 223, 233–35; Breitman, *Last Year*, 37–39, 43–44, 47.

70. Malcolm X with Haley, *Autobiography*, 495 (emphasis added).

71. Farmer, *Remaking Black Power*, 29.
72. Malcolm X with Haley, *Autobiography*, 410–13, 420–29.
73. Malcolm X, "The Ballot or the Bullet," April 3, 1964, in Malcolm X, *Malcolm X Speaks*, 38.
74. Sales, *From Civil Rights to Black Liberation*, 59; Malcolm X, "The Ballot or the Bullet," 38–41; Goldman, *Death and Life of Malcolm X*, 133–38, 147–59.
75. Malcolm X, "Founding Rally of the OAAU," 54.
76. Goldman, *Death and Life of Malcolm X*, 187.
77. Seale, *Seize the Time*, 79; Marine, *Black Panthers*, 36; Newton with Blake, *Revolutionary Suicide*, 121–22. Bloom and Martin, in *Black against Empire* (70, 417n8) argue that no evidence proves that it was written until April 1967. See *TBP*, April 25, 1967, 2.
78. Bloom and Martin, *Black against Empire*, 70–73, 122–23, 300, 426n30; "October 1966 Black Panther Party Platform and Program," *TBP*, May 4, 1968, 7; "Black Panther Party Platform and Program," *TBP*, July 5, 1969, 22.
79. "What We Want Now! What We Believe" in Bloom and Martin, *Black against Empire*, 71–72, quotation on 71.
80. "What We Want. What We Believe" in Foner, *Black Panthers Speak*, 3; "Eldridge Cleaver on Ice," in Cleaver, *Target Zero*, 257.
81. Hayes and Kiene, "All Power to the People," in Jones, *Black Panther Party*, 163–64.
82. Shames and Seale, *Power to the People*, 37; Clemons and Jones, "Global Solidarity," 191; Seale, *Seize the Time*, 40–41; Kelley and Esch, "Black Like Mao," 14–15, 16, 18–20, 23; Newton with Blake, *Revolutionary Suicide*, 72–73.
83. Mao, *Quotations from Chairman Mao Tse-Tung*, 32 (quotation), 33, 48–53.
84. Mao, 29–30, 65–70, 78–80, 90–94, 116–30, 147–52, 165–79; Kelley and Esch, "Black Like Mao," 31.
85. Seale interview by Blackside.
86. Seale interview by Blackside; Kelley and Esch, "Black Like Mao," 22–23; Mao, *Quotations from Chairman Mao Tse-Tung*, 95–97.
87. Seale, *Seize the Time*, 105.
88. Karl Marx, *Theses on Feuerbach*.
89. Seale, *Seize the Time*, 107–22; Eldridge Cleaver, "The Courage to Kill," in Cleaver, *Eldridge Cleaver*, 32–36.

Chapter 2. The Gendered World of the BPP

1. Rahman, "Marching Blind," in Williams and Lazerow, *Liberated Territory*, 188; see also Jeffries, "Conversing with Gwen Robinson," 143.
2. Tracye Matthews, "'No One Ever Asks, What a Man's Place in the Revolution Is': Gender and the Politics of the Black Panther Party 1966–1971," in Jones, *Black Panther Party*, 268–70; Angela D. LeBlanc-Ernest, "'The Most Qualified Person to Handle the Job': Black Panther Party Women, 1966–1982," in Jones, *Black Panther Party*, 309–25; "Black Panther Party Book List," *TBP*, September 14, 1968, 3.
3. Hughey, "Black Aesthetics and Panther Rhetoric," 36.
4. "Armed Black Brothers in Richmond Community," *TBP*, April 25, 1967, 4.
5. Newton, "Fear and Doubt," *TBP*, May 15, 1967, 3–4.
6. Phillips and LeBlanc-Ernest, "Hidden Narratives," 77–78.
7. LeBlanc-Ernest, "Most Qualified Person," 307–8; Jane Rhodes, "Black Radicalism in 1960s California," in Taylor and Moore, *African American Women Confront the West*,

349, 350, 351; Spencer, "Engendering the Black Freedom Struggle," 94–95; Bass and Rae, *Murder in the Model City*, 83; Ang Li, "Panther Women Look Back," NY City Lens, February 25, 2016, https://nycitylens.com/panther-women-look-back/.

8. Matthews, "No One Ever Asks," 283, 286. Lewis drew as "Matilaba": Farmer, *Remaking Black Power*, 62.

9. Minister of Information, "Beauty Contests & the Third World," *TBP*, November 23, 1967, 10.

10. Newton, "Fear and Doubt."

11. Newton, 4.

12. Farmer, *Remaking Black Power*, 57; Kathleen Neal Cleaver, "Women, Power, and Revolution," in Cleaver and Katsiaficas, *Liberation, Imagination, and the Black Panther Party*, 122.

13. Ransby, *Ella Baker and the Black Freedom Movement*, 43–45, 95, 132, 259, 261–62, 274, 291, 300, 305, 319–20, 345, 346–47, 364–65, 369.

14. Ransby, 68–69, 74, 86–88, 119–20, 195, 219, 226, 280, 372.

15. Ransby, 99–100, 232–23, 295–97, 365–68.

16. Ransby, 112 (quotations), 224–26; Hunt, "Planned Failure," 870–71.

17. Gaines, *Uplifting the Race*, 134, 143.

18. McDuffie, "I Wanted a Communist Philosophy," 190.

19. Kay Lindsey, "The Black Woman as a Woman," in Cade, *Black Woman*, 85–89.

20. Toni Cade, "On the Issue of Roles" ibid., 102.

21. K. Cleaver, "Women, Power, and Revolution," 124–25; Spencer, "Engendering the Black Freedom Struggle," 97; Morgan, *Black Arts Movement*, 125.

22. Varda, *Black Panthers*; K. Cleaver, "Women, Power, and Revolution," 124.

23. Quoted in Varda, *Black Panthers*.

24. Hart, "Sister's Section: Black Womanhood No. 1," *TBP*, July 20, 1967, 14; Greene, "The Black Revolutionary Woman," *TBP*, September 28, 1968, 11; Bartholomew, "A Black Woman's Thoughts," *TBP*, September 28, 1968, 11.

25. Farmer, *Remaking Black Power*, 59–61, 68.

26. "Elaine Brown," *Good Times*, March 5, 1971, 10–11.

27. Sandoval, "US Third World Feminism," 270–73, quotation on 272. For intersectional studies and the BPP, see Phillips et al., "Ode to Our Feminist Foremothers."

28. Ula Y. Taylor, "Negro Women Are Great Thinkers," 105, 110–12.

29. Terrell, *Progress of Colored Women*, 7–9.

30. McDuffie, "New Freedom Movement," 82.

31. Farmer, *Remaking Black Power*, 32.

32. Brown, *Taste of Power*, 3.

33. Farmer, *Remaking Black Power*, 82; Culberson, "The Role of a Revolutionary Woman," *TBP*, May 4, 1969, 9.

34. Harper, "Sisters—Comrades at Arms," *TBP*, November 8, 1969, 17.

35. Shakur, "Revolutionary Poem," *TBP*, May 31, 1970, 12.

36. Bird and Shakur, "To Our Sisters in Arms," *TBP*, September 5, 1970, 18.

37. Walston, "Check It Out Sister," *TBP*, September 27, 1969, 15.

38. Hart, "Sister's Section," 11.

39. Ula Y. Taylor, "Negro Women Are Great Thinkers," 105.

40. Jeffries, "Reflecting on Her Life," 133–35.

41. Collins, *Black Feminist Thought*, 222.

42. Bass and Rae, *Murder in the Model City*, 83.

43. Lindsey, "Black Woman as a Woman," 87.

44. "Panther Sisters on Women's Liberation" supplement, *TBP*, September 13, 1969, 12–13. All quotations in this passage are from this article.

45. Candi Robinson, "Message to Revolutionary Women," *TBP*, August 9, 1969, 23.

46. DC [likely Don Cox], "Towards a Revolutionary Morality," *TBP*, March 15, 1970, 14.

47. Judi Douglas, "Birth Control," *TBP*, February 7, 1970, 7.

48. Lee, *For Freedom's Sake*, 21–22, 80–81.

49. LeBlanc-Ernest, "Most Qualified Person," 320–21; Spencer, "Engendering the Black Freedom Struggle," 104–5; Innerparty Memorandum January 24, 1974 HPNC 14: Innerparty Memorandums.

50. Stephania Tyson, "The Question: Why Did I Lie About Wearing a Wig?," *TBP*, April 18, 1970, 13.

51. "Black Women and the Revolution," *TBP*, March 3, 1969, 9.

52. Kathleen Cleaver, "On Eldridge Cleaver," *Ramparts*, June 1969, 4. She received numerous FBI counterintelligence letters alleging that he was cavorting with underage girls. The FBI was not alone in highlighting Cleaver's priapism. Berkeley radical Steve Wasserman suggests that Kathleen Cleaver endured physical abuse and "many and persistent infidelities." Director FBI memo, October 31, 1968, FBIBEO 100–448006, section 4; SAC, San Francisco memo, November 26, 1968, FBIBEO 100–448006, section 5; Wasserman, "Rage and Ruin."

53. Eldridge Cleaver, "The Black Moochie," in K. Cleaver, *Target Zero*, 17.

54. Cleaver, *Soul on Ice*, 49; Mills, "Cleaver/Baldwin Revisited," 50.

55. Cleaver, *Soul on Ice*, 24–26, 126–27.

56. Eldridge Cleaver, "The Autobiography of Eldridge Cleaver," in K. Cleaver, *Target Zero*, 12–13 (first quotation), 17; Cleaver quoted in Gifford, *Revolution or Death*, 78 (second quotation).

57. Eldridge Cleaver, "Uptight in Babylon," in K. Cleaver, *Target Zero*, 68.

58. "Armed Panthers Here," *Berkeley Barb*, February 25, 1967, 1.

59. Cleaver, "Courage to Kill," in Cleaver, *Eldridge Cleaver*, 29.

60. Cleaver, "The Death of Martin Luther King," in Cleaver, *Eldridge Cleaver*, 74, 76.

61. Cleaver, "Uptight in Babylon," 87; Austin, *Up Against the Wall*, 165–66; Cleaver, "Affidavit No. 1," in Cleaver, *Eldridge Cleaver*, 140; Cleaver, "Affidavit #2," in Cleaver, *Eldridge Cleaver*, 86–87; FBI report, Leroy Eldridge Cleaver June 1968, 17 FBIEC section 1; FBI memo, SAC San Francisco, April 12, 1968, FBIEC section 29.

62. Cleaver interview, in Hampton and Fayer, *Voices of Freedom*, 515, quotation on 516; Richard Jensen interview, in Hampton and Fayer, *Voices of Freedom*, 515–16.

63. Quoted in Malloy, *Out of Oakland*, 135.

64. Cleaver, "Affidavit #2," 91 (emphasis added); Warren Wells, field statement, April 8, 1968; "Oakland Police Department Continuation Report" April 6, 1968, HPNC 39: illegible (2).

65. Robert Wright, letter to Charles Garry, May 7, 1968; autopsy report of Bobby James Hutton, April 7, 1968, both HPNC 39: illegible (2); Austin, *Up Against the Wall*, 167.

66. "1218 28th Street," *TBP*, May 4, 1968, 20.

67. Cleaver, "Affidavit #2," 93; G. C. Moore (FBI) memo, June 24, 1968, FBIEC section 1; *OT*, April 25, 1968, quoted in FBI report, "Black Panther Party," April 29, 1968; "Bobby Hutton Murdered," handbill, n.d., both FBIEC section 29; Newton, "A Tribute to Lil Bobby," *TBP*, May 4, 1968, 1.

68. SAC San Francisco memo, October 11, 1968, FBIBEO, section 4.

69. All quotations in this paragraph are from Cleaver, "Stanford Speech," October 1,

1968, in Cleaver, *Eldridge Cleaver*, 142–44. Its themes were repeated numerous times. See, e.g., Schanche, *Panther Paradox*, 69; transcript of Cleaver speech, October 18, 1968, 13; transcript of Cleaver speech, October 4, 1968, 29–30, FBIBEO, part 2.

70. Cleaver, "Message to Sister Ericka Huggins of the Black Panther Party," *TBP*, July 5, 1969, 13.

71. Guevara, *Venceremos!*, 388, quotation on 398.

72. Cleaver, *Soul on Ice*, 23.

73. Huggins, "Oral History," first quotation on 57, 62–63, 66–70, second quotation on 67.

74. Seale, *Seize the Time*, 149, 169, 193, 201–11, 435–46, quotation on 436.

75. Seale, 436–38, quotation on 437.

76. Seale, 442–44, quotations on 444.

77. Regina Jennings, "Why I Joined the Party," 262–63.

78. Spain quoted in Cummins, *Rise and Fall*, 109.

79. Bloom and Martin, *Black against Empire*, 306–7.

80. Newton, "Women's Liberation and Gay Liberation Movements," in Newton, *To Die for the People*, 152–55. The BPP offered tacit support to the Gay Liberation Movement in October 1968, printing a statement by the national chair of the Student Homophile League about the passage of a bill of rights for homosexual citizens, albeit beneath a problematic title. See "Bill of Rights for Homos," *TBP*, October 12, 1968, 17.

81. Landon Williams, "Black Capitalism and What It Means," *TBP*, March 16, 1969, 4.

82. Brown, *Taste of Power*, 306–10, quotation on 310.

83. Brown, 313 (quotation), 369–71, 385. As this suggests, physical punishment was not uncommon in the BPP, with other punishments including an increased physical exercise regimen, imprisonment, and extra duties. Spencer, *Revolution Has Come*, 92–93.

84. Brown, *Taste of Power*, 249.

85. Farmer, *Remaking Black Power*, 82, 212n141.

86. Brown, *Taste of Power*, 367, 445, 447.

87. Mzuri Pambeli, "The Black Panther Party . . . from a Sister's Point of View," *Positive Action*, March–April 2007, http://www.itsabouttimebpp.com/Women_BPP/pdf/Black_Panther_Party_from_a_Sister_View_Point.pdf; Phillips, "Feminist Leadership of Ericka Huggins," 198; Bukhari, *War Before*, 58.

88. Shakur quoted in Josephs, "Whose Revolution Is This," 422; Shakur, *Assata*, 223.

89. Bukhari, *War Before*, 57.

90. Quoted in Rhodes, "Black Radicalism," 348.

91. Quoted in Bloom and Martin, *Black against Empire*, 307.

92. Bukhari, *War Before*, 60.

Chapter 3. BPP Political Philosophy

1. Cleaver, "The Courage to Kill," in Cleaver, *Eldridge Cleaver*, 29, 31.

2. Cleaver, "Courage to Kill," 36.

3. "Eldridge Cleaver on Guarding Betty Shabazz," February 22, 1967, YouTube, https://www.youtube.com/watch?v=uXuKHHWE5Hs.

4. David Mills, "Q&A: Eldridge Cleaver (pt. 2)," *Undercover Black Man* (blog), February 27, 2007, http://undercoverblackman.blogspot.com/2007/02/q-eldridge-cleaver-pt-2.html; Shames and Seale, *Power to the People*, 38; Cleaver, "Bunchy" c. 1971, in K. Cleaver, *Target Zero*, 115; Rhodes, *Framing the Black Panthers*, 100–101; Cleaver, "Affidavit No. 1," 138.

5. Cleaver, "Uptight in Babylon," 78, 80.

6. Cleaver, 79, 86; Cleaver, *Playboy* interview, December 1968, in K. Cleaver, *Target Zero*, 145, 161; *The Black Panthers: Vanguard of the Revolution* at 19:14.

7. "Huey Must Be Set Free!," *TBP*, November 23, 1967, 1.

8. Cleaver, "On the Ideology of the Black Panther Party", *TBP*, June 6, 1970, 12.

9. Cleaver, 12; Lockwood, *Conversation with Eldridge*, 99–100; Nikhil Pal Singh, "Black Panthers and the 'Undeveloped Country,'" 65.

10. "Executive Mandate Number One" in Foner, *Black Panthers Speak*, 41.

11. "The Truth about Sacramento," *TBP*, May 15, 1967, 1, 5; "Black Activists in America," *TBP*, May 15, 1967, 7 (first and second quotations, suggestively positioned next to an excerpt from Malcolm X's "The Ballot or the Bullet"); untitled article, *TBP*, May 15, 1967, 8, which betrays the least influence of Cleaver.

12. "Minister of Defense," *TBP*, May 15, 1967, 3; Morgan, *Black Arts Movement*, 101–2.

13. Minister of Information, "Welfare Recipients Threatened," *TBP*, June 20, 1967, 2.

14. Earl Anthony, "Core City Politics," *TBP*, June 20, 1967, 6. See also Anthony, "A Letter to You Brothers and Sisters," *TBP*, July 3, 1967, 2 (a panegyric to the BPP). Anthony, *Spitting in the Wind* (18–20, 38) suggests that he began informing in late August or early September.

15. Minister for Information, "Police Slaughter Black People," *TBP*, July 20, 1967, 1, 10, 15 (quotations); Minister of Information, "Mother Country Radicals," *TBP*, July 20, 1967, 1, 6.

16. "World of Black Folks," *TBP*, July 20, 1967, 17; "The World of Black People," *TBP*, July 3, 1967, 5. This issue included denunciations of CORE ("CORE Convention Fallout," 2, 22) and the NAACP (Minister of Information, "Old Toms Never Die Unless They're Blown Away," 7, 19); reports on activities in San Francisco (Seale, "Black Panthers Hunters Point," 4, 15, 23; Murray, "Hunters Point Brothers Sock It to the Mayor of SF," 14) and a Black Arts Convention in Detroit (7, 22).

17. Carl Mack, "What Goes Around Comes Around," *TBP*, July 20, 1967, 21; "Brother Dynamite Says," *TBP*, July 20, 1967, 7, 21.

18. Seale quoted in "Press Release from the Black Panther Party," *TBP*, May 18, 1968, 5; Kathleen Cleaver, "Black Lawyers Are Jiving," *TBP*, May 18, 1968, 5, 13.

19. George Murray, "Minister of Education," *TBP*, May 18, 1968, 20; George Murray, "For a Revolutionary Culture," *TBP*, September 7, 1968, 12.

20. Anonymous, "Justice of Injustice," *TBP*, October 5, 1968, 13–14; "Black Panther Party Book List," *TBP*, October 5, 1968, 15.

21. Landon R. Williams, "Law and Order," *TBP*, November 2, 1968, 15.

22. Newton, "Functional Definition of Politics," *TBP*, May 15, 1967, 3–4; "Message on the Peace Movement," *TBP*, September 27, 1969, 10–11; Newton, "To the Black Movement" and "To the Republic of New Afrika," in Newton, *To Die for the People*, 92–100.

23. Newton, "The Correct Handling of a Revolution," in Foner, *Black Panthers Speak*, 40–45, quotation on 44; Newton, "Talks to the Movement," in Foner, *Black Panthers Speak*, 50–66; Rush Greenlee, "A Revolutionary Talks from Cell," *SFE*, June 30, 1968, 1, 17.

24. Newton, "Functional Definition of Politics."

25. Newton, "Message on the Peace Movement."

26. Minister of Information, "Huey Must Be Set Free," *TBP*, November 23, 1967, 1.

27. Minister of Information, "Huey Must Be Set Free," 3, 8.

28. Newton, "The Correct Handling of a Revolution," *TBP*, May 4, 1968, 6; "Gestapo Tactics," *TBP*, May 4, 1968, 22; "Gestapo Tactics," *TBP*, May 18, 1968, 12; "Gestapo Tactics," *TBP*, March 23, 1969, 5; Raymond Lewis, "Apology Demanded of Pig Alioto," *TBP*, No-

vember 2, 1968, 1; "Chief of Staff David Hilliard Speaks at May Day Rally to Free Huey," *TBP*, May 11, 1969, 13–14. See also Keith Hinch, "Fascist Tactics," *TBP*, April 6, 1969, 16.

29. Kathleen Cleaver, "Liberation and Political Assassination," *TBP*, May 18, 1968, 16.

30. Kathleen Cleaver, "Racism, Fascism, and Political Murder," *TBP*, September 14, 1968, 8; Emory Douglas artwork, *TBP*, October 19, 1968, 8.

31. Eldridge Cleaver, "Community Imperialism," *TBP*, May 18, 1968, 10.

32. "Fascism in America," *TBP*, May 31, 1969, 1; "Revolutionary Conference for a United Front against Fascism," *TBP*, May 18, 1968, 2 (quotation); Robyn C. Spencer, "The Black Panther Party and Black Anti-Fascism in the United States," Duke University Press, January 26, 2017, https://dukeupress.wordpress.com/2017/01/26/the-black-panther-party-and-black-anti-fascism-in-the-united-states/.

33. "The Black Panther Party Comes Forth: We Must Develop a United Front against Fascism," *TBP*, May 31, 1969, 12–13.

34. Mercer, "Specters of Fascism," 99, 114.

35. "Sgt. Pepper," "Face of Fascism—Oily and Piggish," *Berkeley Barb*, February 21–27, 1969, 2.

36. Bobby Seale quoted in "What Is the United Front against Fascism?" *TBP*, July 12, 1969, 8.

37. Bobby Seale, "Black Soldiers as Revolutionaries to Overthrow the Ruling Class," *TBP*, September 20, 1969, 2; Seale, "The Ten Point Platform and Program of the Black Panther Party," *TBP*, October 18, 1969, 2 (quotation).

38. Sacramento Branch BPP, "Breaking Capitalism Down," *TBP*, April 20, 1969, 17; "An Interview with the Chief of Staff David Hilliard," *TBP*, April 20, 1969, 18; "The Nature of Guerrilla Warfare," *TBP*, April 20, 1969, 20.

39. "Big Man," "Renegade Philosophy," *TBP*, March 23, 1969, 4; Eldridge Cleaver, "Community Imperialism," *TBP*, April 20, 1969, 14.

40. "We Remember Brother Malcolm," *TBP*, May 19, 1969, 4–10; "Long Live Ho Chi Minh," *TBP*, May 19, 1969, 11; untitled photo collage, *TBP*, May 19, 1969, 12–13.

41. "Chicago Panthers Serve the People," *TBP*, May 31, 1969, 4.

42. Ed Williams, "Capitalism the Enemy of the People," *TBP*, May 31, 1969, 18.

43. Fred Hampton, "You Can Murder a Liberator but You Can't Murder Liberation," in Foner, *Black Panthers Speak*, 138–39, 142–43; Landon Williams, "Black Capitalism and What It Means," *TBP*, March 16, 1969, 4.

44. LeBlanc-Ernest, "Most Qualified Person," 311; Williams, From the *Bullet to the Ballot*, 56–60, 78–80, 128, quotation on 131; Hampton, "You Can Murder," 142.

45. Eldridge Cleaver, "Somewhere in the Third World," *TBP*, July 12, 1969, 12–13; David Hilliard, "What You Are Speak So Loud I Hardly Hear Anything You Say," *TBP*, November 8, 1969, 6.

46. Seale, "Message to All Progressive Force," *TBP*, November 15, 1969, 10.

47. Street, "Shadow of the Soul Breaker," 349–51; Major, *Panther Is a Black Cat*, 126.

48. *Firing Line* transcript, "How Does It Go with the Black Movement?" transmitted February 11, 1973, 7, HPNC 14: Servant Writings (folder 1); Jeffries, *Huey P. Newton*, 128.

49. Newton, "To the National Liberation Front of South Vietnam"; Newton, "On the Middle East," in Newton, *To Die for the People*, 178–81, 191–96.

50. Newton, "A Letter from Huey to the Revolutionary Brothers and Sisters About the Women's Liberation and Gay Liberation Movements," *TBP*, August 21, 1970, 5 (quotation); Director, FBI airtel, September 16, 1970, HPNC 18: untitled; Thomas A. Johnson, "Theme of Black Parleys," *NYT*, September 9, 1970, 32.

51. San Quentin B-00000, "Warning to Pigs"; Ericka, Rose, Penny, "Open Letter to

Angela Davis," both in *TBP*, September 5, 1970, 13; Joan Bird and Afeni Shakur, "To Our Sisters in Arms," *TBP*, September 5, 1970, 18.

52. Newton/Lane interview, September 17, 1970, transcript, 1–2, 4, 9, 10, quotation on 29, HPNC 15: Interview with Huey P. Newton and Mark Lane.

53. Newton/Lane interview, 30–32, 35, 37, 46–49, 114; Newton, message at Boston College, November 18, 1970, *TBP*, January 23, 1971, supplement, B.

54. Newton/Lane interview, 19, 20, 45, 78.

55. Newton/Lane interview, 53–54, quotation on 76.

56. Newton/Lane interview, 79–80.

57. Newton/Lane interview, 119, 124–25, 231.

58. Blake, "Caged Panther," 244.

59. Newton, "To the Revolutionary People's Constitutional Convention," in Newton, *To Die for the People*, 158–62; Katsiaficas, "Organization and Movement," in Cleaver and Katsiaficas, *Liberation, Imagination, and the Black Panther Party*, 146, quotation on 148.

60. FBI memo, December 29, 1970, FBIHPN section 7; transcript at FBI report: Huey Percy Newton, April 29, 1971, 292–369, quotation on 293, FBIHPN section 12; Jeffries, *Huey P. Newton*, 78.

61. Newton speech at Ann Arbor, November 17, 1970, transcript at FBI report: Huey Percy Newton, April 29, 1971, 373–425; "Female" comment in FBI report: Huey Percy Newton, April 29, 1971, 429.

62. FBI report, "Huey P. Newton: Racial Matters—BPP," November 27, 1970, FBIHPN section 7.

63. Newton, message at Boston College, B–C.

64. Newton, C–G.

65. Newton, speech at New York Community College, November 19, 1970, transcript, 2, 4–6, quotation on 6, HPNC 15: H.P.N. at New York Community College.

66. Newton, 8–9.

67. FBI document, "Huey P. Newton: Racial Matters—BPP," 2.

68. See, for example, Newton, "Uniting against a Common Enemy," October 23, 1971, in Newton, *Huey P. Newton Reader*, 235.

69. Newton, "Uniting against a Common Enemy," 236–240; Newton, "The Technology Question," 1972, in Newton, *Huey P. Newton Reader*, 259–65; Narayan, "The Wages of Whiteness in the Absence of Wages," 4–5.

70. Hardt and Negri, *Empire*, xi–xiv, 44–45, 50–52, 137–39, 150–54, 251–54, 306–14, 325–50; Narayan, "Wages of Whiteness," 7.

71. FBI reports, January 10, February 3, February 10, 1971, in FBI report: Huey Percy Newton, April 29, 1971, 247–48, 250.

72. Transcript of Los Angeles television interview, July 16, 1972 (taped June 20), in FBI report, August 30, 1972, 40, FBIHPN section 19.

73. Kai T. Erikson, introduction to Erikson and Newton, *In Search of Common Ground*, 14–16; FBI report: Huey Percy Newton, April 29, 1971, 21–22, 25–29; Freed, letter to Herman [Blake] and Kai [Erikson], July 21, 1971, HPNC 10: Letters from Don Freed.

74. Tape 1 transcript, 1–13, HPNC 32: Yale Press Conference, February 2, 1971; Philip Rosenberg, "A Surprisingly Gentle Confrontation," *NYT Book Review*, September 9, 1973, 48–49. Other sections edited included discussions of the BPP, the manipulation of reactionary intercommunalism, earth's natural resources, and an argument about Newton's rhetoric. Tape 2 transcript, 27–34; Tape 5 (February 4, 1971) transcript, 7–9, 22–23, HPNC 32: Yale Press Conference, February 2, 1971.

75. Tape 2 transcript, 16; Erikson and Newton, *In Search*, 38; Jeffrey Gordon, "Erik Erikson and Huey Newton," May 1971, FBIHPN section 13.

76. Tape 5 transcript, 2–3, Yale Press Conference, February 4, 1971.

77. FBI transcript of Newton speech, Princeton, February 9, 1971, in FBI report: Huey Percy Newton, April 29, 1971, 37–120, quotation on 47.

78. "Afro-American Cultural Center History," http://afam.yalecollege.yale.edu/.

79. All quotations in this paragraph from Newton, "On the Defection of Eldridge Cleaver from the Black Panther Party and the Defection of the Black Panther Party from the Black Community," *TBP*, April 17, 1971, supplement.

80. Spencer, *Revolution Has Come*, 110–13.

81. "Randy Williams on the Black Panther Party," *TBP*, May 8, 1971, 15.

82. Earl Satcher, "To Supreme Servant, Minister of Defense, Huey P. Newton," *TBP*, May 8, 1971, 17.

83. Romaine Fitzgerald, "Prospects for Revolutionary Intercommunal Warfare," *TBP*, May 8, 1971, 16–17.

84. Note Newton's argument at Boston College (November 18, 1970) that the BPP was a Black nationalist organization in 1966.

85. Newton, "On the Defection of Eldridge Cleaver"; Newton, "On the Relevance of the Church," May 19, 1971, in Newton, *To Die for the People*, 68.

86. David Lubell to Newton, June 6, 1972, HPNC 52: Stronghold Consolidated Inc. Newton claimed that Random House paid a $25,000 advance for his conversations at Yale. The BPP received $200,000 for George Jackson's *Blood in My Eye*. FBI surveillance document, January 14, 1971, 4, FBIHPN section 7; contract between Random House and Stronghold, September 28, 1971; Edward C. Bell statement, November 3, 1971; David Lubell to Gwen Fountaine, August 6, 1973, and Scott Paxton, January 7, 1972; Paxton telephone message to Lubell, n.d.; Carol Anderson to Martin Kenner, March 31, 1972; John J. Simon to Lubell, December 1, 1971; Catherine Von Bülow to Newton, November 22, 1971, all HPNC 40: Blood in My Eye; Carol R. Anderson to Lubell, March 6, 1972, HPNC 40: George Jackson Agreement.

87. All quotations in this paragraph from Newton, "Black Capitalism Re-Analyzed I," *TBP*, June 5, 1971.

88. Huey P. Newton, "On Pan-Africanism or Communism," December 1, 1972, in Newton, *Huey P. Newton Reader*, 248–55, quotation on 255.

89. "He Won't Bleed Me: A Revolutionary Analysis of Sweet Sweetback's Baadasssss Song," *TBP*, June 19, 1971, supplement, reproduced in Newton, *To Die for the People*, 112–47. According to the FBI, Newton visited Van Peebles in June 1971. Such was Van Peebles's obnoxiousness that Newton allegedly confided to a colleague (an FBI informant) that "any social message" in Peebles's film "had gotten into the picture by accident." FBI surveillance report: Huey P. Newton, June 25, 1971, 2–3, FBIHPN section 13.

90. Pearson, *Shadow of the Panther*, 234; Innerparty Memorandum #5, August 12, 1972, HPNC 14: Innerparty Memorandums; Hilliard and Cole, *This Side of Glory*, 339.

91. Vanderscoff, "Look'n M'Face and Hear M' Story," 299.

92. Bobby Seale, *Seize the Time*; Street, "Historiography of the Black Panther Party," 354.

93. Newton with Blake, *Revolutionary Suicide*, 54–55, 67–70, 76–77, 82, 116–17, 136, 173, 179–80, 191, 183, 249, 283; Street, "Shadow of the Soul Breaker," 348–49.

94. *Firing Line* transcript, "How Does It Go with the Black Movement?," 1.

95. *Firing Line* transcript, 3; "Firing Line with William F. Buckley Jr."

96. *Firing Line* transcript, 5–7, Buckley quotation on 6.
97. "Who Makes U.S. Foreign Policy"; "Dialectics of Nature"; "Eve, the Mother of All Living"; "The Mind Is Flesh," all in Newton, *Huey P. Newton Reader*, 295–330; Spencer, *Revolution Has Come*, 160.

Chapter 4. The BPP in the Street

1. Shames and Seale, *Power to the People*, 24.
2. E.g., Murch, *Living for the City*, 132–34.
3. Lebel, "Notes on Political Street Theatre, Paris," in Cohen-Cruz, *Radical Street Performance*, 161; Singh, *Black Is a Country*, 203, 205.
4. Cohen-Cruz, "General Introduction" in Cohen-Cruz, *Radical Street Performance*, 1–2, 6.
5. Cohen-Cruz, introduction to Part Three in Cohen-Cruz, *Radical Street Performance*, 119; Boal, "Invisible Theater," in Cohen-Cruz, *Radical Street Performance*, 121–24.
6. Abbie Hoffman, "Museum of the Streets," 1980, https://theanarchistlibrary.org/library/abbie-hoffman-museum-of-the-streets.
7. Murch, *Living for the City*, 91–92, 97.
8. Lefebvre, *Production of Space*, 26.
9. Mitchell, *Right to the City*, 52–54; Fanon, *Wretched*, 66–67; Nayar, *Frantz Fanon*, 85–86.
10. Lebel, "Notes on Political Street Theatre," 180.
11. Marine, *Black Panthers*, 34.
12. Malloy, *Out of Oakland*, 53, 57.
13. Lefebvre, *Production of Space*, 56.
14. Robert Scheer, "Dialectics of Confrontation," *Ramparts*, August 1969, 44.
15. Sabatini, testimony at *People of the State of California v. Huey P. Newton*, Preliminary Examination, April 19, 1966, 3, 5–10, HPNC 7: Huey's Miscellaneous Appeals.
16. Seale, *Lonely Rage*, 190; James D. Callahan, "Record of Arrests," 4, 10, HPNC 7: unnamed; Hillard et al., *Huey*, 13–14, 20; Major, *Panther Is a Black Cat*, 201. Seale, *Seize the Time* (45) recounts the incident without the gun. Newton later claimed that he did not attempt to take the gun; Sabatini disagreed. Keating, *Free Huey*, 183–85; Drew McKillips, "Berkeley Cop Incident Used against Newton," *SFC*, July 22, 1971, 4.
17. Seale, *Seize the Time*, 44–45, 48–49; Keating, *Free Huey*, 183–84; Murch, *Living for the City*, 112.
18. Seale, *Seize the Time*, 109.
19. Seale, 112. See also Shames and Seale, *Power to the People*, 25–26. Seale's quotations (or more likely paraphrases) of Newton remain remarkably consistent. Oakland police recorded a similar incident in April 1967. FBI file, "Black Panther Party for Self-Defense," November 16, 1967, 51–52, FBIEC section 29.
20. Seale, *Seize the Time*, 113.
21. Seale, 115–16.
22. "Merritt College: Home of the Black Panthers" at 26:00.
23. Newton with Blake, *Revolutionary Suicide*, 24–25; Smitherman, *Talkin and Testifyin*, 128–34.
24. Singh, "Black Panthers and the 'Undeveloped Country,'" 81.
25. Curtis Stephen, "Life of a Party," *Crisis*, September/October 2006, 31; Newton with Blake, *Revolutionary Suicide*, 127–28; "Pocket Lawyer of Legal First Aid," *TBP*, May 15, 1967, 5.

26. Seale, *Seize the Time*, 120.
27. Seale, 121–22.
28. Newton with Blake, *Revolutionary Suicide*, 127.
29. Mao, *Quotations from Chairman Mao Tse-Tung*, 35.
30. Newton with Blake, *Revolutionary Suicide*, 129; Zamalin, *Struggle on Their Minds*, 111.
31. Schutzman and Cohen-Cruz, introduction to *A Boal Companion*, 3.
32. Fanon, *Wretched*, 161.
33. Seale, *Seize the Time*, 123–26; Austin, *Up Against the Wall*, 63; "David Hilliard Giving the Black Panther Tour."
34. Cleaver, "Courage to Kill," 23–32; Marine, *Black Panthers*, 54; Seale, *Seize the Time*, 145–52.
35. Bobby Seale interview by Blackside.
36. "Frightening 'Army' Hits the Airport," *SFC*, February 22, 1967, 1.
37. Seale, Blackside interview. See also Hampton and Fayer, *Voices of Freedom*, 365, 366.
38. Cleaver, "Courage to Kill," 36.
39. "Eldridge Cleaver on Guarding Betty Shabazz."
40. Sol Stern, "America's Black Guerrillas," *Ramparts*, September 1967, 25; Zamalin, *Struggle on Their Minds*, 108.
41. Seale, *Seize the Time*, 177; Rhodes, *Framing the Black Panthers*, 69–70; "It's All Legal: Oakland's Black Panthers Wear Guns, Talk Revolution," *SFE*, April 30, 1967, 1.
42. Quoted in Spencer, *Revolution Has Come*, 43.
43. Spencer, 49; Copes et al., "The Lost Cause?," 361; Fagan and Wilkinson, "Guns, Youth Violence, and Social Identity in Inner Cities," 107, 151; Springwood, "Gun Concealment, Display, and Other Magical Habits of the Body," 462–63.
44. Williams, *Negroes with Guns*, 9–10. All Williams quotations in this passage come from this source.
45. Williams, 12, 26, 46; Richard Maxwell Brown, "Violence," in Milner et al., *Oxford History of the American West*, 393–96.
46. Seale, *Seize the Time*, 157, 184, 187; Hampton and Fayer, *Voices of Freedom*, 365–66.
47. Haldeman with DiMona, *Ends of Power*, 83.
48. FBI, "Black Panther Party for Self-Defense," 51.
49. Walter Benjamin, "Theses on the Philosophy of History" in Benjamin, *Illuminations*, 253; Khvostov, *Russian Civil War (1)*, 8, 22, 28, 43.
50. Shames and Seale, *Power to the People*, 42.
51. Mestman, "Last Sacred Image," 24; Anderson, *Che Guevara*, 342, 424, 565.
52. Winkler, "Secret History of Guns"; "Don Mulford—Longtime Assemblyman," *SFC*, March 28, 2000, https://www.sfgate.com/news/article/Don-Mulford-Longtime-Assemblyman-2792988.php.
53. "Penal Code Section 25850 [California]," https://leginfo.legislature.ca.gov/faces/codes_displaySection.xhtml?sectionNum=25850&lawCode=PEN; Leonardatos, "California's Attempts," 976–77; McLaughlin, *Long Hot Summer*, 6–9.
54. Seale, *Seize the Time*, 178; FBI, "Black Panther Party for Self Defense," November 16, 1967, 21; "Merritt College: Home of the Black Panthers" at 33:00; *Eyes on the Prize II*, episode 3, "Power! (1966–68)"; Forte quoted in *The Black Panthers: Vanguard of the Revolution* at 08:10.
55. FBI report, Leroy Eldridge Cleaver, May 8, 1967, 19, 20, FBIEC section 1.
56. *Eyes on the Prize II*, episode 3; Seale, *Seize the Time*, 183–94.

57. Martin Smith, "Incident May Prompt New Control Law," *Sacramento Bee*, May 3, 1967, A1; Seale, *Seize the Time*, 187.
58. Seale, *Seize the Time*, 189.
59. Tyner, "Defend the Ghetto," 112.
60. "Merritt College: Home of the Black Panthers" at 36:00.
61. Emory Douglas interview, conducted by Blackside, Inc.; Major, *Panther Is a Black Cat*, 77–78; Baraka, *Autobiography of LeRoi Jones*, 353.
62. Newton with Blake, *Revolutionary Suicide*, 157–59.
63. "Merritt College: Home of the Black Panthers" at 34:00; Leonardatos, "California's Attempts," 971–72, 973.
64. Leonardatos, "California's Attempts," 969, 972, 976, 980; FBI report, Leroy Eldridge Cleaver, June 1968, 15, FBIEC section 1; "Merritt College: Home of the Black Panthers" at 38:00.
65. "Black Panthers Disrupt Assembly," *SFC*, May 3, 1967, 1; "Interview with Assemblyman Don Mulford," KPIX Eyewitness News, c. May 1967, https://diva.sfsu.edu/collections/sfbatv/bundles/206880; Leonardatos, "California's Attempts," 980.
66. Hilliard and Cole, *This Side of Glory*, 123.
67. Dan Kataoka, "Probation Officer's Report and Recommendation: Huey Percy Newton," October 18, 1978, 4, HPNC 38: Legal Briefs.
68. FBI, "Black Panther Party for Self-Defense," 54; "Trial of Huey P. Newton, Minister of Defense, Black Panther Party," September 3, 1968, 2, FBIHPN section 2.
69. Eberhart, "Stack Lee," 32, quotation on 41.
70. Eberhart, 42.
71. Stern, "America's Black Guerrillas," 25.
72. Newton with Blake, *Revolutionary Suicide*, 113 (quotation), 157.
73. Sorensen, "Humor as a Serious Strategy," 178.
74. Mao, *Quotations from Chairman Mao Tse-Tung*, 39.
75. Fanon, *Wretched*, 29–31, 46–48, 55, 114, 154.
76. See, for example, "Affidavit of Glenn Stafford," April 16, 1968; "Affidavit of Warren William Wells," April 14, 1968, HPNC 39: illegible (2).
77. Bloom and Martin, *Black against Empire*, 66–70; Spencer, *Revolution Has Come*, 56.

Chapter 5. BPP's Social Programs and Local Chapters

1. FBI report: Huey Percy Newton, April 29, 1971, 286–87, FBIHPN section 12; Don Cox, "Organizing Self-Defense Groups," *TBP*, January 30, 1971, 7–8; "Sawed-Off Shotguns," *TBP*, February 20, 1971, 5; "Weapon Safety," *TBP*, February 27, 1971; "The 9mm FN Browning High Power Pistol," *TBP*, March 6, 1971, 13; "The Caliber .45, Automatic Pistol," *TBP*, March 13, 1971, 13.
2. Alkebulan, *Survival Pending Revolution*, 31, 33; Senate Report No. 94–755, 210–11.
3. Shames and Seale, *Power to the People*, 78.
4. "Everywhere It's Raining Bags of Groceries," *TBP*, August 12, 1972, 6.
5. Landon Williams, "Reform or Revolution?," *TBP*, March 3, 1969, 12.
6. Farmer, *Remaking Black Power*, 81.
7. Nelson, *Body and Soul*, 62; Davis and Wiener, *Set the Night on Fire*, 607.
8. Spencer, *Revolution Has Come*, 71; Ryan Nissim-Sabat, "Panthers Set Up Shop in Cleveland," in Jeffries, *Comrades*, 101–5.
9. Alkebulan, *Survival Pending Revolution*, 65–66.
10. Hilliard, *Black Panther Party Service to the People Programs*, 5–80; Jama Lazerow,

"The Black Panthers at the Water's Edge," in Williams and Lazerow, *Liberated Territory*, 114–15.

11. Nelson, *Body and Soul*, 49, 51, 65–69, 77, 88–90, 102–6; Witt, *Black Panthers in the Midwest*, 63–65.

12. Nelson, *Body and Soul*, 105–7.

13. Nelson, "Genuine Struggle and Care," 1746; Nissim-Sabat, "Panthers Set Up Shop in Cleveland," 105–6, 120–21.

14. Duncan MacLaury et al., "The Black Panther Party and Community Development in Boston," in Jeffries, *Black Panther Party*, 115–21.

15. Bob Heard to "sisters and brothers," n.d.; National Free Clinic Council "Statement of Purpose," n.d.; Heard to Huey, March 27, 1973; "Projected Budget: Drug Education Program," n.d.; "Staff Job Description: Community Counselors"; Audrea Jones memo, July 16, 1973, all in HPNC 12: Info on Medical Clinics; Heard memo, August 31, 1973, HPNC 14: George L. Jackson Clinic.

16. "Statistics for Black Community Survival Conference," c. 1972, HPNC 14: Black Community Survival Conference; Nelson, *Body and Soul*, 116–19; "The Sickle Cell 'Game,'" *TBP*, May 27, 1972, 10; "The People's Fight against Sickle Cell Anemia Begins," *TBP*, May 22, 1971, 10.

17. Henry Smith memo, April 5, 1974, HPNC 14: George L. Jackson Clinic; Nelson, *Body and Soul*, 87, 120.

18. Conway and Stevenson, *Marshall Law*, 45–46; Jeffries, "Revising Panther History in Baltimore," in Jeffries, *Comrades*, 22.

19. "The Angela Davis People's Free Food Program and the David Hilliard People's Free Shoe Factory Will Provide Some of the Tools for Our Survival," *TBP*, October 9, 1971, 8; "These Shoes Are New!" *TBP*, October 23, 1971, 11; "All White, Not All Right," *TBP*, January 15, 1971, 13–14; Miriam Ma'at-Ka-Re Monges, "I Got a Right to the Tree of Life," in Jones, *Black Panther Party*, 140; Nissim-Sabat, "Panthers Set Up Shop in Cleveland," 122–27; "Everywhere It's Raining Bags of Groceries," 13–14; Benjamin R. Friedman, "Picking Up Where Robert F. Williams Left Off," in Jeffries, *Comrades*, 61, 76; Jeffries and Tiyi M. Morris, "Nap Town Awakens to Find a Menacing Panther," in Jeffries, *Comrades*, 158–59, 167–69.

20. Katsiaficas, "Organization and Movement," in Cleaver and Katsiaficas, *Liberation, Imagination, and the Black Panther Party*, 146.

21. Witt, "On the Radio with Michael McGee," 152, quotation on 153.

22. Bloom and Martin, *Black against Empire*, 182; "To Feed Our Children," *TBP*, April 27, 1969, 3; Andrew Witt, "Picking Up the Hammer," in Jeffries, *Comrades*, 195–205; Burke and Jeffries, *Portland Black Panthers*, 109–10.

23. Bloom and Martin, *Black against Empire*, 184–85; Ed Buryn, "Suffer Not, Little Children," *TBP*, April 27, 1969, 5; Olsson, *Black Power Mixtape* at 29:00.

24. "Angela Davis Day-Care Center Raided," *TBP*, January 29, 1972, 8, 18; Jeffries, "Revising Panther History in Baltimore," in Jeffries, *Comrades*, 21. The first BPP school opened in Berkeley in June 1969. See "Liberation Means Freedom," *TBP*, July 5, 1969, 3.

25. Ericka Huggins and Angela D. LeBlanc-Ernest, "Revolutionary Women, Revolutionary Education," in Core et al., *Want to Start a Revolution?*, 168–70, 174–77, 180.

26. Bob Lucas, "East Oakland Ghetto Blooms," *Jet*, February 5, 1976, 20–24; Huggins and LeBlanc-Ernest, "Revolutionary Women, Revolutionary Education," in Core et al., *Want to Start a Revolution?*, 172–75.

27. Huggins and LeBlanc-Ernest, "Revolutionary Women, Revolutionary Education," 168–69, 173; E.O.C. Annual Report, February 1975, HPNC 30: Huey's Personal File; Murch,

Living for the City, 182–83; Huggins, "An Oral History with Ericka Huggins," 81–82, 88–89; McCutchen, *We Were Free for a While*, 149, 153, 161.

28. Garcha, "Children and Childhood," 322; Val Douglas, "Vallejo Liberation School," *TBP*, August 9, 1969, 19.

29. "Mad," "The Youth Make the Revolution," *TBP*, August 9, 1969, 19; Val Douglas, "The Youth Make the Revolution," *TBP*, August 2, 1969, 12; Huggins and LeBlanc-Ernest, "Revolutionary Women," 178.

30. Robinson, "Until the Revolution," 188; "Letters to Charles," *TBP*, August 16, 1969, 11.

31. Perlstein, "Minds Stayed on Freedom," 26–27; Garcha, "Children and Childhood," 329; "Oakland Community School Instructor Handbook," 1978, 2, 11, HPNC 65: Oakland Community School Instructor Handbook; Robinson, "Until the Revolution," 195, 198.

32. Lucas, "East Oakland Ghetto Blooms"; Huggins, "Oral History with Ericka Huggins," 56; Murch, *Living for the City*, 179; Robinson, "Until the Revolution," 193–97.

33. Michael Grieg, "Cable-TV Accord with Minorities," *SFC*, November 29, 1972, 3; Philip Hager, "Panthers' New Image" *Los Angeles Times*, December 5, 1972, 25; Angel, "Monthly Fiscal Report," May 3, 1973, HPNC 17: Articles General; "Report on Restaurant Operations," HPNC 17: David Horowitz.

34. Omari L. Dyson, Kevin L. Brooks, and Judson L. Jeffries, "Brotherly Love Can Kill You," in Jeffries, *Comrades*, 223–34, 247.

35. Bill Bancroft, "The Black Panthers Today," *Twin City Sentinel*, May 28, 1972, 19; Larry Little, "Progress Report from Winston-Salem, North Carolina," HPNC 14: General Reports from Chapters; "Free Ambulance Service," *TBP*, June 26, 1971; Friedman, "Picking Up," 62, 76; Nelson, *Body and Soul*, 110.

36. "Bussing Program Growing in Illinois," *TBP*, August 9, 1971, supplement; "FBI Attempts to Stop the People's Free Bussing to Prisons Program," *TBP*, October 9, 1971, 6, 18; "Black Panther Party Community Transportation Program," HPNC 52: BPP Community Transport; Nissim-Sabat, "Panthers Set Up Shop in Cleveland," 122–27.

37. Witt, *Black Panthers in the Midwest*, 61, 77; Witt, "On the Radio with Michael McGee," 154–55.

38. Jeffries, "Reflecting on Her Life," 133.

39. Steve D. McCutchen, "Selections from a Panther Diary," in Jones, *Black Panther Party*, 117 (quotation), 119–20, 127–29.

40. Jeffries, "Conversing with Gwen Robinson," 141–42; Shames and Seale, *Power to the People*, 79; Pharr, *Nine Lives of a Black Panther*, 100.

41. Joseph, *Panther Baby*, 52–56, 63, 133–37, 143; Foster, "Housing Coordinator" notebook, BPP Harlem Branch files, folder 12; Abu-Jamal, *We Want Freedom*, 61.

42. Dyson et al., "Brotherly Love Can Kill You," 220–21; Spencer, *Revolution Has Come*, 74; Abu-Jamal, *We Want Freedom*, 59, quotation on 201.

43. Huggins and LeBlanc-Ernest, "Revolutionary Women," 67; Pacifica Radio Archives, "Revolution for Breakfast," August 14, 1970, https://archive.org/details/pra-BB2540.

44. Jeffrey Zane and Judson L. Jeffries, "A Panther Sighting in the Pacific Northwest," in Jeffries, *On the Ground*, 59–60 (quotation), 61, 67–73.

45. Zane and Jeffries, 76; Dixon, *My People Are Rising*, 74–75, 80–82, 87–88, 109–10, 128–29, 132–33, 140–43, 148–49, 167–68, 178.

46. "Motor City Busses Rolling," *TBP*, January 15, 1972, 8; Joel P. Rhodes and Judson L. Jeffries, "Motor City Panthers," in Jeffries, *On the Ground*, 140, 142, 148, 155–56; Reynaldo Anderson, "The Kansas City Black Panther Party and the Repression of the Black Rev-

olution," in Jeffries, *On the Ground*, 101–4; Ahmad A. Rahman, "Marching Blind," in Williams and Lazerow, *Liberated Territory*, 19.

47. Newton directives, May 3, 1973, January 14, 1974, March 6, 1974, HPNC 14: Directives.

48. Russell Washington, Weekly Reports, July 17–24, 1973, July 24–31, 1973; Jennings, "Weekly Report," July 24, 1973 (quotation), all in HPNC 2: untitled.

49. Charles E. Jones, "Wake Up Georgia, the Panthers Are Here!" in Jeffries, *Black Panther Party*, 32–35, 37–41; Dyson et al., "Brotherly Love Can Kill You," 221; West Oakland Branch memo, n.d., HPNC 14: General Reports from Chapters; Nelson, *Body and Soul*, 94.

50. Interparty Memoranda, July 29, August 3, August 12, August 27, 1972; January 31, March 21, 1974, all in HPNC 14: Innerparty Memorandums; "Draft of Answers to Interrogatories to Huey P. Newton," c. 1977, 19, HPNC 41: H.P.N. Answers to Interrogatories.

51. Arend, *Showdown in Desire*, 32–33, 55, 81–82.

52. Director, FBI airtel, May 15, 1969, quoted in Newton, *War against the Panthers*, 102–3, 103n120.

53. Austin, "Interview with Harold Taylor," 165.

54. Jones, "Wake Up Georgia," 21.

55. Umoja, "Maroon," 202–5; Balagoon, *Look for Me*, 273–74, 282, 296.

56. Joseph, *Panther Baby*, 73–78, 107–8; Editorial, *People's Community News*, May 24, 1970, 8–9, BPP, Harlem Branch files, folder 19; Umoja, "Maroon," 203–9.

57. Newton, untitled memo, HPNC 15: Newton, the Prison, the Prisoner; Burrough, *Days of Rage*, 179, 181–83, 187–92, 197, 202–3; Joseph P. Fried, "2 Policemen Slain by Shots in Back; 2 Men Are Sought," *NYT*, May 22, 1971, 1; Umoja, "Maroon," 214–15.

58. Abu-Jamal, *We Want Freedom*, 189; Austin, "Interview with Harold Taylor," 169–71; Pharr, *Nine Lives of a Black Panther*, 6–12, 102–3, 128–29, 143–48, 161, 164–68; Judson L. Jeffries and Malcolm Foley, "To Live and Die in L.A.," in Jeffries, *Comrades*, 261, 264–71, 278–79.

59. Rhodes and Jeffries, "Motor City Panthers," 169–73; Rahman, "Marching Blind," 189–93, 197, 207–14.

60. Andrew Witt, "Picking Up the Hammer," in Jeffries, *Comrades*, 187–88, 191; Yohuru Williams, "Give Them a Cause to Die For," in Williams and Lazerow, *Liberated Territory*, 245, 250–51.

61. Alkebulan, *Survival Pending Revolution*, 52; Friedman, "Picking Up," 60–61, 64–72; Bancroft, "Black Panthers Today," 19.

62. Conway and Stevenson, *Marshall Law*, 45–48, 55–56, 60–62; Jeffries, "Revising Panther History," 18, 22, 27–36; McCutchen, "Selections from a Panther Diary," in Jones, *Black Panther Party*, 121–26.

63. Jeffries and Morris, "Nap Town Awakens," 157, 160–63.

64. Dyson et al., "Brotherly Love Can Kill You," 238, 240–47; Abu-Jamal, *We Want Freedom*, 195–96.

65. Bruce Fehn and Robert Jefferson, "The Des Moines, Iowa, African American Community and the Emergence and Impact of the Black Panther Party, 1948–1973," in Jeffries, *On the Ground*, 206–8, 212–14; Dixon, *My People*, 123–24, 130–31, 139, 187–88.

66. Jones, "Talkin' the Talk and Walkin' the Walk," in Jones, *Black Panther Party*, 148, 151; Nissim-Sabat, "Panthers Set Up Shop in Cleveland," 107–12, 126–29.

67. Charles E. Jones, "Arm Yourself or Harm Yourself," in Jeffries, *On the Ground*, 20–25.

68. Arend, *Showdown in Desire*, 3, 9–11, 25–26, 62–64, 137–45, 224–25.

Chapter 6. The Cal-Pac Boycott

1. As Robyn Spencer argues, "Although organizational dynamics in Oakland were not representative of nationwide trends, and local chapters exercised considerable autonomy, Oakland's centrality as the organizational headquarters for much of Panther history make [sic] it a critical point of inquiry." Spencer, "Engendering the Black Freedom Struggle," 91.

2. FBI report, "Huey P. Newton," November 27, 1970, FBIHPN section 7; FBI report, "Huey P. Newton," April 29, 1971, 201–7, FBIHPN section 12.

3. Morris Kaplan, "Bomb Plot Is Laid to 21 Panthers," *NYT*, April 3, 1969, 1; Edith Evans Asbury, "2 Panthers' Bail Ordered Revoked," *NYT*, February 9, 1971, 15; Bloom and Martin, *Black against Empire*, 359–62, 476n61; Press release, February 9, 1971, HPNC 15: Newton, the Prison, the Prisoner; English, *Savage City*, 206–8, 216, 225, 246, 285–90, 293–99.

4. Nelson, *Black Panthers: Vanguard of the Revolution* transcript, 92, 95; FBI, "Huey P. Newton," April 29, 1971, 165–74; Hilliard and Cole, *This Side of Glory*, 323–24 (quotation).

5. FBI airtel, SAC San Francisco to Director FBI, September 8, 1970, FBIBEO section 21; SAC WFO to Director, FBI, August 6, 1970, FBIBEO section 20.

6. FBI "Huey P. Newton," April 29, 1971, 213–16; David Rosenzweig, "Ex-Panther Says He Saw Cleaver Kill a Man," *Los Angeles Times*, February 24, 2001, http://articles.latimes.com/2001/feb/24/local/me-29765; Elaine Mokhtefi, "Diary: Panthers in Algiers," *London Review of Books*, June 1, 2017, https://www.lrb.co.uk/the-paper/v39/n11/elaine-mokhtefi/diary; Gifford, *Revolution or Death*, 198–99; "Byron Booth on the Hidden Traitor Renegade Scab," 4, 16, HPNC 30: Hidden Traitor Renegade Scab (hereafter HTRS) attests to Cleaver's guilt.

7. Newton, "On the Defection of Eldridge Cleaver," C–E; "April 6, 1968, 1218 28th St., Oakland, California," *TBP*, March 13, 1971, 16.

8. Various documents in HPNC 15: Hidden Traitor; "To Eldridge Cleaver and His Conspirators," c. 1970; "For Inclusion in *Hidden Traitor Renegade Scab*," n.d.; Newton to Marty Kenner, August 27, 1972, both HPNC 30: HTRS; Random House contract, July 17, 1972, HPNC 41: HTRS. The book remains unpublished.

9. Bloom and Martin, *Black against Empire*, 364.

10. Bennett quoted in White, *Challenge of Blackness*, 114, 112.

11. Chappell, *Waking from the Dream*, 41–42.

12. "Panther Reform," *WP*, January 31, 1972, A4.

13. Bloom and Martin, *Black against Empire*, 379–80.

14. Chappell, *Waking from the Dream*, 34, 126.

15. Obama, *Dreams from My Father*, 139.

16. Bloom and Martin, *Black against Empire*, 347–49, 351.

17. Cal-Pac, "About," 2013, https://web.archive.org/web/20190915071855/http://calpac.mktgkings.com/about/; Pearson, *Shadow of the Panther*, 240–42; Ross K. Baker, "The Transformation of the Panthers," *WP*, February 13, 1972, B1–B2; Potorti, "Feeding the Revolution," 101–2; FBI reports, September 17, October 18, 1971, 11; transcript of Newton–Cal-Pac meeting, July 22, 1971, all in FBIHPN 92–HQ-12718 sections 1 and 2; Undated, untitled document, HPNC 16: Cal-Pac.

18. Pearson, *Shadow of the Panther*, 241–42; Boyette to Newton, July 29, 1971; Newton memo, July 28, 1971, both in HPNC 16: Cal-Pac.

19. SAC, San Francisco memo, October 4, 1972; A. William Olson memo, c. October 1972, both in FBIHPN 92–HQ-13682; "General Investigative Division" memo, August 6,

1971; San Francisco FBI office teletype, August 31, 1971, both in FBIHPN 92–HQ-12718 sections 1 and 2.

20. Newton–Cal-Pac meeting transcript; William Moore, "Berkeley Cop Incident Used against Newton," *SFC*, July 22, 1971, 4.

21. Transcript of Cal-Pac–Newton Meeting, July 30, 1971, 2–3, FBIHPN 92–HQ-12718 sections 1 and 2.

22. Transcript, 6–16; San Francisco FBI teletype, August 31, 1971, 1–2; "Seale Discusses Panthers' Survival Programs," KPIX Eyewitness News, July 31, 1971, https://diva.sfsu.edu/collections/sfbatv/bundles/208067.

23. FBI report, "Huey P. Newton," February 7, 1972, 3, FBIHPN section 17; "Boycott of Bill Boyette's Liquor Store in Oakland," KPIX Eyewitness News, August 13, 1971, https://diva.sfsu.edu/collections/sfbatv/bundles/208069#; "Panthers Give Away Goods at Boycott of Liquor Store," KPIX Eyewitness News, September 18, 1971, https://diva.sfsu.edu/collections/sfbatv/bundles/208075; "Community Members Speak Out against Panthers' Tactics," KPIX Eyewitness News, September 24, 1971, https://diva.sfsu.edu/bundles/208078.

24. FBI reports, August 21, September 21, 1971, 4; San Francisco FBI teletype, August 5, 1971, all in FBIHPN 92–HQ-12718 sections 1 and 2; Seale and Shames, *Power to the People*, 122–25.

25. Potorti, "Feeding the Revolution," 102; "Boycott of Bill Boyette's Liquor Store"; "Panthers Give Away Goods"; "Boyette Wants No Part of the People's Survival Programs," *TBP*, September 25, 1971, 15; "Boyette Talks About Your Momma," *TBP*, October 16, 1971, 3.

26. San Francisco FBI teletype, August 5, 1971; Superior Court of California, County of Alameda, "Order to Show Cause," August 9, 1971, HPNC 16: Cal-Pac; San Francisco FBI teletype, August 10, 1971, FBIHPN 92–HQ-12718 sections 1 and 2; "Merchants Group Accuses Panthers," *SFC*, August 11, 1971, 26.

27. "Why Boycott Boyette?," *TBP*, August 9, 1971, supplement, A, F.

28. "The Black Community Is Boyette's Only Family," *TBP*, August 21, 1971, 15 (quotation), 16.

29. Newton, "Black Capitalism Re-Analyzed II," *TBP*, August 9, 1971, in Newton, *To Die for the People*, 110.

30. "People's Boycott" flyer, n.d., FBIHPN 92–HQ-12718 sections 1 and 2.

31. Notes of KSFX radio show, August 13, 1971, attached to SAC, San Francisco memo, August 16, 1971, 3; two San Francisco FBI office teletypes, August 13, 1971, all FBIHPN 92–HQ-12718 sections 1 and 2.

32. "Boycott of Bill Boyette's Liquor Store in Oakland"; FBI report, August 16, 1971, FBIHPN 92–HQ-12718 sections 1 and 2.

33. "Chairman Bobby Speaks at Boycott Site," *TBP* supplement, August 9, 1971, C. These comments were also reported in the *Oakland Post*. See Potorti, "Feeding the Revolution," 106.

34. Pearson, *Shadow of the Panther*, 244–45.

35. Notes of press conference, September 17, 1971, FBIHPN 92–HQ-12718 sections 1 and 2.

36. Transcript of Cal-Pac meeting, September 10, 1971, 2, 3, 5, 7, 12, HPNC 16: Cal-Pac.

37. FBI report, October 18, 1971, 2–3, FBIHPN 92–HQ-12718 section 2.

38. San Francisco FBI teletype, September 13, 1971 (quotation); FBI report, September 14, 1971, both in FBIHPN 92–HQ-12718 sections 1 and 2.

39. "Panthers' Boycott—Can Blacks Resist?," *OT*, September 23, 1971, 1; "Blacks Unit-

ing to Fight Newton Plan," *OT*, September 24, 1971, 1; "Huey Newton Luxury Life Stirs Growing Resentment," *OT*, September 26, 1971, 1.

40. Durant, *Black Panther*, 143, 142.

41. James L. Browning and Jerry K. Cimmet to Brandon Alvey, November 1, 1971, attached to SAC, San Francisco teletype, May 17 1972, FBIHPN 92–HQ-12718 section 2; Roy Wilkins, "The 'New' Panthers," *New York Post*, February 26, 1972, HPNC 12: Open Letter to Roy Wilkins.

42. Thomas A. Johnson, "Report Assails Inquiry on Slaying of Black Panthers," *NYT*, March 17, 1972, 17.

43. Hopkins memo, January 7, 1972, HPNC 16: Cal-Pac; "Panthers Halt One Boycott," *SFC*, January 16, 1972, 27.

44. San Francisco FBI office teletype, January 17, 1972, FBIHPN 92–HQ-12718 section 2; "Dellums Settles Panthers Dispute," KPIX Eyewitness News, January 15, 1972, https://diva.sfsu.edu/collections/sfbatv/bundles/208079; Transcript of KNBC-TV News segment, January 21, 1972 (quotation on 3), FBIHPN section 17.

45. KNBC-TV News transcript, 4.

46. "Letter to White Businesses," n.d., HPNC 16: Cal-Pac.

47. Wilson, "Attorney, Judge, and Oakland Mayor," 53–55.

48. "Letter to White Businesses," post-January 1972, HPNC 16: Cal-Pac.

49. Hiawatha Roberts to Earl Neil, February 1, 1972; undated flyer, both in HPNC 16: Cal-Pac.

50. Durant, *Black Panther*, 148.

51. "Unity Ends Boycott," *TBP* supplement, January 22, 1972, F.

52. Donald Hopkins letter to Hiawatha Roberts, June 15, 1972, HPNC 16: Cal-Pac.

53. "Barbara" to Newton, c. September 1972; "Statement by Domestic Corporation," May 29, 1972; UBF to Garry, July 20, 1972; Gwen Fountaine, untitled document, October 2, 1972, all in HPNC 11: United Black Fund, Inc.

54. FBI report, January 14, 1971, 2, FBIHPN section 7; FBI reports, January 25, January 26, March 30, April 5, 1971, FBIHPN section 12; Ross K. Baker, "The Transformation of the Panthers," *WP*, February 13, 1972, B1.

55. San Francisco FBI teletype, April 14, 1971, 2, FBIHPN section 11; "Summary of meeting between Philip Kenner and Bette Shertzer," October 17, 1972, HPNC 30: Huey's Personal File.

56. David Lubell, memo, n.d., HPNC 52: Structure for Income Producing Assets and Property; Lubell to Newton and Seale, June 28, 1971; Bette to Gwen [Fountaine], December 5, 1972; Martin Kenner to Gwen and Huey, September 11, 1973; Kenner to Gwen, June 17, 1974; anonymous to Gwen, n.d., all in HPNC 30: Huey's Personal File.

57. Kenner to Fountaine, May 12, June 5, 1972; Kenner to "Servant" (Newton), June 20, July 7, 1972, all in HPNC 30: Martin Kenner; Lubell to Newton, June 6, 1972, HPNC 30: Bert Halvonik; Kenner to Gwen, November 13, 1973, HPNC 52: General Stronghold Corresp; Hilary Maddux to Lubell, February 24, 1972, HPNC 52: Seale Seize the Time tax materials.

58. SAC, San Francisco memo, FBI, October 4, 1972; FBI document, October 18, 1972; San Francisco FBI report, February 8, 1973, 2, all in FBIHPN 92–HQ-13682.

59. "Panthers Lead Protest of Blaxploitation Films," KPIX Eyewitness News, September 27, 1972, https://diva.sfsu.edu/collections/sfbatv/bundles/208083; FBI report, "Huey P. Newton," December 6, 1972, 4, FBIHPN 92–HQ-13682; Newton testimony, *People of the State of California vs. Huey Percy Newton*, transcript, 184–85, 195–96, 203–5, HPNC 8: Court of Appeals.

60. "Memorandum of Agreement," n.d., HPNC 16: Cal-Pac.
61. B. J. Mason, "A Shift to the Middle," *Ebony*, August 1973, 80.
62. Newton, "Black Capitalism Re-Analyzed I," in Newton, *To Die for the People*, 102.

Chapter 7. Bobby Seale for Mayor!

1. Chappell, *Waking from the Dream*, 40; Johnson, *Revolutionaries to Race Leaders*, 89–95, 102–3.
2. "A State of Black Unity in Gary, Indiana," *TBP*, March 18, 1972, 8, 17; Newton, "All Black People Got to Seize the Time for Unity!," *TBP*, April 29, 1972, 2–3; Willie Brown memo, May 11, 1972; Newton to Hopkins, May 5, 1972; Newton to Dellums, June 12, 1972, all in HPNC 11: National Black Political Convention (hereafter NBPC).
3. Johnson, *Revolutionaries to Race Leaders*, 104, 106, 109, 129; NBPC agenda, HPNC 11: NBPC; Chappell, *Waking from the Dream*, 37, 87, 89.
4. Hahn et al., "Cleavages, Coalitions, and the Black Candidate," 513, 517–18; Steven Roberts, "Yorty Is Closing Gap in Los Angeles Mayoralty Race," *NYT*, May 25, 1969, 67.
5. Self, *American Babylon*, 306; Newton, "On the Defection of Eldridge Cleaver," in Newton, *To Die for the People*, 50.
6. Janine DeFao, "John Reading: Former Mayor of Oakland," *SFC*, February 13, 2003, https://www.sfgate.com/bayarea/article/john-reading-former-mayor-of-oakland-his-2670609.php; "Oakland Mayor" (1977), https://www.ourcampaigns.com/RaceDetail.html?RaceID=86235.
7. Eldridge Cleaver, "Black Paper by the Minister of Information," *TBP*, May 4, 1968, 12.
8. "We're Talking About Winning in Oakland," *TBP*, November 9, 1972, 5, quotation on 13.
9. "We Can Take Oakland," *SFE*, November 12, 1972, 1, 17; "Seale Says He'll Take Oakland," *OT*, November 12, 1972, 5.
10. "Voter Information Guide for 1972, General Election," 5–6, 26, 31–36, 42–44, 48, 58. Available at https://repository.uclawsf.edu/ca_ballot_props/774/.
11. "Elections '72," *TBP*, November 16, 1972, 8.
12. Alterman, "Ron Dellums," 39–40; Self, *American Babylon*, 295–97; Bell, *California Crucible*, 230–31; "Berkeley City Council Race, Apr 04, 1967," https://www.ourcampaigns.com/RaceDetail.html?RaceID=546532; "Seale: 'More Black Cops,'" *SFE*, March 6, 1973, 4.
13. Jack Slater, "The Guard Changes in Berkeley," *Ebony*, October 1971, 74–82; Bell, *California Crucible*, 251–54; Alterman, "Ron Dellums," 37, 40–41; Self, *American Babylon*, 297–98.
14. Art Goldberg, "Report on the Political Situation in Berkeley," HPNC 16: Berkeley City Council; Art Goldberg, "Organizing an Earthquake," *University Review*, April 1973, 11, HPNC 25: Bobby Seale for Mayor (hereafter BSM).
15. Goldberg, "Organizing an Earthquake," 13.
16. "Cobb, Seale, Brooks Highlight Political Meet," *California Voice*, December 7, 1972, 1 HPNC 25: BSM.
17. Jerry Carroll, "High Stakes in Oakland Election," *SFC*, April 11, 1973, 4; Murch, *Living for the City*, 197; DeFao, "John Reading"; "Portrait of Mayor Reading," HPNC 15: Bobby Seale Campaign Info (hereafter BSCI); Gayle Montgomery, "Hot Race for Mayor in April," *OT*, January 7, 1973, 40.
18. Malloy, *Out of Oakland*, 178–79; Forbes, *Will You Die with Me?*, 64–66, 71. The FBI estimated a membership of 366 in May 1972, with over two hundred in Oakland. SAC, San Francisco airtel, June 19, 1972, 6–7, in *What We Want, What We Believe*, disc 4.

19. Robert O. Self, "The Black Panther Party and the Long Civil Rights Era," in Lazerow and Williams, *In Search of the Black Panther Party*, 41–42.

20. "Oakland—A Base of Operation!," *TBP* supplement, July 29, 1972, A. (Hereafter cited as "OBO" with date and pages from *TBP* supplement.)

21. "OBO," B-C.

22. "OBO," part 3, August 12, 1972, A.

23. "Families on Welfare—1970"; "Unemployment in Oakland and Some Possible Remedies," both in HPNC 14: BSCI; "OBO," part 32, March 3, 1973, A–C.

24. "OBO," part 20, December 7, 1972, A–D.

25. "OBO," part 9, September 23, 1972, B.

26. "OBO," part 31, February 24, 1973, A–C.

27. "OBO," part 26, January 20, 1973, A–C; "OBO," part 14, October 28, 1972, C (quotation).

28. "OBO," part 8, September 16, 1972, A–C; "Add Racism to the Three 'R's,'" *TBP*, October 28, 1972, 5, 14.

29. "October 1966 Black Panther Party Platform and Program," in Foner, *Black Panthers Speak*, 2 (quotation); "OBO," part 16, November 9, 1972, B–C.

30. "OBO," part 17, November 16, 1972, B–C.

31. "War Machine Docks at the Port of Oakland," *TBP*, September 9, 1972, 7.

32. Bobby Seale memo, c. August 1972, various untitled documents in HPNC 16: WOPC Elections; Press Statement c. August 1972, HPNC 15: BSCI; Self, *American Babylon*, 304–5.

33. "Panthers Sweep Berkeley Elections!," *TBP*, June 10, 1972, 2, 12–3; "O.E.O. Attempts to Unseat the Community," *TBP*, September 16, 1972, 5.

34. James Mott memo to Comrade Huey, c. October 1972; Gene Jones memo, December 16, 1972, both in HPNC 16: Berkeley City Council; Elections Committee memo to Servant, n.d., HPNC 11: Voter Registration Elections Committee (hereafter VREC).

35. Concerned Citizens Committee letter, September 25, 1972, HPNC 15: BSCI.

36. Earl Raymond to Dellums, n.d., HPNC 16: Ron Dellums—Don Hopkins.

37. "Huey Newton Backs Race by Mrs. Chisholm," *NYT*, April 28, 1972, 83; "Huey Newton Arrested," *SFC*, April 28, 1972, 1, 18.

38. LeBlanc-Ernest, "Most Qualified Person," 318; Michael Kissinger, "Joshua Rose (1906–1987)," Black Past, March 31, 2014, https://www.blackpast.org/african-american-history/rose-joshua-1906-1987/; Rhomberg, *No There There*, 153, 169; "Mayor Race—Wide Range of Choices," *OT*, n.d., HPNC 25: BSM; "Guide to the Joshua Rose Papers," https://oac.cdlib.org/findaid/ark:/13030/c85x29pt/.

39. "Notes on the Oakland City Elections," n.d., HPNC 15: BSCI; Carroll, "High Stakes in Oakland Election."

40. Patti Williams memo, March 21, 1973, HPNC 14: BSCI.

41. Community Committee to Elect Bobby Seale and Elaine Brown (hereafter Community Committee) letter, n.d., HPNC 15: BSCI.

42. Sue Soennichsen, "More Than Just a Change in Tactics," *Montclarion*, March 28, 1973, 1, HPNC 25: BSM.

43. Seale, "Statement of Contributions," April 16, 1973, HPNC 14: BSCI; SAC San Francisco, airtel, July 3, 1972, 6, in *What We Want, What We Believe*, disc 4.

44. Weekly Reports by Bill Jennings, February 27–March 5, March 20–27, 1973; Mike Cross, March 20–26, 1973; Mike Ellis and Victor Grayson, March 27, 1973, all in HPNC 2: untitled.

45. Philip Hager, "Panthers' New Image," *Los Angeles Times*, December 5, 1972, 1, 24, 25; Keith Power, "Black Panther Escorts," *SFC*, December 5, 1972, 2; "Black Panthers Call for Funding of S.A.F.E. Program," January 3, 1973, HPNC 11: Senior Citizen "Muggings."

46. "Bobby Seale and Elaine Brown Are the Effective Democrats!"; "People Have a Right to a Job, with or without a Skill," both in HPNC 14: BSCI; Seale to Councilmen, February 14, 1973, HPNC 15: BSCI.

47. "Verified Statements of Candidates," c. February 1973, 10, 11, HPNC 14: BSCI.

48. Seale open letter, January 30, 1973, HPNC 15: BSCI; Community Committee press releases, February 9, March 8, 1973, HPNC 14: BSCI; *Tribune* editorial, February 6, 1973, cited in Community Committee press release, c. February 1973; press release February 15, 1973, all in HPNC 15: BSCI.

49. "Elaine Brown Charges Oakland City Council," March 7, 1973, HPNC 15: BSCI; Fran Dauth, "Secret Meetings Banned by City," *OT*, March 9, 1973, 1.

50. Hager, "Panthers' New Image," 24; "Bobby Seale: From Clenched Fist to the Ballot Box," *WP*, April 13, 1973, A2; "Make Your Vote Count on April 17th," flyer, HPNC 14: BSCI.

51. Seale and Brown election statements; "Biographical Sketch of Bobby Seale"; Sample Municipal Ballot paper, April 17, 1973, all in HPNC 14: BSCI.

52. "Getting the Vote Out," *TBP*, February 10, 1973, 10; "Vote for Survival" lyrics, HPNC 15: BSCI.

53. "City of Oakland Budget Summary for 1972–3 fiscal year," HPNC 14: BSCI; "Use of General Revenue Sharing Funds," n.d., HPNC 16: Revenue Sharing; "Vote April 17th," campaign leaflet, HPNC 25: BSCI.

54. Robert Odell memo, February 20, 1973, HPNC 16: Revenue Sharing.

55. Community Committee press release, March 5, 1973, HPNC 14: BSCI.

56. "Methods of Increasing Revenues to the City," n.d.; "Loss of Federal Funds and Jobs Due to Cuts in Federal Budget for Fiscal Year 1974," n.d., both in HPNC 16: Revenue Sharing.

57. Community Committee press releases, March 5, March 29, 1973, HPNC 14: BSCI.

58. Community Committee press releases, March 7, March 29, 1973; open letter, March 7, 1973, all HPNC 14: BSCI.

59. Tim Findley, "What Bobby Seale Must Do," *SFC*, April 26, 1973, 4; Jerry Carroll, "Reading Props Up a Runoff Menace," *SFC*, May 7, 1973, 4; Gayle Montgomery, "Demos, Labor Seek Mayor Candidate," *OT*, January 16, 1973, 2.

60. "Bobby Seale, the Wild Card," *OT*, April 1, 1973; "Mayor Race," *OT*, April 15, 1973, back page; "The Hottest City Election in Years," *OT*, April 15, 1973, all HPNC 25: BSM.

61. "For Mayor Don't Pick a Panther," HPNC 15: BSCI.

62. "Electing Otho Green Will Mean New Pride for Oakland," HPNC 14: BSCI.

63. Patti Williams memo, March 21, 1973; Montgomery, "Hot Race for Mayor in April"; Carroll, "High Stakes in Oakland Election" (quotation).

64. "Church Labor Democrat" campaign flyer, April 1973, HPNC 25: BSCI; Pete Almeida memo, March 20, 1973, HPNC 14: BSCI.

65. "Together . . . " flyer; "Oakland: It Takes Leadership" flyer, HPNC 14: BSCI; "Verified Statements of Candidates," 2.

66. "Quotations from Reading," n.d., HPNC 15: BSCI.

67. "Total Population and Employment in Major Industries," HPNC 14: BSCI.

68. Bay Area Census: City of Oakland, 1960, 1970, 1980, http://www.bayareacensus.ca.gov/cities/Oakland50.htm, http://www.bayareacensus.ca.gov/cities/Oakland70.htm; Ericka Huggins memos, n.d., July 31, 1972; Elections Committee memo, August 1,

1972; "Notes from Meeting with Comrades"; Minutes of Elections Committee Meeting, June 30 [1972], all in HPNC 11: VREC; "Getting the Vote Out," *TBP*, February 10, 1973, 5, 10–11; "Voter Registration 'Hot Line' Open," *TBP*, February 24, 1972, 5; Community Committee for Greater Voter Registration press release, n.d., HPNC 15: BSCI.

69. Victor Grayson and Russell Washington, report, January 5, 1973, HPNC 2 file: untitled; "Elaine Brown for Councilwoman of Oakland" poster, HPNC 14 file: BSCI.

70. Donald Freed, "Oakland and the World," 1972, HPNC 16: Oakland and the World; Section 4 Weekly Reports, n.d., HPNC 2: untitled; Orlando Vaughn, Weekly Report, March 20–26, 1973, HPNC 2: untitled; Herman Smith memo: Status of Campaign Offices, n.d.; Whites for Bobby Seale, Elaine Brown flyer, both in HPNC 15: BSCI; "Whites for Bobby and Elaine," *TBP*, February 10, 1973, 10.

71. "Event Calender [*sic*] Section [illegible]"; "Calendar for Section 4," n.d.; William Roberts weekly report, January 25–29, 1973; "Bubber" [James Young] to Servant, c. January 1973; various flyers, all in HPNC 2: untitled; various flyers in HPNC 14: BSCI; "Street Operations"; Elections Committee memo, June 22, 1972, both in HPNC 15: BSCI; "Bobby and Elaine Meet the People on Oakland Buses," *TBP*, March 3, 1973, 12.

72. "Notes from Meeting with Comrades Who Are Voter Registrars and 3 Community Campaign Workers," July 2, 1972, HPNC 11: VREC.

73. Ericka Huggins memo, August 4, 1972, HPNC 2: untitled; Elections Committee Memos, July 3, July 19, September 3, 1972; Huggins memo, n.d., all in HPNC 11: VREC; Victor Grason [*sic*], report, December 2, 1972; Victor Grayson and Russell Washington, report, January 5, 1973; Bill Jennings, Weekly Report, December 11, 1972; Billy Jennings, Report, February 3–10 [1973]; Audrea Jones, "Daily Telephone Reports by Section Leaders," February 25, 1973; Reeni, "Section 4—Mexican Community," March 19, 1973, all in HPNC 2: untitled.

74. Section 4 Weekly Reports, c. February 1973, n.d., HPNC 2: untitled; "Why Should the Spanish Speaking Community Vote for Bobby Seale for Mayor of Oakland" flyer, HPNC 15: BSCI.

75. Elbert Howard and William Roberts memo, December 21, 1972; Howard report, December 30, 1972, HPNC 2: untitled; "Why Gay People Should Vote for Bobby Seale and Elaine Brown" flyer, c. March 1973, HPNC 14: BSCI.

76. "Attention All Employees!"; Seale to "Oakland Employer"; press release, November 6, 1973, all in HPNC 14: BPP v Granny Goose; Community Committee press release and letter, April 3, 1973, HPNC 14: BSCI; "Are You Getting Your 2 Hours Leave with Pay?," *TBP*, October 28, 1972, 3.

77. Gene Jones report, January 27, 1973, HPNC 14: Public Relations Weekly Reports.

78. Elections Committee memo, December 5, 1972; Washington and Grayson report, December 29, 1972; Jennings report, December 11, 1972, all HPNC 2: untitled; "66% Support for Bobby for Mayor," *TBP*, May 12, 1973, 12; Community Committee, undated letter "to friends," HPNC 14: BSCI.

79. Innerparty Memorandums, January 3, January 10, January 17, January 31, February 7, February 23, 1973, HPNC 14: Innerparty Memorandums; various documents, HPNC 14: Subscription Drive.

80. McAllister, Two Week Schedule, January 29–February 11, 1973; James Parhms report, April 24–30, 1973; Michael Ellis and Victor Grayson report, February 17, 1973; Section 4, "Meeting January 28, 1973," all HPNC 2: untitled; Goldberg, "Organizing an Earthquake," 13.

81. William Roberts report, January 25–29, 1973, HPNC 2: untitled; press release, Feb-

ruary 22, 1973, HPNC 14: BSCI; press release, February 14, 1973, HPNC 15: BSCI; "F.B.I. Harasses Campaign Workers," *TBP*, February 24, 1973, 4.

82. Chuck McAllister, "Section 9 Activities Report," February 19, 1973, HPNC 2: untitled.

83. "Bobby Seale's Life Threatened," *TBP*, February 24, 1972, 5, 14; Sherry Brown memo, March 16, 1973, HPNC 15: BSCI; Sid Blumenthal, "How the FBI Destroyed the Black Panthers," *Real Paper*, April 24, 1974, 6, HPNC 25: General Write Ups on Oakland.

84. Quoted in Susan and Chuck McAllister, Section 9 Report, c. May 1973, HPNC 2: untitled.

85. "Oakland Mayor," https://www.ourcampaigns.com/RaceDetail.html?RaceID=546530.

86. "Election Results April 17, 1973"; Gayle Montgomery, "Reading Beats Seale Decisively in Runoff," *OT*, May 16, 1973, 1; "Election Results," *Montclarion*, n.d., HPNC 25: BSM.

87. John Sutter, "Why We Lost," HPNC 14: BSCI.

88. "Make Your Vote Count," *TBP*, May 12, 1973, 2; "66% Support for Bobby for Mayor," *TBP*, May 12, 1973, 3; figures from *TBP*, May 12, 1973, 13; Carroll, "Reading Props Up."

89. Frances memo, April 30, 1973, HPNC 15: BSCI; "Vote May 15th" flyer, HPNC 14: BSCI; "Dellums Endorses Seale for Mayor," *OT*, April 26, 1973, HPNC 2: untitled; "Coretta King Endorses Bobby," *TBP*, May 12, 1973, 3.

90. "OBO," part 42, May 12, 1973, A–D.

91. "Statements by Reading, Seale," *OT*, May 11, 1973, HPNC 25: BSM; Carroll, "Reading Props Up."

92. John Sutter, "Why We Lost."

93. Don Martinez, "Reading in Easy Win over Seale," *SFE*, May 16, 1973, 1; "Bobby Seale: From Clenched Fist"; Gayle Montgomery, "Reading Beats Seale Decisively in Runoff," *OT*, May 16, 1973, 1, 16.

94. "Preliminary Vote Analysis & Comparison April 17 to May 15," HPNC 15: BSCI.

95. "Treasurers Campaign Statement," May 1973, HPNC 15: BSCI; Montgomery, "Reading Beats Seale" 1; Gayle Montgomery, "Reading, Seale in Five-Day Drive," *OT*, May 10, 1973, 5.

96. Pearson, *Shadow of the Panther*, 249; "We've Only Just Begun," *TBP*, June 2, 1973, 5; written reports: section 4, May 22–28, 1973; section 7, May 29, 1973; Bubber Young, c. May 1973; Russell Washington, July 25–July 9, 1973; Area Five, June 26–July 2, 1973, all in HPNC 2: untitled.

97. Shilts, *Mayor of Castro Street*, 80.

98. "Elections Central" memo, May 22, 1973; written reports: Bill Jennings, July 4–11, July 24, 1973; Area 2, June 27–July 2, July 11, 1973; Russell Washington, June 25–July 9, July 17–25, 1973; James Young, July 18–24, 1973, all in HPNC 2: untitled.

99. Written reports: Washington, September 6–12, 1973; Area Five, August 29–September 5, 1973; Steve Long, September 6, September 12, 1973; Area #3, August 15–28, 1973, all in HPNC 2: untitled; Seale, *Lonely Rage*, 292, 296–302, 305; Brown, *Taste of Power*, 333–36, 349–52.

100. Goldstein, "Huey Newton Comes Home," 4; Self, *American Babylon*, 310–16; Malloy, *Out of Oakland*, 218–22.

101. Pearl Stewart and Lance Williams, "City Audit Questions Panthers' Spending," *OT*, March 14, 1978, HPNC 19: General Articles; Pearl Stewart and Lance Williams, "Black Panther Bail Forgeries Exposed," *OT*, February 5, 1978, 1, 5; Pearl Stewart and Lance Williams, "Huge Tax Lien against Panthers," *OT*, May 21, 1978, 1, 16.

102. Weir and Noyes, "Behind the Story," in *Raising Hell*, 261, 266, 268; Coleman and Avery, "Party's Over"; Paul Grabowicz, "Huey's Reign of Terror," *Berkeley Barb*, July 7–13, 1978, 3; Lance Williams, "Newton Files $6 Million Libel Suit," *OT*, August 17, 1978, 17.

103. Spencer, *Revolution Has Come*, 191–95; JoNina [Abron] memo, October 1, 1980, HPNC 63: Booker T. Lewis.

104. Officer's Statement, December 4, 1979, HPNC 6: 1979 DMV case; "Newton Drunk Charges Dropped," *OT*, December 27, 1979, HPNC 3: News Clippings and Magazines; Order of Suspension: Huey P. Newton, September 22, 1980, HPNC 45: Personal File Huey; OPD arrest report, May 6, 1980, HPNC 11: Huey's Columbia Contract; Lowell Jensen to Ronald Locke, February 19, 1981, HPNC 31: Court Trans.

Chapter 8. The Trial of Huey P. Newton

1. Marine, *Black Panthers*, 101–2; "Interview with Lt. John Ream, OPD," November 21, 1968, HPNC 14: Servant's Second Trial; "Officer Frey Just Wasn't a Good Cop," *TBP*, August 9, 1971, 2, 5, 9; Pearlman, *Sky's the Limit*, 325.

2. Coleman and Avery, "Party's Over," 25.

3. "Record of Arrests," 3, HPNC 7: unnamed; Marine, *Black Panthers*, 79–82; Keating, *Free Huey*, 7, 19, 32–33.

4. Charles Garry, undated fragment, 8, HPNC 42: illegible name; Keating, *Free Huey*, 26–30; Fortner, "The 'Silent Majority' in Black and White," 272.

5. Garry and Goldberg, *Streetfighter in the Courtroom*, 7–14, 97; "Transcript of a Seminar given 3/9/71 in the Common Room of Branford College, Y[ale] U[niversity]," 4–5, HPNC 33: Newspaper Clippings.

6. Garry, undated fragment, 2 (quotation), 3–5, HPNC 42: illegible name; Pearlman, *Sky's the Limit*, 332, 354–55; Garry and Goldberg, *Streetfighter in the Courtroom*, 131.

7. Ward Just, "The Making of a Martyr," *WP*, July 28, 1968, B2.

8. Keating, *Free Huey*, 49; Berger, *Captive Nation*, 177–222.

9. Jim Neubacher, "Garry: Snatching Panthers from the Belly of the Monster," *Michigan Daily*, November 19, 1970, HPNC 33: Newspaper Clippings.

10. Garry and Goldberg, *Streetfighter in the Courtroom*, 99; *Huey P. Newton vs. Kaiser Foundation Hospital et al.*, December 5, 1967, HPNC 38: Testimony and Statements.

11. Keating, *Free Huey*, 53; Garry, undated fragment, 9–13; *People vs. Newton*, February 1, 1968, 17, HPNC 35: illegible (third on reel); Garry and Goldberg, *Streetfighter in the Courtroom*, 99 (quotation).

12. Rhodes, *Framing the Black Panthers*, 118–19.

13. Bloom and Martin, *Black against Empire*, 108–9; Joel Wilson, "Invisible Cages," in Lazerow and Williams, *In Search of the Black Panther Party*, 194, 204; "New Left on Coast Begins Ballot Drive," *NYT*, August 16, 1967, 18.

14. Rhodes, *Framing the Black Panthers*, 122–23; Robinson, *Black Nationalism*, 1–2.

15. FBI telegram, October 28, 1967, FBIHPN section 1; FBI report, "The Black Panther Party for Self Defense," November 16, 1967, 16, 23 FBIEC section 29; Shames and Seale, *Power to the People*, 29.

16. Hilliard and Cole, *This Side of Glory*, 141, 182.

17. Seale, *Seize the Time*, 240–41.

18. Seale, 240; Pearlman, *Sky's the Limit*, 342, 351–52; "Backers Pack Court for Huey," *Berkeley Barb*, December 15–21, 1967, 1, 3.

19. "Panthers & Radicals," *Berkeley Barb*, January 19–25, 7.

20. "How It Went Down: Convention in Expert Hands," *Berkeley Barb*, March 22–28, 1968, 5.

21. Newton, "Executive Mandate No. 2," *TBP*, July 1, 1967, 6; Joseph, *Stokely*, 87–99, 161–63.

22. Austin, *Up Against the Wall*, 129–32; Eldridge Cleaver, "Bunchy," in K. Cleaver, *Target Zero*, 131; Forman, *Making of Black Revolutionaries*, 522, 525–27, 530–31.

23. Pugh, *Huey!*; Rhodes, *Framing the Black Panthers*, 127.

24. Joseph, *Stokely*, 243; FBI letter, March 5, 1968, 1–3; transcript of speeches at February 18, 1968, rally, Los Angeles, 13; FBI report, "Huey Percy Newton," May 24, 1968, 15, all in FBIHPN section 1; Pugh, *Huey!*.

25. "Huey Must Be Set Free," *TBP*, March 16, 1968, 20.

26. Audio recording of Bobby Seale speech at "Huey Newton Birthday Rally February 17, 1968 (Bobby Seale, H. Rap Brown, Stokely Carmichael)," https://archive.org/details/pra-BB5471.

27. "H. Rap Brown and Stokely Carmichael Address the Black Panthers," https://archive.org/details/pra-BB1708.

28. "H. Rap Brown and Stokely Carmichael Address the Black Panthers" (quotation); "H. Rap Brown and Stokely Carmichael in Oakland," KQED News, February 17, 1968, https://diva.sfsu.edu/collections/sfbatv/bundles/189468.

29. Ture quoted in Carson, *In Struggle*, 280.

30. Morry Wright, "If the Pigs Don't Kill Cleaver, Watch Him," *Berkeley Barb*, August 2–8, 1968, 11.

31. FBI transcript, February 18, 1968, rally, Los Angeles, 36–43 (quotations on 40, 42), FBIHPN section 1.

32. FBI transcript, 47–56, quotations on 49, 56.

33. FBI transcript, 57–84.

34. Seale, *Seize the Time*, 256–57; "Interview with Bobby Seale," KPIX Eyewitness News, February 25, 1968, https://diva.sfsu.edu/collections/sfbatv/bundles/206866; "Complaint for Injunction and Declaratory Relief," April 19, 1968, HPNC 7: illegible (fifth on reel); Newton, "Executive Mandate No. 3: March 1, 1968," in Newton, *To Die for the People*, 12–13 (quotation).

35. Rout, *Eldridge Cleaver*, 62, 100, 134, 164.

36. Pearlman, *Sky's the Limit*, 355; Rhodes, *Framing the Black Panthers*, 131; Weingarten, *Gang That Wouldn't Write Straight*, 116–23.

37. Joan Didion, "Black Panther," *Saturday Evening Post*, May 4, 1968, in *Reporting Civil Rights: Part Two*, 676, quotation on 679.

38. Didion, 678.

39. Welsh, "Huey, the Police, and the White Community," *TBP*, March 16, 1968, 14.

40. "Huey Must Be Set Free," *TBP*, March 16, 1968, 20.

41. Rhodes, *Framing the Black Panthers*, 145, 149.

42. Henry Weinstein, "'Free Huey': A White Man's View," *Daily Californian*, May 20, 1968, 15; "Huey Must Be Set Free."

43. "Free Huey, Free Huey," *SFC*, July 16, 1968, 1, 16; "Bobby Seale Describes Police Conduct at Alameda Courthouse," KTVU News, July 15, 1968, https://diva.sfsu.edu/collections/sfbatv/bundles/220766.

44. "Panthers Trial in Police Death Opens," *WP*, July 16, 1968, A3; Rhodes, *Framing the Black Panthers*, 153; "2500 in a March at Trial on Coast," *NYT*, July 16, 1968, 14.

45. "Trial of Huey P. Newton," FBI memos, July 22, 1968, 2; July 29, 1968, 1; August 16, 1968, 3, all in FBIHPN section 2.

46. FBI teletype, "Trial of Huey Newton," August 8, 1968, FBIHPN section 2.
47. "Free Huey at the U.N.," *TBP*, September 14, 1968, 3.
48. Just, "Making of a Martyr."
49. James Schreiber, "Crossroads Trial: Nation's Life at Stake," *Berkeley Barb*, July 19–25, 1968, 3.
50. Forman, *Making of Black Revolutionaries*, 526.
51. Carson, *In Struggle*, 282; Pearlman, *Sky's the Limit*, 397; "World Awaits Verdict: Free Huey or the Sky's the Limit!," *TBP*, September 7, 1968, 1; FBI memo, July 16, 1968, FBIHPN section 2; "Bobby Seale Calls for Huey P. Newton's Release," KPIX Eyewitness News, c. August 1968, https://diva.sfsu.edu/collections/sfbatv/bundles/190419.
52. "October 1966 Black Panther Party Platform and Program," *TBP*, May 4, 1968, 7.
53. Henry Weinstein, "'Free Huey': A White Man's View," *Daily Californian*, May 20, 1968, 16.
54. Seale, *Seize the Time*, 277; Pearlman, *Sky's the Limit*, 467–68.
55. Garry and Goldberg, *Streetfighter in the Courtroom*, 142.
56. "Bobby Seale Calls for Huey P. Newton's Release"; Wallace Turner, "Black Panthers, White Power: Violent Confrontation on Coast," *NYT*, July 20, 1968, 10.
57. Garry and Goldberg, *Streetfighter in the Courtroom*, 105–6.
58. Garry and Goldberg, 105–6; Pearlman, *Sky's the Limit*, 377–78; "Motion to Quash the Entire Master Panel and Jury Venire," *People vs. Newton*, June 6, 1968, 9, 10 (quotations), HPNC 7: illegible name (fifth on reel).
59. "Third Session: The Embattled Jury Tape #6," n.d., 5, HPNC 33: Newspaper Clippings; "Plan to Delay Trial of Newton Snagged," *NYT*, July 17, 1968, 17; Garry and Goldberg, *Streetfighter in the Courtroom*, 106–7; "Complaint for Injunction and Declaratory Relief," *Newton et al. vs. City of Oakland et al.*, April 19, 1968, 9–11, HPNC 7: illegible name (fifth on reel).
60. Pearlman, *Sky's the Limit*, 412, 416; Moore, *Special Rage*, 139–40; voir dire examinations of prospective jurors number 11, 9, *People vs. Newton*, 605–11, 634–36, HPNC 44: Court of Appeal of the State of California (hereafter Court of Appeal).
61. Keating, *Free Huey*, 71; Garry and Goldberg, *Streetfighter in the Courtroom*, 107–8; examinations of prospective jurors 3, 7, 8: *People vs. Newton*, 675, 896, 952, HPNC 44: Court of Appeal; Terry A. Reim, "From Alameda County How Far to Alabama?" *Berkeley Barb*, July 26–August 1, 1968, 5; Blauner, "Sociology in the Courtroom: The Search for White Racism in the Huey Newton Voir Dire" manuscript, 9–12, HPNC 45: illegible (first on reel).
62. "Meet Your New Assistant United States Attorney General," *CLO News*, March–April 1981, 1 HPNC 45: illegible (first on reel); Jensen, "A Life Dedicated to the Administration of Justice and Legal Reform," 1, 22–3, 60; Blauner, "Sociology in the Courtroom," 17–18.
63. Blauner, "Sociology in the Courtroom," 15–16, 22 (quotation), 23, 25–26; Ward Just, "Newton Trial … Microcosmic Oakland Drama," *WP*, July 24, 1968, A6; Pearlman, *Sky's the Limit*, 422–23.
64. Keating, *Free Huey*, 75–76; Pearlman, *Sky's the Limit*, 427–29; Wallace Turner, "State Opens Case of Black Panther," *NYT*, August 6, 1968, 16.
65. Moore, *Special Rage*, 154.
66. Garry and Goldberg, *Streetfighter in the Courtroom*, 100, 112–13; "Supplementary Memorandum of points and authorities in support of motion under penal code section 995," *People vs. Newton* no. 41266, HPNC 7: illegible name (fifth on reel); Moore, *Special Rage*, 156–57.

67. Garry and Goldberg, *Streetfighter in the Courtroom*, 114–17; Pearlman, *Sky's the Limit*, 434–45; "Gutting of Herbert Heanes," 8–13, HPNC 38: Testimony and Statements.

68. Garry and Goldberg, *Streetfighter in the Courtroom*, 110, 118–19; Statement: Henry Grier, HPNC 38: Testimony and Statements.

69. Grier testimony, August 9, 1968, *People vs. Newton*, 2107, 2136–42, 2147–50, HPNC 44: Court of Appeal; Keating, *Free Huey*, 102–6; "Gutting of Henry Grier," 6–13; transcript of police radio, October 28, 1967, 6–7, both in HPNC 35: illegible (first on reel). In private, Garry's team denounced Grier's testimony as "poppycock." See "Gutting of Henry Grier," 3.

70. Ross testimony, August 12, 1968, *People vs. Newton*, 2244–58, HPNC 44: Court of Appeal; Garry and Goldberg, *Streetfighter in the Courtroom*, 122 (quotation); Pearlman, *Sky's the Limit*, 439.

71. *People vs. Newton*, August 13, 1968, 2262–334 (quotation and context: 2281–82), HPNC 44: Court of Appeal; Garry and Goldberg, *Streetfighter in the Courtroom*, 123–27; notes from Ross grand jury testimony, 2–4, HPNC 35: illegible (seventh on reel); "Gutting of Grand Jury Testimony," 10, HPNC 38: Testimony and Statements; transcript of Garry/Ross interview, July 28, 1968, 1–3, HPNC 35: illegible (first on reel).

72. Garry and Goldberg, *Streetfighter in the Courtroom*, 101–2; transcript of John Davis interview, 14–15, 18–22, 27–30, 67–71, HPNC 34: illegible name (fifth on reel); *People of the State of California vs. Huey P. Newton*, appeal filed May 29, 1970, HPNC reel 34 file: illegible (first on reel), 11–12; "LCF 8993 JB Supplement: Recapitulation," HPNC 38: Testimony and Statements; Garry/Ross interview transcript, 2; Keating, *Free Huey*, 41, 43.

73. Moore, *Special Rage*, 171–72; Wallace Turner, "Bullet Evidence in Panther Trial," *NYT*, August 15, 1968, 20; *People vs. Newton* appeal, 12–13; John Davis interview, 10–11, 46–47, 68, 70.

74. Garry and Goldberg, *Streetfighter in the Courtroom*, 127.

75. Wallace Turner, "Newton Trial Hears He Had Marijuana Fragments in Pocket When Shot," *NYT*, August 16, 1968, 13; Jan Bashinski and Melvin Torley testimonies, *People vs. Newton*, 2617–18, 2621–31, HPNC 44: Court of Appeal.

76. Pearlman, *Sky's the Limit*, 442–43; Thomas Finch testimony, *People vs. Newton*, 2357–67, HPNC 44: Court of Appeal; Mary Jane Aguilar, "Doctor Apologizes to Huey," *TBP*, November 23, 1967, 6; "Gutting of Transcripts VII thru XI," 9–10 (quotation), HPNC 38: Testimony and Statements.

77. Garry and Goldberg, *Streetfighter in the Courtroom*, 128–31; Wallace Turner, "Defense Opens Case in Newton Trial," *NYT*, August 20, 1968, 22; Wallace Turner, "Family Testifies in Panther Trial," *NYT*, August 21, 1968, 28; McKinney testimony, *People vs. Newton*, 3011–16, HPNC reel 44: Court of Appeal.

78. Garry and Goldberg, *Streetfighter in the Courtroom*, 132–38; *People vs. Newton* appeal, 14–15; Newton testimony, *People vs. Newton*, 3093–94, 3100–101, 3105–36, HPNC reel 44: Court of Appeal; Hopper and Lisak, "Why Rape and Trauma Survivors."

79. Keating, *Free Huey*, 160–61; *People v. Newton*, 4908 transcript, 2–4, appendix A, 1–3, 8–9, HPNC reel 10 folder: 1964 Prior felony conviction; Newton B-17121, "Social Evaluation," October 23, 1968, 7–8, Huey P. Newton Inmate Record; Sabatini testimony at *People of the State of California v. Huey P. Newton*, C-11738 Preliminary Examination, April 19, 1966, 3, HPNC 7: Huey's Miscellaneous Appeals; Sabatini testimony in *People vs. Newton*, August 27, 1968, 3474–76, 3480, HPNC 33: illegible (second on reel); Drew McKillips, "Berkeley Cop Incident Used against Newton," *SFC*, July 22, 1971, 4.

80. Newton testimony, August 23, August 26, 1968, *People vs. Newton*, 3316–17, 3321–27, HPNC 33: illegible (second on reel); Newton testimony, August 23, August 26, 1968,

People vs. Newton, 3137–85, 3194–263, 3267–84, 3284–99, HPNC 44: Court of Appeal; Garry and Goldberg, *Streetfighter in the Courtroom*, 139–41; "Did Not Kill Cop, Panther Leader Says," *Chicago Tribune*, August 23, 1968, B18.

81. Keating, *Free Huey*, 186–92; Blake redirect testimony, August 26–27, 1968, *People vs. Newton*, 3342–45, 3365–66, 3372, 3374, HPNC 33: illegible (second on reel).

82. Pearlman, *Sky's the Limit*, 461; Diamond redirect testimony, *People vs. Newton*, August 27, 1968, 3407–11 HPNC 33: illegible (second on reel).

83. Garry closing statement, *People vs. Newton*, 3607–79 (quotation on 3676–77), HPNC reel 66 file: *State of California v Newton* #3 (hereafter State #3).

84. Jensen closing statement, *People vs. Newton*, 3680–734, HPNC 66: State #3.

85. Garry and Goldberg, *Streetfighter in the Courtroom*, 146–48; Wallace Turner, "Testimony Is Read to Newton Jurors," *NYT*, September 7, 1968, 38.

86. Wallace Turner, "Newton Predicts an Armed Revolt," *NYT*, September 8, 1968, 32.

87. Garry and Goldberg, *Streetfighter in the Courtroom*, 150 (quotation); Newton, "Huey's Statement on Racist Verdict," *TBP*, September 14, 1968, 2.

88. Bloom and Martin, *Black against Empire*, 199; masthead, *TBP*, September 14, 1968, 1.

89. Street, "Shadow of the Soul Breaker," 343.

90. FBI airtel, March 4, 1968, 3 FBIBEO 100–448006 section 1; Rhodes, *Framing the Black Panthers*, 164–65.

91. Newton, "Executive Mandate Number One," "The Correct Handling of a Revolution," in Foner, *Black Panthers Speak*, 41, 40–45, quotation on 44.

92. Tim Findley, "Newton's Message at Berkeley Party," *SFC*, February 17, 1969, 8; "Message from Huey," *TBP*, March 3, 1969, 2.

93. Stew Albert, "Freeing Huey: Here's How to Do It," *Berkeley Barb*, April 25–May 1, 1969, 3.

94. Pearlman, *Sky's the Limit*, 500–501.

95. "Message from Huey, June 2, 1970," *TBP*, June 6, 1970, 3.

96. Malcolm X, "Message to the Grass Roots," in Malcolm X, *Malcolm X Speaks*, 8; Caldwell, "Young White Army Rallies to Newton," *NYT*, August 7, 1970, 14.

97. "Mistrial Called in Newton Trial," *NYT*, August 9, 1971, 13; "Oakland Prosecutor Decides Not to Retry Huey Newton," *WP*, December 16, 1971, A3; Keating, *Free Huey*, 254–73; Moore, *Special Rage*, 243–44.

98. Hilliard and Cole, *This Side of Glory*, 131–33; John Davis interview, 20–22, 48–52, 69; Newton with Blake, *Revolutionary Suicide*, 235.

99. FBI teletype, August 6, 1970, FBIBEO 100–48006 section 20.

Chapter 9. The FBI and the BPP

1. Director, FBI airtel, September 16, 1970, HPNC 18: untitled, emphasis added.

2. Robert O. Self, "The Black Panther Party and the Long Civil Rights Era," in Lazerow and Williams, *In Search of the Black Panther Party*, 45.

3. Burrough, *Days of Rage*, 133–35; "US Admits Wiretapping David Hilliard's Home," *TBP*, June 3, 1972, 2; Hoerl and Ortiz, "Organizational Secrecy," 596.

4. SAC, San Francisco memo, FBI, April 10, 1967; FBI report, "Huey Percy Newton," May 10, 1967, both in FBIHPN section 1; D. W. Bacon to J. Walter Yeagley, June 17, August 9, October 3, 1968, all in FBIHPN section 2.

5. Burrough, *Days of Rage*, 71.

6. FBI file: Berton Schneider, March 17, 1975, HPNC reel 61: FBI File Berton Schneider #1.

7. Michael Kelly, "Perot Shows Penchant for Seeing Conspiracy," *NYT*, October 26, 1992, A12.

8. SAC San Francisco airtel, May 14, 1969, 5; "FBI Agent William A. Cohendet, History edited from a video produced by Roz Payne," 3, both in *What We Want, What We Believe*; Cohendet oral history, *FBI Agents*; SAC San Francisco airtel, January 20, 1971; Director, FBI airtel, June 30, 1970, both in FBIHPN section 3.

9. Donald Freed, "Body Counting the Panthers: Genocide of Exaggeration," *Los Angeles Free Press*, March 12–18, 1971, 1, 3; Epstein, "The Black Panthers and the Police."

10. Brown, *Taste of Power*, 165–67; Brown, "US Organization," 295–97; Davis and Wiener, *Set the Night on Fire*, 442–48; "3 Men Convicted of Murder in Black Nationalist Feud," *NYT*, September 11, 1969, 30; SAC, Los Angeles airtel, August 10, 1970, HPNC 18: untitled; "Black Ex-Agent's Mission Impossible," *TBP*, April 24, 1976, 1, 14–15.

11. Wesley Swearingen oral history, *FBI Agents*; "Declaration of Darthard Perry," February 4, 1978, HPNC 64: Declaration of Darthard Perry; Rapoport, "Meet America's Meanest Dirty Trickster"; Swearingen, *FBI Secrets*, 82–83.

12. Everett-Karenga interview with Carson (my thanks to Prof. Carson for access); Brown, *Fighting for US*, 9–17.

13. Brown, *Fighting for US*, 4; Brown, "US Organization," 144–45; Halisi, *Quotable Karenga*, 23–25.

14. Brown, *Fighting for US*, 18, 69–70, 76–77; Halisi, *Quotable Karenga*, 14, 19; Malcolm X, letter from Accra, Ghana, May 11, 1964, in Malcolm X, *Malcolm X Speaks*, 62–63; Malcolm X, "Founding Rally of the OAAU," 54–55, 63.

15. Brown, *Fighting for US*, 15–16, 50, 70, 85–86, 132–42; Halisi, *Quotable Karenga*, 10, 29, 31.

16. Carson, foreword in Brown, *Fighting for US*, viii; "Black Panther Party Book List," *TBP*, December 21, 1968, 14; "Revolutionary Posters," *TBP*, October 12, 1968, 4; Carson, *In Struggle*, 283; Everett-Karenga interview; Brown, *Fighting for US*, 78–79, 88; "Black Panther Party Book List," *TBP*, September 14, 1968, 6; Kilgore, "Black Leadership in Los Angeles," 149–50.

17. Fanon, *Wretched*, 119–66; Akinyele Omowale Umoja, "Repression Breeds Resistance," in Cleaver and Katsiaficas, *Liberation, Imagination, and the Black Panther Party*, 6–7.

18. Brown, *Fighting for US*, 108–10; Brown, "US," 270; Karenga, "Kawaida," 129–30, 145; Horne, *Fire*, 199–204; Huey P. Newton, "To the Black Movement," 93; Lockwood, *Conversation with Eldridge Cleaver*, 112; "Los Angeles Panthers Await Justice for US Organization," *TBP*, February 2, 1969, 4.

19. Brown, *Fighting for US*, 39, 40, 80, 83, 95–96; Pharr, *Nine Lives of a Black Panther*, 69; Brown, *Taste of Power*, 142–43, 176; Horne, *Fire This Time*, 199–204; Churchill and Vander Wall, *Agents of Repression*, 42–43, 63, 80; Jeffries, "Hanging Out with Al Amour," 126; Jeffries and Foley, "To Live and Die in L.A.," in Jeffries, *Comrades*, 266–67; "Oral History with Ericka Huggins," 46; Newton with Blake, *Revolutionary Suicide*, 129–30, 132; Seale, *Seize the Time*, 139–46; Brown, *Taste of Power*, 123–25.

20. Anthony, *Spitting in the Wind*, 7–9, 35–38, 46–47.

21. Moore memo, September 27, 1968; Director, FBI memo, September 30, 1968, both FBIBEO section 4.

22. SAC Los Angeles memo, October 14, 1968, FBIBEO section 4; SAC Los Angeles, November 29, 1968, FBIBEO section 5.

23. Director, FBI memo, October 31, 1968, FBIBEO section 4; SAC Los Angeles memo,

December 12, 1968, FBIBEO section 6; Director, FBI memo, December 31, 1968, FBIBEO section 6; G. C. Moore memo, November 5, 1968, FBIBEO section 4.

24. Director, FBI memo, November 25, 1968, FBIBEO section 5; O'Reilly, *Racial Matters*, 304–9.

25. "Declaration of Darthard Perry"; Swearingen oral history, *FBI Agents*.

26. SAC, Los Angeles, memo, November 29, 1968; Ward Churchill, "To Disrupt, Discredit, and Destroy," in Cleaver and Katsiaficas, *Liberation, Imagination, and the Black Panther Party*, 88, 93; SAC San Diego memo, November 22, 1968, FBIBEO section 5.

27. SAC Los Angeles memo, December 12, 1968; SAC Los Angeles memos, January 2, January 16, 1969, all in FBIBEO section 6.

28. SAC Los Angeles memo, February 26, 1969, FBIBEO section 7.

29. SAC Los Angeles memo, March 3, 1969, FBIBEO section 8.

30. Winston A. Grady-Willis, "The Black Panther Party: State Repression and Political Prisoners," in Jones, *Black Panther Party*, 370; Austin, *Up Against the Wall*, 232–37.

31. SAC San Diego memo to Director, FBI, February 27, 1969, FBIBEO section 7.

32. SAC San Diego memo, January 20, 1969, FBIBEO section 6; SAC San Diego memos, February 12, February 27, March 12, 1969, FBIBEO section 8; Austin, *Up Against the Wall*, 232–34, 239–40; Austin, "Interview with Harold Taylor," 160–61; Churchill, "To Disrupt, Discredit, and Destroy," 94.

33. Austin, *Up Against the Wall*, 232; "Ron Karenga (Pig)," *TBP*, September 6, 1969, 10 (quotation).

34. Emory Douglas, "A Pig, Is a Pig, Is a Pig, Is a Pig!!," *TBP*, August 23, 1969, 1.

35. Jeffries and Foley, "To Live and Die in L.A.," 278–81; Ronald Freeman and Wayne Pharr testimony in Nelson, *Black Panthers: Vanguard of the Revolution*, 1:25:50, 1:27:08; Davis and Wiener, *Set the Night on Fire*, 454–56, 464–68; LeBlanc-Ernest, "Most Qualified Person," 315.

36. Austin, "Interview with Harold Taylor," 165–68.

37. Bass and Rae, *Murder in the Model City*, 3–10, 22, 28, 30–31; Williams, *Black Politics/White Power*, 140; "Oral History with Ericka Huggins," 54–62.

38. Bass and Rae, *Murder in the Model City*, 3 (quotation), 26; Newton comments post-August 1970 in FBI report, Huey P. Newton, October 15, 1971, HPNC 31: illegible name; Swearingen, *FBI Secrets*, 82.

39. Williams, *Black Politics/White Power*, 99; Bass and Rae, *Murder in the Model City*, 64 (quotation).

40. Bass and Rae, *Murder in the Model City*, 26–27, 30.

41. Paul Bass, "Black Panther Torture 'Trial' Tape Surfaces," *New Haven Independent*, February 21, 2013, https://www.newhavenindependent.org/article/rackley_trial_tape_surfaces.

42. Bass and Rae, *Murder in the Model City*, 15–19, 35, 37–38, 41–42; Austin, *Up Against the Wall*, 294.

43. "Chief Was 'Astonished' by Indictment of Seale," *SFC*, April 4, 1972, 1, 24; Bass and Rae, *Murder in the Model City*, 33, 71, 74, 98, 169; John Bancroft, "Lonnie McLucas New Haven 9 Trial, Daily Report #31," August 14, 1970, HPNC 60: New Haven Miscellaneous Information.

44. Bass and Rae, *Murder in the Model City*, 173, 181–88, 196–98, 202–5; "Lonnie's Trial," August 4/6, 1970; "Panther Trial News," August 17, 1970, both in HPNC 60: New Haven Miscellaneous Information; Damian Formisano, "Seale Freed, Heads for Coast," *New Haven Register*, May 29, 1971, 1.

45. Bass and Rae, *Murder in the Model City*, 166, 191–92, 209–12.

46. Williams, *Black Politics/White Power*, 127, 129, 132, 135–36; Bass and Rae, *Murder in the Model City*, 88, 99, 102, 116, 127–35, 261.

47. Lane interview with Newton, September 17, 1970, 105–6.

48. Williams, *Black Politics/White Power*, 129, 135.

49. Jon Rice, "The World of the Illinois Panthers," in Theoharis and Woodard, *Freedom North*, 52; Forbes, *Will You Die With Me?*, 72; Dixon, *My People Are Rising*, 108, 230, 259; Pharr, *Nine Lives of a Black Panther*, 224, 231–32; Brown, *Taste of Power*, 9, 144, 298, 351, 371, 444; Hilliard and Cole, *This Side of Glory*, 234–35.

50. Bass and Rae, *Murder in the Model City*, 263.

51. Quoted in Pearson, *Shadow of the Panther*, 233.

52. Tackett, "Rumor and Revolution," 56–57.

53. Bass and Rae, *Murder in the Model City*, 262.

54. "All Panthers Beware," *TBP*, February 17, 1969, 9 (quotation); Williams, *Black Politics/White Power*, 138–39.

55. Rice, "World of the Illinois Panthers," 53.

56. Williams, *From the Bullet to the Ballot*, 167, 174–80; Churchill, "To Disrupt, Discredit, and Destroy," 84; Ronald Koziol, "Black Panther Financial Aid by Communists Is Revealed," *Chicago Tribune*, February 14, 1969, 3; Ronald Koziol, "Find Panthers Feed Only a Few Children," *Chicago Tribune*, September 18, 1969, A5; Ronald Koziol, "Black Panther Records Show Misuse of Funds," *Chicago Tribune*, September 19, 1969, 5.

57. Interviews conducted by Blackside, Inc., with William O'Neal, Bobby Rush, Flint Taylor.

58. Williams, *From the Bullet to the Ballot*, 175–76; O'Neal and Rush interviews.

59. O'Neal interview; "Shoot-Out Deaths Are Ruled Murder," *NYT*, December 25, 1969, 59; "Chicago Policeman, Panther Associate Killed in Shootout," *WP*, November 14, 1969, A3 (quotation).

60. "No Quarter for Wild Beasts," *Chicago Tribune*, November 15, 1969, 10.

61. O'Neal and Rush interviews; Interview with Deborah Johnson, conducted by Blackside, Inc.

62. Williams, *From the Bullet to the Ballot*, 182–85; Taylor interview; Churchill, "To Disrupt, Discredit, and Destroy," 106.

63. Haas, *Assassination of Fred Hampton*, photo section 11; Jeffries et al., "Mark Clark's Tenuous Place in History," 9.

64. Edward Lee and William Currie, "Panther Apartment Sealed; Report New Evidence Found," *Chicago Tribune*, December 18, 1969, 4; Taylor interview; Interview with Howard Saffold, conducted by Blackside, Inc.; "Hanrahan's Indictment for Bad Lying," *TBP*, September 18, 1971, 5–6, 16; Haas, *Assassination of Fred Hampton*, 83–127, 151–53, 163–348.

65. Lane interview with Newton, 57–58 (emphasis added).

66. Jeffries and Foley, "To Live and Die in L.A.," 266–67; Rice, "The World of the Illinois Panthers," 50, 54–56; Williams, *From the Bullet to the Ballot*, 60, 62–63, 66, 74–77, 86–89.

67. Ervin, "The Last Hours of William O'Neal"; Robert Blau, "Panther Informant Death Ruled Suicide," *Chicago Tribune*, January 18, 1990, S1, S6.

68. Phillip J. O'Connor, "Informant in Panthers Raid Killed by Auto," *Chicago Sun Times*, January 17, 1990, 12.

69. Maurice Possley, "FBI Informant Cleared of Role in 1972 Slaying," *Chicago Tribune*, October 2, 1984, A5.

70. "Eyes on the Prize Reviews," https://web.archive.org/web/20160405234627

/http://www.pbs.org/wgbh/amex/eyesontheprize/about/press.html; Henry Mayer, "With Eyes Still on the Prize," *NYT* Book Review, January 28, 1990, 12 (quotation).

71. "A Nation of Law?," season 2, ep. 6 of Eyes on the Prize, February 19, 1990, https://www.imdb.com/title/tt0896125/?ref_=fn_al_tt_2.

72. Blau, "Panther Informant Death Ruled Suicide."

73. O'Neal interview.

74. Spencer, *Revolution Has Come*, 178.

75. Joan Kelley, "Plaintiff Black Panther Party's Responses to Interrogatories," n.d., BPP v. Levi, 74–92, 100–110, 116–17, 125–28, HPNC 66: BPP vs Levi folder #4; "Plaintiff Huey P. Newton's Answers to First Interrogatories," July 1978, BPP v. Levi, 17–18; "Complaint (civil rights) for Damages and Demand for Jury Trial," Eldridge Cleaver and Kathleen Cleaver v. Charles Bates, Estate of J. Edgar Hoover, Robert E. Savage, Joseph E. Smith, John Mitchell, Richard G. Kleindienst, Richard Helms, Winton M. Blount, June 30, 1977, esp. 6 (quotation), 7–8, 11, HPNC 53: Eldridge Cleaver.

76. Newton letter to Johnson, September 13, 1977, FBIHPN section 21.

77. George Lardner, "Nominee for FBI Withdraws; Bell Defers Search," *WP*, November 30, 1977, A1.

78. Seth Rosenfeld, "Man Who Armed Black Panthers Was FBI Informant, Records Show," Reveal, August 20, 2012, https://revealnews.org/article/man-who-armed-black-panthers-was-fbi-informant-records-show/; Bloom and Martin, *Black against Empire*, 47–48; "Richard Aoki interviewed by Dolly Veale" in Ho with Antonio et al., *Legacy to Liberation*, 319.

79. "Richard Aoki interviewed," 320–23, 326–27, 331; Rosenfeld, *Subversives*, 419–22, 640–43; Fujino, *Samurai among Panthers*, 140–41.

80. Fred Ho, "Fred Ho Refutes the Claim That Richard Aoki Was an FBI Informant," *San Francisco BayView*, August 21, 2012, https://sfbayview.com/2012/08/fred-ho-refutes-the-claim-that-richard-aoki-was-an-fbi-informant/.

81. Scott Kurashige, "Each Generation Must Discover Its Own History: Some Thoughts on the Richard Aoki Debate," NewBlackMan (in Exile), August 27, 2012, https://www.newblackmaninexile.net/2012/08/each-generation-must-discover-its-own.html; Diane Fujino, "Where's the Evidence Aoki Was FBI Informant?" *SFC*, August 22, 2012, http://www.sfgate.com/opinion/openforum/article/Where-s-the-evidence-Aoki-was-fbi-informant-3808396.php; Elbert "Big Man" Howard, "Elbert 'Big Man' Howard on Richard Aoki," *Blackbird Press News* (blog), August 26, 2012, https://blackbirdpressnews.blogspot.com/2012/08/elbert-big-man-howard-on-richard-aoki.html.

82. Weir and Noyes, *Raising Hell*, 263–67, 269.

83. Rosenfeld, "FBI Files Reveal New Details about Informant Who Armed Black Panthers," Reveal, September 7, 2012, https://revealnews.org/article/fbi-files-reveal-new-details-about-informant-who-armed-black-panthers/; quotation from Fred Ho, "An Analysis of Seth Rosenfeld's FBI Files on Richard Aoki," *San Francisco BayView*, September 7, 2012, https://sfbayview.com/2012/09/an-analysis-of-seth-rosenfelds-fbi-files-on-richard-aoki/.

Chapter 10. Prison and the (Un)making of the BPP

1. Malcolm X, "Message to the Grassroots," in *Malcolm X Speaks*, 8.

2. Newton, "The Prison, The Prisoner and Society," 2, HPNC 15: The Prison, The Prisoner + Society.

3. Hilliard and Cole, *This Side of Glory*, 183, 192–97, 255, 259, 261, 266–67, 271, 332, 373–

74, 382; Brown, *Taste of Power*, 217; "Hilliard Sentenced in Police Shootout," *NYT*, July 3, 1971, 8.

4. Cummins, *Rise and Fall*, 117–18, 125; "What We Want Now! What We Believe," *TBP*, May 15, 1967, 3.

5. David Mills, "Q&A: Eldridge Cleaver (pt. 2)," *Undercover Black Man* (blog), February 27, 2007, http://undercoverblackman.blogspot.com/2007/02/q-eldridge-cleaver-pt-2.html.

6. Gifford, *Revolution or Death*, 54–55 (66–67 outlines the shaky foundations of Cleaver's 1958 conviction); Cummins, *Rise and Fall*, 3–4, 8–15; Simon, "From the Big House," 221–22.

7. "Editors' Introduction," Wilkinson, *Prison Work*, x–xvi; Cummins, *Rise and Fall*, 19, 63–92; Janssen, "From the Inside Out," 131; Eldridge Cleaver, "Prisons," in *Ramparts* and Browning, *Prison Life*, 101; Malcolm X with Haley, *Autobiography of Malcolm X*, 255–87.

8. FBI, "Leroy Eldridge Cleaver," May 8, 1967, 2, 5–8, 12; SAC San Francisco memo, May 9, 1967, 2, both in FBIEC section 1; Cleaver, *Soul on Fire*, 70 (quotation), 73.

9. Lockwood, *Conversation with Eldridge Cleaver*, 84–85; Cleaver, "On Eldridge Cleaver," *Ramparts*, June 1969, 6; Cummins, *Rise and Fall*, 73–79; Gifford, *Revolution or Death*, 50, 62, 80–81, 91, 94, 97–98, 111–12, 115–17.

10. Pepper and Pepper, *Straight Life*, 273, 280–83, 294–95, 298–99, 307 (quotation), 331.

11. Cleaver, *Soul on Ice*, 17–18 (quotations), 24–25, 108–12, 130, 133–35.

12. Pepper and Pepper, *Straight Life*, 303–4.

13. Gifford, *Revolution or Death*, 6; Cleaver, "On Eldridge Cleaver," 6, quotation on 8.

14. Schanche, *Panther Paradox*, 159, 177, 188, 200–201; FBI report, "Appearance of Leroy Eldridge Cleaver ... October 10, 1968"; Director FBI memo, October 21, 1968; Cleaver speech, October 18, 1968, 5, all in FBIBEO part 2; Marvin X, "Eldridge Cleaver: A Memoir," chap. 11, 17, https://blackbirdpressnews.blogspot.com/2012/04/eldridge-cleaver-memoir-by-marvin-x.html; Brown, *Taste of Power*, 227–28; Lockwood, *Conversation with Eldridge Cleaver*, 24–26; T. D. Allman, "The 'Rebirth' of Eldridge Cleaver," *NYT Magazine*, January 16, 1977, 31; Julia Herve, "Message to the Central Committee," April 2, 1970, 5–9, HPNC 15: Hidden Traitor; Connie Matthews to David Hilliard, April 28 [1971?]; "Byron Booth on the Hidden Traitor Renegade Scab"; James A., "Report on Black Panther Party International Section," 21, 22, all in HPNC 30: Hidden Traitor Renegade Scab; Mokhtefi, "Diary."

15. G. C. Moore memo, May 14, 1970; SAC San Francisco airtel, May 28, 1970, FBIBEO section 19; Director, FBI teletype, January 22, 1971; Director, FBI airtel, January 20, 1971; Director, FBI airtel, December 18, 1970 SAC, Los Angeles airtel, December 3, 1970, all FBIBEO section 23.

16. Brown, *Taste of Power*, 220–28, quotation on 223; "Anti-Imperialist Delegation—1970," HPNC 30: Hidden Traitor Renegade Scab; Wu, *Radicals on the Road*, 166, 169–70.

17. Seale, *Seize the Time*, 196–202, 219–30; Seale, *Lonely Rage*, 94–95, 113, 127, 184–85; FBI telegram, October 28, 1967, FBIHPN section 1.

18. Murch, *Living for the City*, 162; Epstein, "Special Supplement"; J. Anthony Lukas, "2 'Chicago 8' Defendants Say They Were 'Kidnapped' on Coast by Marshalls," *NYT*, September 28, 1969, 60; Seale, *Seize the Time*, 345, 349; Ronald Koziol, "Rubin, Seale Taken from Jail for Trip to Riot Trial Here," *Chicago Tribune*, September 13, 1969, N3; J. Anthony Lukas, "Judge Drops Contempt Citations against 4 Defending the 'Chicago 8,'" *NYT*, September 30, 1969, 1, 35.

19. J. Anthony Lukas, "'Party' Disrupts Chicago 8 Court," *NYT*, October 23, 1969, 24.

20. J. Anthony Lukas, "Seale Put in Chains at Chicago 8 Trial," *NYT*, October 30, 1969, 1; William Chapman, "Judge Vows to Bar New Outbursts at Trial of '8,'" *WP*, November 1, 1969, A3.

21. Epstein, "Special Supplement"; Bass and Rae, *Murder in the Model City*, 113–14; Seale, *Lonely Rage*, 264–77; Hilliard and Cole, *This Side of Glory*, 257.

22. Newton trial testimony, March 13, 15–16, 19, 1979, 13–14, HPNC 8: Court of Appeals; Newton with Blake, *Revolutionary Suicide*, 103–4, 107–8.

23. Street, "Shadow of the Soul Breaker," 343 (for a fuller discussion of Newton's prison experience, on which the following section is based, see 336–49); FBI memos, September 30, 1968; February 14, 1969, FBIHPN HQ105–165429 section 2.

24. "Social Evaluation," October 23, 1968, 7–9 (quotation 7), Newton Inmate Record.

25. Newton with Blake, *Revolutionary Suicide*, 76–80; Fanon, *Wretched*, 200–250.

26. "Huey Political Prisoner," *Berkeley Barb*, November 10–16, 1967, 5; "Stop!" *Berkeley Tribe*, n.d.; Byron Robertson, "Interview with the Minister for Defense," *TBP*, October 4, 1969, 13; "Case Summary Newton B–17121," October 23, 1968, Newton Inmate Record.

27. FBI reports, "Huey Percy Newton," February 14, 1969, 21; February 17, 1970, 4–5a, FBIHPN section 3; Blake, "The Caged Panther," 237–40; L. S. Topper, untitled document, March 3, 1969, Newton Inmate Record; "Report of Violation of Institution Rules," April 1969, HPNC 10: unnamed; "Why Huey," *TBP*, May 25, 1969, 2; Newton, "Prison: Where Is Thy Victory" draft, HPNC 12: Prison: Where Is Thy Victory.

28. Newton trial testimony, *People v. Newton*, July 27, 1971, HPNC 35: illegible name (second on reel); Newton with Blake, *Revolutionary Suicide*, 198, 271, 278–79.

29. Gifford, *Revolution or Death*, 98–99, 103–6, 110, 121; Richardson, *Bomb in Every Issue*, 68–69; Eldridge Cleaver, "Letters from Prison," *Ramparts*, August 1966, 16–26.

30. Newton with Blake, *Revolutionary Suicide*, 103–5, 289; Digby Diehl, "An Interview with Huey Newton," *WP*, August 16, 1972, A22; Newton, "Prison, Where Is Thy Victory?," *TBP*, January 3, 1970, 13.

31. Lockwood, "*Playboy* Interview," 88.

32. Grassian, "Psychiatric Effects of Solitary Confinement"; Hresko, "In the Cellars of the Hollow Men," 11–12; Haney, "Mental Health Issues in Long-Term Solitary and 'Supermax' Confinement," 132, 137–38, 140–41; Haney, "Psychological Impact of Incarceration," 41–43; de Viggiani, "Unhealthy Prisons," 118, 123.

33. Hiestand and Smith, "Of Panthers and Prisons," 3–4, 57 (first quotation), 61; Diehl, "Interview," A22 (second quotation).

34. Newton with Blake, *Revolutionary Suicide*, 106.

35. Romano, "If the SHU Fits," 1096–115; Grassian, "Psychiatric Effects of Solitary Confinement," 345–46, 367–72, 380–81; Blake, "Caged Panther," 239, 242, 245.

36. "A Conversation with Huey P. Newton," *TBP*, February 18, 1978, 15, 16.

37. "Two Interviews with Ericka Huggins," 61–63; Grassian, "Psychiatric Effects of Solitary Confinement," 328; Guevara, "Man and Socialism in Cuba," in Guevara, *Venceremos!*, 398.

38. Fujino, "Spiritual Practice for Sustaining Social Justice Activism," 82.

39. Gifford, *Revolution or Death*, 127–28, 130–31, 135, 136.

40. Shames and Seale, *Power to the People*, 179.

41. Lockwood, "*Playboy* Interview," 90; de Viggiani, "Unhealthy Prisons," 117, 122, 124; Haney, "Psychological Impact," 38–41.

42. Newton with Blake, *Revolutionary Suicide*, 300, 314–15.

43. Haney, "Psychological Impact of Incarceration," 40, 46–47; Hipp et al., "Parolee Recidivism in California," 950, 952.

44. Major, *Panther Is a Black Cat*, 126.

45. Brown, *Taste of Power*, 251–52.

46. Brown, 256; Jerry LeBlanc, "A Panther at Bay," *Boston Globe Magazine*, December 6, 1970, 38; FBI teletypes, August 4, 7, 9, 1970; FBI "informative note," August 8, 1970, all FBIHPN section 4; Director FBI, airtel, August 24, 1970, 2, FBIBEO section 21 (quotation).

47. FBI memo, January 28, 1971, quoted in Newton, *War Against the Panthers*, 99n71.

48. U.S. Congress, Senate, Book III, Final Report of the Select Committee to Study Governmental Operations with Respect to Intelligence Activities, 94th Congress, 2nd Session, 1976, 200–207 (hereafter cited as Church Committee); FBI surveillance report, June 25, 1971, FBIHPN section 13.

49. Lockwood, "*Playboy* Interview," 74; FBI, "Huey Percy Newton," December 2, 1970, FBIHPN section 7; Brown, *Taste of Power*, 258 (quotation).

50. Hilliard et al., *Huey*, 177–81, 195; Brown, *Taste of Power*, 266; Tim Findley, "Huey Newton: Twenty-Five Floors from the Street," *Rolling Stone*, August 3, 1972, 30; Church Committee, 201–5, 219–20; FBI "Counterintelligence Program against Huey P. Newton," n.d., 9–12, HPNC 1: Freedom of Information Counterintelligence Program against HPN; Newton and Gwen Fountaine declarations, *People of State of California v. Huey P. Newton*, 64624A and 65919, 108–16, 139–40, HPNC 8: Court of Appeals; "Newton's Neighbor Fires on Police," *SFE*, February 18, 1973, B8; Walt Thompson, "What's Left of the Black Left?" *Ramparts*, June 1972, 52.

51. Scott and Gendreau, "Psychiatric Implications of Sensory Deprivation in a Maximum Security Prison," 340; San Francisco office memo, April 16, 1971, FBIHPN section 11; Brown, *Taste of Power*, 266; Forbes, *Will You Die with Me?*, 88–89; Lockwood, "*Playboy* Interview," 74; Tim Findley, "The View from Newton's 'Prison,'" *SFC*, February 18, 1971, 1, 20.

52. Findley, "Huey Newton," 30.

53. Hilliard and Cole, *This Side of Glory*, 302, 318, 321; Rowland Evans and Robert Novak, "Huey Newton's Tour Falls Flat," *WP*, December 6, 1970, C7.

54. Forbes, *Will You Die with Me?*, 73–75, 87.

55. "February 17th: Something to Commemorate," *TBP*, February 19, 1972, 2, 19.

56. LeBlanc, "Panther at Bay," 44.

57. SAC San Francisco airtel, May 1, 1972, 2, *What We Want, What We Believe*, disc 4; Hilliard et al., *Huey*, 194 (quotation).

58. Church Committee, 204; Stephen Lee Kies (FBI) memo, October 11, 1973, HPNC 31: illegible; Forbes, *Will You Die with Me?*, 81, 147, 150, 163, 167–70; David Harris, "Huey's Last Stand," 1–3, 5, 8–11, HPNC 40: "Huey's Last Stand" (an article submitted to but never published by *Rolling Stone*; David Harris, email to author, February 22, 2013); Charles Garry surveillance file, May 5, 1972, 2, HPNC 7: FBI File Charles Garry; FBI, "Huey Percy Newton," November 22, 1974, HPNC 30: "HPN Legal Brief"; "Sweet Sounds of Forgiveness," *OT*, August 18, 1978, 1; Coleman and Avery, "Party's Over," 33–35, 41–43; Alonzo Herbert Miller testimony, August 23, 1973, *People of the State of California vs. Huey P. Newton and Robert Bay* transcript, HPNC 12: KDIA and Marlon Scott.

59. Brown, *Taste of Power*, 256, 271, 274, 293; Hilliard and Cole, *This Side of Glory*, 299; Greenhill, "Science of Stimulant Abuse," 210–13.

60. Brown, *Taste of Power*, 271, 282, 285, 298–99, 347–48, 353, 365, 438–40; Hilliard and Cole, *This Side of Glory*, 340, 350, 352–53, 365; "A Conversation with Huey P. Newton," 16; Hilliard et al., *Huey*, 195, 260–61.

61. Joel Dreyfuss, "On Trial with Huey Newton," *Village Voice*, March 12, 1979, 23; San Francisco FBI memo, August 30, 1974, 3, FBIHPN section 21; Washton, *Cocaine Addiction*, 12, 21–25, 32, 44–45, 53–54.

62. San Francisco FBI Field Office report, November 22, 1974, HPNC 31: illegible; "Newton Forfeits $42,000 Bail," *WP*, August 24, 1974, A4; Hilliard et al., *Huey*, 212–17, 226–29.

63. Newton, *War Against the Panthers*; Weir and Noyes, "Behind the Story," in *Raising Hell*, 261, 266–68; Paul Grabowicz, "Huey's Reign of Terror," *Berkeley Barb*, July 7–13, 1978, 3.

64. Berger, *Captive Nation*, 98–101, 116; Colley, "War without Terms," 271–75.

65. "Judge and 3 Slain on Coast as Convicts Hold Up Court," *NYT*, August 8, 1970, 1; Hilliard and Cole, *This Side of Glory*, 301–2; Berger, *Captive Nation*, 103–8, 130–38; Jackson letter to Newton, February 21, 1971, HPNC 15: Hidden Traitor.

66. Berger, *Captive Nation*, 109–11; Jackson, *Soledad Brother*, 27.

67. Jackson, *Blood in My Eye*, 213–16; Random House/Stronghold contract, September 28, 1971; Edward Bell statement, November 3, 1971; David Lubell to Gwen Fountaine, August 6, 1973, all in HPNC 40: Blood in My Eye.

68. "Bobby Seale on the Death of George Jackson," August 22, 1971, HPNC 1: Press Statement from HPN on Geo. Jackson.

69. "Funeral of Jonathan Jackson and William Christmas," KPFA audio recording, August 15, 1970, now held by Pacifica Radio Archives; "George Jackson on His Brother Jonathan," KRON-TV Newswatch, August 15, 1970, https://diva.sfsu.edu/collections/sfbatv/bundles/228228.

70. "To Eldridge Cleaver and His Conspirators," n.d., HPNC 15: Hidden Traitor; FBI report "Huey P. Newton," April 29, 1971, 213–16.

71. "Statement by Huey P. Newton," HPNC 40: Blood in My Eye; Berger, *Captive Nation*, 119–20; Bob Dylan, "George Jackson," CBS single, 1971, http://www.bobdylan.com/songs/george-jackson/.

72. "Statement by Huey P. Newton, Minister of Defense of the Black Panther Party, at the Revolutionary Memorial Service for George Jackson," *TBP* supplement, September 4, 1971, G.

73. "Interview with George," *TBP*, August 28, 1971, 6–7, quotation on 7 (emphasis added).

74. "On the Soledad Brothers' Pre-Trial Hearing," *TBP*, June 26, 1971, 12–13; "San Quentin Branch of the Black Panther Party Demands the Immediate Freedom of Romaine 'Chip' Fitzgerald," *TBP*, June 26, 1971, 15.

75. "5,000 Blacks May Go to Prison by December," *TBP*, August 21, 1971, center page.

76. "Press Statement by Huey P. Newton," c. September 1971, HPNC 15.

77. "Attica Is Everywhere," *TBP*, October 16, 1971, 7.

78. Kenner to Newton, March 27, 1972, HPNC 40: George Jackson Estate.

79. "Interview with George," 19; George Jackson, last will and testament, August 21, 1971, HPNC 40: Folder 4: George Jackson.

80. FBI Director airtel, March 4, 1968, 3, FBIBEO part 1.

81. "George Jackson on Membership of the BPP," *TBP*, September 18, 1971, 10–11.

Epilogue. Remembering the BPP

1. Peter Baker and Richard Fausset, "Work of Selma 'Not Yet Over' President Says," *NYT*, March 8, 2015, 1.

2. "Black Panther Party 50th Year Anniversary—Rally and Concert!" Black Matters US, October 22, 2016, https://blackmattersus.com (no longer available); "Black Panther Party 50th Anniversary," https://www.eventbrite.com/e/black-panther-party-50th-anniversary-tickets-25604896936#.; Angela Hill, "Black Panthers Celebrate 50th Anni-

versary, Looking at Then and Now," East Bay Times, October 6, 2016; Katie Parish, "City Council Approves Renaming Grove after Black Panther Member," Oakland North, October 5, 2016, https://oaklandnorth.net/2016/10/05/city-council-approves-renaming-grove-after-black-panther-member-hears-from-mayor-schaaf/.

3. Quoted in Hill, "Black Panthers Celebrate 50th Anniversary."

4. Oakland Museum of California, "What Do You Feel Is the Legacy of the Black Panther Party?," 2016, YouTube, https://www.youtube.com/watch?v=T7wgjAtoK_4.

5. Oakland Museum of California, "How Did Being in the Black Panther Party Change Your Life?," 2016, YouTube, https://www.youtube.com/watch?v=12F_fxWzufA.

6. Shames and Seale, *Power to the People*, 200.

7. Tammerlin Drummond, "Amid Backlash, National Park Service Yanks $98,000 Grant for Black Panther Party Legacy Project," East Bay Times, October 27, 2017.

8. Hilliard et al., *Huey*, 281; Pearson, *Shadow of the Panther*, 316–18, 321–23.

9. Funeral of Dr. Huey P. Newton transcript, available with subscription at alexanderstreet.com.

10. Funeral transcript; Pearson, *Shadow of the Panther*, 331–32; JoNina Abron et al., "People's Revolutionary Alumni" press letter, February 1990, HPNC 60: BPP material; Bobby Seale et al. to "friend," n.d., HPNC 60: Political Articles, Speeches.

11. Street, "Historiography of the Black Panther Party," 353, 360, 363–66, 368–70; Arch Puddington, "*The Shadow of the Panther*, by Hugh Pearson," Commentary, September 1994, https://www.commentary.org/articles/arch-puddington-2/the-shadow-of-the-panther-by-hugh-pearson/; Abigail Thernstrom, "Huey Newton: The Whole Story," *Wall Street Journal*, August 15, 1994, A9; Christopher Lehmann-Haupt, "On the Rise and Fall of Huey Newton," *NYT*, June 30, 1994, C18; Horowitz, *Radical Son*, 442; Henderson, "Lumpenproletariat as Vanguard?," 171–99.

12. Don Terry, "Soul on Wheels: A Bus Tour of Black Panther Turf," *NYT*, November 10, 1997, A14; Hilliard interview, 2002; "Black Panther Legacy Tour"; "David Hilliard Giving the Black Panther Tour" (quotation); Reed, *Blues City*, 86.

13. Reed, *Blues City*, 144.

14. Foote, *Shadowed Ground*, 80–81, 96.

15. See posts at Lil Bobby Hutton Park Facebook page, https://www.facebook.com/pages/Lil-Bobby-Hutton-Park/164126690265526.

16. Terry, "Soul on Wheels"; "David Hilliard Giving the Black Panther Tour" (quotation).

17. Justin Allen, "A Black Panther's Guide to Oakland," *Creosote Journal*, July 26, 2011, http://creosotejournal.com/2011/07/black-panthers-guide-to-oakland/.

18. "David Hilliard Giving the Black Panther Tour"; Hilliard interview, 2002; Reed, *Blues City*, 134, 139; Kate Coleman, "All Aboard: Off the Pig," *LA Weekly*, February 11, 1998, https://www.laweekly.com/all-aboard-off-the-pig/.

19. Hilliard and Cole, *This Side of Glory*, 182–88, 193–95; "Black Panther Legacy Tour"; "David Hilliard Giving the Black Panther Tour" (quotation).

20. Rahman, "Marching Blind," in Williams and Lazerow, *Liberated Territory*, 197; Austin, "An Interview with Harold Taylor," 162.

21. Terry, "Soul on Wheels" (quotation); Hilliard interview, 2002; Sam Diaz, "Oakland Tour Explores Black Panther Heritage," *Seattle Times*, November 16, 1997, https://archive.seattletimes.com/archive/?date=19971116&slug=257251; Rick DelVecchio, "Tour of Black Panther Sites," *SFC*, October 25, 1997, http://www.sfgate.com/news/article/Tour-of-Black-Panther-Sites-Former-member-shows-2825056.php.

22. Hilliard interview, 2002; Coleman, "Last Panther," 1, 9–11; Huey P. Newton Foun-

dation, "About the Foundation," https://hueypnewtonfoundation.org/about-the-foundation.

23. "The Black Panther Party Trademark Information," last updated March 17, 2022, https://www.bizapedia.com/trademarks/the-black-panther-party-85316352.html; "Burn Baby Burn," https://www.trademarkia.com/burn-baby-burn-78500148; "Revolutionary Hot Sauce," https://www.trademarkia.com/revolutionary-hot-sauce-78500157; "Black Panther Party," https://www.trademarkia.com/the-black-panther-party-78960001; "Burn Baby Burn Hot Sauce," https://web.archive.org/web/20140426111906/http://www.blackpanthertours.com/burn_baby_burn_order.html; *Dr. Huey P. Newton Foundation, Inc. v. Cafepress.com, Inc.*, https://docs.justia.com/cases/federal/district-courts/new-york/nysdce/1:2011cv03476/379534/1.

24. Coleman, "Last Panther," 9–10; Kate Coleman, "A Black Panther's Last Hurrah," Salon, March 2, 2000, https://www.salon.com/2000/03/06/hilliard/.

25. Nasstrom, "Between Memory and History," 341; Wertsch and Roediger, "Collective Memory," 324.

26. Nasstrom, "Between Memory and History," 347.

27. Pearson, *Shadow of the Panther*, 264; Horowitz, "Black Murder Inc."; Perkins, *Autobiography as Activism*, 102–3 (electronic pagination); Coleman and Avery, "Party's Over," 33; Perkins, "Inside Our Dangerous Ranks," in Springer, *Still Lifting, Still Climbing*, 100–103.

28. Brown, *Taste of Power*, 363–65; Horowitz, *Radical Son*, 244–50; Pearson, *Shadow of the Panther*, 271–72, 288, 290, 328, 346; Browning, "Strange Journey of David Horowitz," 34–35.

29. David Horowitz, "Black Murder Inc.," *Front Page*, December 13, 1999, transcript available at http://lists.village.virginia.edu/lists_archive/sixties-l/0843.html; Austin, *Up Against the Wall*, 402; Spencer, *Revolution Has Come*, 174.

30. Nasstrom, "Between Memory and History," 345–46.

31. Street, "Historiography of the Black Panther Party," 366.

32. Forbes, *Will You Die with Me?*, 191–214, 221–22, 234, 250, 262–66, 276–79, quotation on 279.

33. Rodriguez, "Former Black Panther Marshall Eddie Conway"; Joseph, *Panther Baby*, 253–80.

34. Kane, "Ex-Panther Continues to Push for Change"; Johnson, "Black Panther Reunion."

35. Forbes, "Not Your Daddy's Reunion."

36. Lewis, "Abandoned Pasts, Disappearing Futures," 86; Nasstrom, "Between Memory and History," 342.

37. Jennings, "The 35th Anniversary of the Black Panther Party," http://whgbetc.com/mind/bpp-35th-ann.html (no longer available); Forbes, "Not Your Daddy's Reunion"; "Black Panther Party 35th Year Reunion and Conference Schedule," April 18, 2002, http://www.itsabouttimebpp.com/reunions/35th/full_scheduled.html.

38. Forbes, "Not Your Daddy's Reunion."

39. Johnson, "Black Panther Reunion."

40. Quoted in Christopher Brown, "All Power to the People: The 40th Anniversary of the Black Panther Party," October 16, 2006, http://cbgonzo.blogspot.com/2006/10/all-power-to-people-40th-anniversary.html.

41. Johnson, "Black Panther Reunion." See also Shih and Williams, *Black Panthers*.

42. Reed, *Blues City*, 188; "About Juneteenth," https://berkeleyjuneteenth.org/aboutjuneteenth-2/.

BIBLIOGRAPHY

Archival Sources

Black Panther Party Harlem Branch files, Schomburg Center for Research in Black Culture, Manuscripts, Archives, and Rare Books Division, New York Public Library

Eldridge Cleaver FBI file (available via ProQuest History Vault; cited as FBIEC)

FBI COINTELPRO Black Extremist (available via vault.fbi.gov and ProQuest History Vault; cited as FBIBEO)

Huey P. Newton collection, microfilm at Northumbria University (cited as HPNC [reel number]: [file name]).

Huey P. Newton FBI file (available via ProQuest History Vault; cited as FBIHPN).

Huey P. Newton Inmate Record, California State Archives, Sacramento

INTERVIEWS

Douglas, Emory. Interview with author, San Francisco, June 28, 2001. Audio recording and transcript in author's collection.

Everett-Karenga, Ron. Interview with Clayborne Carson, October 4, 1977. Personal collection of Clayborne Carson.

Hilliard, David. c. 2002. Available with subscription at alexanderstreet.com.

Huggins, Ericka. An Oral History with Ericka Huggins conducted by Fiona Thompson. 2007. Oral History Center, Bancroft Library, University of California, Berkeley. http://digitalassets.lib.berkeley.edu/.

Interviews conducted by Blackside, Inc. for *Eyes on the Prize II: America at the Racial Crossroads 1965 to 1985*. Washington University Libraries, Film and Media Archive, Henry Hampton Collection at http://digital.wustl.edu/:

    Douglas, Emory. October 13, 1988.
    Johnson, Deborah. October 19, 1988.
    Newton, Huey P. May 23, 1989.
    O'Neal, William. April 13, 1989.
    Rush, Bobby. October 20, 1988.
    Saffold, Howard. October 18, 1988.
    Seale, Bobby. November 4, 1988.
    Taylor, Flint. October 18, 1988.

Jensen, Judge D. Lowell. "A Life Dedicated to the Administration of Justice and Legal Reform." Interview conducted by Lisa Rubens and Marcia Jensen, 2005–6. Regional Oral History Office, Bancroft Library, University of California, Berkeley. https://digicoll.lib.berkeley.edu/record/218477?ln=en.

Kilgore, Thomas, Jr. "Black Leadership in Los Angeles." UCLA Oral History Program transcripts, Bancroft Library, UC Berkeley.

Ralph J. Bunche Oral History Collection. Moorland-Spingarn Research Center, Howard University (cited as RJBOHC).

Vanderscoff, Cameron. "'Look'n M'Face and Hear M' Story': An Oral History with Professor J. Herman Blake." 2014. UC Santa Cruz Regional History Project. https://escholarship.org/uc/item/4m01p3bz.

Wilson, Lionel. "Attorney, Judge, and Oakland Mayor." Interview conducted in 1985 and 1990 by Gabrielle Morris, Regional Oral History Office, Bancroft Library, University of California, Berkeley, 1992. https://digicoll.lib.berkeley.edu/record/217816?ln=en.

FILMS AND DOCUMENTARIES

"Black Panther Legacy Tour (Copyright 2015 by the Dr. Huey P. Newton Foundation)." Available with subscription at alexanderstreet.com.

"David Hilliard Giving the Black Panther Tour." Available with subscription at www.alexanderstreet.com.

Eyes on the Prize II: America at the Racial Crossroads, 1965–1985. Episode 3, "Power! (1966–68)." PBS DVD, 2010.

"Merritt College: Home of the Black Panthers." 2014. https://www.youtube.com/watch?v=54wYflGYMrw.

Nelson, Stanley, dir. *The Black Panthers: Vanguard of the Revolution*. 2015.

Olsson, Göran. *The Black Power Mixtape, 1967–1975*. 2011.

———. *Concerning Violence: Nine Scenes from the Anti-Imperialistic Self-Defense*. 2014.

Pugh, Sally. *Huey!* American Documentary Films, 1968. San Francisco Bay Area Television Archive. https://diva.sfsu.edu/.

Van Peebles, Melvin. *Sweet Sweetback's Baadasssss Song*. 1971.

Varda, Agnès. *Black Panthers*. 1968. http://www.eastofborneo.org/. The website misidentifies *Black Panthers* as *Huey*, Varda's other documentary about the BPP.

What We Want, What We Believe. Richmond, Vt.: Newsreel Films, 2006. Includes *Off the Pig*; *FBI Agents*.

Newspapers and Periodicals

Atlantic
Berkeley Barb
Berkeley Tribe
The Black Panther Black Community News Service and *The Black Panther Intercommunal News Service* (referred to as TBP)
Boston Globe
Chicago Tribune
Daily Californian
Ebony
Guardian (London)
Jet
Los Angeles Times
Mercury News
New York Times (referred to as *NYT*)
Oakland North
Oakland Tribune (referred to as *OT*)
Ramparts
Rolling Stone
San Francisco Chronicle (referred to as *SFC*)
San Francisco Examiner (referred to as *SFE*)
SFGate
Twin City Sentinel (Winston-Salem)
Village Voice
Wall Street Journal
Washington Post (referred to as *WP*)

Published Sources

Abu-Jamal, Mumia. *We Want Freedom: A Life in the Black Panther Party*. Boston: South End, 2004.

Alkebulan, Paul. *Survival Pending Revolution: The History of the Black Panther Party*. Tuscaloosa: University of Alabama Press, 2007.

Alterman, Eric. "Ron Dellums: Radical Insider." *World Policy Journal* 10 (Winter 1993/94): 35–46.
Anderson, Jon Lee. *Che Guevara: A Revolutionary Life.* London: Bantam, 1997.
Anthony, Earl. *Spitting in the Wind: The True Story Behind the Violent Legacy of the Black Panther Party.* Malibu, Calif.: Roundtable, 1990.
Arend, Orissa. *Showdown in Desire: The Black Panthers Take a Stand in New Orleans.* Fayetteville: University of Arkansas Press, 2009.
Austin, Curtis. "An Interview with Harold Taylor." *Journal of African American Studies* 21 (2017): 159–71.
———. *Up Against the Wall: Violence in the Making and Unmaking of the Black Panther Party.* Fayetteville: University of Arkansas Press, 2006.
Balagoon, Kuwasi. *Look for Me in the Whirlwind: The Collective Autobiography of the New York 21.* New York: Vintage, 1971.
Baraka, Amiri. *The Autobiography of LeRoi Jones.* Chicago: Lawrence Hill, 1997.
Bass, Paul, and Douglas W. Rae. *Murder in the Model City: The Black Panthers, Yale, and the Redemption of a Killer.* New York: Basic, 2006.
Bell, Jonathan. *California Crucible: The Forging of Modern American Liberalism.* Philadelphia: University of Pennsylvania Press, 2012.
Benjamin, Walter. *Illuminations.* London: Jonathan Cape, 1970.
Berger, Dan. *Captive Nation: Black Prison Organizing in the Civil Rights Era.* Chapel Hill: University of North Carolina Press, 2014.
Bignardi, Irene. "The Making of *The Battle of Algiers*." *Cineaste* 25, (2000): 14–22.
The Black Panthers: Vanguard of the Revolution. Transcript in author's collection. Courtesy of Stanley Nelson.
Blake, J. Herman. "The Caged Panther: The Prison Years of Huey P. Newton." *Journal of African American Studies* 16 (2012): 236–48.
Bloom, Joshua, and Waldo E. Martin Jr. *Black against Empire: The History and Politics of the Black Panther Party.* Berkeley: University of California Press, 2013.
Breitman, George. *The Last Year of Malcolm X: The Evolution of a Revolutionary.* New York: Merit, 1967.
Browning, Frank. "The Strange Journey of David Horowitz." *Mother Jones,* May 1987, 27–38.
Brown, Elaine. *A Taste of Power: A Black Woman's Story.* New York: Anchor, 1992.
Brown, Scot. *Fighting for US: Maulana Karenga, the US Organization, and Black Cultural Nationalism.* New York: New York University Press, 2003.
———. "The US Organization: African-American Cultural Nationalism in the Era of Black Power, 1965 to the 1970s." PhD diss., Cornell University, 1999.
Bukhari, Safiya. *The War Before: The True Life Story of Becoming a Panther, Keeping the Faith in Prison and Fighting for Those Left Behind.* Edited by Laura Whitehorn. New York: Feminist Press, 2010.
Burke, Lucas N. N., and Judson L. Jeffries. *The Portland Black Panthers: Empowering Albina and Remaking a City.* Seattle: University of Washington Press, 2016.
Burrough, Bryan. *Days of Rage: America's Radical Underground, the FBI, and the Forgotten Age of Revolutionary Violence.* New York: Penguin, 2015.
Cade, Toni, ed. *The Black Woman: An Anthology.* New York: Mentor, 1970.
Cameron, Christopher. "The New Negro Renaissance and African American Secularism." In *New Perspectives on the Black Intellectual Tradition,* edited by Keisha N. Blain, Christopher Cameron, and Ashley D. Farmer, 99–114. Evanston, Ill.: Northwestern University Press, 2018.

Carson, Clayborne. *In Struggle: SNCC and the Black Awakening of the 1960s.* Cambridge, Mass.: Harvard University Press, 1981.

Castledine, Jacqueline. "'In a Solid Bond of Unity': Anticolonial Feminism in the Cold War Era." *Journal of Women's History* 20 (2008): 57–81.

Chappell, David L. *Waking from the Dream: The Struggle for Civil Rights in the Shadow of Martin Luther King, Jr.* New York: Random House, 2014.

Childs, Matt D. "An Historical Critique of the Emergence and Evolution of Ernesto Che Guevara's *Foco* Theory." *Journal of Latin American Studies* 27, no. 3 (October 1995): 593–624.

Churchill, Ward, and Jim Vander Wall. *Agents of Repression: The FBI's Secret Wars against the Black Panther Party and the American Indian Movement.* Boston: South End, 1990.

Cleaver, Eldridge. *Eldridge Cleaver: Post-Prison Writings and Speeches.* Edited by Robert Scheer. New York: Random House, 1969.

———. *Soul on Fire.* Waco, Tex.: Word Books, 1978.

———. *Soul on Ice: Selected Essays.* London: Jonathan Cape, 1969.

Cleaver, Kathleen, and George Katsiaficas, eds. *Liberation, Imagination, and the Black Panther Party: A New Look at the Panthers and Their Legacy.* New York: Routledge, 2001.

Cleaver, Kathleen, ed. *Target Zero: A Life in Writing, Eldridge Cleaver.* New York: Palgrave, 2006.

Clemons, Michael L., and Charles E. Jones. "Global Solidarity: The Black Panther Party in the International Arena." *New Political Science* 21 (1999): 177–203.

Cohen-Cruz, Jan, ed. *Radical Street Performance: An International Anthology.* London: Routledge, 1998.

Coleman, Kate. "The Last Panther." *Heterodoxy*, February 1998.

Coleman, Kate, and Paul Avery. "The Party's Over." *New Times*, July 10, 1978.

Colley, Zoe. "War without Terms: George Jackson, Black Power and the American Radical Prison Rights Movement, 1941–1971." *History* 101 (2016): 265–86.

Collins, Patricia Hill. *Black Feminist Thought.* 2nd ed. London: Routledge, 2009.

Conway, Marshall "Eddie," and Dominique Stevenson. *Marshall Law: The Life and Times of a Baltimore Black Panther.* Edinburgh: AK Press, 2011.

Coogler, Ryan, and Joe Robert Cole. *Black Panther* adapted screenplay. https://static1.squarespace.com/.

Cooper, Anna Julia Haywood. *A Voice from the South: by a Black Woman of the South.* Xenia: Aldine Printing House, 1892. Available at https://www.gutenberg.org/.

Cooper, Brittney C. *Beyond Respectability: The Intellectual Thought of Race Women.* Chicago: University of Illinois Press, 2017.

Copes, Heith, Tomislav V. Kovandzic, J. Mitchell Miller, and Luke Williamson. "The Lost Cause? Examining the Southern Culture of Honor through Defensive Gun Use." *Crime and Delinquency* 60 (2014): 356–78.

Cummins, Eric. *The Rise and Fall of California's Radical Prison Movement.* Stanford, Calif.: Stanford University Press, 1994.

Davis, Mike, and Jon Wiener. *Set the Night on Fire: L.A. in the Sixties.* London: Verso, 2020.

DeCaro, Louis A., Jr. *On the Side of My People: A Religious Life of Malcolm X.* New York: New York University Press, 1996.

de Viggiani, Nick, "Unhealthy Prisons: Exploring Structural Determinants of Prison Health." *Sociology of Health and Illness* 29 (2007): 115–35.

Dixon, Aaron. *My People Are Rising: Memoir of a Black Panther Party Captain*. Chicago: Haymarket, 2012.

Durant, Sam, ed. *Black Panther: The Revolutionary Art of Emory Douglas*. New York: Rizzoli, 2007.

Eberhart, George M. "Stack Lee: The Man, the Music, and the Myth." *Popular Music and Society* 20 (1996): 1–70.

English, T. J. *The Savage City: Race, Murder, and a Generation on the Edge*. Edinburgh: Mainstream, 2011.

Epstein, Edward Jay. "The Black Panthers and the Police: A Pattern of Genocide?" *New Yorker*, February 13, 1971.

Epstein, Jason. "A Special Supplement: The Trial of Bobby Seale." *New York Review of Books*, December 4, 1969.

Erikson, Erik H., and Huey P. Newton. *In Search of Common Ground: Conversations with Erik H. Erikson and Huey P. Newton*. New York: Norton, 1973.

Ervin, Michael. "The Last Hours of William O'Neal." *Chicago Reader*, January 25, 1990.

Fanon, Frantz. *The Wretched of the Earth*. Translated by Constance Farrington. London: Penguin, 1967.

Fagan, Jeffrey, and Deanna L. Wilkinson. "Guns, Youth Violence, and Social Identity in Inner Cities." *Crime and Justice* 24 (1988): 105–88.

Farmer, Ashley D. "Mothers of Pan-Africanism: Audley Moore and Dara Abubakari." *Women, Gender, and Families of Color* 4 (2016): 274–95.

———. *Remaking Black Power: How Black Women Transformed an Era*. Chapel Hill: University of North Carolina Press, 2017.

Foner, Philip S., ed. *The Black Panthers Speak*. New York: Da Capo, 1995.

Foote, Kenneth E. *Shadowed Ground: America's Landscapes of Violence and Tragedy*. Rev. ed. Austin: University of Texas Press, 2003.

Forbes, Flores. "Not Your Daddy's Reunion: Black Panthers 35 Years Later." *Village Voice*, n.d. http://www.itsabouttimebpp.com/reunions/35th/NotYourDaddysReunion.html.

———. *Will You Die with Me? My Life and the Black Panther Party*. New York: Atria, 2006.

Forman, James. *The Making of Black Revolutionaries*. Seattle: University of Washington Press, 1997.

Fortner, Michael Javen. "The 'Silent Majority' in Black and White: Invisibility and Imprecision in the Historiography of Mass Incarceration." *Journal of Urban History* 40 (2014): 252–82.

Fujino, Diane C. *Samurai among Panthers: Richard Aoki on Race, Resistance, and a Paradoxical Life*. Minneapolis: University of Minnesota Press, 2012.

———. "A Spiritual Practice for Sustaining Social Justice Activism: An Interview with Ericka Huggins." In *Black Power Afterlives: The Enduring Significance of the Black Panther Party*, edited by Diane C. Fujino and Matef Harmachis, 79–90. Chicago: Haymarket, 2020.

Gaines, Kevin K. *Uplifting the Race: Black Leadership in the Twentieth Century*. Chapel Hill: University of North Carolina Press, 1996.

Gallen, David, ed. *Malcolm X: As They Knew Him*. New York: Carroll & Graf, 1992.

Garcha, Kiran. "Children and Childhood in Black Panther Party Thought and Discourse." *Journal of African American Studies* 23 (2019): 320–34.

Garry, Charles, and Art Goldberg. *Streetfighter in the Courtroom: The People's Advocate*. New York: Dutton, 1977.

Giddings, Paula J. *Ida: A Sword among Lions*. New York: HarperCollins, 2008.
Gifford, Justin. *Revolution or Death: The Life of Eldridge Cleaver*. Chicago: Lawrence Hill, 2020.
Goldman, Peter. *The Death and Life of Malcolm X*. 2nd ed. Urbana: University of Illinois Press, 1979.
Goldstein, Joshua. "Huey Newton Comes Home." *Grapevine*, July-August 1977.
Gore, Dayo F., Jeanne Theoharis, and Komozi Woodard, eds. *Want to Start a Revolution? Radical Women in the Black Freedom Struggle*. New York City: New York University Press, 2009.
Grassian, Stuart. "Psychiatric Effects of Solitary Confinement." *Journal of Law and Policy* 22 (2006): 325–83.
Greenhill, Laurence L. "The Science of Stimulant Abuse." *Psychiatric Annals* 35 (2005): 210–14.
Guevara, Che. *Guerrilla Warfare*. Lincoln: University of Nebraska Press, 1985.
———. *Venceremos!: The Speeches and Writings of Che Guevara*. Edited by John Gerassi. New York: Clarion, 1968.
Haas, Jeffrey. *The Assassination of Fred Hampton: How the FBI and Chicago Police Murdered a Black Panther*. Chicago: Lawrence Hill, 2010.
Hahn, Harlan, David Klingman, and Harry Pachon. "Cleavages, Coalitions, and the Black Candidate: The Los Angeles Mayoralty Elections of 1969 and 1973." *Western Political Quarterly* 29 (1976): 507–20.
Haldeman, H. R., with Joseph DiMona. *The Ends of Power*. New York: Times, 1978.
Halisi, Clyde, ed. *The Quotable Karenga*. Los Angeles: US Organization, 1967.
Hampton, Henry, and Steve Fayer. *Voices of Freedom: An Oral History of the Civil Rights Movement from the 1950s through the 1980s*. London: Vintage, 1995.
Haney, Craig. "Mental Health Issues in Long-Term Solitary and 'Supermax' Confinement." *Crime and Delinquency* 49 (2003): 124–56.
———. "The Psychological Impact of Incarceration: Implications for Postprison Adjustment." In *Prisoners Once Removed: The Impact of Incarceration and Reentry on Children, Families, and Communities*, edited by Jeremy Travis and Michelle Waul. Washington, D.C.: Urban Institute Press, 2003.
Hardt, Michael, and Antonio Negri. *Empire*. Cambridge, Mass.: Harvard University Press, 2000.
Harrison, Nicholas "Based on Actual Events . . . : Pontecorvo's *Battle of Algiers*, 40 Years On." *Interventions* 9 (2007): 335–39.
Henderson, Errol A. "The Lumpenproletariat as Vanguard? The Black Panther Party, Social Transformation, and Pearson's Analysis of Huey Newton." *Journal of Black Studies* 28 (1997): 171–99.
Hiestand, Fred, and Jim Smith. "Of Panthers and Prisons: An Interview with Huey P. Newton." *National Lawyers' Guild Practitioner* 29 (1972): 57–65.
Hilliard, David. *The Black Panther Party Service to the People Programs*. Albuquerque: University of New Mexico Press, 2008.
Hilliard, David, and Lewis Cole. *This Side of Glory: The Autobiography of David Hilliard and the Story of the Black Panther Party*. Boston: Little, Brown, 1993.
Hilliard, David, with Keith and Kent Zimmerman. *Huey: Spirit of the Panther*. New York: Thunder's Mouth, 2006.
Hipp, John R., Joan Petersilia, and Susan Turner. "Parolee Recidivism in California: The Effect of Neighborhood Context and Social Service Agency Characteristics." *Criminology* 48 (2010): 947–79.

Ho, Fred, with Carolyn Antonio, Diane Fujino, and Steve Yip, eds. *Legacy to Liberation: Politics and Culture of Revolutionary Asian Pacific America*. New York: Big Red Media, 2000.

Hoerl, Kristen, and Erin Ortiz. "Organizational Secrecy and the FBI's COINTELPRO-Black Nationalist Hate Groups Program, 1967–1972." *Management Communication Quarterly* 29 (2015): 590–615.

Hopper, James, and David Lisak. "Why Rape and Trauma Survivors Have Fragmented and Incomplete Memories." *Time*, December 9, 2014.

Horne, Gerald. *Fire This Time: The Watts Uprising and the 1960s*. New York: Da Capo, 1997.

Horowitz, David. *Radical Son: A Generational Odyssey*. New York: Free Press, 1997.

"How Does It Go with the Black Movement?" Firing Line with William F. Buckley Jr., January 23, 1973. https://youtu.be/XUicVnx1UKU.

Hresko, Tracy. "In the Cellars of the Hollow Men: Use of Solitary Confinement in U.S. Prisons and Its Implications under International Laws against Torture." *Pace International Law Review* 18 (2006): 1–27.

Huggins, Erica, Tony Platt, and Cecilia O'Leary. "Two Interviews with Ericka Huggins." *Social Justice* 40 (2014): 54–71.

Hughey, Matthew W. "Black Aesthetics and Panther Rhetoric: A Critical Decoding of Black Masculinity in *The Black Panther*, 1967–1980." *Critical Sociology* 35 (2009): 29–56.

Hunt, Irvin J. "Planned Failure: George Schuyler, Ella Baker and the Young Negroes' Cooperative League." *American Quarterly* 72 (2020): 853–79.

Jackson, George. *Blood in My Eye*. London: Jonathan Cape, 1972.

———. *Soledad Brother: The Prison Letters of George Jackson*. London: Jonathan Cape, 1971.

Janssen, Volker. "From the Inside Out: Therapeutic Penology and Political Liberalism in Postwar California." *Osiris* 22 (2007): 116–34.

Jeffries, Judson L., ed. *The Black Panther Party in a City Near You*. Athens: University of Georgia Press, 2018.

———. *Comrades: A Local History of the Black Panther Party*. Bloomington: Indiana University Press, 2007.

———. "Conversing with Gwen Robinson." *Spectrum* 5 (2016): 137–45.

———. "Hanging Out with Al Amour." *Journal of African American Studies* 21 (2017): 124–27.

———. *Huey P. Newton: The Radical Theorist*. Jackson: University Press of Mississippi, 2002.

———. *On the Ground: The Black Panther Party in Communities across America*. Jackson: University Press of Mississippi, 2010.

———. "Reflecting on Her Life in the Party: Conversations with Connie Felder." *Journal of African American Studies* 21 (2017): 128–37.

Jeffries, Judson, Omari L. Dyson, and Charles E. Jones. "Mark Clark's Tenuous Place in History." *Journal of African American Studies* 21 (2017): 6–25.

Johnson, Cedric. *Revolutionaries to Race Leaders: Black Power and the Making of African American Politics*. Minneapolis: University of Minnesota Press, 2007.

Johnson, Christopher. "Black Panther Reunion Looks Back 40 Years." *News and Notes* transcript, National Public Radio, December 26, 2006. https://www.npr.org/templates/story/story.php?storyId=6677032.

Johnson, Marilynn S. *The Second Gold Rush: Oakland and the East Bay in World War II*. Berkeley: University of California Press, 1993.

———. "War as Watershed: The East Bay and World War II." *Pacific Historical Review* 63 (1994): 315–31.
Jones, Charles E., ed. *The Black Panther Party [Reconsidered]*. Baltimore: Black Classic, 1998.
Jones, Claudia. *An End to the Neglect of the Problems of the Negro Woman!* National Women's Commission, CPUSA reprint, 1949.
Joseph, Jamal. *Panther Baby: A Life of Rebellion and Reinvention*. Chapel Hill, N.C.: Algonquin, 2012.
Joseph, Peniel E. *Stokely: A Life*. New York: Basic, 2014.
Josephs, Samuel. "Whose Revolution Is This? Gender's Divisive Role in the Black Panther Party." *Georgetown Journal of Gender and the Law* 2 (2008): 403–26.
Kane, Gregory. "Ex-Panther Continues to Push for Change." *Baltimore Sun*, October 28, 2006.
Karenga, M. Ron. "Kawaida and Its Critics: A Socio-Historical Analysis." *Journal of Black Studies* 8, no. 2 (December 1977): 125–48.
Keating, Edward M. *Free Huey: The True Story of the Trial of Huey P. Newton for Murder*. Berkeley: Ramparts, 1970.
Kelley, Robin D. G., and Betsy Esch. "Black Like Mao: Red China and Black Revolution." *Souls* 1 (1999): 6–41.
Khvostov, Mikhail. *The Russian Civil War (1): The Red Army*. Oxford: Osprey, 1996.
Lazerow, Jama, and Yohuru Williams, eds. *In Search of the Black Panther Party: New Perspectives on a Revolutionary Movement*. Durham, N.C.: Duke University Press, 2006.
Lee, Chana Kai. *For Freedom's Sake: The Life of Fannie Lou Hamer*. Chicago: University of Illinois Press, 1999.
Lefebvre, Henri. *The Production of Space*. Translated by Donald Nicholson-Smith. Oxford: Blackwell, 1991.
Leonardatos, Cynthia Deitle. "California's Attempts to Disarm the Black Panthers." *San Diego Law Review* 36 (1999): 947–96.
Leovy, Jill. *Ghettoside: A True Story of Murder in America*. London: Vintage, 2014.
Lewis, David. "Abandoned Pasts, Disappearing Futures: Further Reflections on Multiple Temporalities in Studying Non-Governmental Organisation Worlds." *Critique of Anthropology* 36 (2016): 84–92.
Lockwood, Lee. *Conversation with Eldridge Cleaver*. New York: McGraw-Hill, 1970.
———. "*Playboy* Interview: Huey Newton." *Playboy*, May 1973, 73–90.
Macey, David. *Frantz Fanon, A Life*. London: Granta, 2000.
Madrigal, Alexis C. "The Racist Housing Policy That Made Your Neighborhood." *Atlantic*, May 22, 2014.
Major, Reginald. *A Panther Is a Black Cat*. Baltimore: Black Classic, 1991.
Malloy, Sean L. *Out of Oakland: Black Panther Party Internationalism during the Cold War*. Ithaca, N.Y.: Cornell University Press, 2017.
Mao Tse-Tung. *Quotations from Chairman Mao Tse-Tung*. New York: Bantam, 1967.
Marine, Gene. *The Black Panthers*. New York: Signet, 1969.
Marx, Karl. *A Contribution to the Critique of Hegel's Philosophy of Right*. 1844. Marx/Engels Internet Archive at https://www.marxists.org/.
———. *The Eighteenth Brumaire of Louis Bonaparte*. 1852. Marx/Engels Internet Archive at http://www.marxists.org/.
———. *Theses on Feuerbach*. 1845. Marx/Engels Internet Archive at https://www.marxists.org/.

McCutchen, Steve D. [Lil' Masai]. *We Were Free for a While: Back to Back in the Black Panther Party*. Baltimore: Publish America, 2008.

McDuffie, Erik S. "A 'New Freedom Movement of Negro Women': Sojourning for Truth, Justice, and Human Rights during the Early Cold War." *Radical History Review* 101 (2008): 81–106.

———. "'I Wanted a Communist Philosophy, But I Wanted Us to Have a Chance to Organize Our People': The Diasporic Radicalism of Queen Mother Audley Moore and the Origins of Black Power." *African and Black Diaspora* 3 (2010): 181–95.

McLaughlin, Malcolm. *The Long, Hot Summer of 1967: Urban Rebellion in America*. New York: Palgrave Macmillan, 2014.

McMurry, Linda O. *To Keep the Waters Troubled: The Life of Ida B. Wells*. New York: Oxford University Press, 1998.

Mercer, Ben. "Specters of Fascism: The Rhetoric of Historical Analogy in 1968." *Journal of Modern History* 88 (2016): 96–129.

Mestman, Mariano. "The Last Sacred Image of the Latin American Revolution." *Journal of Latin American Cultural Studies* 19 (2010): 23–44.

Mills, Nathaniel. "Cleaver/Baldwin Revisited: Naturalism and the Gendering of Black Revolution." *Studies in American Naturalism* 7, no. 1 (Summer 2012): 50–79.

Milner, Clyde A., II, Carol A. O'Connor, and Martha A. Sandweiss, eds. *The Oxford History of the American West*. Oxford: Oxford University Press, 1994.

Mitchell, Don, *The Right to the City: Social Justice and the Fight for Public Space*. New York: Guilford Press, 2003.

Moore, Gilbert. *A Special Rage*. New York: Harper & Row, 1971.

Morgan, Jo-Ann. *The Black Arts Movement and the Black Panther Party in American Visual Culture*. New York: Routledge, 2019.

Murch, Donna Jean. *Living for the City: Migration, Education, and the Rise of the Black Panther Party in Oakland, California*. Chapel Hill: University of North Carolina Press, 2010.

Narayan, John. "The Wages of Whiteness in the Absence of Wages: Racial Capitalism, Reactionary Intercommunalism and the Rise of Trumpism." *Third World Quarterly* 38 (2017): 2482–2500.

Nasstrom, Kathryn L. "Between Memory and History: Autobiographies of the Civil Rights Movement and the Writing of Civil Rights History." *Journal of Southern History* 74 (2008): 325–64.

Nayar, Pramod K. *Frantz Fanon*. London: Routledge, 2013.

Nelson, Alondra. *Body and Soul: The Black Panther Party and the Fight against Medical Discrimination*. Minneapolis: University of Minnesota Press, 2011.

———. "Genuine Struggle and Care." *American Journal of Public Health* 106 (2016): 1744–48.

Newton, Huey P. *The Huey P. Newton Reader*. Edited by David Hilliard and Donald Weise. New York: Seven Stories Press, 2002.

———. *To Die for the People: The Writings of Huey P. Newton*. Edited by Toni Morrison. New York: Writers & Readers, 1972.

———. *War against The Panthers: A Study of Repression in America*. New York: Harlem River, 1996.

Newton, Huey P., with J. Herman Blake. *Revolutionary Suicide*. New York: Penguin, 2009.

Obama, Barack. *Dreams from My Father*. Edinburgh: Canongate, 2007.

Ogbar, Jeffrey O. G. *Black Power: Radical Politics and African American Identity*. Baltimore: Johns Hopkins University Press, 2004.

O'Reilly, Kenneth. *"Racial Matters": The FBI's Secret War on Black America, 1960–1972.* New York: Free Press, 1989.

Pearlman, Lise. *The Sky's the Limit: People v. Newton, the Real Trial of the 20th Century?* Berkeley, Calif.: Regent, 2012.

Pearson, Hugh. *Shadow of the Panther: Huey Newton and the Price of Black Power in America.* Reading, Mass.: Da Capo, 1994.

Pepper, Art, and Laurie Pepper. *Straight Life: The Story of Art Pepper.* New York: Da Capo, 1994.

Perkins, Margo. *Autobiography as Activism: Three Black Women of the Sixties.* Jackson: University Press of Mississippi, 2000.

Perlstein, Daniel. "Minds Stayed on Freedom: Politics and Pedagogy in the African American Freedom Struggle." *Radical Teacher* 69 (May 2004): 23–28.

Perry, Bruce. *Malcolm: The Life of a Man Who Changed Black America.* New York: Station Hill, 1991.

Pharr, Wayne. *Nine Lives of a Black Panther: A Story of Survival.* Chicago: Lawrence Hill, 2014.

Phillips, Mary. "The Feminist Leadership of Ericka Huggins in the Black Panther Party." *Black Diaspora Review* 4 (2014): 187–218.

Phillips, Mary, and Angela LeBlanc-Ernest. "The Hidden Narratives: Recovering and (Re)Visioning the Community Activism of Men in the Black Panther Party." *Spectrum* 5 (2016): 63–89.

Phillips, Mary, Robyn C. Spencer, Angela D. LeBlanc-Ernest, and Tracye A. Matthews. "Ode to Our Feminist Foremothers: The Intersectional Black Panther Party History Project on Collaborative Praxis and Fifty Years of Panther History." *Souls* 19 (2017): 241–60.

Pope, Ricky J., and Shawn T. Flanigan. "Revolution for Breakfast: Intersections of Activism, Service, and Violence in the Black Panther Party's Community Service Programs." *Social Justice Research* 26 (2013): 445–70.

Potorti, Mary. "'Feeding the Revolution': The Black Panther Party, Hunger, and Community Survival." *Journal of African American Studies* 21 (2017): 85–110.

Ramparts Magazine and Frank Browning, eds. *Prison Life: A Study of the Explosive Conditions in America's Prisons.* New York: Harper & Row, 1972.

Ransby, Barbara. *Ella Baker and the Black Freedom Movement: A Radical Democratic Vision.* Chapel Hill: University of North Carolina Press, 2003.

Rapoport, Roger. "Meet America's Meanest Dirty Trickster." *Mother Jones*, April 1977, 18–23, 59–61.

Rebman, Christine. "Eighth Amendment and Solitary Confinement: The Gap in Protection from Psychological Consequences." *DePaul Law Review* 49 (2000): 567–619.

Reed, Ishmael. *Blues City: A Walk in Oakland.* New York: Crown, 2003.

Reid, Donald. "Re-Viewing *The Battle of Algiers* with Germaine Tillion." *History Workshop Journal* 60 (2005): 93–115.

Reporting Civil Rights: Part Two, American Journalism, 1963–1973. New York: Library of America, 2003.

Rhodes, Jane. *Framing the Black Panthers: The Spectacular Rise of a Black Power Icon.* New York: New Press, 2007.

Richardson, Peter. *A Bomb in Every Issue: How the Short, Unruly Life of Ramparts Magazine Changed America.* New York: New Press, 2009.

——— . "The Perilous Fight: The Rise of *Ramparts* Magazine." *California History* 86 (2009): 22–43, 68–69.
Robinson, Dean E. *Black Nationalism in American Politics and Thought*. Cambridge: Cambridge University Press, 2000.
Robinson, Robert P. "Until the Revolution: Analyzing the Politics, Pedagogy, and Curriculum of the Oakland Community School." *Espacio, Tiempo y Educación* 7, no. 1 (2020): 181–203.
Rodriguez, Anthony Bayani. "Former Black Panther Marshall Eddie Conway on Revolutionary Political Education in the Twenty-First Century." *Journal of African American Studies* 21 (2017): 138–49.
Romano, Sally Mann. "If the SHU Fits: Cruel and Unusual Punishment at California's Pelican Bay State Prison." *Emory Law Journal* 45 (1996): 1089–138.
Rooney, Adrienne. "*The Battle of Algiers* and Colonial Analogy in the Panther 21." *Journal of African American Studies* 23 (2019): 455–75.
Rosenfeld, Seth. *Subversives: The FBI's War on Student Radicals, and Reagan's Rise to Power*. New York: Farrar, Straus & Giroux, 2012.
Rout, Kathleen. *Eldridge Cleaver*. Boston: Twayne, 1991.
Sales, William W., Jr. *From Civil Rights to Black Liberation: Malcolm X and the Organization of Afro-American Unity*. Boston: South End, 1994.
Sandoval, Chela. "US Third World Feminism: The Theory and Method of Oppositional Consciousness in the Postmodern World." In *Feminism and "Race,"* edited by KumKum Bhavnani, 261–80. Oxford: Oxford University Press, 2001.
Schanche, Don. *The Panther Paradox: A Liberal's Dilemma*. New York: Van Rees, 1970.
Schutzman, Mady, and Jan Cohen-Cruz, eds. *A Boal Companion: Dialogues on Theatre and Cultural Politics*. New York: Routledge, 2006.
Scott, G. D., and Paul Gendreau. "Psychiatric Implications of Sensory Deprivation in a Maximum Security Prison." *Canadian Psychiatric Association Journal* 14 (1969): 337–41.
Seale, Bobby. *A Lonely Rage*. New York: Times, 1978.
——— . *Seize the Time: The Story of the Black Panther Party*. London: Arrow, 1970.
Self, Robert O. *American Babylon: Race and the Struggle for Postwar Oakland*. Princeton, N.J.: Princeton University Press, 2003.
Shakur, Assata. *Assata: An Autobiography*. Chicago: Lawrence Hill, 2001.
Shames, Stephen, and Bobby Seale. *Power to the People: The World of the Black Panthers*. New York: Abrams, 2016.
Shih, Brian, and Yohuru Williams. *The Black Panthers: Portraits from an Unfinished Revolution*. New York: Nation, 2016.
Shilts, Randy. *The Mayor of Castro Street: The Life and Times of Harvey Milk*. London: Penguin, 1993.
Simon, Jonathan. "From the Big House to the Warehouse: Rethinking Prisons and State Government in the 20th Century." *Punishment and Society* 2 (2000): 337–41.
Singh, Nikhil Pal. *Black Is a Country: Race and the Unfinished Struggle for Democracy*. Cambridge, Mass.: Harvard University Press, 2004.
Smitherman, Geneva. *Talkin and Testifyin: The Language of Black America*. Boston: Houghton Mifflin, 1977.
Sorensen, Majken Jul. "Humor as a Serious Strategy of Nonviolent Resistance to Oppression." *Peace and Change* 33 (2008): 167–90.
Spencer, Robyn. "Engendering the Black Freedom Struggle: Revolutionary Black Wom-

anhood and the Black Panther Party in the Bay Area, California." *Journal of Women's History* 20 (2008): 90–113.

———. *The Revolution Has Come: Black Power, Gender, and the Black Panther Party in Oakland*. Durham, N.C.: Duke University Press, 2016.

Springer, Kimberley, ed. *Still Lifting, Still Climbing: African American Women's Contemporary Activism*. New York: New York University Press, 1999.

Springwood, Charles Fruehling. "Gun Concealment, Display, and Other Magical Habits of the Body." *Critique of Anthropology* 34 (2014): 450–71.

Street, Joe. "The Historiography of the Black Panther Party." *Journal of American Studies* 44 (2010): 351–75.

———. "The Shadow of the Soul Breaker: Solitary Confinement, Cocaine, and the Decline of Huey P. Newton." *Pacific Historical Review* 84 (2015): 333–63.

Swearingen, M. Wesley. *FBI Secrets: An Agent's Exposé*. Boston: South End, 1995.

Tackett, Timothy. "Rumor and Revolution: The Case of the September Massacres." *French History and Civilization* 4 (2011): 54–64.

Taylor, Quintard, and Shirley Ann Wilson Moore, eds. *African American Women Confront the West, 1600–2000*. Norman: University of Oklahoma Press, 2008.

Taylor, Ula Y. "'Negro Women Are Great Thinkers as Well as Doers': Amy Jacques-Garvey and Community Feminism in the United States, 1924–1927." *Journal of Women's History* 12 (2000): 104–26.

Terrell, Mary Church. *The Progress of Colored Women: An Address Delivered before the National American Women's Suffrage Association, at the Columbia Theater, Washington, D.C., February 19, 1898, on the Occasion of Its Fiftieth Anniversary*. Washington, D.C.: Smith Brothers, 1898.

Theoharis, Jeanne F., and Komozi Woodard, eds. *Freedom North: Black Freedom Struggles Outside the South, 1940–1980*. New York: Palgrave, 2003.

Tyner, James A. "'Defend the Ghetto': Space and the Urban Politics of the Black Panther Party." *Annals of the Association of American Geographers* 96 (2006): 105–18.

Tyson, Timothy B., *Radio Free Dixie: Robert F. Williams and the Roots of Black Power*. Chapel Hill: University of North Carolina Press, 1999.

Umoja, Akinyele K. "Maroon: Kuwasi Balagoon and the Evolution of Revolutionary New Afrikan Anarchism." *Science and Society* 72 (2015): 196–220.

U.S. Congress, Senate. Book III, *Final Report of the Select Committee to Study Governmental Operations with Respect to Intelligence Activities, Supplementary Detailed Staff Reports on Intelligence Activities and the Rights of Americans*, 94th Congress, 2nd Session. Washington, D.C.: Government Printing Office, 1976.

Washton, Arnold M. *Cocaine Addiction: Treatment, Recovery, and Relapse Prevention*. New York: Norton, 1989.

Wasserman, Steve. "Rage and Ruin: On the Black Panthers." *Nation*, June 5, 2013.

Weingarten, Marc. *The Gang That Wouldn't Write Straight: Wolfe, Thompson, Didion, Capote and the New Journalism Revolution*. New York: Three Rivers, 2005.

Weir, David, and Dan Noyes. *Raising Hell: How the Center for Investigative Reporting Gets the Story*. Reading, Mass.: Addison Wesley, 1983.

Wertsch, J. V., and H. L. Roediger. "Collective Memory: Conceptual Foundations and Theoretical Approaches." *Memory* 3 (2008): 318–26.

White, Derrick E. *The Challenge of Blackness: The Institute of the Black World and Political Activism in the 1970s*. Gainesville: University Press of Florida, 2011.

Wilkinson, William Richard. *Prison Work: A Tale of Thirty Years in the California Department of Corrections*. Columbus: Ohio State University Press, 1995.

Williams, Jakobi. *From the Bullet to the Ballot: The Illinois Chapter of the Black Panther Party and Radical Coalition Politics in Chicago*. Chapel Hill: University of North Carolina Press, 2013.

Williams, Robert F. *Negroes with Guns*. Reprint ed. Detroit: Wayne State University Press, 1998.

Williams, Yohuru. *Black Politics/White Power: Civil Rights, Black Power, and the Black Panthers in New Haven*. St. James, N.Y.: Brandywine, 2000.

Williams, Yohuru, and Jama Lazerow, eds. *Liberated Territory: Untold Local Perspectives on the Black Panther Party*. Durham, N.C.: Duke University Press, 2008.

Winkler, Adam. "The Secret History of Guns." *Atlantic*, September 2011.

Witt, Andrew. *The Black Panthers in the Midwest: The Community Programs and Services of the Black Panther Party in Milwaukee, 1966–1977*. New York: Routledge, 2013.

———. "On the Radio with Michael McGee." *Journal of African American Studies* 21 (2017): 150–58.

Wu, Judy Tzu-Chun. *Radicals on the Road: Internationalism, Orientalism, and Feminism during the Vietnam Era*. Ithaca, N.Y.: Cornell University Press, 2013.

X, Malcolm. *By Any Means Necessary: Speeches, Interviews and a Letter by Malcolm X*. Edited by George Breitman. New York: Pathfinder, 1970.

———. *Malcolm X Speaks: Selected Speeches and Statements*. Edited by George Breitman. New York: Grove, 1965.

X, Malcolm, with the assistance of Alex Haley. *The Autobiography of Malcolm X*. London: Penguin, 1968.

Zamalin, Alex. *Struggle on Their Minds: The Political Thought of African American Resistance*. New York: Columbia University Press, 2017.

Zolberg, Aristide, and Vera Zolberg. "The Americanization of Frantz Fanon." *Public Interest* 9 (Fall 1967): 49–63.

INDEX

Abron, JoNina, 126–7, 186
Abu-Jamal, Mumia, 16, 94–5, 173
Afro American Association 7, 114, 136, 153
al Amin, Jamil Abdullah, 27, 135, 136–7, 186
Anthony, Earl, 58, 97, 155, 204n14
Anticolonialism xii, 2, 10, 13, 20–27, 33, 57, 58, 59, 138, 154, 179, 186. *See also* Fanon, Frantz
Aoki, Richard, 165–6
armed struggle, 19, 20, 21, 22, 26, 27, 49, 57, 59, 61, 97, 102, 148. *See also* Black Panther Party police patrols; guerrilla warfare; self-defense
Avakian, Bob, 134, 136; steals American flag, 138

Baker, Ella, 29, 39
Bambara, Toni Cade, 39–40, 44
Baraka, Amiri, 83, 154
The Battle of Algiers (Pontecorvo), 26–7
Bennett, Lerone, Jr., 102–3
Berkeley, 7, 74–5, 82, 114, 117, 122, 141, 148, 165, 194
Bin Wahad, Dhoruba, 97, 101, 171
Bird, Joan, 43, 62–3, 96, 101
Black Liberation Army, 96–7
BlackLivesMatter, 3
Black Nationalism, 22, 23, 24, 32, 35, 42, 102–3, 114, 134, 136, 153–4; BPP and, 2, 13, 19, 54, 58, 67, 155
Black Panther (film), xii
The Black Panther (newspaper), 5, 7, 37, 49, 55, 76, 92, 95, 108, 120, 124, 126, 161, 186, 177–8; Free Huey campaign and, 56, 136, 138–9, 147; gender in, 37–44 *passim*, 46, 53; Oakland: A Base of Operation series, 115–7, 125; political ideology in, 57–60, 62–3, 64, 87, 105–6, 112, 156, 157, 181–2
Black Panther Party: Cal-Pac boycott, 14–15, 104–111, 114, 188; criminality/underground activity, 10, 63, 68, 84, 86, 91, 95, 96, 103, 126, 178; clothing of, 35, 55, 78, 79, 81–2, 117, 120, 135, 136; electoral campaigns, 3, 8–9, 14, 15, 93, 95, 112–26 *passim*; finances of, 8, 49, 90, 93–4, 95, 98, 101, 109, 118–9, 126, 134, 167, 180, 182, 183, 184, 207n86; gay rights and, 52–3, 54, 62, 122, 156, 203n80; historiography of, 9, 11, 12, 20, 73, 88, 112, 165–6, 186–7, 189, 191, 196n26, 214n1; image of, 57, 74, 79, 81, 84–5, 96, 113, 117, 119, 120, 124–5, 132, 138, 147, 182, 183, 185, 189; memory of, 12, 16, 185–94; police patrols, 3, 7, 14, 37, 75–78, 80–81, 85–86, 119, 150, 165, 166; political education within 13, 23, 46, 56, 60, 90, 91; and prisons, 10, 16, 51, 58, 66, 124, 149, 154, 167–84; psychological impact of membership, 3, 11, 37, 96, 98, 151, 152, 156, 159, 160–1, 162, 163, 189, 190, 192–4; referenced in popular culture, xi–xii; repression of, 2–3, 12–13, 37, 85–6, 87, 96, 97–9, 123, 131–184; Ten Point Platform and Program, 11, 32–33, 51, 116, 121, 133, 142, 148, 168, 188
Black Panther Party Chapters, 5–7, 14, 88–89; Atlanta, 95; Baltimore, 44, 94, 98; Boston, 90, 95; Brooklyn, 5; Chicago, 5, 26, 60–1, 161–3, 165; Cleveland, 88–89, 90, 99; Des Moines, 95, 99; Detroit, 26, 36, 95, 97–8; Harlem, 5, 94, 97; Houston, 99; Indianapolis, 91, 98; Jamaica, 5; Los Angeles, 5, 8, 44, 88, 90, 94, 97, 152–8, 163, 165; Milwaukee, 89, 91, 93–4, 98; New Bedford, 89; New Haven, 95, 158–61; New Orleans, 5, 96, 99, 165; New York City, 5, 26, 89, 90, 94, 96–7, 101, 158; Philadelphia, 5, 31, 91, 93, 94–5, 98–9; Portland, 91; Sacramento, 60; San Diego, 157; San Francisco, 90, 152; Seattle, 5, 95, 99; Winston-Salem, 93, 98
Black Panther Party programs, 6, 8, 62, 63, 87–100, 110–11, 113, 114, 119, 182, 186, 187, 188–9; breakfast, 34, 60–1, 63, 87, 91, 93–9 *passim*, 154, 194; busing, 89, 93–4, 95, 97, 184; clothing, 89, 90–91, 93, 97, 105, 117; education, 9, 87, 89–93, 95, 100, 119, 126–7, 211n24; food, 14, 88–91 *passim*, 93, 95, 97, 105, 109, 113, 117, 122; health care, 88, 89–90, 93, 94, 95, 97, 99, 117, 119, 154, 189, 194
Black Power, 8, 112–13, 132, 137, 140, 141

251

Blake, J. Herman, 63, 68, 139, 146, 174
Boyette, Bill, 104–8, 110, 188
Brown, Elaine, 8–9, 41–3, 53, 69, 113, 126, 153, 154, 176, 191–2; 1973 election campaign, 113, 115, 118, 119–20, 121, 124
Brown, H. 'Rap' *See* al Amin, Jamil Abdullah
Bukhari, Safiya, 53–54

Cal-Pac, 14–15, 101, 103–111, 114, 188
Capitalism, 22, 24, 25, 31, 38, 39, 73, 93; Black capitalism, 15, 67–8, 70, 91, 102–3, 109; BPP approach to, xi, 12–13, 14, 20, 25–26, 32, 34, 45, 53, 56, 58–65 *passim*, 69, 88, 90, 91, 92–3, 99–100, 103, 104, 106, 108, 109–110, 115–6, 133, 168, 183, 186, 189–90. *See also* Newton, Huey P., "Black Capitalism Re-Analyzed"
Carmichael, Stokely. *See* Ture, Kwame
Carter, Alprentice "Bunchy," 8, 15, 88, 152–6, 163
Chavez, Cesar, 121, 122
Civil rights movement, 2, 6, 8, 13, 28, 39, 74, 83, 103, 120, 131, 133, 185; BPP criticisms of, 10, 20, 22, 24, 57, 139, 148
Clark, Mark, 8, 15, 97, 152, 161–4
Class, 25, 28, 33, 112–3, 120, 151, 153; BPP analysis of, 6, 24, 33, 35, 41–2, 58, 60, 64, 68, 70, 85, 108, 115, 116, 122, 154, 168–9, 184; intersectional analysis 6, 38, 39, 47, 54, 90; Fanon and, 22–3, 24, 28, 154
Cleaver, Eldridge, 137, 154, 165, 189, 202n52; BPP activities, 7, 8, 82, 85, 113, 134, 138, 140, 149; gendered views, 13, 47–51, 52, 54, 87, 183; in exile, 8, 47, 101, 102, 171–2; Marxism and, 34; Newton and, 8, 55–56, 57, 59, 66–67, 69–70, 78, 97, 101–2, 179, 181, 182; prison and, 16, 47, 48, 51, 138, 154, 167, 169–72, 176, 183, 184; thought of, 38, 49–51, 57, 58, 59, 60, 61, 62, 79, 113, 169, 170–1, 180
Cleaver, Kathleen, 14, 88, 191, 193; BPP activities, 37, 39, 40, 138, 183; thought of, 40, 58, 59, 139; Eldridge Cleaver and, 47, 165, 171, 202n52
COINTELPRO. *See* Federal Bureau of Investigation
Coleman, Kate, 126, 166, 179, 190
Combahee River Collective, 44
Cooper, Anna Julia, 23, 28, 39
Coto, Joseph, 118, 122, 124
Cox, Don, 26, 87
Cuba, 8, 9, 28–29, 38, 59, 60, 69, 82, 101, 107, 171, 178. *See also* Guevara, Ernesto "Che"

Davis, Angela, 132, 180, 181
Dellums, Ron, 107–8, 112, 114, 117, 125, 136
Democratic Party, 32, 59, 103, 114, 117, 118, 121, 122, 124, 140, 172
Didion, Joan, 137–8
Douglas, Emory, 26, 38, 59, 83, 102, 107, 108, 154, 157, 186
Dowell, Denzil, 7
Dunbar, Jim, 101–2, 106
Dylan, Bob, 181

Erikson, Erik, 65

Fanon, Frantz, 7, 20–1, 68, 69, 89; BPP and, 10, 13, 19–20, 21, 23–4, 25–6, 33, 34, 35, 57–61 *passim*, 63, 67, 76, 77, 85, 89, 98, 132, 134, 148, 154, 174, 180; *The Wretched of the Earth*, 19, 21–31 *passim*, 74, 148
Fascism: as BPP rhetorical trope, 59–60, 61, 157
Federal Bureau of Investigation: and BPP social programs, 96; and BPP's decline, 8, 10, 151, 158, 160–1, 165; harassment of BPP members, 8, 14, 15, 50, 96, 98, 101, 123, 156, 159, 160, 171, 173, 202n52; in Chicago, 8, 15, 152, 161–3, 164; in Los Angeles, 8, 15, 97, 136–7, 152, 153, 155–8; in New Haven, 15, 152, 158, 159–60; infiltration of BPP, 8, 15, 58, 97, 98, 152, 153, 155, 158–66; internal structure, 155–6; and Newton, 3, 62, 64, 65, 101–2, 107, 147, 151, 165, 176–7, 178, 183; monitoring of BPP, xi, 49, 62, 64, 65, 81, 87, 96, 104–5, 107, 109, 137, 138, 150, 151–2, 153, 156–7, 160, 161, 172, 185, 204n14, 207n89; problematic nature of archival record, 10–11, 165–6
Federal Housing Authority, 4–5
Feminism, 23, 39–47, 53–54
Forbes, Flores, 97, 192–4
Forte, Sherwin, 79, 82
Free Huey campaign, 2, 7, 15, 40, 47, 114, 120, 132–4, 135, 136–40, 147–8, 150, 154
Frey, John, 15, 30, 55–6, 85, 102, 131–2, 140, 142–7 *passim*, 149

Garry, Charles, 15, 58, 108, 132–3, 136, 137, 139, 140–7, 150, 152, 172, 179–80
Gender, 13, 19, 23; BPP and, 29, 35, 36–54, 73, 79, 88, 92–5, 117, 118, 159, 168; Fanon and, 21, 26; Robert F. Williams and, 29
Goldberg, Art, 12, 114
Green, Otho, 107, 114, 121, 123, 124

252 INDEX

Greene, Linda, 41
Grier, Henry, 143, 145, 146–7, 149
guerrilla warfare, 23, 26, 27, 29–30, 33, 59, 60, 66–7, 96
Guevara, Ernesto "Che," 13, 19, 20, 34, 35, 69, 89; beret of, 82, 147; thought of, 29–30, 51, 98, 176, 180
Guns: BPP attitude towards, 35, 37, 42, 43, 46, 49, 53–4, 55, 75–6, 77, 79, 87, 91, 102, 147, 189; BPP possession of, 7, 36, 40, 55, 57, 75–85 *passim*, 123, 165–6; as gesture of power, 77, 78–81, 83, 85; control laws, 7, 76, 83–4, 86; in Newton trial, 142–6, 149; role in other liberation struggles, 20, 27–8, 29, 33, 77

Hair, xii, 40, 46, 51, 193–4
Hampton, Fred, 8, 14, 15, 60–62, 69, 97, 100, 107, 152, 161–4
Hart, Judy, 41, 43–44
Heanes, Herbert, 131, 140, 142–3, 144, 145, 146, 147, 149
Hilliard, David, 68, 101, 168, 171, 173, 191, 192; and BPP ideology, 13, 21, 60, 61, 187, 188–90; and guns, 85, 189; and Newton, 13, 84, 149, 178, 180, 186, 188
Homophobia, 48, 62, 87, 156
Hoover, J. Edgar, 8, 96, 150, 151, 155, 156, 157, 165, 182, 183
Howard, Elbert "Big Man," 60, 122, 166
Huggins, Ericka, 45, 53, 69, 122, 178, 186; and BPP ideology, 44, 53, 54; and BPP school, 9, 92; in New Haven, 15, 65, 95, 158–60, 173; and prison, 51, 176
Huggins, John, 8, 15, 152, 153, 156
Hutton, Bobby, 8, 49, 77, 85, 102, 171, 185, 187–8, 189

Internationalism, xii, 2, 13, 14, 20, 22–3, 28, 30–1, 33–34, 58–9, 61–2, 69, 99

Jackson, George, 8, 16, 179–82, 183–4
Jackson, Jesse, 103, 110, 125
Jackson, Jonathan, 8, 16, 179–81
Jacques-Garvey, Amy, 23, 42, 43–44
Jennings, Regina, 26, 52
Jensen, Lowell, 141–2, 143–4, 145, 146, 149, 150
Jones, Audrea, 46, 95, 118
Jones, Claudia, 13, 23, 42
Jones, LeRoi. *See* Baraka, Amiri

Karenga, Maulana, 136, 137, 153–5, 156, 157
Kelley, Joan, 95, 118

King, Dr. Martin Luther, Jr., 8, 27, 49, 103, 139, 147, 154, 177, 189

Lewis, Tarika, 37, 38, 76, 79, 186
Liberalism, 2, 7, 28, 115, 119, 126
lumpenproletariat, 22–23, 25–26, 27, 28, 30, 33, 39, 48, 57, 62, 66, 154, 167, 168, 180

Mao Zedong, 13, 19, 20, 33, 34, 35, 60, 69, 77, 85, 88
Marx, Karl, 22, 24, 34–35, 63, 64, 169
Marxism, 22–3, 34, 169, 170, 179; BPP and, 2, 13, 14, 19–20, 22, 34–5, 58, 59, 60, 61, 64–5, 67, 154, 171, 180, 186
masculinism, 35, 39, 118; BPP and, 13, 19, 20, 23, 26, 36–8, 40, 41, 44–5, 47–55 *passim*, 81, 160, 168; Cleaver and, 13, 38, 48–9, 170–1, 183; Robert F. Williams and, 29–30
McKinney, Gene, 131, 142, 144, 145, 149
Milk, Harvey, 126
Moore, Queen Mother Audley, 31, 39
Mulford, Donald, 57, 82, 83–4

National Black Political Convention, 112
Neil, Earl, 107, 108, 148, 181, 186, 193
Neoliberalism, 16, 65, 115, 117, 121, 189–90
New Left, 7, 20, 30, 54, 148, 182
Newton, Huey P., 16, 24, 35, 53, 78, 81, 120, 151, 158; after 1970 release from prison, 1, 2, 3, 9, 14–15, 30, 56, 62–70, 109, 111, 112, 113, 117, 126–7, 165, 176–9, 184; arrests of, 1–2, 7, 30, 55–56, 59, 75, 84, 85, 127, 131–2, 144–5, 208n16; before the BPP, 7, 74–5, 153; "Black Capitalism Re-Analyzed," 15, 67–8, 70, 91, 101, 103, 104, 105, 106; in Cal-Pac dispute, 104–5, 106, 107, 108; and Cleaver, 8, 48, 55, 66–67, 69–70, 97, 101–2, 171–2, 179, 181, 182; "The Correct Handling of a Revolution," 59, 145, 148; drugs and, 69, 127, 178–9, 188; "Executive Mandate Number One," 57, 58–9, 82, 83, 148; and guns, 75–7, 80–1, 83, 84, 85, 98, 111, 145, 148, 149, 165; intercommunalism, 8, 64–5, 67, 69, 111; as legend, xii, 55–56, 57, 66, 79, 81, 84, 135, 136, 138, 139, 140, 147–8, 177–8, 180, 186, 188; and prison; 1–2, 8, 16, 38, 58, 60, 68, 147–8, 149, 167–8, 171, 173–8, 179, 181, 183–4; *Revolutionary Suicide*, 68–9, 76, 109; thought of, 8, 13, 14, 15, 19–22 *passim*, 25–32 *passim*, 35, 37, 38, 41, 46, 49, 52, 54, 55, 62–70, 99, 108, 110, 111, 137, 147–8, 149, 163, 167, 174–5, 180, 181, 182, 207n89; trials

Newton, Huey P. (continued) of, 8, 15, 40, 132–3, 138, 140–7, 148–50, 172, 181
Nixon, Richard, 90, 103, 109, 114, 124, 151, 168, 182; madman theory of, 81

Oakland, xii, 3–9 *passim*, 4, 15, 25, 80–1, 85, 112, 114, 121, 122, 125, 126, 138, 140, 146, 194; BPP and, xi, 1, 70, 73–4, 90, 92–3, 94–5, 103, 104, 105, 108, 111, 115–26, 132–3, 136, 138, 185–8, 194
Oakland Police Department, 1, 6, 25, 35, 74–78, 80–1, 84, 85–6, 119, 121, 123, 131–2, 142, 144, 147, 149–50, 176, 177, 188. *See also* pigs; police
Oakland Tribune, 107, 114, 118, 119, 121, 126, 133
Obama, Barack, 185
O'Neal, William, 152, 161–4

Peace and Freedom Party, 8, 112, 133–4, 155, 156
pigs, 46, 47, 75–6, 87, 91, 120, 157, 158. *See also* Police
Police, 2, 14, 161, 162–4; brutality, 3, 6, 8, 25, 32, 60, 93, 95, 96, 97–9, 123–4, 131–2, 138, 157–8, 164. *See also* Oakland Police Department, pigs
Pratt, Elmer "Geronimo," 155, 173
Prison. *See* Black Panther Party and prisons; specific individuals

Rackley, Alex, 15, 65, 152, 156, 158–61, 172, 173
Ramparts, 7, 47, 55, 57, 78–9, 82, 138, 174
Reading, John, 15, 113–8 *passim*, 120, 121, 123, 124, 125–6
Reagan, Ronald, 49–50, 82–3, 182
redlining, 4, 5, 6
Reed, Ishmael, 187, 194
Republican Party, 32, 102, 113, 114, 118, 125
Revolutionary Action Movement, 7, 31, 33, 74
Revolutionary People's Constitutional Convention, 62, 63, 98
Richmond (Ca.), 7, 25, 81, 84
Robinson, Candi, 45–46
Ross, Dell, 140, 143–4, 145, 149
Rush, Bobby, 26, 162, 164

Sabatini, Eugene, 74–5, 145, 208n16
Sacramento, 1, 7, 57, 60, 82–3, 84, 85, 172
San Francisco, 7, 26, 59, 78, 80, 126, 152, 165, 168, 172
San Francisco Chronicle, 121, 138

San Francisco Examiner, 59, 79, 82, 177
San Quentin Prison, 169, 170–1, 174, 179, 180, 181, 182
Schneider, Bert, 118, 152
Seale, Bobby, xii, 11–12, 33, 109, 134, 135, 137, 138, 153, 178, 188, 191; 1973 election campaign, 3, 8, 15, 109, 112–3, 115, 118–126; before the BPP, 31, 33, 74–5; birthday cake arrested, 172; and Cal-Pac, 105, 106; gendered ideas, 51–52; and golf, 121; and New Haven, 15, 65, 159, 172–3; and Newton, 7, 9, 32, 68, 75–9, 81, 136, 138, 165; and prison 16, 59, 83, 84, 136, 168, 172, 173; thought of, 19–20, 22, 24, 25–30 *passim*, 34, 35, 58, 60, 62, 73, 79, 80, 82–3, 85, 87, 106, 139, 140, 181, 186
Self-defense, 6, 19, 20, 26, 27–29, 32, 33, 61–2, 84, 87, 153, 174, 194. *See also* armed struggle; Black Panther Party police patrols Fanon, Frantz; Williams, Robert F.; X, Malcolm
Shabazz, Betty, 7, 55, 78, 79
Shakur, Afeni, 43, 62–3, 101
Shakur, Assata, 53–54, 97, 173
Sojourners for Truth and Justice, 23, 31, 42
Soul Students Advisory Council, 7, 33, 75
Stender, Fay, 140, 143, 179–80
Stern, Sol, 7, 79, 145
Stronghold corporation, 109, 118–9, 126
Student Nonviolent Coordinating Committee, 8, 39, 133–4, 136, 139, 163
Sweet Sweetback's Baadasssss Song, 68

Tabor, Michael Cetewayo, 63, 101, 171
Taylor, Harold, 11, 96, 97
Trotsky, Leon, 82
Trump, Donald, 3–4
Ture, Kwame, 134, 135, 136, 137, 146, 158
Tyson, Stephania, 46–47

United Front Against Fascism, 59–60
United Nations, 31, 33, 138
US organization, 11, 136, 153–7

Varda, Agnès, 9, 40–41
Vietnam war, 62, 104, 114, 140, 152; antiwar movement, 8, 58, 133–4
Voting Rights Act, 1965, 2, 103

Watts, 2, 5, 7, 153
Wells, Ida B., 13, 19, 27
Wilkins, Roy, 107

Wilson, Lionel, 9, 15, 108, 113, 126
Williams, Landon, 53, 58, 61, 68, 87–88, 158, 159
Williams, Robert F., 7, 13, 19, 35, 37, 57, 76, 79–80, 85; thought of, 20, 27–29, 30, 31, 80

X, Malcolm, 7, 29, 34, 48, 55, 68, 153, 168, 170; BPP and, 7, 13, 19–20, 25, 33, 34, 35, 49, 55–6, 58, 60, 78, 132, 138, 149, 168, 177–8, 180; referenced in popular culture, xii; thought of, 20, 30–32, 33, 60, 153, 167, 171, 180, 149

Yale University, 65–66
Yippies, 73–74

Since 1970: Histories of Contemporary America

Jimmy Carter, the Politics of Family, and the Rise of the Religious Right
    by J. Brooks Flippen

Rumor, Repression, and Racial Politics: How the Harassment of Black Elected Officials Shaped Post–Civil Rights America
    by George Derek Musgrove

Doing Recent History: On Privacy, Copyright, Video Games, Institutional Review Boards, Activist Scholarship, and History That Talks Back
    edited by Claire Bond Potter and Renee C. Romano

The Dinner Party: Judy Chicago and the Power of Popular Feminism, 1970–2007
    by Jane F. Gerhard

Reconsidering Roots: Race, Politics, and Memory
    edited by Erica L. Ball and Kellie Carter Jackson

Liberation in Print: Feminist Periodicals and Social Movement Identity
    by Agatha Beins

Pushing Back: Women of Color–Led Grassroots Activism in New York City
    by Ariella Rotramel

Remaking Radicalism: A Grassroots Documentary Reader of the United States, 1973–2001
    edited by Dan Berger and Emily K. Hobson

Deep Cut: Science, Power, and the Unbuilt Interoceanic Canal
    by Christine Keiner

America's Other Automakers: A History of the Foreign-Owned Automotive Sector in the United States
    by Timothy J. Minchin

Public Religions in the Future World: Postsecularism and Utopia
    by David Morris

Goldwater Girls to Reagan Women: Gender, Georgia, and the Growth of the New Right
    by Robin M. Morris

Here Are My People: LGBT College Student Organizing in California
    by David A. Reichard

Black Revolutionaries: A History of the Black Panther Party
    by Joe Street

www.ingramcontent.com/pod-product-compliance
Lightning Source LLC
Chambersburg PA
CBHW032141230426
43672CB00011B/2414